To Michael Candela -

Enjoy the book.

Kathleen Coakley

For
The
People

Alameda County in 1947

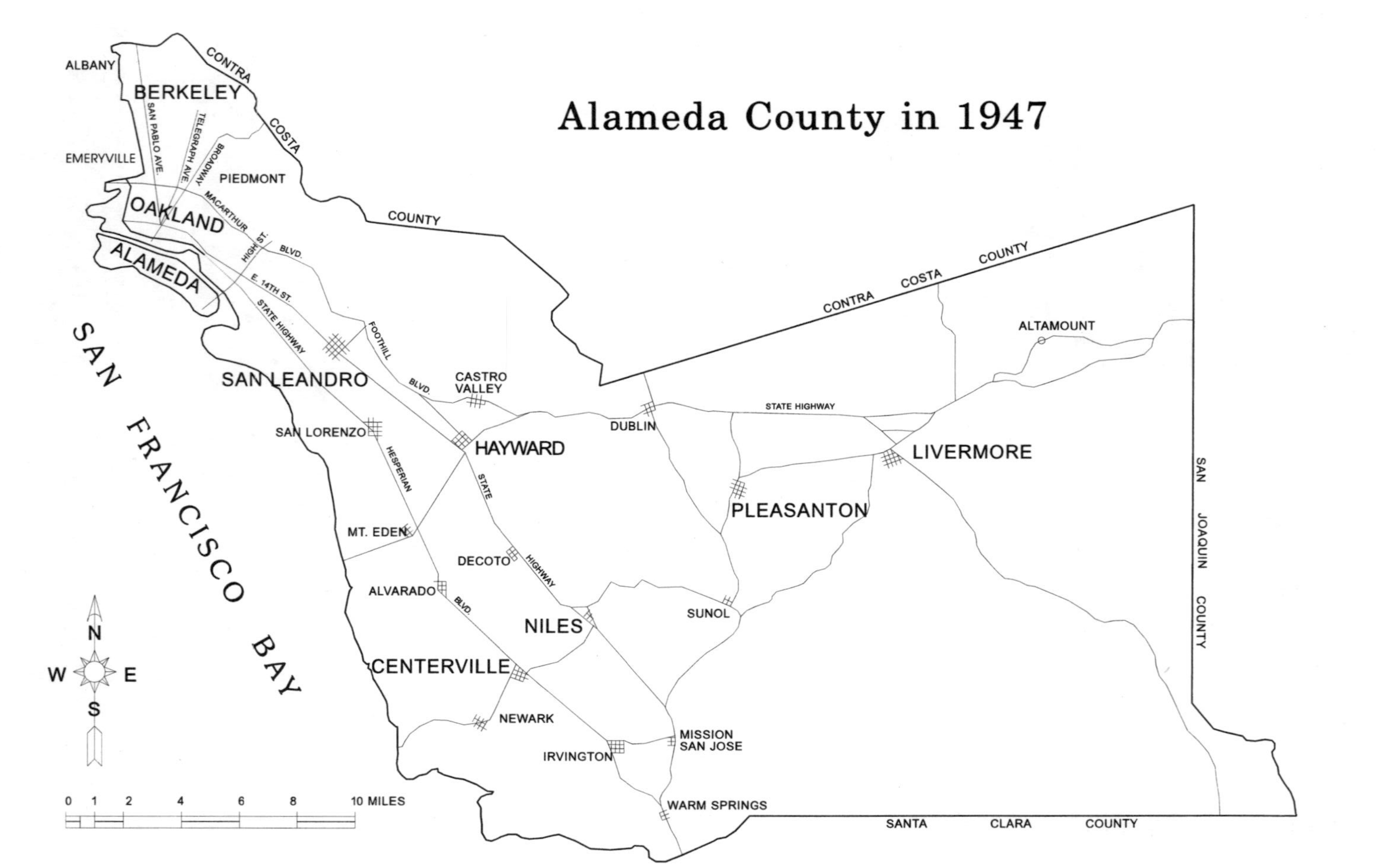

For The People

Sixty Years of Fighting for Law and Order

by

J. Frank Coakley

District Attorney Emeritus of Alameda County

Western Star Press

Orinda, California

1992

Printed on acid–free paper

Published by Western Star Press
P. O. Box 2108
Orinda, California

Book design by VF Graphics

Manufactured in the United States of America

Cataloging-in-Publication Data

Coakley, J. Frank (James Francis), 1897–1983.
For the people : sixty years of fighting for law and order / by J. Frank Coakley.
p. cm.
Includes bibliographical references and index.

1. Coakley, J. Frank (James Francis), 1897–1983. 2. California.—District Attorney (Alameda County)—History. 3. Criminal law 4. Crime & criminals 5. Criminal justice, Administration of—United States 6. Law enforcement—United States 7. Law enforcement—California—Alameda County—Case studies 7. Public prosecutors—California—History 8. Biography—Warren, Earl b. 1891 I. Title

KFC1199.A43A8C6 1992 345.794'6501 92-60983
ISBN 0-9630466-0-8

FIRST EDITION: November 1992

0 9 8 7 6 5 4 3 2 1

To my devoted and very patient wife

Kathleen

and our children

Thomas, Clare and John

Table of Contents

Table of Contents vii

Foreword xi

Publisher's Preface xii

Introduction xix

Acknowledgments xxiii

1 Early History 1

2 Ezra Decoto 1918—1925 12

The Probation Department 12
Prohibition 13
Decoto's Attorneys 15
Movie Stars 16
The Bank President 17
And a Man with Influence 17
The Country Judges 19
A Case of Libel 20
The Pigeon Drop 21
Office Rumors 23

3 Earl Warren 1925—1938 24

The Bail Bonds Broker Scam 36
Bessie Ferguson 37
Graft in Emeryville 38
Street Paving Graft 42
The Disappearing Wife 43
The Cleaning & Dyeing Racket 44
An Unethical Attorney 47
Warren Stays On 49
Fraud 50
Golet Oil Company 52
Lusitania, Inc. 53
Cox Chemical 55

The Acme Builders Swindle 62
The Free Lot Racket 65
A Speculating Loan Company 69
Phony Baloney Insurance 70
The Poisoner 70
The Constitutional Amendment of 1934 74
Yacht Bandits 77
Alameda Graft 81
Liquor Law Graft 84
Warren's Ship Murder Case 85
A Case of Mistaken Identity 88
An Unusual Drunk Driving Case 89
An Exceptional Manslaughter 91
A Case of Armed Withdrawal 92
Warren as Administrator and Politician 94
Warren Runs for Higher Office 95

4 *Ralph E. Hoyt 1939—1947* 98
Corruption on the Bench 99
Police Brutality 101
A Fruit Shake Case 103
White Hibiscus Claire De Lune 112
Officer Johnston 112
Tunnel Road Rapists 114
Proven Oil Land For Sale 116
Leona Vlught 119
Inside Job 120

5 *Civil Defense 1940—1961* 122
Red Alert!—Enemy Planes Approaching 123
Doing our Part for the Duration 126

6 *J. Frank Coakley 1947—1969* 129
The Attorney General's Gang 129
Drug Bust 138
Automotive Salvage Fraud 142
The Boxing and Wrestling Investigation 147

Fish & Game Bribery 148
More Bank Robbers 149
The McClure Case 153
Grand Juries 158
Prostitutes & Reporters 163
Smut 165
Accessory to a Psychopath 171
Preachers & Charlatans 173
Cold Blooded Murder 178
Stephanie Bryan 190
Officers Frey and Heanes 200
Ambush in West Oakland 210
Corruption in the Assessor's Office 212

7 *Riots & Demonstrations* 217
Slate 219
San Francisco's Turn 221
The Free Speech Movement 223
The Vietnam Day Committee 236
Stop the Draft Week 247
Burn, Baby, Burn 251
People's Park 255
Aftermath of the 60's 260

8 *D. Lowell Jensen 1969—1981* 265
Chowchilla School Bus Kidnaping 267
Cyanide Bullets 273
The Ultimate Miranda Case 276
Other Miscellaneous Cases 276

9 *Civil Public Law* 277
Bridges 279
The Key System 281
Freeways 285
Private Schools 286
Livermore Valley Water 287
The Coliseum 289
The School Department 292

The School Department 292
Miller's Opus and Other Indexes 296
Code of County Ordinances 297
The Athletic Safety Committee 298
Collaborating with the City Attorneys 300
Polio Vaccinations 300
The Loss of the Welfare Burden 301
The Civil—Criminal Split 303

Appendix A: District Attorneys of Alameda County & Chief Assistants 307

Appendix B: Office Employees in 1982 309

Appendix C: Other Official Positions Held By Staff Personnel 314

Appendix D: Former Staff 319

Appendix E: Proceedings on Sentence in People v. Huey P. Newton 325

Index 327

About The Author 347

Foreword

For over half a century, under the direction of a succession of able lawyers dedicated to excellence in their profession, the District Attorney's Office of Alameda County has been the model of a great public law office. Earl Warren was district attorney from 1925 to 1938 when he moved to the office of attorney general of California. Ralph Hoyt succeeded him and served as district attorney from 1939 to 1947. J. Frank Coakley held the job from 1947 until his retirement in 1969. Lowell Jensen served until 1981, when he resigned to accept a position of assistant attorney general of the United States and was succeeded by John Meehan.

Frank Coakley came to work in this office in 1923, was directly involved in its operation for 46 years, and has been a close observer of its operations in the years since he retired. I was a resident of Alameda County during all but the last 5 years of Coakley's tenure as district attorney. My own interests and research relating to criminal justice brought me in contact with him frequently. What I saw was a man of unimpeachable character—honest, incorruptible, incredibly hard working. He saw the world in a somewhat sharper division between good and bad than most of us did—but no one doubted that he was a vital leader on the side of good in our society.

This book then is written from a special vantage point. The author has been in and of the office for 60 years. He holds strong views about many of the things which happened during that period and he writes about them as he saw them. The book should be seen as reflecting his views about the period, the office, the cases, and the personnel. It is not necessary to agree with everything said to make this book stimulating and useful to read.

At a time of unprecedented increase in serious crime and of much criticism of the administration of justice, this history of the performance of a great public office coming from a person who has had a lifetime of involvement in it is refreshing, interesting, and well worth reading.

Edward L. Barrett
Professor of Law
University of California, Davis

Publisher's Preface

This book tells the story of the Alameda County, California District Attorney's Office from its beginnings to the early 1980's. To a great extent, it embodies the personal memoirs of J. Frank Coakley, the district attorney from 1947 to 1969. But, Frank's intention was to do more than write of his exploits—rather, to tell a history of the office he was a part of for 60 years and which he personally administered as its "Chief" for 22 years.

Frank joined the office in February of 1923 after graduating from Boalt Hall, the School of Law at the University of California's Berkeley campus. The Alameda County District Attorney's Office was small then—only twelve attorneys in total. During Frank's first year, Earl Warren was promoted to chief assistant, having been in the office only three years as a deputy. During those early years, Frank Coakley and Earl Warren became fast friends, both prosecuting many cases—some of the more important of which are related in this book. These two men, whose friendship would last throughout the rest of their lives, were to leave their marks on the office as no one before or since.

Perhaps typical of district attorney's offices of the era, Alameda County's was antiquated, it's operation having changed little in decades. As the post–World War I era became a time of rapid change throughout American society, so grew the challenges facing local law enforcement. The old ways of administering justice had limitations that became increasingly apparent.

In 1925, Warren succeeded Ezra Decoto as district attorney. Warren's era was marked by growth, both in the number of cases and in their variety. The changes happening in society meant the District Attorney's Office had to change, too, and Warren was the right man for the times. As time passed, Warren's era in the office became one of transformation, from an office where deputies worked cases alone and maintained simultaneous private law practices, to one where the staff collaborated on cases and devoted their time and talents exclusively to the District Attorney's Office.

It was Warren who personally set the tone for the future growth of the office. Above all else, it was to be a clean office—untouchable by corruption or graft, and fearless of any outside political pressure. In the first few years under Warren, the office challenged the corrupt political machine that had run the county. He prosecuted the various vice operations and official fraud and corruption that machine had allowed or protected. Careful to first obtain the support of the business community and the citizenry at large, Warren laid a solid groundwork of evidence and corroborated testimony before bringing his cases to the grand jury.

Warren quickly assumed the mantle of Champion of Good Government which would ultimately lead him to success in state elective office and appointment as Chief Justice of the United States Supreme Court. Under Warren the District Attorney's Office was to be the advocate for the people, and strict professional propriety was to be observed by all the staff, publicly and privately.

Warren began a practice of reliance on new law school graduates to fill his growing staff of deputies. This practice had many practical effects: first, it provided a blank sheet on which Warren could create his own idea of what a good prosecutor should be—no bad habits to be unlearned, no petty professional jealousies or worldly cynicism to be got round; second, it provided the young law school graduate with what Warren remembered he wanted most when he had first graduated—lots of practical and varied experience; third, a deputy who was less susceptible to enticement or compromise—who had no large family to support, and who could work long hours for months on end without destroying his family life; and fourth, a cadre of friends who would later become political allies as they spread out into other posts across the state, in law enforcement, the criminal bar, the bench, the legislature and elsewhere.

While district attorney, Warren used his considerable political skills directly to expand the political independence and influence of the office, and the tradition of that independence and influence became his greatest legacy when he moved on to higher positions in government. While attorney general and governor, Warren was in a position to protect and enhance what he had built in Alameda County, and he did so, but, in the years that followed Warren's appointment to the U.S. Supreme Court in 1953, it fell to Frank Coakley to build upon and extend Warren's legacy.

By the time Frank took office as the district attorney in 1947, he was an accomplished prosecutor. Meticulous and dogged in building a case, forceful and clever in the courtroom, he seldom lost. Once becoming the district attorney, he could not afford the time to personally prosecute cases. His prosecution of Burton Abbott for the kidnaping and murder of Stephanie Bryan was a rare exception. Rather, his personal influence was magnified manyfold as the manager, the coach, the "Chief."

In hiring deputies, Frank followed Warren's practice of reliance on new law school graduates. He himself taught classes at the University of California and St. Mary's College. Many members of his staff also became part–time adjunct professors and lecturers at local colleges. Frank believed in continuing education, and he became a leader in advancing the skills of prosecutors, not only in his own office, but across the nation. This aspect of the office is one to which Frank pays particular attention in the following pages.

Much more so than Warren had done, Frank Coakley focused on the education of new lawyers. His devotion to teaching young lawyers and lawyers–to–be grew out of his natural altruism, but it surely had a profoundly important political impact—possibly as profound as Warren's ultimately was—as his "Coakley College" graduates spread out in government and the legal community. Certainly, the Reagan eras, in both California and the nation, have seen the rise to high office of many of these graduates.

Almost unique at the time, the Alameda County District Attorney's Office handled both the criminal and civil legal work of the county until 1966, when the office of County Counsel was created. What a wonderful educational opportunity that work was for many of the "students" at "Coakley College." Although Frank treats the civil work of the office separately, devoting a single chapter at the end of this book, it was very much as important to the county and integral to the office as the criminal side. It gave the office a distinctly balanced character and involved it much more in the routine operations of county government than it otherwise would have been.

Related to the civil legal work was the civil defense job the office was given from 1940 to 1961, and to which Frank also devotes a separate chapter. At first glance, such a mission seems foreign to the charter of a district attorney's office. But in 1940, the most well–organized entity in the county was the District Attorney's Office. As the office which supervised and coordinated the various law enforcement organizations throughout the county, and since such organizations would be the manpower for disseminating warnings and information to civilians and otherwise managing their protection, it was natural to coordinate the military–civilian interface through the District Attorney's Office.

The societal changes which first appeared in the 1920's and 30's, during Warren's era, did not end after World War II. In fact, in Alameda County those changes accelerated. Huge numbers of people, including large numbers of blacks, had immigrated to the Bay Area to work in the shipyards and other war–related work. Wartime public housing, built for those workers, became their postwar homes as most decided to stay. While Alameda County had experienced a steady growth in its ethnically and racially diverse population throughout its history, the changes in the population's numbers and racial mix experienced during and after World War II were unprecedented. The added demands placed upon all public agencies, from schools to public works to law enforcement, were unaccustomedly great. But the public management of the county was adaptable, and the District Attorney's Office played a major role in its adaptation.

Frank's era as district attorney saw great changes, not only in the character of Alameda County and its district attorney's office, but in the law itself. His era witnessed the rise of judicial activism by the U.S. Supreme Court, of which a principal proponent was his old friend, Chief Justice Earl Warren. Overturning centuries–old legal precedents, the Warren court embarked on a judicial revolution, issuing new federal rules and procedures that some would call anti–law enforcement and that certainly complicated the pursuit of justice in criminal cases. Without mentioning the Chief Justice, Frank relates in this book the seeming irrationality of such decisions and their impact upon the District Attorney's Office. Such arguments as Frank presents here are still heard today in the controversy over our more conservative current Supreme Court. Perhaps these issues are not yet entirely moot.

Frank's establishment of the National District Attorneys Association and his intimate affiliation with the California District Attorneys and Peace Officers Associations were critically important to the fight for law and order in California and the nation. One cannot imagine what our law enforcement and judicial systems would be like today if an organization imbued with Frank Coakley's moral integrity and forceful determination had not fought the political battles to defend the law–abiding from those whose professional lives are devoted to defending criminals. While it is sadly true that our government's legislative branch has often been dominated by criminal defense lawyers, the influence of the organizations Frank was instrumental in founding and leading has been great.

When he retired in 1969, Frank was given a lifetime appointment to a newly created position—District Attorney Emeritus. He was provided an office in the courthouse where he continued to work with his successors, providing advice when asked and generally maintaining a presence in the District Attorney's Office. As the years of his retirement wore on, he spent more and more of his time researching and writing the manuscript for this book. In 1983, Frank Coakley passed on from mortal life. A few weeks before he died, he completed the manuscript for the book which you now hold in your hands.

Those reading this book who knew Frank will hear his voice in the words written hereafter. Those not privileged to know him personally before, will come to do so. His voice was often loud in volume and sharp in tone. He usually spoke his mind with piercing force and deliberate directness. In his prosecutorial heyday he would hammer out his courtroom arguments, delivering phrases like body punches. When not engaged in arguing a case, his pugnacious voice resembled that of an athletic coach. His temper was often short and he was frequently impatient, anxious to push forward on whatever project he or his staff was working. Just as a boxing coach believes his own truth, so Frank seemed always to know the truth and was easily aroused to argument. The lines between right and wrong seemed often to be more sharply drawn in his mind than in others around him. The obfuscation and theatrical irrelevancies that are the stock–in–trade of many defense attorneys were anathema to Frank, the veteran prosecutor. To Frank, the purpose of the justice system was to accomplish justice, and that which misled or obscured the facts was an obstacle to be fought through.

The objective for his office was not a conviction, per se, but justice. Warren had established the policy that no one would be charged unless a careful examination of the evidence was convincing of his guilt; if the prosecutor later became convinced of an accused's innocence, the case would be dropped; if he were convinced of a convicted defendant's innocence, he would earnestly seek his vindication. That policy is, still today, the guiding philosophy of the Alameda County District Attorney's Office, in no small measure thanks to J. Frank Coakley.

Those who knew Frank privately saw in him the occasional deep–seated doubts and petty faults we all have that make us human, but in Frank Coakley those doubts and faults were overridden by his will to accomplish justice. He believed in the ideals of good government, and he proved that one man can make a difference.

Frank had enormous faith—in God, in himself, in his family, in his staff and friends, in his country, and in his profession. He was genuinely deeply religious, and from that religious faith, he drew much of his strength. He attended Mass at least once a week, and saw to it that his family did so as well. As gruff and polemical as he sometimes seemed, he cherished a surpassing love for and devotion to his family and his community.

In the times of frustration—when his prosecutors lost a case, or when the U.S. Supreme Court, led by his early colleague, Chief Justice Earl Warren, began to deconstruct the rules of law enforcement—Frank Coakley, although he stood as a staunch advocate for law and order and would express seemingly palpable pain on suffering a loss, would, nevertheless, defend the system itself against its critics, maintaining his allegiance to his profession. He believed in sticking to the rules (win or lose, one always played by the rules), and, indeed, his friendship with Earl Warren survived to the end of their lives. Perhaps this story tells a side of Warren that may not be well understood, or has been forgotten, by many of his critics.

As the reader will note, this book reflects the almost consuming attachment and commitment Frank had to his office. Just as any long–time coach might feel such devotion to his team that he would endeavor to proclaim the drama of its great victories, Frank felt compelled to do the same in his short retirement. It was his ambition to record the story of the office to which he had dedicated so much of his life—perhaps as a testimony of his devotion to it. If his tone sometimes sounds bragging, we hope the reader will accept the testimonials of others which accompany Frank's own words as substantiating his prideful opinions; he truly had much of which to be proud.

In editing this book, we have tried to put Frank's manuscript in as readable a form as possible, without taking Frank's voice out of the text—for it is his voice that really is the essence of this book. In our task, we have had the assistance of several people, whom we would like to thank. They are: Kitty Coakley, Frank's devoted wife; Tom and John Coakley and Clare Klinge, his children; Charlie Klinge, his grandson; Jack Meehan, current district attorney of Alameda County; Ninfa Wood, Jack's executive secretary; Tom Orloff, chief assistant district attorney of Alameda County; Richard Reid, property manager in the Alameda County District Attorney's Office; Officer Don Burnett and Departmental Historian Phil McArdle of the Oakland Police Department; and, once again, Anne Marie, James and Dorothy Dierke for their helpful index of the manuscript.

THE PUBLISHER

Introduction

The District Attorney's Office of Alameda County, California, has had a long and consistent record of high quality performance in the administration of criminal justice, civil public law work, and of leadership in law enforcement.

Raymond Moley, architect of the New Deal and director of surveys of municipal law enforcement operations in various metropolitan areas once said "The District Attorney's Office of Alameda County is the best in the nation."

The late Augustin Donovan, distinguished lawyer, judge and a governor of the California state bar, in his *History of the Bench and Bar* wrote:

> "The District Attorney's Office of Alameda County has been an exemplar of excellence in law enforcement which has stood out throughout the entire nation. Numerous articles, pamphlets and news stories of national circulation and consequence bear testimony to this acknowledged fact. Through the years Alameda County witnessed a group of the most outstanding district attorneys in all the history of the state."

Jerome Skolnick in his book *Justice Without Trial: Law Enforcement in a Democratic Society* referring to the administration of justice in the city of Oakland in Alameda County, wrote:

> "The prosecutor's office, the police department, and the office of the public defender are generally of as high quality in facilities, pay, and national renown as those of any middle–sized city in the United States. . . . The salutary reputation of Westville's (Oakland) criminal justice machinery extends throughout the United States and even abroad. During my visit to Eastville (an Eastern city) several high–ranking officials of the police department there expressed strong interest in coming to Westville to learn its operating procedures. Consequently, since Westville is generally regarded as a model of efficiency and modernity, its administration of criminal law cannot be claimed to be representative of the United States as a whole. On the contrary, it would be more accurate to consider

> it as an example of the top stratum of American criminal justice administration."[1]

Geoffrey C. Hazard, Jr., in his review of Skolnick's book, wrote:

> "Its (Oakland) criminal justice apparatus is renowned for its integrity and technical efficiency. . . . Hence, the subject of study is a law enforcement mechanism operating in a fairly typical urban milieu at what is in practical terms of today's United States an optimum level. Because the (Oakland) law enforcement mechanism is so good, the fact that it endures major subsisting problems has sharpened significance."[2]

Chief Justice Earl Warren, while on the United States Supreme Court, in conversation with me often said: "The District Attorney's Office of Alameda County has been, through the years, the finest public law office in the nation. A history should be written about it while a few of us are left who know the story. We should do it." Since I retired, I have been urged many times by other persons to do it.

As administered by Warren, the position of district attorney became in fact as well as theory the chief public law office of the county with great potential for leadership in law enforcement throughout the state and nation. Eventually it became a full–time career job with far–reaching opportunities to improve the quality of justice. In the course of time, the District Attorney's Office of Alameda County achieved nation–wide prestige and influence. That influence was continued and enhanced through the years to the present time. It is fitting therefore that some highlights in the story of this remarkable office be written while a few survive who were a part of it.

Such a history may be helpful to those who follow in this office and to others engaged in law enforcement and the administration of justice. Obviously, in a book like this, one could not cover but a

[1] Jerome H. Skolnick, *Justice Without Trial: Law Enforcement in a Democratic Society*,(Wiley, New York, 1966)
[2] Geoffrey C. Hazard, *American Bar Foundation Book Review*, No. 3, 1967

small fraction of the enormous number of cases that passed through a major metropolitan public law office over the course of several decades. The intent has been, by careful selection, to relate the cases which have had the most impact on the office and the community which it has served. The full extent of the outstanding performance of the persons who served in the office during the sixty years of my association with it cannot be adequately related in these pages. It is, in fact, the quality of that service which has compelled me to believe that, even in this small way, a record of it should be preserved.

Whatever image the office may have developed was due to the character and performance of a carefully selected and well trained staff. Selection was by personal interview. There was no civil service. Training was essentially in–service, which we combined with a continuing mutual helpfulness, hard work, camaraderie, and a policy of which a prime tenet was to give the accused the benefit of any reasonable doubt. There was certainly no policy that everyone accused should be convicted or even charged. In fact, the practice was to screen facts well before charging so that no one would be charged if a careful consideration of the legal evidence left a reasonable doubt.

The period of the 1930's through the 1960's was a bruising period for law enforcement officials who were trying to do a conscientious job of maintaining law and order. That during a critical period after World War II, the state of California was not inundated by organized crime and corruption in high places was due to the combined efforts and leadership of Governor Earl Warren, Warren Olney's Organized Crime Commission, and, of course, the District Attorney's Office of Alameda County.

That nationwide efforts of the New and Old Left to overthrow the "Establishment" in campus unrest, the anti–Vietnam War movement and other episodes of unlawful mass protest and riots were abated and attempts at obstructing justice and smearing law enforcement institutions by radical Left activists were successfully combated, at least in Northern California, was due in large measure to the professionalism of the law enforcement agencies of Alameda County under the direction of the District Attorney's Office, the Sheriff's Department and the Oakland and Berkeley police departments.

That a rapid expansion of the narcotics traffic under international mobster Waxey Gordon, "Trigger Abe" Chapman and 26 other co–conspirators across the nation was curtailed with their conviction in what Harry J. Anslinger, director of the United States Bureau of Narcotics, said was one of the most important trials in the history of the Bureau, was due also to the prompt and adept action of the District Attorney's Office of Alameda County in cooperation with Bureau agents in the early stages of the investigation.

That these and other forms of individual and organized crime were successfully combated and the rights of the law–abiding citizens of our community were preserved and enhanced was in no small measure due to the continuous efforts of the District Attorney's Office of Alameda County.

It is hoped that this story will be a significant contribution to the literature of local government, generate a better understanding of problems involved and perhaps serve to stimulate improvement in law enforcement and the administration of justice.

Because of the tortuous contours of decisions in California courts concerning the law of privacy, it was deemed advisable to use pseudonyms for names of possibly still–living persons who were convicted of crimes, although the real names appear in countless official records and legal publications throughout the nation.[3]

J. Frank Coakley

[3]Ed. Note: Throughout the text such pseudonyms are indicated by an asterisk (*).

Acknowledgments

Special mention must be made of Dorothy Bate who served for seventeen years with outstanding ability and dedication in positions of senior stenographic reporter and executive secretary in the District Attorney's Office of Alameda County. Her able assistance made it possible for me to get the National District Attorneys Association started, and, during its early formative years, to act as first president and director of its successful development. Her faithful assistance and that of Inspector Lawrence Cappelli, Barbara Klatt, Draga Canaday and other members of the stenographic pool contributed in large measure to the completion of this book. Appreciation must also be expressed to Anne, James and Dorothy Dierke for their help with the index.

Special mention should also be made of the generous assistance of the *Oakland Tribune/Eastbay Today* newspaper in providing photographs for inclusion in this book and to the *Tribune* photographers who, in shooting countless photographs of significant events—some of which are related herein—performed an important public service to our community.

For
The
People

1

Early History

Some account of the conditions that prevailed in California before and after it became a state is pertinent to the difficulties and problems encountered by officials of local government and particularly of peace officers, prosecutors and judges through the years that followed. That they succeeded in overcoming these conditions as soon as they did and bringing order out of the chaos is indicative of their character, courage and ability.

For an unknown period of time prior to 1848, when Alta California was ceded to the United States by Mexico in the Treaty of Hidalgo, this territory had been inhabited by various nomadic tribes of Indians who lived off what fish and wild game they could catch and what edible vegetation they could forage from the sometimes arid soil.

In the early 16th century, Spaniards from Europe, exploring the Western Hemisphere, among them Alarcon, came to what is now California. Beginning in 1769, the King of Spain, growing apprehensive over the activities of Russian and English hunters in parts of his New World domain, commissioned Spanish Franciscan missionaries and soldiers to begin colonizing California and Christianizing its native Indians. Between 1769 and 1823 Spanish missionaries and soldiers built a chain of missions, presidios and pueblos from San Diego to Sonoma, about sixty miles north of San Francisco.

There they met Russians who had crossed over the ice from Siberia to Alaska. The Russians had traveled south along the west coast of North America, hunting fur–bearing sea mammals and establishing communities along the coast of Northern California. In about the middle of the 19th century, shortly before the discovery of gold, the Russians, unaware of the wealth that lay below the ground of California, sold to Americans the properties which they had explored and developed, and traveled back to Alaska and Siberia.

Likewise unaware of the wealth beneath the ground, English and French fur traders from Canada hunted and trapped in the mountains of Northern California and natives of other countries also explored the territory. The flags of Russia, England and Portugal flew briefly over California as various explorers landed and departed after varying periods of exploration. Spain, and later the Republic of Mexico, stayed longer and did a fair job of developing the territory and civilizing the Indians.

In 1776, while the Founding Fathers were debating the Declaration of Independence, Mission Dolores and the Presidio at San Francisco were established by Spanish priests and soldiers. In 1848, by the Treaty of Hidalgo, as renegotiated in the Gadsen Treaty (1851), Mexico ceded to the United States the vast area now covered by the states of Texas, California, Arizona, Nevada, Utah, New Mexico and parts of Wyoming and Colorado.

Under the Treaty of Hidalgo, the negotiating representatives of the United States promised to pay Mexico $15 million for this area and to compensate the Republic of Mexico for damage by marauding Texas Indians in Mexico. This amount was later reduced summarily by Congress to $10 million and the United States reneged on payment of the Mexican claims for the damages caused by the Indians. General and President Santa Anna, who had once again returned to power in Mexico through connivance with the United States, was in need of money and the United States drove a hard bargain.

Spaniards, whose forebears had braved the hazards of exploration centuries before, and Mexicans, who had occupied and colonized the territories of the Western Hemisphere in the name of Spain and Mexico, felt unfairly treated and betrayed by the cupidity of their leaders. Naturally they were reluctant to capitulate to the invaders from the United States and other countries who moved in to take over their property. The bitterness and polarization that ensued remain to this day, as Mexican cheap labor imported to work the farms of the Sunbelt states are scorned as alien "wetbacks" while other racial minorities are given preferential treatment. Language and cultural differences have persisted and exacerbated relations between Mexican– and Anglo–Americans through the years, contributing to a distorted law enforcement problem.

The Treaty of Hidalgo, among other conditions, provided that Mexicans living in the newly ceded territory would be citizens of the United States—a condition which in practice had little effect upon the treatment imposed by Anglo–Americans on the Mexicans. In fact, the United States reduced Mexico to the status of a conquered nation, and Mexicans, although vastly outnumbering Anglo–Americans before 1848, were discriminated against and treated like aliens in lands they felt rightfully belonged to them. Their ranches were taken from them, their political power—or the potential for it—was usurped, and their social position was demolished.

Throughout the Southwest the Mexicans were supplanted socially and economically and left with menial tasks. A new stereotype of the Mexican–American emerged as an unskilled worker, uninterested and incapable in politics or education. Unknown to Mexico at the time the treaty was negotiated, gold was discovered in California, and shortly after the treaty was signed the gold rush was on. Countless thousands from all over the world swarmed into California in a mad search for gold and a chaotic scramble began.

By the time that a few leaders, under the direction of Stephen J. Field,[4] got around to organizing a state government, life in California was a hodgepodge of races, languages, cultures and ad hoc justice. Race, language and cultural differences still prevail among a large segment of the population so that official election documents in certain locations under law must be printed in Spanish, Chinese and other languages as well as English, and in many schools the curricula must include courses in "English as a Second Language." Now in

[4]Field later became a justice of the Supreme Court of California and of the Supreme Court of the United States.

California, after 130 years, Chinese, Mexicans, Blacks, Filipinos, Vietnamese, Caucasians and other races are integrated by school busing from districts in which they live.

The Indians aside, the Spanish from Mexico to Sonoma had been on the ground longest and had lived, worked and colonized under a loose laissez faire adaptation of European Continental legal systems. In Northern California from Sonoma to Oregon, Russians, English and French fur traders had lived under whatever legal systems they had brought with them from their respective countries. The Anglo–Americans brought adaptations of the Anglo–Saxon systems under which they had lived in the eastern and midwestern United States.

During the two years that California was a territory of the United States, things continued largely as they had been under Spanish and Mexican rule. There was no constitution, no statutory law and no uniform legal discipline. Under the Spanish, with their missionaries, soldiers and alcaldes, and what legal discipline had filtered down through the centuries from Justinian via Spain and Mexico, the legal system was part Continental, part ecclesiastic and part military. With Anglo–Americans and other racial groups it was ad hoc and peremptory. Persons desirous of law and order, who had been reared according to the legal systems of their mother countries, vied with each other according to recollections of their legal rights and customs, and their efforts to establish and live according to a formal legal system often compounded the confusion. For several years there was even a question whether California should be a slave or non–slave state, and although this was resolved in favor of non–slavery, many laws and practices of the deep South persisted.

Two legal heritages predominated, namely: the European Continental non–jury inquisitorial system of the Spanish countries, and the accusatory adversary Common Law of England and the United States. With the signing of the peace treaty between the United States and Mexico in 1848 and the cession of California, there was some hangover of the Continental system. For a long time the Alcalde system of the Spanish–Mexican occupation, under which non–lawyers acted as arbitrators and judges of disputes and wrongdoing, continued. A species of the Alcalde system is still reflected in some counties of the state where non–lawyer justices of the peace may preside in civil matters, in infractions punishable by fine only, in criminal offenses not punishable by a jail sentence or by stipulation of a defendant or his counsel in a criminal proceeding involving a charge punishable by a county jail sentence.

Josiah Royce described conditions in California after the discovery of gold as a "society morally and socially tried as no other American community ever has been tried" and the later 1850's in California were characterized by the historian Hubert H. Bancroft as "a period of moral, political and financial blight." An account of conditions in the new State of California is contained in the Preface of Volume I of *California Reports*,[5] written by Nathaniel Bennett, one of the three original justices of the California Supreme Court. In his preface, Bennett describes the chaos and confusion which was spawned by the Mexican revolution and the separation of Mexico from Spain, and which continued in the years following the treaty. Further accounts of conditions in early California and the legal problems prevailing at and following the admission of the state to the Union are contained in an Appendix of Volume I of the *California Reports*.[6]

Justice was often prompt and peremptory without benefit of legal formalities. If the culprit was not disposed of in the area of the crime and he managed to escape the scene, his disposition might occur in a shoot–out with a constable, a sheriff or a posse. From time to time there were lynchings.

In 1855, an armed mob broke into an Oakland jail, took a prisoner by force from the jailer, carried him to an adjoining township and lynched him. He was charged with horse stealing, at that time a capital offense. Lynching of persons charged with or suspected of crimes occurred well into the 20th century. In the 1920's, the bodies of three ex–convicts involved in the killing of a policeman were found hanging from a tree in a public park in Santa Rosa. In the

[5]Nathaniel Bennett, Reports of cases determined in the Supreme Court of the State of California, Vol. I (1850-1851), with notes on California reports (San Francisco, Bancroft-Whitney Company, 1906)
[6]Ibid., pp. 559—604

1930's, two persons awaiting trial in San Jose for kidnaping and murder were taken forcibly from the county jail by a mob and lynched by hanging from a tree in a plaza across the street from the jail. No one involved in the lynchings was prosecuted. Between the admission of California to the Union and the turn of the century, in lieu of formal judicial proceedings, vigilante committees frquently apprehended, tried and quickly dispensed a final justice. There were no appeals.

Occasionally a district attorney accompanied the sheriff and assisted in pursuing the criminal. In the celebrated case of *People v. Ford* in 1914, a district attorney and deputy sheriff were killed and the sheriff and a constable were beaten in an attempt to quell a riot precipitated by a gang of radical members of the Industrial Workers of the World.[7]

On January 16, 1935, four escaping San Quentin prisoners, heavily armed with guns that had been smuggled in to them, kidnaped and took as hostages Warden James Holohan, four prison board members and two prison guards. District Attorney Al Bagshaw of Marin County, with Undersheriff Edmund Blum, joined a posse of Sonoma County in a chase that ended in a shoot–out with the prisoners at Valley Ford in which the leader of the escape, a very dangerous police–hating ex–convict, was shot dead by Bagshaw, who had been inducted into his office as district attorney nine days before.

The last half of the 19th century was a particularly hazardous time for law enforcement officers. A sheriff would ride his horse into wild uninhabited areas in pursuit of a criminal, and, upon finding him, would have to shoot it out. The best shot won. Either the sheriff did not return or if he did, it was with the dead criminal strapped to the back of his saddle. On occasion, when a sheriff killed his prey in a shoot–out, he left the body where it lay to be buried by friends of the deceased or devoured by hawks or predatory animals.

Harry Morse, a colorful and courageous sheriff of Alameda County from 1863 to 1877, was such an officer. After his tenure as

[7] *People v. Ford* (1914) 25 Cal.App 388

sheriff, he worked for Wells Fargo Company, a stagecoach operation. One of the highwaymen who periodically robbed their stagecoaches was the infamous "Black Bart." Until Morse and James Hume ran him down and arrested him, "Black Bart" had never been apprehended.

In 1852, the California Legislature created Alameda County by carving out parts of Santa Clara and Contra Costa counties on the east side of San Francisco Bay. The area stretched along the Bay for about 100 miles and from the bayshore over the hills and across Livermore Valley to San Joaquin County, an area of some 847 square miles. The Livermore Valley is a large flat valley surrounded by rugged hills that provided secluded havens for stagecoach robbers and other outlaws who preyed upon the rancheros of the area. On the whole, the terrain, climate and soil conditions of Alameda County provided excellent opportunities for cattle and sheep raising, agriculture, viticulture, and industrial and maritime development which, in due course over the years, presented a wide variety of law enforcement and civil public law problems. The county was sparsely populated; the main growth and activity having been concentrated across the Bay in San Francisco.

The first county seat was in a small settlement called New Haven in the vicinity of the present district of Alvarado in the south–county city of Union City and not far from the bayshore where shallow draft boats carried farm products and hides to San Francisco and returned with merchandise. In 1857 the county seat was moved to San Leandro. After an earthquake which demolished the jail and courthouse, it was moved back to New Haven, later to San Leandro again, then to Clinton in Brooklyn Township east of Oakland and finally in 1872, after considerable controversy, to Oakland where the county's legal business was conducted in a courthouse at Fifth and Broadway.

A hall of records was constructed across the street from the courthouse on Broadway and another building was constructed at Fifth and Washington, adjacent to the courthouse, to house the Sheriff's Department and the County Jail, where public hangings were conducted by the sheriffs until the legislature changed the place of executions to San Quentin, across the Bay in Marin County. On one occasion, after a speech at a Native Sons of the Golden West dedication of a plaque identifying the site of the old courthouse at Fifth and Broadway, one of the audience told me that he had witnessed hangings conducted by sheriff's men a short distance from where we were standing.

In general, law enforcement involved run–of–the–mill crimes such as murder, robbery, burglary, larceny, assault and rape. Among other offenses, cattle rustling (which continues to occur) was (and still is) a penitentiary offense. Murder and certain other offenses, including horse–stealing, carried the death penalty.

Immigrants, frustrated by their failure to prospect successfully for gold, turned to farming, cattle and sheep raising and other business, often on land upon which they squatted and summarily appropriated illegally. A portion of Alameda County became known as Squattersville. Over the years before the Treaty of Hidalgo the governments of Spain and Mexico had made grants of vast land areas to soldiers and missionaries without carefully defined boundaries.

Hidalgo, Father of Mexican independence, and other dedicated liberal, idealistic missionary priests of 17th and 18th century Mexico, pioneered freedom, Christianizing and general betterment of conditions among the natives of America. For their efforts they were executed by greedy buccaneers who sought to exploit and profit by the work of the impoverished natives. Under the tutelage of the missionaries in skills of husbandry brought from Europe, the natives had helped to develop in choice locations in California numerous lush farms and great herds of cattle and sheep. Because of poorly defined boundaries of these properties, countless disputes arose as to ownership, spawning much violence and litigation that continued into the 20th century and caused no end of trouble for law enforcement and the administration of justice.

Many of the district attorneys of Alameda County came to the position from private practice and, after relatively short periods in the office, became judges or returned to private practice to become leaders in the social and political life of the county and state. For names of all district attorneys of Alameda County and their terms of service, see Appendix A. Among the more prominent of these were:

George M. Blake (1856—1857) who served as a member of the City Council, mayor and city attorney of Oakland.

William Van Voorheis (1858—1859) who, after two years in office as the district attorney of Alameda County, served as the city attorney of Oakland.

In addition to his service as district attorney, William H. Glascock served as the superintendent of the Oakland city schools and as a country judge.

After his service of two years as district attorney, W. W. Crane served as a city council member and mayor of Oakland.

Stephen G. Nye became a Superior Court judge, and, following his service as a judge, became a state senator.

A. A. Moore served as district attorney from 1872 to 1876. After his service as district attorney he practiced law in Oakland for several years with George Reed, who later became a district attorney. A. A. Moore also practiced law in San Francisco where his brilliant performance in defense of Calhoun, alleged bribe–giver of the Market Street Railway case of San Francisco, brought him statewide fame. His son–in–law, Donald McClure, served in the District Attorney's Office after World War I under Ezra Decoto.

John R. Glascock, son of William H. Glascock, after two years as district attorney, became mayor of Oakland and later the first representative of Alameda County in Congress.

Henry Vrooman, who first worked as a blacksmith and as a member of the Oakland volunteer fire department, studied law while blacksmithing and was admitted to the Bar in 1874. Thereafter he became a deputy district attorney under A. A. Moore. He served as city attorney of Oakland from 1876 to 1877, during which time he mapped out a plan of reform resulting in elimination of the floating indebtedness, reduction of taxes to the lowest figure ever known in the history of city government, and, when he left the City Attorney's Office, the general fund of the city treasury had a substantial surplus.

While city attorney, he rendered an opinion that San Antonio Creek was a public water highway and as such could not be legally obstructed by any private person or company. At that time this water was a shallow slough barely deep enough at low tide for a row boat.

It was later dredged to a depth of 35 feet—deep enough to accommodate ocean–going vessels—and became known as the Oakland Estuary and Inner Harbor.

As district attorney when the Alameda County Board of Supervisors was about to allow certain claims that he said it was not authorized to allow, he stood firm in his position as "law officer of the county." He told them that they were bound by his opinion and threatened to call them before the grand jury if they ignored his advice.

While he was district attorney, his private practice grew to such an extent that, rather than neglect county business, he resigned. He was very successful in private practice. Among his many clients was the politically powerful Southern Pacific Railway Company and the Oakland Bank of Savings.

In 1882 Vrooman was elected state senator from Alameda County and, while in that position, became a powerful leader in the Legislature and in affairs of the state. Among many laws that he authored as a member of the state Legislature was one concerning street construction financing, which at the time was badly needed by the growing cities of the state. He was followed in the office of district attorney by E. M. Gibson.

E. M. Gibson served as district attorney of Alameda County from 1880 to 1883. He had fought in many famous battles of the Civil War as a Union soldier and had lost a leg in combat at the Battle of Gettysburg. In 1885 he became a Superior Court judge and served until 1891.

Samuel P. Hall served as district attorney for three terms, 1883 to 1889. He served as a Superior Court judge from 1897 to 1905 and on the District Court of Appeal from 1905 to 1913.

George W. Reed served four years as district attorney, from 1889 to 1893. In later years he was senior partner in the law firm of Reed, Nusbaumer and Bingamin, where I practiced law before entering the District Attorney's Office.

Charles E. Snook served as district attorney from 1893 to 1899, during which time Lincoln S. Church served as his chief assistant. Snook and Church left the District Attorney's Office to pursue a growing private practice in what became one of the more prominent law firms of the county. Church served as a Superior Court judge from 1919 to 1943.

John J. Allen succeeded Snook as district attorney and served from 1899 to 1907. Allen later became a Superior Court judge.

Everett J. Brown served as district attorney from 1907 until September 1908, at which time he was appointed to the Superior Court.

William H. Donahue was appointed on that date to succeed Brown and was reelected in 1910. He served until December 2, 1912, at which time he was appointed to the Supreme Court.

William H. Hynes, Donahue's chief assistant, was appointed to succeed Donahue on December 2, 1912, elected in 1914 and served until April 5, 1918. He resigned to join Judge Donahue in what became one of the leading law firms in the county.

2

Ezra Decoto 1918—1925

In 1918, Ezra Decoto, who had served several years as a deputy district attorney under William H. Hynes, was appointed to the vacancy. He was elected district attorney in 1918 and reelected in 1922.

THE PROBATION DEPARTMENT

During Decoto's administration, a socially prominent liberal activist, Anita Whitney, and other members of the radical Industrial Workers of the World were charged with and convicted of violations of the Criminal Syndicalism Law of California. They were sentenced to state prison and their sentences were affirmed on appeal by the California District Court of Appeal. Earl Warren participated in the prosecution of one of these cases. In 1927 the United States Supreme Court affirmed the conviction of Whitney. Many years later, the United States Supreme Court expressly overruled the case in a *Per Currian* opinion while Chief Justice Warren was a member of the Court[8]

For a few months during 1902 the defendant in this case had been the first unofficial (unpaid) probation officer in Alameda County.

[8] *Brandenburg v. Ohio* (1969) 395 U.S. 444 (23 L.Ed.2d 430, 89S.Ct. 1827); *In re Harris*, (1971) 20 Cal.App.3d 632.

The first officially appointed probation officer of Alameda County was a young attorney by the name of Ezra Decoto. Appointed on June 4, 1904, he was paid $50 per month through subscriptions sought by the Oakland Club, a civic group. He accepted the position on appointment by the Superior Court stating that he "would visit the courts twice a week and do what he could toward securing probation in some cases." In 1905, Decoto was provided with three deputy probation officers. Some years later, as district attorney, Decoto castigated publicly the then–probation officer for being too lenient. By 1979 the staff of the county Probation Department would consist of eight hundred persons.

PROHIBITION

During Decoto's administration, the 18th Amendment to the U.S. Constitution—Prohibition—became effective. Between 1919, when the California Legislature ratified the constitutional proposal, and 1933, when the 21st Amendment was ratified, repealing the 18th Amendment, considerable time of office personnel was consumed in the investigation and prosecution of violations of Prohibition laws.

In 1913, the Legislature had passed a law making prostitution illegal and enacted a Red Light Abatement Act under which premises used for purposes of prostitution could be locked up for a period of a year in a civil action. During Prohibition, the Legislature also enacted a law under which premises where violations of Prohibition laws occurred could be abated and padlocked for a period of up to a year through a civil action without a jury. During Decoto's and Warren's administrations, over one hundred abatement cases resulted in padlocking premises where Prohibition laws were violated.

During Decoto's administration, there was occasional needling by the press. This bothered him and probably precipitated his move to the Railroad Commission. On one occasion, a daily paper came out with a series in glaring headlines about vice conditions in Emeryville. These articles were based upon reports of a local minister who claimed to have visited, incognito, certain of the places where various forms of vice prevailed.

Decoto made a sincere and earnest effort to enforce all laws including the laws regarding Prohibition. He did not drink or smoke himself and he did not permit smoking or drinking in the District Attorney's Office. "No smoking" signs throughout the office notified staff and customers alike of the policy. If a deputy or customer wanted to smoke, he went outside the office to do so.

Decoto was in great demand as a public speaker, especially at dinners where he entertained with a repertoire of humorous stories in dialect. Although he did not go into court often, when he did he was a formidable advocate. He could be quite pontifical.

Over the years before the 1950's, there were relatively few changes in criminal law. A district attorney with previous criminal trial experience could go into court without worrying about the possibility of being surprised by some recent departure from precedent. Year after year the law remained virtually the same.

When two Superior Court judges, Lincoln S. Church and Fred V. Wood, sitting in bank, decided that mere possession of an alcoholic beverage for personal use only, without evidence of intent to sell, was not unlawful, Decoto was quite disturbed because he believed this would weaken enforcement of the law. Traffic in and use of alcoholic beverages grew apace and the so–called "speakeasy," "blind pig" and "gin mill" came into existence and increased in numbers and patronage. The public grew apathetic about liquor law enforcement and there were not enough policemen to provide consistent comprehensive enforcement.

In fairness it should be said that, by and large, city policemen—at least in Alameda County—tried to enforce the liquor laws. Generally, jurors were not so enforcement–minded. Liquor law violators generally waived jury trial or pleaded guilty and were fined or given short sentences in the county jail.

Driving while under the influence of liquor was then a crime triable as a felony in the Superior Court and punishable by imprisonment in state prison or by a misdemeanor punishment of fine or county jail confinement. This law was later changed, and driving while drunk, in the absence of injury to another person, became a misdemeanor, generally punished with a fine.

As the use of the automobile increased, the number of drunk driving cases increased and added greatly to criminal calendars in courts of misdemeanor jurisdiction. Increased penalties, including imprisonment and loss of license for repetition of this offense, caused attorneys to plead not guilty, demand trial by jury, and maneuver for assignment or transfer of cases to courts where they thought certain judges were more lenient than others. This practice, known as "judge shopping," added to court calendar congestion and delay. In our modern day, electronic automated processing of misdemeanor calendars by clerks or other attachés mitigates, somewhat, that process.

DECOTO'S ATTORNEYS

Earl Warren was appointed deputy district attorney by Decoto at the bottom salary of $150 a month on May 1, 1920, to fill a vacancy left by O. D. Hamlin, Jr., who had served in the office under Hynes and Decoto from 1915. Hamlin went into private practice with Donahue and Hynes. Later, he was appointed to the Superior Court by Governor Warren, to the United States District Court and to the United States Court of Appeals by President Eisenhower.

Harry Styles and I were appointed deputy district attorneys by Decoto on February 21, 1923. There were then twelve attorneys in the office, viz. Ezra Decoto, Frank Shay, Earl Warren, Ralph Hoyt, Fred Donahue, Donald McClure, Agnes Polsdorfer, James Walsh, Frank Mitchel, Preston Higgins, Wade Snook and Milton Sevier. Now, 60 years later, there are 126 lawyers in the office.

During my first two years in the District Attorney's Office, my assignment was what was called the "country run," which involved handling whatever business was pending in the six justice courts of south–county located in San Leandro, Hayward, Niles, Centerville, Livermore and Pleasanton. It was, in fact, like riding circuit. This assignment took a day and a half. Now there are three branch offices with 24 deputies full–time covering the same territory.

With the exception of Centerville, the judges of south–county justice courts were non–lawyers. If any legal problems arose, they leaned on the District Attorney's Office, although for the most part they could, and did, decide cases according to their own common sense—which was usually sound. We were careful not to charge anyone with an offense unless we were satisfied with the proof. Rarely was there a not guilty plea.

MOVIE STARS

Before the California Highway Patrol was established by the state Legislature, traffic control in southern Alameda County was handled by county motorcycle officers who were on the payroll of the District Attorney's Office. In about 1912, during that period when motorcycle officers worked for the District Attorney's Office, the movie industry came west and started making movies in Niles under the name of Essanay. They built a large barn–like building at Niles for the studio. Many of the early movies were made there. If Oakland had had the kind of live–wire Chamber of Commerce that Los Angeles had in those days, maybe the movie business would have been in Alameda County instead of Hollywood. In the group of actors and actresses were Bronco Billy Anderson, Wallace Beery, Ben Turpin, Marie Prevost, Charlie Chaplin, Mabel Normand, Marie Dressler, Vick Potel and others of Keystone comedy fame.

Wallace Beery had a high–powered souped–up Mercer. At that time the road from Niles to San Jose was a relatively straight, two–lane, unpaved road. For dinner, Beery used to drive from Niles to San Jose, where there were some very good Italian restaurants in which Beery indulged freely of the good Italian wine. On his return to Niles, he would drive through San Jose and Milpitas, which were in Santa Clara County—usually at excessive rates of speed.

The Santa Clara County officers were never able to clock him. So, after several futile efforts, one of them got a complaint and warrant for his arrest for reckless driving. The bail on the warrant was $200. It was sent to Decoto who gave it to Leon Solon, one of our traffic officers, to execute. Solon and Beery were good friends.

When he had the opportunity, he encountered Beery, presented the warrant and told him that he was under arrest.

Beery said, “Well, what do I do now?”

“The bail is $200,” Solon replied. “If you want to go to trial you can be tried on the charge or you can forfeit the bail.”

Beery reached into his pocket, pulled out a handful of five, ten and twenty dollar gold pieces and said, “Here, take $200.”

“No,” Solon said, “I can’t do it that way, you have to put it up with the judge,” which he did and paid the fine. Leon used to say, “Beery was a great guy and everyone liked him, but I had a hell of a time keeping him out of jail.”

THE BANK PRESIDENT

On another occasion, Solon gave a ticket for speeding to August May, who was the president of the Bank of America. There were relatively few automobiles and few speeding arrests in those days. When Leon sent the stubs through to Decoto, who was August May’s brother–in–law, Decoto got a laugh out of it and thought it was a good joke on his brother–in–law.

So, May was charged and the case came up before Judge Mattos, who was the justice of the peace in Centerville. Mattos was president of a competing bank in south–county and knew May quite well. He likewise enjoyed the situation and relished the opportunity of confrontation with his competitor in court under the circumstances. May pleaded guilty and Mattos imposed the maximum penalty.

AND A MAN WITH INFLUENCE

Louie Eicke, another of the district attorney’s traffic officers and a long–time and highly respected resident of Hayward, patrolled the area around Hayward and in Dublin Canyon between Dublin and Hayward, then a sparsely inhabited cattle country. The road between Dublin and Hayward was two lanes and had many dangerous curves.

One day, he gave a speeder a ticket in Dublin Canyon, and told him he would have to appear before Judge Harder in Hayward the following Monday. During the week, the speeder came to my office in the old courthouse, introduced himself as a very important citizen of Stockton, a friend of the governor and many other high–ranking officials in Sacramento.

He said, "I assume that you will dismiss this thing and there will be no more trouble about it."

"We don't do things that way in this county," I told him firmly.

"What do you mean?" he replied. "I never have to worry about speeding tickets in *my* county!"

"You will have to worry about this one, and you had better be at Judge Harder's court at ten o'clock on Monday," I said.

Furious, he shouted, "I'll get your job and I'll get Eicke's job, too!"

"O.K.," I retorted, "but you had better be there, or there will be a warrant for your arrest."

He was there on Monday morning, pleaded not guilty and demanded a jury trial. The citation charged him with speeding at 38 miles an hour, which was unlawful and particularly hazardous under the conditions at that time in Dublin Canyon. He asked for a month's continuance. Judge Harder said that the case would go to trial immediately, whereupon he ordered the constable to go out and get a jury panel.

The constable brought in about twenty jurors, whom he summoned on the street in the neighborhood of the court, and the jury was quickly selected. Louie Eicke testified that the man was going better than 38 miles an hour and passing other cars on the curves. The defendant testified and took issue with Louie Eicke's testimony.

In my summation to the jury I said: "The question here is whether or not Louie Eicke is telling the truth or whether this defendant is telling the truth. It is up to you. If you believe Louie, the verdict should be guilty."

Louie was well known and liked by practically everyone in south–county. He had always been fair and honest. The jury was out about three minutes and came in with a verdict of guilty. Judge Harder imposed a fine of $100 on the defendant. The defendant did not have $100 cash, so the judge directed the constable to take him into custody and deliver him to the sheriff at the county jail in Oakland. In due course the defendant raised the money and was released. Country judges believed that prompt justice was a deterrent.

THE COUNTRY JUDGES

The justice of the peace was an elective, part–time office. The justice usually had other employment. William Gannon, judge in San Leandro and Eden Township Justice Court, worked in a bank. Jacob Harder, Eden Township justice of the peace in Hayward, was a realtor and director of the Hayward Unified School District. Ralph Richmond of Niles, later a county supervisor, was a grocer. Judge Mickle, a Justice Court judge of Washington Township, was a country lawyer in Centerville. Fitzgerald, the justice of the peace of Murray Township in Livermore, was a blacksmith in the Livermore Valley, which was predominately cattle, sheep and wine country. Fitzgerald did a thriving business as a blacksmith. Livermore later became the site of one of the leading rodeos of the West.

Judge Patrick Quinn, justice of the peace of Pleasanton Township, had been a carriage and railroad car painter, a craft that he learned after coming to the United States in 1865 from Tipperary County, Ireland. Before settling in Pleasanton in 1880, he had worked at his trade on cars of the New York Central and Pennsylvania railroads and on street cars in San Francisco. In 1898, he was elected justice of the peace of Pleasanton Township, a position that, as of 1925 when I was riding circuit on the "country run," he had held continuously, and which he could continue to hold as long as he desired. During this period he also held the office of city recorder of Pleasanton. His continuous service as judge exceeded that of any other judge in California. He had been elected and reelected repeatedly without opposition. A history of Alameda County published in 1928 characterized Judge Quinn as "a man of clear–headed judgment and a sound sense of justice and fairness. He has to a marked degree commanded the confidence and esteem of his fellow citizens."

William Davis, as mayor of Pleasanton, presided in the Mayor's Court of the city of Pleasanton. He was also owner–publisher and editor of the Pleasanton weekly newspaper.

These country judges, as they were called, were well known and highly respected men of their communities. The jurisdiction of these courts in civil cases was in claims up to $300 and in criminal cases in misdemeanors for which the maximum punishment was six months or $500, or both. In my time in the District Attorney's Office I never heard of a serious complaint concerning their work, and there was never an appeal or *denovo* proceeding in any case over which they had presided. With the growth of the county and the advent of automobiles, the volume of their case loads increased markedly, and eventually, by constitutional amendment, most of the Justice of the Peace Courts became Municipal Courts.

A CASE OF LIBEL

A case of considerable significance during Decoto's regime was a criminal libel case entitled *People v. Phillip Riley.* Riley published a scurrilous weekly paper in which he lampooned and often libeled public officials. Riley's *Free Press*, as it was called, was sold for a nickel by the street vendors who sold daily newspapers. It probably had the largest non–paying circulation of readers per issue of any paper in the state. Other than Riley's comical distortion of facts ridiculing incumbent politicians and persons prominent in community affairs, the news content of the *Free Press* was nihil.

Because criminal libel was a misdemeanor, the case was filed in the Oakland Police Court and tried by jury there, a rare proceeding then in the courts of misdemeanor jurisdiction. Decoto assigned Earl Warren and Carlisle Crosby to prosecute the case. After three trials in which the jury disagreed each time, the case was dismissed.

Riley's attorney filed a civil action for damages against the surety companies in the United States District Court in San Francisco on official performance bonds of Decoto, the chief of police and the judge under the diversity of citizenship law. The official bonds contained hold–harmless clauses as to the sureties, so I handled the litigation in the United States District Court and the United States Court of Appeals which ruled in favor of the defendant bond companies. In doing so, these courts held that judges and prosecutors had an absolute immunity from liability in an action for damages for any injury caused in the performance of their official duties, and extended such immunity to police in execution of process legal on its face.

Jim Oakley, one of the deputies in the Civil Division of the District Attorney's Office, who handled civil actions against county officials, used to call the Riley case his bible because it enabled him to get such cases summarily dismissed without trial. It also helped district attorneys in other jurisdictions who were subjected to harassment suits.

THE PIGEON DROP

One of the first cases I prosecuted during Decoto's regime involved the #1 man of a "pigeon drop" bunco team. The victim was a little old man named Johnson, age 75, who had toiled all of his adult years prospecting in the gold fields of the Yukon and Klondike. He had saved about $8,000 which he had in a savings account in a Seattle bank. Infirm and crippled with rheumatism, he had come to San Francisco in 1924 with the thought of buying a little chicken ranch around Petaluma to live out his days in peace and quiet in the comparative warmth of Sonoma County.

While Johnson was standing on the Market Street sidewalk in San Francisco, looking at the buildings and the traffic, a young Italian named Bergoni, the #1 man in the pigeon drop team, engaged him in idle conversation and began to cultivate him. Bergoni questioned him about what he was doing in San Francisco, where he was from, and where he was staying. Bergoni suggested that they have some coffee. They parted on a pleasant note.

The next day Bergoni encountered Johnson, his new–found Alaskan friend, supposedly by accident, and suggested that they ride across the Bay on a ferry boat to see Oakland. While walking in Oakland, Bergoni and Johnson were encountered by the #2 member of the team, who excitedly showed a wallet containing what appeared to be several thousands of dollars and important documents that he said he had just found on the street.

The #2 man and Bergoni discussed what to do with the wallet. Johnson suggested that they look in the wallet to see who the owner was. The #2 man did so and found a name and address. He said he would contact this person about the ownership of the wallet and the money. The #2 man left and returned in a little while saying that the man he contacted properly established his ownership of the wallet and wanted to give a substantial reward by giving information to a sure–fire investment in a certain stock.

Shortly thereafter, the #3 member of the team appeared, further identifying the wallet and discussing the stock investment matter. At this point Bergoni and the #2 man suggested that inasmuch as Johnson was with them when the wallet was found he should be permitted to participate in the reward. But the #3 man said that Bergoni and the #2 man and Johnson would have to show that they were people of substance and had the necessary funds to invest. Johnson was asked if had any money. He said he had money in a bank in Seattle.

He was taken to a bank in Oakland, where arrangements were made for the transfer of his account in the Seattle bank to the Oakland bank. Johnson had the passbook for his account in the Seattle bank showing some $8,000 on deposit, so the transfer of funds was accomplished without delay.

With Johnson's money now in the Oakland bank, #3 then said Bergoni and #2 and Johnson should put up $8,000 apiece to manifest their honesty and good faith and their ability to capitalize on the stock investment. So it was suggested that Johnson withdraw $8,000, which he did, and put it in a small satchel that he was permitted to hold. In due course, Bergoni and #2 appeared and, opening the satchel, put into it what seemed to be large rolls of greenbacks purporting to represent $16,000. The satchel was left in Johnson's custody and arrangements were made to meet at Johnson's hotel the next day, whereupon they separated.

When they did not appear, Johnson opened the satchel and found his money gone and that the two rolls of what appeared to be currency were pieces of newspaper cut the size of currency with a few greenbacks on the outside of the rolls. Johnson went to the San

Francisco Police and was directed to the Oakland Police Pepartment. A complaint was filed, and, shortly thereafter, Bergoni was arrested.

I was assigned to prosecute the case. In preparing for trial, I spent many hours talking with Johnson. It was a heart–rending experience. Johnson was extremely depressed, saying that since the loss of his money he had several times thought of suicide. He had lost everything and was too old to go back to prospecting. He was in a state of complete frustration and confusion.

The significance of this case is the seriousness and tragedy of a bunco case. The typical bunco artist is a professional thief, absolutely ruthless in his operation. The victim of the robber, burglar or pickpocket loses what he may have on his person or in his home, but the victim of the bunco man generally loses everything and is usually one who can ill afford to do so. I once heard Earl Warren, addressing a convention in Oakland, say that he hated a bunco man worse than a murderer. Early in his career in the District Attorney's Office, Warren had prosecuted a bunco case. When the victim of a crook, especially an elderly victim, is stripped of a life's savings, the prolonged frustration from which he cannot recover is often worse than death.

OFFICE RUMORS

During his time in the District Attorney's Office, Decoto had developed a substantial private practice. After his second election to the office of district attorney in 1922, rumors started to the effect that he would move on to other public office in which he could better continue his private practice. Such a spot was the California Railroad Commission. There was speculation as to who would succeed him if his move came before the next election in 1926.

3

Earl Warren 1925—1938

In 1923, Theodore Witschen, an able lawyer who handled the Board of Supervisors' work, resigned to become chief counsel for Miller and Lux, one of the nation's largest cattle producers and meat packers. Decoto appointed Warren to Witschen's position and assigned him to handle Witschen's work with the Board of Supervisors. Warren won favor with three of the five supervisors, viz. Charles Hyer, Ralph Richmond and John Mullins, who voted for him for district attorney when Decoto was appointed to the Railroad Commission on January 12, 1925, by Governor Friend Richardson, who also favored Warren for district attorney.

There were several attorneys on the staff senior to Warren at the time. Frank Shay, the assistant in charge of the criminal work and the chief trial attorney, outranked all the attorneys including Warren. Shay, an older man who in his youth had been a sailor and a pal of Jack London, had many friends among the judges, county officials and attorneys in private practice. When Witschen resigned, it was thought that Shay would be next in line for the top spot if Decoto left the office. Michael Kelly, a political leader in the county who had great influence with the Board of Supervisors, favored Shay and had actively supported three of the five supervisors, viz. Chairman William Hamilton, Rudy Staats and John Mullins. In voting for Warren, Mullins offended Kelly and at the next election for county supervisor he was defeated. The day Warren was appointed district attorney, Shay left the office and never returned. He had spent many years in the District Attorney's Office, and he was greatly disappointed. He practiced law for a short while and then retired to his ranch near Gilroy in the Santa Clara Valley.

Warren made some changes in the staff assignments. He moved Ralph Hoyt and Wade Snook to the two positions of assistant district attorney in the main office. At this time there was one branch office at the Oakland City Hall which serviced the Oakland Police Department and the two Police Courts. Milton Sevier had been one of the two prosecutors at the Oakland Police Court. The other prosecutor there was Fred Donahue, brother of former District Attorney William Donahue.

The position of prosecuting attorney in the Oakland Police Court was actually part time. The two Police Court judges, Edward Tyrrell and William Hennessey, generally finished their calendars before noon. The judges and the Police Court prosecutors had non–conflicting private practices and as soon as the calendars were finished, they returned to their law offices. Cases on the calendar of the Police Court were predominantly of chronic alcoholics and prostitutes and sentences varied. If the City Jail needed a cook, a drunk with a long record of arrests who was known to be a good cook might receive an extended period of confinement, during which he would serve time as cook and trustee with certain privileges. When released, he was well dried out unless a trustee who did janitorial work around the City Hall had managed to get some liquor at a nearby bar and had shared an occasional covert drink with him.

Sevier, an able trial lawyer, upon transfer to the "main office," as it was called, was assigned to the calendars in the two Superior Court departments which handled felony criminal cases. The main office assignment apparently cut into Sevier's private practice and after several months he moved back to the part–time work of the Police Court. I was then appointed chief deputy. A month later in May, 1926, Wade Snook resigned to join his father, a former district attorney, in private practice. I was then appointed assistant district attorney in Snook's place.

At this time, 1926, two positions of assistant district attorney were top spots on the payroll with salaries of $300 a month each. The range of salaries for lawyers in the office was from $1,800 a year to $5,000 for the district attorney. The salary of the district attorney was later increased by the Legislature from $417 to $600 a month, where it remained during Warren's incumbency. All of the lawyers could, and most did, handle non–conflicting private practice.

There was only one investigator, George Helms, in the office at this time. There was no public defender until 1927, when the position was created under the county Charter which was adopted by a vote of the people in 1926. Willard Shea was appointed public defender by the Board of Supervisors and served without assistance until Raymond Ferrario of Livermore became his first assistant. Later, Kennett Forsman became a deputy public defender. By 1979, the Public Defender's Office had grown to 101 lawyers and 26 investigators. Incidentally, all salaries were reduced ten percent during the Great Depression of the 1930's.

Howard Bacon succeeded Judge Hennessey on the Oakland Police Court. Not long thereafter, a man walked into his office and shot him dead. He was succeeded by Christopher Fox, who later became a Superior Court judge.

Judge Tyrrell, who served for many years on the Police Court, was a self–educated lawyer, a colleague of Governor Hiram Johnson in politics and, at one–time, a state senator. While a young man, he had contracted tuberculosis and gone to Arizona to live. While there, he studied shorthand and supported himself by working as a court reporter until he recovered and returned to Oakland. A genial redheaded Irishman of great understanding and common sense, he was highly respected and had a legion of friends. He left the Police Court in 1936, when he was appointed to the Superior Court, where he served with distinction until he retired.

He and George "Chick" Wade were close friends from the days when they were boys in west Oakland. One of Wade's functions as county clerk was to issue marriage licenses. Many of the licensees had no preference as to who would perform the marriage ceremony and would ask Wade or one of his deputies how to make arrangements. During his service in the Police Court, Judge Tyrrell was always willing and available for this service, except when he might be playing the horses, sitting with his friends Ben Woolner and Walter Harris in his box on the finish line at Bay Meadows, Tanforan or Golden Gate Fields. Through the years I handled many cases before Judge Tyrrell. The countless attorneys who appeared before him often wished, as I did, that we had more judges like the "redhead." During his retirement, after the revolution in criminal law, the judge remarked to me: "I am glad I am not on the bench now. I'd be reversed every month"—a monstrous self–denigration because appeals from his decisions were extremely rare and he was never reversed.

The appointment of Earl Warren marked an important transition in the operation of the District Attorney's Office of Alameda County. Prior to his appointment, the tempo of the office had been slow and easy—a reflection of the laissez–faire condition of the time, a period when the position of district attorney was a stop gap in a lawyer's career during which time he increased his private law practice, enhanced his reputation and aspired to other employment, such as appointment to the bench or return to a more lucrative practice. It was a period also of more camaraderie among judges and opposing counsel in litigation; when counsel and a judge would repair at noon recess to a convenient restaurant for a leisurely meal and oftentimes settlement of the lawsuit.

Many years before World War I, Oakland had become the terminal of three transcontinental railroad systems: the Southern Pacific, the Santa Fc and the Western Pacific Rio Grande. A branch of the Great Northern connected with the Western Pacific in Northern California and Great Northern freight trains came to Oakland on Western Pacific tracks. It was also a terminal of considerable coastwise interstate and intrastate railroad and highway traffic. However, there was no serious crime problem. The population and industrial growth of Alameda County was gradual. Oakland was called the "bedroom" of San Francisco. With shipbuilding and other war activities, there was a heavy influx of people during World War I. Following World War I, the population and industrial growth of Alameda County, and particularly Oakland, was accompanied by a steady growth in the work of the District Attorney's Office in both criminal and civil public law matters. When Warren became district attorney in 1925, the population of the county was about 400,000.

Warren proved to be a shrewd administrator and innovator, with plenty of savvy and courage. Tom Stark, owner, publisher and editor of a daily Santa Barbara newspaper and a quite successful and powerful life–long California Democrat, once said to me, "Warren is a master politician." Warren ran for election seven times: for district attorney three, attorney general one and governor three. He won easily each time.

Before entering the District Attorney's Office, he served as a clerk for the Judicial Committee of the Assembly—the lower house of the state Legislature—where he acquired some knowledge of legislative procedures; a knowledge which he used to advantage in later years. With Decoto's approval, he got one of his friends in the Legislature to introduce a bill to provide a secret fund for each district attorney's office in the state to be used for investigative purposes. This proved to be very helpful to district attorneys.

It did not take Warren long to start changing the operation of the office. One of the first things was the filing system, which had to be coordinated, in form and content, with the filing systems of the courts and the County Clerk's Office. This was a big improvement and long overdue. Work hours were theoretically Monday through Saturday forenoon. Warren was not district attorney long before some deputies and Hoyt and I were working much longer hours. Warren caused the cramped space of the main office in the old courthouse at Fifth and Broadway, built in 1874, to be cut up into smaller rooms to accommodate anticipated increases in personnel and to provide a combination library and conference room.

In the District Attorney's Office of Los Angeles County, a scholarly and able lawyer named Charles Fricke, who taught law collaterally, had initiated a modest continuing legal education program in his office. Fricke later became a Superior Court judge and authored a number of books on criminal law and procedure. His program consisted of weekly meetings of the lawyers on the staff at which they reviewed recent decisions in criminal law of the California Supreme Court and District Courts of Appeal.

Warren sent me to Los Angeles to find out about it. I discussed it with Fricke, returned to Oakland and helped Warren initiate an in–service continuing education program, which became part of weekly meetings in the main office. The attorneys in the main office met with Warren every Saturday morning from 8:30 a.m. until we finished. At that time, I was teaching collaterally at night at Saint Mary's College Law School in Oakland. Warren asked me to review the decisions of the higher courts of California which appeared weekly in the advance publications. The reviews and discussion of the decisions were subsequently extended to include decisions of the United States Supreme Court affecting law enforcement. Before 1950, few decisions of that court concerned criminal law, especially in application to state law enforcement. Later, review of the appellate decisions was rotated weekly among the lawyers of the main office staff. This chore greatly increased after the 1950's.

Ultimately, the in–service continuing legal education program of our office increased so much that it became a full–time assignment of one deputy, John Meehan, sometimes called the "Wizard of Warrants." Meehan produced a monthly publication in which recent decisions of the California appellate courts and the United States Supreme Court involving criminal law were analyzed, summarized and their impact upon the administration of criminal justice discussed. This publication was called *Point of View* and was widely distributed not only to deputies but to judges and law enforcement officers throughout the county and state.

Meehan was singularly qualified to handle this assignment. Reared in San Francisco in an atmosphere of law enforcement, his distinguished father was a Captain in the San Francisco Police Department. Like his father, Meehan became dedicated to service in law enforcement. Upon his admission to practice, I appointed him a deputy in the District Attorney's Office. During Lowell Jensen's administration, Meehan's weekly oral review of recent criminal law decisions was videotaped and distributed to the seven branch offices. Under Meehan, the in–service continuing education program became one of the best—if not the best—in the United States.

During Warren's administration, the size of the staff, although growing steadily, was such that the lawyers could be assembled for the Saturday morning meetings in the library. At these meetings, in addition to reviewing decisions and pending cases, legal and policy problems were discussed and solutions proposed. This live, case–by–case Socratic dialogue, in which Warren participated personally, was a most stimulating and helpful kind of continuing education in the operation of a district attorney's office in both criminal and civil public law matters. It was also helpful politically. Woe betide the deputy who, in an office meeting, asked a stupid question or pronounced a puerile thesis. Warren was quick to demolish puerility in discussion. Although not bookish or of scholarly bent, he had a prodigious memory, strong personal predilections, and an uncanny sense of what the law was or ought to be and of the right solution to a problem.

Under Warren, a second branch office with one deputy was opened in Berkeley to service the police departments of Berkeley and Albany and the courts in those cities. George Perkins, grandson of United States Senator Perkins, was the first deputy in charge of this office, followed by Arthur Sherry. The two men had graduated from Boalt Hall law school at the University of California and, over a period of years, became distinguished trial lawyers. Perkins went into private practice. Sherry, after service in the United States Air Force during World War II, returned to serve in the District Attorney's Office for several years and later served as an assistant in the California Attorney General's Office, as counsel for Governor Warren's Organized Crime Commission, as director of the Ford Foundation/American Bar Association study of prosecutions in the United States, and as successor to Warren Olney III as a professor of criminal law at Boalt Hall. Sherry said that the continuing education program in the District Attorney's Office of Alameda County was the best in the nation. As director of the Ford Foundation/American Bar Association study of prosecutions throughout the United States, Sherry was certainly in a position to make such an appraisal.

A branch office was set up in Hayward in the 1930's to handle the criminal business of the District Attorney's Office south of Oakland.

After World War II, as the population of the county increased, branch offices were set up in the cities of Alameda, San Leandro, Fremont and Livermore. Before the Hayward branch office was set up in south county, James C. Walsh, Sr. rode the circuit and handled this territory. Walsh left the office to run for county supervisor.

It was considered impolitic and was contrary to office policy for a person, while in the District Attorney's Office, to run against an incumbent candidate for another office. Walsh's son subsequently became a deputy in the District Attorney's Office and in the California Attorney General's Office and a judge of the Municipal Court in Oakland.

Among other changes effected by Warren was a speed–up of the movement of felony cases through the Superior Court departments. The California Penal Code required a felony case to be tried within 60 days of arraignment, unless time was waived by the defendant. This was a requirement more honored in the breach because it was the practice of defense counsel to waive time and move for continuance, a request invariably concurred in by the District Attorney's Office and the Court. Defense counsel usually wanted more time to collect their fee. Delay also generally helped the defense. Consequently there was a steady backlog of cases set for arraignment or trial.

At that time there were few pretrial motions challenging sufficiency of evidence or methods by which the defendant was arrested or evidence obtained, such as is now the norm. Under the long–standing rule of Anglo–Saxon law prevailing in the United States and throughout the British Commonwealth, a challenge to the method of arrest or seizure of evidence did not lie (i.e., it was not sustainable in the law). It made no difference how the arrest was made or the evidence obtained. Consequently, a trial could be moved along expeditiously if the Court and counsel so desired.

Not long after Warren was appointed, his friend Leon Gray was appointed to the Superior Court bench, and the two collaborated to eliminate the customary time waivers and continuances. This was vigorously opposed by defense counsel—to no avail. Over their persistent protests, cases were promptly set for plea or trial and tried on the date set or as soon thereafter as a trial time and court were available. The result was that guilty pleas increased and cases went to trial within the 60 day period. Our target date was 30 days, which was achieved in Judge Gray's department. There was little so–called "plea bargaining" and no sentence bargaining.

Police brought their evidence to the District Attorney's Office for legal evaluation before issuance of complaints. Occasionally a lazy, incompetent, overly optimistic police inspector might oversell his case, but the faults or habits of such policemen surfaced eventually, and their subsequent presentations were closely scrutinized and more cautiously handled. If a mistake occurred in charging because the legally admissible evidence fell short of proof beyond a reasonable doubt and was discovered before trial, the case could and would be dismissed, or if mitigating circumstances indicated the charge should be reduced, this could and would be done. It was a matter of policy in the District Attorney's Office that a citizen accused of a crime was entitled to have a competent legal appraisal of the proof against him made before he was subjected to the stigma, expense and ordeal of defending the charge, and this regardless of whether another citizen or the police had demanded a complaint.

As a result of the calendar speed–up and more careful pre–charge review of the evidence presented, we were able to operate in Alameda County with two regular criminal departments well into the 1950's when the so–called revolution in criminal law began to take its toll with countless time–consuming and often frivolous pretrial proceedings. Reasonably prompt disposition of cases after arrest makes for better and less costly law enforcement. I believe it also makes for less crime.

During his early years as district attorney, Warren increased the staff by appointing attorneys who had been in private practice for some time. Among these were Richard H. Chamberlain, Leonard J. Meltzer, Charles D. Wehr, Maurice J. Bleuel, George C. Perkins, Robert M. Ford, Howard Wilke and Nathan Harry Miller. A few years later he favored young law school graduates. Among these were Marshall Ricksen, James H. Freeman, Joseph Murphy, Lawrence Fletcher, Theodore A. Westphal, William Maxfield, Cecil

Mosbacher, Cameron W. Wolfe, Arthur H. Sherry, Folger Emerson, Stanley C. Smallwood and Joseph Schenone. This policy was continued after Warren became attorney general.

A substantial percentage of the Alameda County Bar worked in the District Attorney's Office before going into private practice. Many of them became judges in the state Municipal and Superior Courts and in federal courts. Some went on to the United States Attorney General's Office and to positions in state government. There was a personal satisfaction in training these young men and women and in seeing so many of them go on to other public service or to successful private practice and prestigious stature in their profession and communities.

Before Warren became district attorney, practically all investigative work in criminal cases was done by police, constables or sheriff's men. In the cities of Oakland, Berkeley, Piedmont, Albany and Alameda the sheriff's office did no police work. In the smaller cities and communities of the county, the sheriff assisted the police and the township constables. The latter were elected county officials who were largely responsible for keeping the peace in their townships. We decided to supplement investigations in murder cases by having personnel of the District Attorney's Office enter the case in its initial stage, in fact as soon as a likely suspect was found. Of course, as in most criminal cases involving violence—murder, robbery, burglary or rape—it camc to thc attention of the police, sheriff or constable first. We worked out a system whereby, in homicide cases, a team from the District Attorney's Office interviewed the suspect as soon as the police finished talking to him and we could proceed without interfering with the police. It was our policy to keep any mention of our participation in the police investigation out of the media, although this was not always possible.

In the early years, the district attorney's team consisted of myself, an inspector and a stenographic court reporter who could qualify to testify to the accuracy of the transcription of his or her notes. Later, we were able to employ directly in the District Attorney's Office our own stenographers, whose shorthand speed were adequate and who could likewise qualify to testify in court. As soon as we were notified by police of a murder and they had a suspect in custody, the district attorney's team went to the scene of the crime or to the police department to interview the suspect. This was often at night, by the way, when most murders occurred.

As far back as I can remember, if the victim of a violent assault was in danger of death and his doctor was willing to advise him that he was about to die, a deputy from our office would be summoned by the police to take a dying statement which, if made by the victim in contemplation of death, would no longer be considered legally as hearsay, but would become admissible at the murder trial.

In questioning a suspect there was no *Miranda* admonition. The method used was by simple question and answer concerning the facts. The suspect would be asked his name, age, occupation, address, and what had happened in connection with the crime. The reporter wrote and transcribed every word of the interview from beginning to end, so that a proper foundation could be laid in court, as required by law, that the defendant's statement was free and voluntary. As a rule, only one officer, the stenographer, the interviewer and the suspect were present, so no claim of intimidation could be made.

This method continued until the *Miranda*[9] decision in the United States Supreme Court. We continued to interview suspects and arrestees after *Miranda* but confessions dropped off, which made developing proof beyond a reasonable doubt more difficult. It should be said in fairness that district attorneys and police officers adjusted promptly to the *Miranda* and other restrictive decisions of the Supreme Court as well as the decisions of the courts of their own states. The *Miranda* formula was reproduced on cards which police officers carried and used. There was little trouble in the courts about police and prosecutor compliance. However, other decisions of the higher courts often posed problems in areas of probable cause for arrest of suspects and search and seizure of evidence. Probable cause, which is basic with respect to arrest of suspects and search and seizure of evidence, is not something which can be measured mathe-

[9] *Miranda v. Arizona* (1966) 384 U.S. 436

matically. It is flexible and may differ according to the circumstances of particular cases.

In August of 1926, a year and a half after Warren was appointed district attorney, he had to run for election. As opponents, he had T. L. Christensen, who proved to be a perennial candidate in each of Warren's next two campaigns, and Preston Higgins, a former deputy district attorney under Ezra Decoto who had entered private practice with Frank Shay. The campaign against Higgins was spirited but Warren won handily. Higgins was tabbed by Warren as a candidate of the underworld.

In 1926, the District Attorney's Office drafted a home–rule freeholder's Charter for the county, which the Board of Supervisors and the voters approved. Under the Charter, all department heads and county employees with the exception of the District Attorney's Office were under Civil Service. Warren did not want Civil Service for the District Attorney's Office. This gave the district attorney complete control over hiring and firing of office personnel. The Charter gave the Board of Supervisors full power to pass county ordinances, create official positions and appropriate funds for the operation of county government.

For many years thereafter, in fact until after World War II, the public defender had no investigative help. As previously mentioned, a very fine gentleman and friend of Warren's who had been a clerk of the District Court of Appeal, Willard Shea, was appointed public defender. He could represent only indigent persons in criminal and civil cases. It turned out that he had little or no time for indigent civil cases. These had to be handled by legal aid attorneys or public interest volunteers, generally young lawyers who wanted experience. Before the public defender was appointed, defendants in criminal cases who were unable to employ counsel were represented by volunteers or court appointed attorneys. Great progress has been made in the last few years in legal services for the poor. Now in Alameda County, in a criminal case with more than one indigent defendant, the defendants are provided separate counsel at the expense of the county.

THE BAIL BONDS BROKER SCAM

Shortly after Warren's appointment in 1925, a case broke involving a bail bonds broker who was indicted for grand theft. In the course of the investigation of this case, it developed that certain bail bonds brokers were operating in collusion with certain policemen and attorneys.

Upon arrest, the policeman would arrange for a certain broker to put up the bail and the broker would designate a certain attorney to represent the defendant. The attorney's fee was split with the broker and the broker split his fee, which generally was ten percent of the amount of the bail, with the policeman. In cases where defendants failed to appear, bail forfeitures were usually not pressed by prosecutors or judges. If filed at all, long delayed actions by the counties to collect on forfeitures were permitted to ride along on court calendars for years while delinquent brokers profited by sale of collateral which they had required defendants or their families to put up.

The whole bail system was loosely handled and was conducive to corruption. This was particularly true in San Francisco where the machinations of certain bail brokers, who wielded awesome political power in local and state government, precipitated a number of scandals in that city. Warren labeled the whole operation as handled by the brokers "a leech upon the judicial system."

At Warren's request, a luncheon meeting of the long dormant Bar Association of Alameda County was called by its perennial president Augustin "Mike" Donovan, a close friend of Warren, at which conditions in the bail bonds system were exposed and denounced. As a result, the unsavory operations of the bail bonds brokers and their impositions upon the courts were cleaned up, and conditions in which defendants were often pawns of policemen, bail brokers and attorneys were eliminated.

BESSIE FERGUSON

In the 1926 election for sheriff of Alameda County, Burton F. Becker, chief of police of the city of Piedmont, ran on a strict law enforcement platform against Frank Barnett who had been sheriff for a quarter of a century.

A few months before the election, Barnett's name was bandied about in connection with the mysterious disappearance of a woman named Bessie Ferguson, a buxom blonde of easy virtue in her mid–twenties. Bessie was quite a playgirl who lived at home with her mother. She was also a clever extortionist who was blackmailing a number of prominent married men. Her modus operandi was to have a love affair with an affluent well–known married man and, after a while, claim she was pregnant, refuse abortion and shake her boyfriend down for child support. She had a number of ardent lovers. She used her sister's baby as part of her act. Her medical history, revealed after her death, showed she was incapable of becoming pregnant.

After her disappearance, rumors spread that Barnett was one of her lovers. According to her mother, the last time she saw her, Bessie said she had a date with Sheriff Barnett. Shortly after her disappearance, pieces of her clothing, blonde hair attached to a piece of human scalp and certain things identified as Bessie's were found in a swamp along the shore of San Francisco Bay in Contra Costa County. A few days later, a sack containing pieces of human bones from which the flesh had been removed was found in a slough of the Bay between Oakland and Alameda. Parts of a human jaw were in the sack to which were attached teeth identified by a dentist as being those of Bessie.

All pertinent evidence was presented to the Alameda County grand jury but it was patently insufficient, so there was no indictment. The sack and other evidence were preserved and stored in the evidence room of the District Attorney's Office against the day when something might turn up to support a prosecution. The bones, teeth and other evidence are still there.

During the primary election of 1926 one of the Hearst newspapers in the East Bay supported Warren's opponent, Preston Higgins, and pressured Warren to prosecute the Ferguson case. As a matter of fact, before the grand jury had even met, Warren had informed the press in confidence of the facts he had in the Ferguson case. The exploitation of the evidence by the East Bay Hearst reporter was a breach of confidence.

Warren had a meeting with the publishers of all the Bay Area newspapers and presented, in confidence and off–the–record, all the evidence he had in the case. It was obviously and admittedly insufficient. John Francis Neyland, chief counsel for the Hearst papers, was outraged and he published an editorial in which he condemned strongly the tactics of the publisher of the local East Bay Hearst paper who had been exploiting the case and caused him to be summarily discharged. With respect to this episode, Warren commented privately to me that he had "learned that you cannot tell things off–the–record to anyone or it may come back in unpredictable ways to plague you."

The Ferguson case was a sexy sensational "who–done–it," and both Becker and the press pilloried Barnett and Bessie's other paramours, although legal proof of guilt was lacking.

GRAFT IN EMERYVILLE

Burton Becker also accused Sheriff Barnett of not doing anything about vice conditions in Emeryville, a small city of about 3,000 population located on the east shore of San Francisco Bay between Oakland and Berkeley. From before the turn of the century, Emeryville had been the site of Shellmound Park, a popular picnic and recreation resort named after mounds of oyster and crab shells piled up through the centuries by the Indians. It was also the site of a famous racetrack. Tracks of the Southern Pacific Railroad Company, which rimmed San Francisco Bay, ran between Shellmound Park and Golden Gate Fields racetrack. Before World War I, the celebrated Lincoln Beachey and other early aviators tested their airplanes and put on flying exhibitions at the Emeryville racetrack. It was there that

Beachey practiced his famous daredevil stunt flying for his day–and–night exhibitions over the Marina at the 1914–15 World's Fair in San Francisco. One day, the wing of a new single–wing plane snapped off during one of his experimental flights and Beachey was killed. Aviation was in its infancy.

Ferryboats crossed the Bay between San Francisco and Oakland, and connected with the railroads and street cars, often carrying people to the park and track in Emeryville. This was a time when few people owned automobiles. There were no auto ferries. Emeryville grew around the racetrack and slowly became a town of industrial plants. It soon proliferated with saloons, bordellos and Chinese lotteries, well patronized by Bay Area residents and students from the University of California at Berkeley. Warren called Emeryville "a vice ridden cancer of crime." Before the 18th Amendment, the Red Light Abatement Act, and the big drive in the early 20th century by the Anti–Saloon League, the Woman's Christian Temperance Union and other organizations against liquor, gambling, horseracing and prostitution, Emeryville was a hotbed of vice. The atmosphere was certainly not conducive to anyone's attempt at closing the town, and this attitude continued even after Prohibition and the Puritan Revolution.

By 1926, when Becker was belaboring Emeryville in his law and order campaign against Barnett, vice conditions there had been about the same for many years. Under the minuscule city government and tiny city police force, vice continued without giving the police trouble, and Barnett, who might have done something about it, did nothing. His own staff was very small and he had plenty to do in the growing unincorporated area of southern Alameda County. He probably never considered usurping the responsibility of the Emeryville Police Department for policing the city. However, he was defeated by Becker in the general election in November 1926.

Not long after the election, rumors began to circulate that the new sheriff, Burton Becker, was beginning to organize a setup whereby he would permit illegal activities in liquor, prostitution, slot machines, Chinese lotteries and other gambling to operate in consideration of payoffs to him or his representatives. He became sheriff on

January 2, 1927, and his graft setup began to function immediately. Warren confirmed the rumors, talked to Becker about them and told him it would have to stop. Becker defied Warren and told him to mind his own business.

In order to combat Becker's illegal activities, Warren asked the Board of Supervisors to create ten investigator positions and to appropriate $25,000 for investigation purposes, pursuant to the home–rule county Charter which had been drafted by the District Attorney's Office, passed by the Board and approved by the electorate in the 1926 election. The Board did so and the District Attorney's Office was in the business of policing Emeryville and some other parts of the county with respect to vice. In due course, the district attorney's inspectors, as the investigators were called, were also supplementing the work of the police departments and initiating investigations in various cases other than vice, such as police misconduct, graft, consumer fraud and special cases.

It should be said here that a district attorney's office which has its own investigators can render a more competent and efficient performance and service to the community than one which has to depend upon investigators who are on the payroll of another department, such as a police or sheriff's department. Warren was determined to have a clean county. Obviously, his office could not eliminate bootlegging, prostitution and gambling completely. Nevertheless, with only ten district attorney's inspectors, accorded the cooperation of honest policemen under competent direction, and by effective use of the grand jury and the other staff of the District Attorney's Office, the county was kept relatively clean. Raids and arrests by inspectors of the District Attorney's Office and honest policemen reduced to a trickle Becker's graft, because he was not staffed to give any protection outside of the unincorporated area of the county. At that time this area was largely agricultural and cattle country and not heavily populated. During 1927, the first year of Becker's incumbency, a few recalcitrants continued to take chances, but eventually they got the message that they could be arrested by the district attorney's men anyway and they discontinued the payoffs to Becker.

Becker's bag man was Fred Smith, an automobile dealer in San Leandro. Smith had become involved in grand theft at his automobile business and was indicted. He disappeared and was missing for almost three years, in spite of intensive efforts to locate him. Finally, Lieutenant Oscar Jahnsen, one of the district attorney's inspectors, arrested Smith in Los Angeles. In accordance with a provision of California law, Warren offered Smith immunity from prosecution on the grand theft charge against him in exchange for his testimony concerning his collection of bribes as bag man for Becker. He agreed to do so and he and his wife testified before the grand jury. Becker, his undersheriff, two of his deputies and an attorney involved with Becker in the payoffs, were indicted for conspiracy to solicit and accept bribes. At trial in 1930, they were convicted and sentenced to state prison.

After a short interim, during which Grant Miller, the coroner of Alameda County, acted as sheriff, the Board of Supervisors appointed Michael Driver, a one–time mayor of Berkeley. Driver had owned and operated a horse–and–wagon express business which, during Driver's time, had involved driving the horses himself. As sheriff, Driver was provided with a county automobile to supervise his territory. He insisted on driving the automobile himself. His county car was frequently in the garage with a variety of bent fenders and other indentations. He did not readily adjust from horses to automobiles. However, Driver was thoroughly honest, as were his successors, Jack Gleason, Frank Madigan, Tom Houchins, Glen Dyer and Charles A. Plummer

After Becker's conviction, there was no trouble with bootlegging, prostitution or gambling in the unincorporated territory under the jurisdiction of the sheriff's office. Bootleggers and Chinese gamblers continued to operate in Emeryville, where Warren's men raided and made arrests.

Because Warren was not satisfied with the juries summoned in the Emeryville City Court, he decided to file complaints in the Berkeley Justice Court. On a hearing of a petition for a writ of prohibition to bar the court in Berkeley from proceeding in a case, the Supreme Court of California held that the Berkeley court had concurrent jurisdiction with the City Court of Emeryville because Emeryville and Berkeley were both located in Oakland Township.[10] As a result of this precedent, Warren continued to file complaints against Emeryville bootleggers and gamblers in the Berkeley court, which policy reduced the volume of vice cases in Emeryville. Judge Edgar, a non–lawyer justice of the peace in Berkeley, was tough on all law violators including speeders whom he often sentenced to jail. Motor vehicles passing from Oakland, Emeryville or Albany into Berkeley usually slowed down to a lawful speed.

STREET PAVING GRAFT

A highly publicized case during Warren's first term involved graft and inferior work performed on street paving contracts in the city of Oakland. In violation of public bidding requirements, for some years paving companies in a conspiracy had been rigging prices on street contracts which, among other things, specified that a certain patented material had to be used in paving Oakland's streets. Actually the material was simply a specified mixture of otherwise common ingredients. Members of the conspiracy controlled the patented material.

Faithful performance bonds of contractors were routinely signed under oath by menial employees of the contractors and falsely certified as financially sufficient to comply with legal requirements. The contractors were indicted for making false oaths on the performance bonds. A city of Oakland commissioner of streets—who was paid by successful bidders a cent a foot on streets laid in which the specified patented paving material was used—was indicted, tried and sentenced to state prison. A leader of a state–wide corrupt paving combine was also convicted and sentenced to state prison. Other officials involved in conflict of interest situations resigned.

The thing which triggered the street paving investigation was the poor quality of streets and curbs installed by the contractors. Had

[10] *Proctor v. Justice's Court of the City of Berkeley* (1930) 209 Cal.39.

the street work been of good quality, knowledge of the payoffs would probably not have surfaced and Warren and the grand jury may never have known about it. These were impact cases which caused the city of Oakland to change the structure of its government from a commission form to a council–manager type. Since that time, the government of Oakland has been free of graft.

THE DISAPPEARING WIFE

Another case of interest resulted in a first–degree murder verdict with life imprisonment, although there was no autopsy or even evidence of a dead body at the time of trial. The defendant, who lived with his wife and children, became enamored with another woman and told his wife he was going to leave her. She protested vehemently, and, during the night, while she and the children were asleep, he killed her with a hammer, scraped the flesh off of her bones and put the flesh in a sack. He sawed the bones into pieces, burned the pieces in a stove and disposed of the remnants of the incinerated bones in a garbage can. The next day he told the children and neighbors that his wife had disappeared.

The police concluded that there was insufficient evidence to support a charge and closed the case. Harry Piper, an inspector in the District Attorney's Office, continued the investigation, and, under a magnifying glass, discovered some spots in a crack on the head–board of the bed in which the defendant's wife used to sleep. He also found in the bedroom a very small piece of hard substance which he suspected might be bone. He had the Western Laboratory, which did our laboratory work, analyze the spots and the piece of hard substance. The spots proved to be human blood of the deceased's type and the hard substance proved to be human bone. Further investigation developed no trace of the defendant's wife. She had been a most exemplary wife and mother and there was no evidence to indicate a desire to desert her family and children. The investigation also disclosed her husband's affair with the other woman.

He was indicted and convicted of murder first–degree and sentenced to imprisonment for life.

After the verdict and sentence, the defendant's attorney told Warren that his client had confessed to him that he had killed his wife and thrown the sack containing her flesh off a bridge over a slough of the San Joaquin River. The defendant could not be prosecuted again because he had been in jeopardy on the murder charge. The defendant and his attorney were taken to the spot below the bridge where divers found the sack containing the human flesh of his wife.

The reason for the attorney disclosing his client's confession was that the client had given him the deed to his home as a fee. The deed was in joint tenancy of the defendant and his wife. In the absence of positive proof that his wife was dead, legal title to the property could not be transferred to the attorney. The attorney later was prosecuted for criminal fraud in another case and joined his client in state prison.

THE CLEANING & DYEING RACKET

The year 1930 was a busy period which involved several important trials. In addition to the cases previously mentioned involving the sheriff's department and the government of the city of Oakland, there was a case involving the cleaning and dyeing business, patterned as a daughter of a racket which started in Chicago. It involved organization of the retail and wholesale cleaning and dyeing business, including all owners, employees, and independent contract drivers of trucks which transported clothes and material between wholesale plants and retail shops.

Bock, a protege of the man who pioneered the first Chicago cleaning and dyeing racket, moved to Southern California where he proceeded to organize a similar racket in the Los Angeles metropolitan area. The *modus operandi* was to organize the retail cleaners and dyers into a dues–paying organization on the representation that, through the organization, prices and profits would be increased. At this point the price of cleaning and pressing a man's suit was forty–nine cents.

At the same time, the inside workers and drivers of the wholesale plants would be organized into a union, and the independent drivers who picked up their residential customers' clothes and took them to a wholesale plant would be organized into another dues–paying group.

There would be a fee of $7.50 to become a member of the retailers association and monthly dues of $2.50, which would be increased from time to time at the whim of the organizer, who pocketed the dues without any accounting. The dues of the inside and outside plant workers were to be paid by the plant owners and their wages were to be thus increased. Eventually the racket leaders would demand a part ownership of certain plants and a substantial amount of the profits, likewise without any accounting. Plants which did not cooperate would be damaged or closed down by strikes and other harassment. An effort was also made to control the wholesale plant drivers who were independent contractors. At first inducement and later intimidation, threats, extortion and sabotage were used in an effort to organize the retailers, wholesalers and drivers.

In the Midwest, bombs, or so–called "pineapples," were exploded in stores, plants and trucks which did not cooperate and follow orders. The leader of the organization of the retail shops, after getting a substantial percentage of the shop owners into the organization, would raise the dues and order the retailers to raise the price of cleaning to a certain figure, generally about double the going rate. After getting control of a wholesale plant owner, either by intimidation or mutual agreement, the wholesale price of cleaning would be raised and likewise the amount charged by the independent drivers. Once control of retailers, plant employees, drivers and wholesale plant owners was accomplished, wages would be raised and profits would be increased—but first a big cut would be taken off the top for the racketeer organizers. Eventually the racketeers would take over the management of the plant.

Of course, complete organization and control could not be achieved, but a substantial amount could be—as in Chicago—by intimidation and actual damage and destruction of the businesses of those who would not cooperate. A suit of clothes with dye in the lining would be left for cleaning at a retail store of a proprietor who would not join the association or raise prices when ordered to do so. When this suit was put in the vat of cleaning fluid at the wholesale plant with hundreds of other suits, the dye would spread throughout the fluid and spoil all of the clothes in the whole batch. Various other means of duress or compulsion were also used.

Bock and his henchmen effected a substantial amount of control in Southern California and then moved to San Francisco where they tried to effect organization of the racket along similar lines. They did not get too far in San Francisco because a Chicago–type racket or shakedown by interlopers was not to be tolerated by San Francisco police. If any payoff racket were to be tolerated in San Francisco it would be locally controlled. San Francisco, a heavy tourist haven, had always been an open city where gambling, prostitution and bootlegging by local entrepreneurs were more or less condoned, but outside operators were not welcome.

So, after an abortive attempt to organize a cleaning and dyeing racket in San Francisco, Bock moved to the East Bay and started to organize retailers and drivers in collusion with a wholesale plant to which the retail business would be directed. A confederate of Bock's started organizing the retailers, and Bock, after making a deal with a wholesale plant owner, went to work on the independent drivers and the inside and outside workers. A substantial percentage of retailers joined the retail association and started paying dues, and drivers started transporting the clothes of the retailers association to the wholesale plant, with Bock cutting in on the overriding profits. To control such a racket, association members must comply with the orders of the racket leaders. Gimov, co–leader with Bock of the racket, passed the word to the members of his retailer association to double the prices of their services.

One retail member, the owner of Drake Cleaners in Oakland, paid his dues but refused to change his prices. His price for cleaning and pressing a man's suit continued to be forty–nine cents. He was threatened with harm or damage to his business if he did not raise his prices. In this racket there were other ways of intimidating recalcitrant dealers than simply planting "pineapples" or dye bombs—

with which the trade had become familiar. One night, a rack of ladies' garments was sprayed with a destructive acid, causing holes in the fabrics of the garments. The offense was reported to the Oakland Police Department but the culprit was not known and the police were unable to identify him.

One day, after a period of seven months had transpired, a man named Delaney walked into the Oakland Police Department and said "I am the one you have been looking for. I did the spray job at Drake Cleaners."

He said that Bock had promised him $500 to spray the clothes and had provided him with the necessary equipment. He said Bock had welshed on their agreement and, because he was a dope addict, fingered him to the police in San Francisco, as a result of which he was arrested and served six months in the County Jail. It was a matter of revenge. Of course he expected and received immunity in consideration of his testimony. Bock and the others were indicted for conspiracy to commit malicious mischief, which was an alternative felony in California.

After the trial had proceeded for some weeks, the trial judge, Homer R. Spence, declared a mistrial because a juror—in violation of instructions—had discussed the case with another juror. Eventually the defendants pleaded guilty. So far as is known, since this prosecution there have been no attempts to start this type of Chicago racket in Alameda County. Without Delaney's testimony, it is doubtful whether Bock and his confederates would have been charged or convicted. The double cross by Delaney and his subsequent testimony was a lucky break for law enforcement. Occasionally such a break occurs when, and from sources, least expected.

AN UNETHICAL ATTORNEY

There were also other cases in the early 1930's of more than ordinary importance. One of these cases which attracted considerable publicity involved an able trial lawyer who was unscrupulous at times in dealing with his clients. One of his ploys was to tell his client that he had a close association with the judge in the case, and that for a certain amount of money he could get the judge to dismiss the case or render a favorable judgment. This was an attempt to obtain money by false pretenses and in some cases he succeeded in obtaining money by such fraud. The irony of the thing was that the attorney was very competent and had been quite successful in the trial of cases. In most instances, he could have obtained a good retainer and earned a substantial fee for handling the cases properly. But he over–indulged at times, procrastinated and succumbed to the quick and easy way of making money without earning it.

His downfall was an Italian immigrant who had been arrested by federal agents during Prohibition for operating a still in the basement of his home. The charge against him, as with so many other cases during Prohibition, had dawdled along in the federal courts in San Francisco and had eventually been dismissed by the government. The charge had been preying on the Italian's mind for years, so he went to see the attorney for advice. The attorney obtained a retainer and later demanded additional fee payments, supposedly to represent him in court. The Italian talked to his boss about it, who suspected something was wrong. The boss brought the Italian to the District Attorney's Office, where I interviewed him and checked the status of the case in the court. I found that the case had been dismissed some years before.

The attorney was indicted, tried and convicted. There were two trials. Two jurors hung out for acquittal in the first trial. In the second trial an aide to the defendant, sitting near a door outside of a room where the jury was deliberating, was in a position to hear the jury foreman tell the bailiff that the jury had a verdict. The aide telephoned the defendant who failed to appear when his office was notified by the court clerk that the jury had a verdict.

The jury was locked up for six days and nights while an intensive statewide search was made for the defendant. At about two o'clock in the morning, a Santa Monica policeman saw a man running in the middle of the street in his underclothes, waiving his arms and yelling "Al Capone is a racketeer." The officer took the man, who was drunk, into custody. When questioned by Lt. Thomas Carr in police headquarters, the man gave a fictitious name. Carr suspected that he might be the missing defendant and telephoned me. The description which I gave Carr fitted the man, who after sobering up finally disclosed his true name.

He was returned to court. The jury returned its verdict of guilty, and the defendant was sentenced to state prison. He waived appeal. At that time, by a previous decision of the California Supreme Court, a defendant had to be present at all stages of a felony trial including the return of a verdict. Immediately as a result of this case, the state Legislature, which was in session at the time, enacted a law providing that if a defendant deliberately absented himself, a felony trial could proceed in his absence. Further investigation of the case disclosed that a former rumrunner client of the defendant had driven him from Oakland to Southern California when he learned that the jury had a verdict, and had hidden him out in a house in Santa Monica. The rumrunner was indicted, tried and convicted as an accessory after the fact.

During my time in the office, eight lawyers were prosecuted for criminal offenses. The California Bar Association had a skeleton investigative process which deferred action until procedures by local bar committees had exhausted efforts to determine facts and compromise complaints. The local bar committee, consisting of local lawyers busy with their own private business, had little time or inclination for pressing complaints against fellow practitioners. Consequently, final action would not often be taken on client complaints. Trial level judges likewise avoided taking action for contempt of court against lawyers who should have been punished for contemptuous conduct. In recent years, however, under prodding by the American Bar Association and the Chief Justice of the United States Supreme Court, state bar associations have stepped up disciplinary proceedings against unethical attorneys.

WARREN STAYS ON

In early 1930, before the cases broke involving the Sheriff's Office and the Oakland city government, Warren had told the grand jury that he did not intend to run again for election. He had had ten years in the District Attorney's Office, which he said was much longer than he intended to stay when he first entered the office. His first desire and ambition had been to become a trial lawyer in private practice, but he had become so engrossed and fascinated with the work of the District Attorney's Office that time had passed quickly. His salary as district attorney was then $500 a month. He was married and children were coming along. Eventually he and his wife, Nina, had five children plus Jimmy Meyers, Nina's son by her former husband (deceased), who was adopted by Warren.

With the advent of the cases against the Sheriff's Office, Oakland city government and the paving contractors, Warren changed his mind and said he could not leave under the circumstances, so he ran for reelection as district attorney in 1930 and again in 1934. The law business in private practice fell off so badly during the Depression years of the 1930's that it was a poor time to be starting a private practice. Had he left the District Attorney's Office in 1930 to enter private practice, he may never have pursued a political career or risen to the position of Chief Justice.

FRAUD

Criminal fraud—also known as white collar crime, bunco, or confidence game—has been around for a long time. In the more flagrant hard core bunco or confidence game situations, the Brooklyn Bridge has been sold to gullible victims for large amounts of money countless times, as has the gleaming gold brick. When embezzlements, in–house speculations, investment frauds, obtaining money by false pretenses and consumer frauds are included, the take by the crooks has been estimated to run from fifty to as high as two hundred billion dollars a year.

This kind of crime is generally committed by a person known to the victim, directly or indirectly. At least it is not committed by force, violence, fear or at the point of a gun. The weapons are cultivation of trust and confidence and abuse thereof, duplicity, guile, trickery and a keen psychologic sense of the innate weakness of many humans to make a quick easy profit on what appears to be a sure thing.

The inventive genius of the crook to exploit current conditions and his ability to design crooked schemes is boundless, as is his ruthless capacity to inflict great harm upon his victims. The take is often substantial, as is the loss to persons who can ill afford to lose. The psychological trauma and distress of the victim is generally very severe.

The concoctions and maneuvers of the "bunco artist," as he is sometimes called, are often very subtle, clever and complex. In an investment bunco he will stress confidence and secrecy and if expedient, as in the sale of phony securities, cut in victims by promises of commissions or shares in the prospective—and usually illusive—profits. The investigation and prosecution of so–called white collar crime is often difficult. Victims, characteristically trustful and optimistic, cling to their hope and recoil from cooperating with law enforcement.

Even when some victims do cooperate, proof of fraud and the falsity of representations made by the crook involve much hard and time–consuming investigative work and, in some cases, costly expert testimony. To be effective in such cases, the investigator and the prosecutor must have a flare for this type of work and much patience and perseverance. The average police or sheriff's department or the average prosecutor's office is not geared for this kind of work, either because of lack of qualified personnel or lack of interest, or both. Consequently, in many jurisdictions white collar crimes get short shrift, especially where police and prosecutors are overloaded with increasing volumes of murders, robberies, muggings, burglaries, rapes, other crimes of violence, narcotics, drunkenness, prostitution, traffic and just keeping the peace.

The average bunco artist and white collar crook is aware of this condition and will take a chance on testing the climate of law enforcement in a community for effective prosecution of this type of crime. If he finds out that law enforcement is effective, he will give such a community a wide berth. From the time that Warren became district attorney, great emphasis was put on white collar crime cases and the effort was invariably successful. Consequently, over the years there were relatively few such cases. However, occasionally such a case would surface and there would be a vigorous and relentless prosecution. Among such cases were: Golet Oil Company; Lusitania, Inc.; Cox Chemical and Processing Company; Acme Builders; and the free lot racket.

GOLET OIL COMPANY

Crowley* and his wife arrived in Oakland in 1923 and started to circulate. Crowley took a position with a company of which Davis* was the owner. Within a short time, Crowley was selling interim certificates representing interests in a highly secret enterprise, which he said was located in Mexico. Supposedly, it involved production of oil by a Mexican company named Golet Oil, a merger of several large oil companies and certain oil tycoons, among them E. L. Doheney.

Crowley's wife, a smart woman, started giving lectures in psychology and how to make friends and succeed in business. Her lectures caught on and she soon developed quite a following of women who spread the word of her "message for success." Gradually and subtly she dropped hints of her husband's success in the Golet Oil Company and of enormous profits to be made. Word spread fast and it was not long before her listeners, their husbands and friends were clamoring for the privilege of investing in Golet.

Esposito,* an old–time bunco artist, played the role of a mystery man and occasionally wrote to Crowley, supposedly from Mexico, about Golet prospects and progress. Eight rather well–known men about town joined Crowley in selling Golet interim certificates, and receipts began to mount. From time to time, Esposito sent letters to Crowley, reporting progress in the merger deal and urging continued secrecy. The reports turned out to be false, and Esposito, descendant of a prominent San Francisco family, proved to be a clever crook. In a relatively short time, receipts from sales of certificates amounting to close to one million dollars came in, most of it being forwarded to Esposito, who was gambling heavily at a racetrack and swank casino resort near Tiajuana, Mexico. Crowley, his wife and friends later claimed they had not thought to check on Esposito's background or with any responsible people in Mexico or elsewhere who might be in a position to know about Golet or if there ever were such a company.

As usually happens in crooked enterprises, funds dwindled and dividends failed to materialize, followed by unending excuses and, in due course, by complaints to the police and the District Attorney's Office. Crowley, his wife, Davis and others who were selling certificates and taking their commissions out in certificates were summoned by the Oakland Police Department for interrogation by Captain of Inspectors Richard McSorley, Inspector Bodie Wallman and District Attorney Warren.

Because of favorable impressions and friends made in the community by Crowley and his wife, Warren was in doubt as to whether to file charges against them. However, after further questioning, Captain McSorley bellowed, "It's a skin game—lock 'em up!" And so Warren had one of his first big cases to prosecute and just a short time before the primary election in August 1926, when he would have to run for office the first time. Captain McSorley's instinct was right because subsequent investigation proved that the representations concerning Golet Oil were false and that the whole thing was a swindle. Esposito, Crowley, his wife and Davis were charged with several counts of grand theft and the salesmen were charged with violation of the Corporate Securities Act.

Wade Snook and I prosecuted the grand theft cases, and, after a hung jury at the first trial, Crowley, his wife and Davis were convicted in the second trial and sentenced to state prison. Crowley, his wife and Davis claimed they had been deceived by Esposito. The salesmen were convicted of violations of the Corporate Securities Act and either sentenced to county jail or fined. Esposito pleaded guilty and was sentenced to state prison. These cases were of importance to Warren because the convictions and sentences came practically on the eve of his first election.

LUSITANIA, INC.

The case of Lusitania, Inc., another business fraud operation, was patterned after the successful and legitimate Bank of Italy and Transamerica operations. Like the Bank of Italy and Transamerica programs, Lusitania, a holding company for Pittsburg Building and Loan Company and Victory Mutual Life Insurance Company, was designed to have a racial or ethnic appeal. Whereas Bank of Italy and Transamerica were targeted originally at Italians, the name Lusitania was adopted because of its strong appeal to people of Portuguese descent, of which there were a large number in Alameda County who were quite wealthy. Many Portuguese immigrants, who had worked hard on the farms of Southern Alameda County and saved substantial amounts of money, invested in Lusitania and lost everything.

Lusitania's vaunted holdings consisted of: the charter of a practically dormant building and loan association known as Pittsburg Building and Loan Association; a few vacant lots of questionable value in a swamp near Vallejo; and the charter of an inactive, completely worthless mutual life insurance company with no clients and no assets or reserves. Lusitania was incorporated in the state of Nevada and received permits to sell stock in Nevada and California.

Domingo* and Davalos,* promoters of the scheme, rented space in a good building centrally located in downtown Oakland and launched upon an intense sales campaign with the help of a staff of salesmen, mostly of Portuguese descent who could speak Portuguese fluently, and heavy advertising in Portuguese publications and on local radio stations broadcasting in the Portuguese language. The representations in the publications, on the radio and by the salesmen were a combination of half–truths and gross falsifications as to the assets of the company. Although a large amount of stock was sold, much of the receipts were dissipated on promotion, salaries, commissions and other expenses. The operation really did not get off the ground. When no dividends appeared and the lavish promises of the advertising campaign failed to materialize, purchasers of the stock began to grumble and eventually began streaming into the District Attorney's Office to press charges.

The theory of the prosecution was that the whole operation was a conspiracy initiated by Domingo and Davalos, and that money received from the public in the sale of stock was obtained by false pretenses. Although Domingo and Davalos did not personally sell any stock, evidence was introduced which showed that they were the promoters and directed the activities of the sales staff. The first trial ended in a hung jury.

During the first trial, I noticed that Domingo and Davalos were well adorned with emblems of the Masonic fraternity on their lapels, on chains on their vests and on rings on their fingers; also that defense counsel were likewise so adorned. After the trial, a juror who was a member of a Masonic organization, told Warren that certain Masons on the jury refused to convict. At the next trial Warren assigned George Perkins to assist me. Throughout the trial, Perkins, a past master of his Masonic lodge, was likewise well arranged with Masonic identification on lapel, watch chain and finger. The defendants were convicted in the second trial and sentenced to San Quentin.

COX CHEMICAL

Cox Chemical was another business fraud which garnered millions of dollars and defrauded hundreds of persons—lawyers, doctors, bankers, brokers and others who should have known better. It also had some of the big oil companies worried for awhile as to the representations of Moore* and his colleagues that they had a new cold catalytic process for extracting gasoline from crude oil. Such a process could save the oil companies billions of dollars. There had been speculation for years in chemical circles about the possibility that, by some cold process or mixture of ingredients, gasoline might, without heat and cracking, be separated from crude oil or, at least, the yield of gasoline from crude oil might be greatly increased.

The irony of this promotion was that it started from scratch with no money and no administrative, business, promotional or technical expertise. Moore and a fellow worker, Rey,* became acquainted while doing menial work in California oil fields. Moore was simply an illiterate roustabout with no collegiate or technical training in geology, chemistry or petroleum engineering. Rey, although a more articulate, educated and personable individual, likewise had no technical training other than what he may have absorbed while working in the oil fields. While working with Santa Maria crude oil, Moore stumbled onto the fact that this very thick, heavily emulsified oil contained a high percentage of water which could be separated easily from the oil by a patented dehydrating chemical used in the trade, known as Treatolite, or even by simple carbolic acid or carbolic crystals. With a little practice, one could pour a few drops of Treatolite or carbolic acid or drop a few carbolic crystals into a bottle of Santa Maria crude oil and in a few minutes a clear fluid, which was water, would separate from the oil.

Moore played around with this dehydration process, adding other ingredients such as tobacco, salt and shale to the mixture, which he would put into a bottle containing the crude oil. He would then shake the bottle vigorously and a clear fluid would separate from the oil. Whether he and Rey thought they had only a better dehydrator, no one other than they themselves will probably ever know, but they should have known. They were told often enough by experts that the clear fluid in the bottle which separated from the oil was plain water and certainly not gasoline.

In any event, by the time the matter came to our attention Cox Chemical and Processing Company had several salesmen and an elaborate chemical plant with considerable acreage isolated in rugged hills east of Hayward in Alameda County. There, Moore would perform in a chemical laboratory his legerdemain of separating fluid, which he said was gasoline, from the black Santa Maria crude in a bottle. This would occur before a group of prospective purchasers of the certificates representing units of interest and participation in a contract between Moore and Rey. Without further probing, customers would be herded to other parts of the property and shown some buildings and a variety of brightly polished machinery and pipes. Moore, who was a fair carpenter and mechanic, had, with the help of hired craftsmen, put together an imposing array of what looked like a going chemical plant, attractively arranged and painted in red, white and blue colors, all surrounded by a heavy steel mesh fence topped with barbed wire.

Salesmen were on hand to answer questions and take orders for the inevitable certificates of interest. Inquisitive persons were told that because of the great value of Moore's secret formula, management had to be very careful about the necessary red tape of incorporating and obtaining from the government permits to issue and sell shares of stock. Management was, however, proceeding to become incorporated and stock would be exchangeable for the interim certificates. As a matter of fact, in the latter stages of the promotion a very reputable lawyer in Los Angeles did get Cox Chemical incorporated and was endeavoring to obtain a permit to sell stock. Another reputable Los Angeles lawyer, who got into the operation early, conceived and approved the interim certificate of interest method of raising money. He was told by the California Corporation Department that the sale of the certificates was a sale of securities in violation of law. However, he, Moore, Rey and the salesmen forged ahead in defiance of the Corporation Department with the assurance that they would, in due course, incorporate and obtain a permit to sell stock. Word concerning an invention with possibilities of potentially great wealth travels fast, and soon many people were clamoring to invest and make a fortune.

Moore did not demonstrate his crude–oil–in–the–bottle separation trick to more–sophisticated persons, like chemists and others with some knowledge of petroleum production. If he had, an expert could readily discover the fraud by pouring off the clear fluid and smelling it or lighting a match to it—being water, it would neither smell like gasoline nor burn. For such observers Moore would pour a quantity of crude oil in one end of a mechanical apparatus he kept in another building. After a short while, about fifty to seventy percent of the volume of crude oil input would emerge from the other end of the apparatus in the form of a clear fluid which was actually gasoline.

If legitimate, such a yield by a simple cold process would, of course, be a fabulous innovation in the oil industry and of tremendous value. Some petroleum scientists had speculated for years over the possibility that some catalytic process might be discovered by which the yield of cracking gasoline from crude oil could be increased. Dr. Arnold O. Beckman, a young Ph.D. in petroleum chemistry from the California Institute of Technology, was employed by one of the large oil companies to study Moore's operation. He spent some time at the plant in the Hayward hills probing and interrogating. It did not take him long to discover that Moore had little knowledge of chemistry or petroleum engineering. Moore did not perform the crude–oil–in–the–bottle separation trick but he did put crude oil in his mechanical apparatus, started the machinery and out came gasoline in a yield of fifty to seventy percent of the quantity of the crude input.

After considerable probing over Moore's vigorous protest, Beckman discovered that a pipe was attached to the middle of the apparatus, leading from a container of gasoline, and, by a valve arrangement, the crude oil could be blocked and the gasoline run into the emerging pipe.

Rey, who was neither a machinist nor a scientist, was present at the plant one day while Beckman was investigating. Beckman told him that the whole thing was scientifically improbable and a colossal fraud. Rey professed ignorance of technical aspects and said: "I hope you're wrong. I don't know it is a phony."

Moore had nothing to say. Rey from time to time had been making trips to New York and sending letters back to Moore and the salesmen for the consumption of investors to the effect that big New York money and oil interests were going to buy in. These representations were false. The letters stimulated sales and smothered fires of dissatisfaction among impatient investors. The selling continued with increasing numbers of people buying interim certificates.

The state Corporation Department referred the case to the District Attorney's Office. Warren, with George Perkins and an inspector, visited the Hayward plant and talked with the attorney for the firm. The attorney argued with Warren that what they were doing was legal. At this point, no one had made a complaint to the District Attorney's Office or requested prosecution of anyone connected with the operation.

After some time had passed, a stockbroker in Portland, Oregon, who had bought certificates and persuaded some of his clients to do so as well, finally became dissatisfied. He located a client who had paid $210 to one of the Cox Chemical salesmen in Alameda County for a certificate. He persuaded this investor to go with him to the District Attorney's Office to press a charge for criminal fraud—obtaining money by false pretense. Reluctantly, the investor came to our office with him.

Deputy District Attorney Perkins, who had been assigned to the case, was away on vacation. I was not familiar with details of the case, but, being in charge of the Criminal Division of the office, I talked for some time with the broker and the Alameda County investor he had in tow. I telephoned Warren that evening and reported the matter to him. When he heard that the proposed victim complainant's loss was only $210, just barely over the $200 minimum amount for a felony charge of grand theft, he demurred to initiating a prosecution on the ground that to prosecute on a $210 loss in an operation allegedly as large as Cox Chemical would be incongruous. "As you know," I said, "I have not worked on this case and I am not familiar with the details. Perkins has not been able to find anyone to sign a complaint. Now at least we have a willing victim to get it off the ground."

The next day we discussed it again and found out that Moore, Rey, the sales group and a committee of investors were meeting in San Francisco. We decided to go ahead with an investigation. Lieutenant Oscar Jahnsen and some of his inspectors went with the Portland broker and his victim to the meeting at the St. Francis Hotel. Jahnsen was an impetuous type; as a Prohibition agent he used to crash "speakeasies" and grab the liquor bottles before the bartender could sweep them into a hole in the floor and down a chute to break on rocks below. At the hotel, Jahnsen decided to arrest Moore and Rey, and he seized their briefcases containing Cox Chemical documents.

This was before the exclusion rule of *People v. Cahan*[11] or *Mapp vs. Ohio*[12] when evidence was admissible at a trial regardless of how it was obtained. Such a seizure of documents without a search warrant, had it occurred after the decision of the California Supreme

[11] *People v. Cahan* (1955) 44 Cal.2d 434
[12] *Mapp vs. Ohio* (1961) 367 U.S. 643

Court in *People v. Cahan* would have rendered the evidence inadmissible and jeopardized all subsequent investigation and indictments. The documents seized on this occasion contained names of numerous investors and other information helpful to our investigation. Moore and Rey were brought to our office and questioned by Warren and myself. A complaint was filed charging Moore and Rey with a violation of the Corporate Securities Act. The plant at Hayward was examined, photographs were taken and other pertinent evidence was seized. The exclusion rule, by the way, has never prevailed in the countries of the British Empire from which we inherited our basic Anglo–Saxon legal system.

Alameda County investors identified in the seized papers were interviewed and the case was prepared for presentation to the grand jury, pursuant to our policy of using the grand jury in selected and complicated cases. At that time, the law permitted subpoenas of suspects or arrestees and their interrogation before the grand jury. They could, of course, advise with counsel before entering the grand jury room or leave the room during the interrogation to advise with their counsel. Also, they could refuse to testify on Fifth Amendment grounds that their testimony might tend to incriminate them.

As is so often the case in a get–rich–quick operation such as Cox Chemical, early investors tell friends and friends tell other friends. In the telling, original representations are embellished and exaggerated, and the word travels fast. Once started, a lot of selling is done by persons who never talked to or had any contact with the originators of the scheme or promotion. Most of the investors make no investigation of the project and have no personal or verified knowledge about it. When such persons start selling for compensation and personal profit and make factual representations which they do not know to be true, they can do much damage by inducing other people, often friends, to invest. This was true in the case of Cox Chemical. Persons who were compensated for selling were selling securities in violation of the law. Principals like Moore and Rey in a crooked scheme like Cox Chemical must be held criminally responsible for illegal sales made by salesmen, and salesmen who make sales by false representations are likewise responsible criminally.

Indictments were returned against Moore, Rey and three salesmen. The Los Angeles attorney was charged with a violation of California Blue Sky laws.[9] A woman who did a lot of selling disappeared before trial and was never heard of again. After a lengthy jury trial, the defendants were convicted and sentenced to state prison.

While preparing for trial, I had the help of a number of leading experts in petroleum technology, whose curiosity had been aroused by Moore's representations and the possibility of his having discovered some new catalytic process for refining gasoline. Among experts who testified were a University of California professor, who had written the standard text on petroleum production, a noted authority and Ph.D. in chemistry from Princeton, and Arnold Beckman of the California Institute of Technology.

During his testimony at the trial, Moore attempted to demonstrate the merits of his invention. He mixed certain ingredients into Santa Maria crude oil and proceeded to distill the mixture in a glass distillation beaker heated over a Bunsen burner. The result of Moore's demonstration was a dismal failure. As he mixed various ingredients I asked him to name each ingredient and had it marked for identification. When he came to a certain dark fluid, supposedly a part of his secret formula, which he said contained shale from his Hayward property, I examined it carefully. It smelled like Treatolite, a well–known patented dehydrating agent in common use in the trade. Beckman, who was present, agreed and later in testimony verified his opinion by a test that it was Treatolite. Obviously, Moore was trying to deceive the Court and jury.

This and other cases demonstrated the importance of thorough preparation and use of the most competent expertise available. Our office was fortunate in having access to some of the best experts from the University of California at Berkeley, Stanford University at Palo Alto, local oil companies and private laboratories. Because of

[9]Blue Sky laws regulate the sale of stocks, bonds, etc., for the protection of the public from fraud. The name Blue Sky Law comes from a comment made by a proponent of the first such law who said certain business groups were trying to "capitalize the blue skies."

increasing limitations on admissibility of evidence in criminal trials, forensic evidence has become more important and necessary in law enforcement. As a result, collegiate institutions and in–service continuing education programs include courses in their curricula and give degrees in criminalistics. The Federal Bureau of Investigation (FBI) conducts an excellent program in forensic evidence in its training curriculum at the National Academy at Quantico. This training is also available to law enforcement personnel throughout the nation. Continuing education courses are also made available to law enforcement personnel on a local basis by the FBI, the National College of District Attorneys and other programs.

As a result of a steady advance through the years, the continuing education program of the District Attorney's Office of Alameda County is probably one of the best in the nation. The Oakland Police Department and the Alameda County Sheriff's Office have excellent crime laboratories—criminalists and facilities which are available on a continuing basis for use by the District Attorney's Office and other police departments.

THE ACME BUILDERS SWINDLE

Another business fraud was operated in the 1930's by a building contractor under the name of Acme Builders. His game was repair and renovation of homes. He advertised freely and talked and moved fast in getting his victims' signatures on contracts. To sell his wares, he would paint a glowing word picture of how a home or a room or a kitchen would look after the alteration. Upon selling his prospective victim, he would get as large a down payment as possible. He would start work on the job, try to milk more money out of the homeowner, meanwhile removing windows, doors, plumbing and other fixtures which he would move or haul away either to sell or use on another job. With the job partially completed, he would move on to another.

The frustration, anxiety and disappointment suffered by his victims were very great. Many of his victims were elderly persons who had lived in their homes for years. He resorted to stalling and excuses when threatened with prosecution, contending that his delinquency was a civil failure to perform under a contract and was not criminal. Hiring a lawyer to sue was futile because what assets he had were well hidden.

After several citation hearings in our office, at which the contractor stalled and persisted in claiming it was not a criminal matter, we obtained an indictment charging him and his secretary, who aided and abetted his fraud, with a conspiracy to cheat and defraud by false promises and conspiracy to commit theft of the fixtures he had removed. Similar offense evidence was used to prove fraudulent intent. After a lengthy trial in which many victims related their unhappy experiences, the defendants were convicted. The contractor was sentenced to San Quentin and his secretary received a misdemeanor penalty.

After his release from state prison, he turned up operating the same as before, this time victimizing homeowners on repair jobs financed by Federal Housing Administration (FHA) loans. He would discount his contract and loan with a bank, get the money quickly, and again not finish the job. The banks, if unable to collect from the victims, were reimbursed and made whole by the FHA. Thus, the federal government and banks made it easy for crooks.

A group of crooked salesmen would come into a city, affiliate with an unscrupulous building contractor and ring doorbells in a poorer section of the community. They would get housewives to sign contracts and promissory notes for the home repairs, which the salesman represented would cost nothing because the house would be shown as a model and each referral would reduce the amount of the contract until the debt was reduced to zero.

Other dishonest so–called "suede shoe" salesmen swept like locusts through communities, pressuring gullible homeowners into signing contracts and promissory notes under similar circumstances for home repairs such as electric wiring, aluminum siding, painting, roofing, asphalt driveways and furnace repair. Obtaining homeowner signatures to notes and contracts and receiving their commissions from the crooked operators or contractors, they then would move quickly on to other communities.

The promoter discounted the loan with a bank or other lending agency. If the victim homeowner defaulted, the lending agency was reimbursed by the FHA and the federal government was left with an uncollectible obligation. The crooked promoter contractor or the bank lost nothing because the FHA made no effort to recover from them. The loss to the federal government through the years on such transactions must have been tremendous.

The only thing the salesmen wanted was the signature of a resident on a form contract and promissory note—any resident with an equity in a home, howsoever small the equity might be, and regardless of ability to pay. There was no check on solvency or credit rating. With each contract and note signed by a homeowner, the salesman received a commission from the operator who employed him. The operator in turn took the contract and note to a bank or finance company where he sold the paper at a big discount.

With part of the proceeds of what he received from the bank or finance company, he would employ an unscrupulous contractor to do the work, which generally was a cheap inferior job actually worth much less than the contract figure. It would seem that when the same operator was discounting building repair loans which terminated frequently in defaulting payments, the bank should take appropriate measures to protect the federal government from loss. I wondered sometimes whether some bank managers were in collusion with certain operators or contractors in buying contracts at a discount to make the volume of the business of their branches look good.

Whenever we received a complaint from a victim of one of the "referral" deals we prosecuted. No doubt many victims did not complain and sooner or later stopped making payments on the notes, often defaulting on their home mortgage payments, moving out and leaving an empty house to be stripped by vandals. The net result was that the federal government, and eventually the taxpayer, was the loser.

Here again was a situation where an inept bureaucracy of the federal government and the United States Department of Justice was either not geared or not inclined to pursue necessary investigations and prosecutions. One wonders if this is another situation like that of defaulting student loans where hundreds of millions in defaults continue to mount.

I was invited one time to speak to a meeting in San Francisco of bankers and visiting FHA executives. I took advantage of the occasion to tell them what I knew—and what they most probably knew as well—was going on with respect to home repair loans. I said if the practice was not cleaned up and stopped some bank executives might find themselves before one of our grand juries to explain why it cannot be stopped. I also said that the failure of the federal government to take appropriate action to prosecute in situations where the federal government was being ripped off by the banks and finance companies was deplorable. It seemed to me that there was a marked decline in "referral" deals and complaints received after that, at least in Alameda County.

This consumer–business fraud racket became so prevalent that the California Legislature enacted legislation designed to give the gullible public some measure of protection. Because of our experience, we assisted the Legislature in drafting this legislation and accelerated enforcement. Richard Chamberlain, Cecil Mosbacher, Arthur Sherry, Alan Lindsay, Fred Drucker, Edwin Meese, Herbert Ellingwood, Carl Anderson, Richard Iglehart and Lieutenant Lloyd Jester, members of the District Attorney's Office, served as representatives of law enforcement and as legislative advocates.

THE FREE LOT RACKET

In what became known as the "free lot" racket, Carlson,* a multi–millionaire street contractor and subdivider, with the assistance of fast–talking salesmen and "bird dog" menials, operated in the Bay Area for several years. At crowded public gatherings, such as county fairs, circuses, picnics and conventions, temporary concession booths would be set up with signs advertising free lots. In the booths, spielers urged the passing crowd to win a "free lot" by simply signing one's name and address on a card, half of which would be torn off and dropped into a barrel; the other half of the card would be given to the signer.

Carlson owned a number of real estate tracts situated in the hilly suburbs around Oakland and San Francisco. In these tracts there were a variety of lots, some of which were quite attractive and others very unattractive and of little or no value. Some of the tracts, located on rolling hilly terrain, afforded excellent panoramic views of San Francisco Bay.

The cards in the barrels would be sorted in Carlson's office by clerks who would arrange them according to districts and distribute bunches of sorted cards to men who then called on the persons whose names were signed on the cards. These calls were generally made in the evening between 6:00 p.m. and 8:30 p.m. The agent, or bird dog, as he was known in the racket, would greet the signer of the card with a cheerful statement to the effect that the signer had won a lot and that if he or she so desired, an appointment would be made for a fee of $2.50 to meet a representative of the company at an office downtown for transportation to a subdivision to see the lot which had been won. If the signer agreed, the appointment was made.

Card signers who appeared at the company's office would be greeted by a salesman who was expensively arrayed with a large diamond stickpin adorning his necktie and rings on his fingers. The salesmen were fast–talking, high–pressure operators who believed that first impressions of affluence and success were helpful. They explained to the signers that they would be taken to a subdivision to see the lots which had been won. Each of these salesmen drove a highly polished Pierce Arrow automobile.

Arriving at the subdivision, a signer would be shown the lot which he or she had supposedly won. This lot was in a most undesirable location on the side of a very steep, almost inaccessible canyon where it would be practically impossible to build. Invariably, the signer would decline to accept the lot. Whereupon, the salesman would say that there were other very attractive lots in the subdivision for sale upon which a credit of a certain amount for the lot which had been won would be given. The signer would then be shown a knoll lot with a panoramic view.

If the signer succumbed to the fast–moving blandishments of the salesman and agreed to buy the more attractive lot, he would be presented with a form contract to sign. This form was printed with blank spaces for the name of the purchaser, date, lot number, purchase price, credit for the won lot and monthly payments. These items would be quickly inserted by the salesman and handed to the purchaser with a pen to sign. The action was fast with little, if any, time to reconsider. The salesman retained the signed document, and no copy would be given to the signer unless he demanded it.

Among other conditions in fine print on the contract was a clause which provided that title to the property remained with the seller until payments on the contract were completed, and, in the event of default or late payment of a monthly installment, the total amount theretofore paid plus interest was forfeited to Carlson's company.

Upon audit, the books of the company showed that an average of 78% of the persons who signed contracts to purchase did not finish payments and eventually forfeited the property and payments. When one of the 22% who had completed payment requested a deed to the property, the salesman would take him or her (or both if husband and wife) to the subdivision and try to switch them to a more attractive and more expensive lot with an apparently generous credit for the lot upon which full payment had been made.

If the victim agreed, a new contract for an increased purchase price was executed on the spot with similar terms and conditions. In the case of the person or persons who refused to be switched and demanded a deed, they would be told that a deed would be sent. This was in the period of the Depression when there was little new building and defaulting on payments was common. The person who, in the first instance, demanded the original won–lot and made enough of a fuss, would receive a deed to the unbuildable lot, after interminable delay and run–around. The number of such persons was extremely small. The company played the law of averages on this and took their chances that rarely would a signer demand a deed to an undesirable lot.

When we investigated the cases of victims who had completed payments and received deeds, we found that the properties described in their deed were not the properties they had been shown and had selected, and the properties described in the deeds were quite inferior and undesirable. Frequently, the same lot had been sold to many different persons. During the investigation of this case we would take groups of lot purchasers, along with a surveyor from the County Surveyor's Office, to their lots. We would instruct an individual purchaser to stand on the lot he thought he had bought. We would then have the surveyor locate on a map the lot described in the purchase contract or deed. Generally the two lots were different and the lot described in the contract or deed was poorly situated. Photographs were taken of the purchaser standing on the lot he thought he had purchased and of the surveyor standing on the lot described in the contract or deed.

Upon discovery of the fraud, the consternation of a victim who had been making payments on a purchase contract for years in anticipation of having a nice home attractively situated in the tract was overwhelming. It was especially so when several victims had their pictures taken standing on the same lot they each thought they had bought. Needless to say, their testimony at the grand jury hearing and at trial was effective. Carlson and his salesmen were indicted for grand theft and, after a lengthy trial, convicted and sentenced to state prison for long terms.

Among other things, it developed that sidewalk curbing and pavement work on one of the subdivisions were inferior and cracking up. The engineering consultant employed by the subdivider on this improvement was a county official, who officially approved engineering aspects of subdivisions in unincorporated territory where the subdivisions were located. When the trial jury returned its verdict, attached to the verdict was a recommendation that the relationship between the subdivider and the county official be investigated. That night the official committed suicide.

The irony of it all was that thirty years later, as south–county grew and developed, some parts of the tracts became quite valuable, but this did not unravel the tangled mess or make good the harm to the keenly disappointed victims.

While the loss and chagrin of the victims and the family of the official who committed suicide was extraordinary, this was partially offset by the excellent attitude and cooperation of the deputies in the county official's office and in the District Attorney's Office, who put in countless hours of overtime without extra compensation to help in putting the case together for effective presentation at the grand jury hearing and the trial. At that time—the 1930's—cooperation, an excellent attitude and uncompensated overtime by county employees was par for the course. Public service and participation in law enforcement was considered a privilege and a satisfying experience. Five–day, forty–hour weeks were not the norm in the District Attorney's Office, or in other county offices.

A SPECULATING LOAN COMPANY

Then there was the case of a San Francisco loan and discount company which did some business in other Bay Area counties during the middle and late 1920's. This was before the financial crash of 1929, when securities were still soaring on the stock exchanges and people were borrowing money wildly to buy stocks on margin.

This particular loan and discount company advertised and broadcast over radio that generous loans would be made on securities to be held as collateral. When persons called at the company offices in San Francisco and other places, they were told that their stock would be held in a safe and returned when the loan was paid. The fine print in the loan document authorized the company to return stock in kind upon repayment of the loan. The actual practice of the loan company was to sell daily at the market all securities received as collateral on loans.

The owner of the loan company figured that the market would turn down and that he could buy back the hypothecated stocks at lower prices. In other words, he was shorting the market and gambling with his customers' stock. However, the market kept going up during the mid–1920's, and, as borrowers came in to redeem their stocks, the loan company, buying stocks at rising prices to supply their customers' demands for return of their securities, ran out of money and became insolvent. The owner of the loan company was indicted and convicted.

In the prosecution I took the position that the loan document was vitiated by fraud and that the state was not bound by the hedging clause in fine print which authorized the company to sell the hypothecated stock and replace it upon payment of the loan. This position was affirmed by the appellate court.

The irony of it was that, had the owner of the loan company been able to hold out for a couple of years until the market turned down, he would have made a fortune. He would have been able to deliver stock in kind and amount to borrowers upon payment of the loans and probably no one would have complained.

PHONY BALONEY INSURANCE

An unscrupulous operator named Constantine,* with his brood of nineteen pitchmen, moved in on Hayward and began promoting a health insurance racket. The pitchmen would represent to prospective victims a health insurance policy promising unlimited sick benefits at a price of $37 a year. There was no permit to operate from the state Insurance Department. There were no reserves whatever behind the insurance and the coverage was worthless. Constantine and his cohorts were indicted for a felony conspiracy to cheat and defraud and to obtain money by false promises with no intent of performing such promises. Constantine pleaded guilty and was sentenced to state prison. His crew of salesmen suddenly disappeared from California and were never heard of again. Fortunately, Constantine's "phony baloney insurance" racket, as he himself labeled it in unguarded moments, was discovered soon after it started and the losses were few.

THE POISONER

Louis Gosden, a 31 year old carpenter, and his wife, Laura, had been married about four years at the time of her death on November 20, 1934, at which time their daughter, Joyce, age three, was living with them in Oakland. On September 27, 1934, Gosden had purchased strychnine at a local drug store under the ficticious name of

"L. N. Larsen" and had given a fictitious address. He had told the druggist that the strychnine was to "kill a kitty," although the Gosdens had no cats.

At about 7 p.m. on the day of her death, Laura Gosden became ill. At around 11 p.m., Mrs. Gonsalves, a next–door neighbor, from her bathroom window saw Gosden and his wife in the kitchen of their home, which was across the driveway from Mrs. Gonsalves' bathroom. Mrs. Gonsalves heard Mrs. Gosden ask Gosden to go across the street to the Cereghinos and phone for a doctor. She told him also to hurry. The Gosdens had no phone.

Gosden went outside and walked back and forth for about an hour along the driveway under his kitchen window, in plain view of Mrs. Gonsalves. During this time he made no effort to get a doctor. Mrs. Gonsalves could hear Mrs. Gosden crying "I am dying." At about 1 a.m. Mrs. Gosden called out for Mrs. Gonsalves. At this time Gosden went into his home and upbraided his wife for calling Mrs. Gonsalves. Upon Mrs. Gonsalves' arrival, Gosden went across the street to the Cereghinos' and asked Mr. Cereghino to phone for a doctor.

Dr. Ream arrived at the Gosden's home in about ten minutes. He found Mrs. Gosden on the kitchen floor. He remained with her until her death about a half hour later.

That day, Gosden called a funeral parlor and ordered a $500 funeral for his wife, offering as proof of his ability to pay for the funeral two accidental death policies on the life of his wife. The proof was rejected by the funeral director for the reason that the policies were payable only in case of accidental death and the death certificate showed death was due to pneumonia. It was suggested that an autopsy be performed to show that death was due to ptomaine poisoning as contended by Gosden, but, upon discovery that death by poison was not covered by the policies, that idea was abandoned.

On the day his wife died, Gosden procured Lydia Sandborn, a girl about seventeen years of age, ostensibly to take care of his daughter, Joyce. Apparently Gosden had known Lydia before his wife's death. Lydia then lived at Gosden's home, taking care of Joyce and performing other domestic duties. Gosden had sexual intercourse with Lydia within a week after his wife's death. They cohabited for three months until Lydia was taken into custody by the juvenile authorities and Gosden was charged with contributing to her delinquency.

An investigation of the death of Laura Gosden, begun by the District Attorney's Office after Gosden was initially jailed on the contributing charge, disclosed that Gosden had been married before, in October of 1927, to a girl, seventeen years of age, named Vivian Taylor. On January 16, 1928, Vivian had died suddenly under circumstances that strongly indicated her death was due to strychnine poisoning. Just a week before Vivian's death, Gosden had procured a policy of insurance upon her life, payable to himself as beneficiary. He had attempted to collect the amount called for by this policy after her death, but was informed that he could not do so since there had been no medical examination of Vivian, as required by the policy.

The investigation further developed that Gosden's marriage to Vivian was, in fact, his second marriage. He had married a woman named Tillie in August of 1921. She had left him in 1925. In September of 1925, Gosden had had that marriage annulled on the ground that Tillie had been a minor at the time of their marriage.

Tillie told investigators she had left Gosden because she feared for her life. "Several times he threatened to kill me," she said. "At other times he urged me to take out insurance but I was afraid to do so."

The investigation also disclosed two prior unsuccessful attempts by Gosden to take out policies of insurance upon the life of his mother, with himself as beneficiary. The attempts to obtain life insurance upon his mother were made after Vivian's death and before Laura's death. Both attempts failed because Gosden gave a fictitious address in his application for such insurance. Gosden's mother had no knowledge of these applications for insurance upon her life.

Upon exhumation of Laura's body and examination of the contents of her stomach by the county pathologist, the presence of strychnine was discovered. At the time of his arrest, Gosden denied the purchase of the strychnine. A short time after Gosden's arrest, a small bottle, corresponding in size and shape with the bottle sold to Gosden by the druggist, was found under Gosden's house by Inspector Jester of the District Attorney's Office.

When interrogated, Gosden said he had bought the poison for use in killing rats at his father's place in Sunnyvale and had prepared poisoned meat for that purpose in his garage in Oakland. He said he threw the bottle under the house to keep his young daughter from getting hold of it. Investigators probed the recent poisoning of a score of dogs in the vicinity of Sunnyvale, in the belief that their deaths might have been "experiments" in the effects of strychnine.

At his trial, Gosden testified: that his wife knew of his purchase of the poison and had access to it up to the time of her death; that she was in usual good health until 7 p.m. on the evening of her death; that at about 10:30 p.m. she said she was getting worse; that he suggested getting a doctor but she declined; that later in the evening he went for a doctor but returned without one because the stores were all closed and he could not get to a phone (although the Cereghinos lived across the street and Gonsalves next door, both of whom had phones).

It was shown at Gosden's trial that the balance in his sole bank account was only slightly over $50 at the time he took out the three life insurance policies on Laura's life with himself as the beneficiary. Two of these policies were payable in case of accidental death and one was payable in the event of death due to natural causes. These policies were procured by Gosden in September 1934, about two months before Laura's death—coincidental with his purchase of the strychnine.

Gosden's counsel was a brilliant young lawyer named Melvin Belli, recently graduated from law school at the University of California at Berkeley, trying his second case. Before this trial, Belli had two other clients, McKay and Christie, in another county, who were convicted of first–degree murder and executed. A few years later, Earl Warren, as a candidate for attorney general of California, on the platform with Belli, who was supporting him, remarked that the Gosden case wiped out half of Belli's law practice, at which point Belli quipped "all of it." Belli went on to fame and fortune in the trial of civil cases, where he was labeled by the media as the "King of Torts." He also pioneered—with eminent success—continuing legal education in civil trial subjects.

Incidentally, Belli contributed to the training of Edwin Meese III, in a murder case successfully prosecuted by Meese while the latter was a deputy district attorney in Alameda County before going to Sacramento to serve as secretary to Governor Reagan. Meese, by the way, developed into a very competent trial lawyer who participated with Dave Dutton, Lowell Jensen and Charles Morehouse in the investigation and prosecution of the "Free Speech Movement" campus unrest cases at the University of California at Berkeley (see chapter 7). Meese also acted as an assistant to the grand jury.

Gosden was convicted of murder first–degree without a recommendation for life imprisonment by the jury—which at the time meant a death penalty. The law in California was changed later by the Legislature to require a specific recommendation by the trial jury that the defendant receive the death penalty in a case for which the death penalty was an alternative to life imprisonment. Later changes in the law provided for bifurcated separate trials as to guilt, sanity and penalty.

In considering the Gosden case, one wonders how many other cases of murder by poison occur throughout the nation, and how many have escaped prosecution because of incompetence or negligence on the part of coroners or doctors with no special knowledge of toxicology and forensic medicine.

THE CONSTITUTIONAL AMENDMENT OF 1934

At the Gosden trial, Judge Frank M. Ogden, a former deputy district attorney of Alameda County, took advantage of a new constitutional amendment permitting a trial judge in a criminal case to comment on the evidence and on the testimony and credibility of particular witnesses. This was the first trial in California in which a trial judge's comments on the evidence and credibility of a witness were made as part of his instructions. This constitutional provision was part of a state constitutional Initiative package proposed by the California police and district attorneys organizations to strengthen law enforcement. This Initiative package included a proposal to permit comment by the court or prosecutor on the failure of a defendant to testify in a criminal trial, or, if he did testify, to comment upon his failure to explain or deny incriminating facts against him.

In its 1965 decision in *Griffin v. California*[10], the United States Supreme Court held the California comment rule to be a violation of the Fifth and Fourteenth Amendments' guarantees of due process, and reversed a death sentence conviction in an opinion in which Chief Justice Warren took no part, and from which Justices Stewart and White vehemently dissented.

Justice Harlan's concurrence in the majority opinion was modified as follows:

> "I agree with the court that within the *federal* judicial system the Fifth Amendment bars adverse comment by federal prosecutors and judges on a defendant's failure to take the stand in criminal trial, a right accorded him by that amendment. And given last Term's decision in *Malloy v. Hogan*,[11] that the Fifth Amendment applies to the states in all its requirements (under the Fourteenth Amendment), I see no legitimate escape from today's decision and concur with it. I do so, however, with great reluctance, since for me the decision exemplifies the creeping paralysis with which this court's recent adoption of the 'incorporation' doctrine is infesting the operation of the federal system. . . I would not, but for *Malloy,* apply the no comment rule to the states."

Justice Stewart's dissent, joined in by Justice White, veritably demolishes the majority opinion on historical, legal, just, practical, and common sense grounds, pointing out the California comment rule is a normal, fair procedure abundantly sanctioned and supported by most respectable legal authorities; among others by: "The Model Code of Evidence, American Bar Association, American Law Institute, and the weight of scholarly opinion."

The Supreme Court opinion said nothing about a trial Court comment on the credibility of witnesses or the weight of evidence—a procedure followed in the courts of the British Commonwealth and federal courts of the United States from time immemorial.

[10]*Griffin v. California* (1965) 380 U.S. 609
[11]*Malloy v. Hogan* (1964) 378 U.S. 1

However, since the *Griffin* decision, comment by trial judges in California courts concerning credibility has had such a tortuous experience on appeal in the higher courts of the state that any such comment by the trial Court is rarely, if ever made, with the result that the trial judge in California has returned, or regressed, to his former status "of a mere referee or automaton as to the ascertainment of the facts."[12]

There were other measures in the Initiative package of 1934 designed to strengthen law enforcement and improve the administration of justice. One provided that a defendant in a criminal felony case other than capital or life without parole, in the presence of his counsel and with the consent of the magistrate and district attorney, may plead guilty in the Municipal or Justice Court to the offense charged or any offense included therein. The defendant would then be committed to the sheriff and the case certified to the Superior Court for sentence.

Another part of the package enlarged the Attorney General's Office, increasing his powers as the chief law officer of the state and increasing his salary to that of an associate justice of the Supreme Court.

Other parts concerned competitive examinations for civil appointments and redefined the selection and election process for judges of the Appellate and Supreme Courts.

Research and drafting of the proposals in the Initiative package were done by Richard Chamberlain, Stanley Smallwood, and District Attorney Earl Warren, who was secretary of the California District Attorneys Association at the time. The proposals were passed overwhelmingly at the general election in November 1934, and became law in January 1935.

The Initiative package was supported by the California Sheriffs and District Attorneys Associations, the State Chamber of Commerce, the California Bar Association, the San Francisco Common-

[12]*People v. Ottey* (1936) 5 Cal.2d 714

wealth Club, the press, and numerous prestigious civic organizations and leaders.

The passage of that Initiative package was an important personal achievement by Warren which gave him statewide exposure and probably influenced his decision to pursue a political career.

YACHT BANDITS

Lloyd Sampsell and Ethan Allen McNabb had known each other for about six years before they robbed the College Avenue branch of the Oakland Bank in Oakland on April 17, 1929. They may have met first at San Quentin Prison, where both served time on robbery and other felony convictions from Los Angeles. Sampsell and McNabb had both served in the United States Navy during World War I. Sampsell's father was a businessman of means in Los Angeles. Both McNabb and Sampsell were resourceful, poised, articulate, and clean–cut. If they had applied their abundant talents to legitimate pursuits, they might have been quite successful.

In March of 1929 they were together in Seattle, Washington. With them was a woman who was living with Sampsell under the name of Lillie Swanson.* Sampsell was also known as Leslie Swanson.

Sampsell, McNabb and Lillie came from Seattle to California by automobile about April 8th, and rented an apartment at 805 Leavenworth Street in San Francisco. After the robbery of the bank on April 17th, they went to Long Beach, where they stayed a few days at the posh Virginia Hotel under assumed names. They returned to San Francisco by plane and stayed at the Palace Hotel until May 1st, at which time they flew to Seattle.

In Seattle, Sampsell and McNabb purchased a seagoing yacht, reconditioned it and sailed it to San Francisco. Lillie was with them on this trip. This was no mean achievement of seamanship. The Pacific Ocean from Seattle to San Francisco along the Washington, Oregon and Northern California coasts can be very rough and is usually fogbound. Again they rented an apartment at 805 Leavenworth Street and two days later Sampsell and McNabb robbed the Dwight Way branch of the Bank of America in Berkeley.

An automobile registered to Lillie Swanson had been shipped to Los Angeles. At the request of either the Los Angeles Police Department or a California parole agent in Los Angeles, the Seattle Police Department developed information showing that the automobile had been shipped to Sampsell and McNabb in Los Angeles, but the shipping invoice had been mailed to 805 Leavenworth Street, San Francisco. This information was transmitted by Los Angeles authorities to the San Francisco Police Department, who visited the apartment on Leavenworth Street. There they found McNabb, Sampsell and Lillie together with identifiable loot of the bank robberies in Alameda County.

The arresting officers found a variety of deadly weapons and ammunition in the apartment, including fully–loaded Colt automatic pistols, a .38 caliber Winchester automatic rifle equipped with a Maxim silencer and 155 cartridges. McNabb had a bill of sale for these guns in his wallet. The search of the apartment was without an arrest warrant or a search warrant. This was before the exclusion rule of *People v. Cahan*[13] and *Mapp v. Ohio.*[14] Their possession of these weapons was a felony because Sampsell and McNabb had previous felony convictions.

They were labeled by the media as the "yacht bandits." It was reported in the press that Sampsell and McNabb were involved in a far–flung bank robbery ring which operated along the Pacific Coast. As District Attorney, Earl Warren prosecuted this case personally before Alameda County Superior Court Judge Homer R. Spence, whom Warren, as governor, later appointed to the California Supreme Court. Sampsell and McNabb were identified by witnesses to the Alameda County robberies, tried, convicted and sentenced to California state prison on the robbery charges.

Before trial, while in custody of the Berkeley police, Sampsell and McNabb made a break for freedom and might have succeeded but for

[13]*People v. Cahan* (1955) 44 Cal.2d 434
[14]*Mapp v. Ohio* (1961) 367 U.S. 643

the fact that in their haste they ran into a dead–end corridor and were captured. Between their arrest and sentence, Sampsell and McNabb boasted repeatedly that they could not be held. While awaiting, trial Sampsell made one break for liberty, and, twice during the trial, jurors were threatened with death if they voted for conviction.

While in prison, the door of Sampsell's cell was found drilled in such a manner that he could have gotten out and obtained two heavy automatic pistols with extra ammunition, which were discovered accidentally in a keg partially filled with nails. A prisoner working on reconstruction of a building inadvertently overturned the keg and exposed a package containing the guns and ammunition.

In another escape attempt, Sampsell and McNabb dug a tunnel under the prison walls. This project was aborted after their extended absence was discovered. Sampsell and McNabb were found in the tunnel which ended under the warden's residence. They were still digging when discovered.

In another escape attempt, Sampsell and McNabb eluded prison guards and hid themselves in a narrow trench under the floor of the prison blacksmith shop. They had been missing for a week before being discovered.

In a conspiracy with other prisoners, McNabb attempted another escape while armed with a crude, self–made pistol, which apparently had been fashioned in a prison machine shop by McNabb or some other prisoner. McNabb at one time had been employed as a machinist and had considerable skill in the use of machine tools. During a violent struggle which resulted with a guard, the pistol carried by McNabb was triggered accidentally. A prisoner who was not involved in the escape conspiracy was hit by a bullet and died from the wound. As a result, McNabb was tried and executed in 1934 by hanging.

On September 15, 1947, Sampsell was released from state prison on parole. On March 27, 1948, he and a companion attempted to rob the Seaboard Finance Company in San Diego. In the course of this attempt Sampsell killed a customer and got away in a commandeered car. He was caught a year later.

Sampsell was tried and convicted of murder and assault with a deadly weapon. He acted as his own attorney, with some help from appointed counsel on the automatic appeal. He was executed in the gas chamber in 1950. This case resulted in legislation which required that a jury in a first–degree murder case must be instructed by the court that separate unanimous approval of the death penalty and written specification with respect to the penalty in a separate verdict must be made by the jury.

In the Oral History Project of the Bancroft Library at the University of California, Berkeley, concerning Warren is a collection entitled "Perspectives on the Alameda County District Attorney's Office." In his interview for this project Judge Spence said:

> "Earl (Warren) was a very active district attorney, not only in administering his office, but also in trying some of the more difficult cases. . . Earl had some tough matters there (while district attorney) and he proceeded with them very fearlessly. Whenever someone would suggest that Earl 'take it easy on some man,' Earl would say, 'Well, I promise you he will have a fair, but vigorous prosecution.' Earl tried several cases before me, one of the most interesting being the Yachting Bandits Case involving Sampsell and McNabb."

Among Justice Spence's comments referring to this case were the following:

> "They (Sampsell and McNabb) sailed out of Seattle in the yacht 'Sovereign.' They came down with credentials they'd gotten somehow, made their way to the St. Francis Yacht Club (one of the most prestigious and exclusive in the nation), obtained guest cards and kept their yacht there. They apparently led a very respectable life aboard the yacht, but they also took an apartment uptown. Sampsell and McNabb operated out of the apartment in robbing banks.
>
> "These fellows had terrible criminal records behind them. Sampsell was an interesting fellow. Both of them were interesting. Sampsell was one of the most convincing liars on the stand that I had ever seen. He did more to bring sympathy from a jury than any crook I have ever known. Very smooth, and very sweet dispositioned, apparently, as he put on his charm. But McNabb was just the opposite. He was mean and ill–tempered. Finally,

> on devastating cross–examination he said, 'I don't want to answer any more questions.' Earl (Warren) said, 'That's all,' and let him go.
>
> "But afterwards, I think I mentioned to you, McNabb fashioned a gun while in San Quentin and shot it out trying to make an escape out of San Quentin. Prior to that time, both he and Sampsell had disappeared I think for twenty–six days inside the prison walls. They found them under the floor (of the warden's home) in the kitchen. Somebody had been passing food down to them. Sampsell was then transferred to Folsom."

While at Folsom State Prison, Sampsell persuaded a prison officer to let him out on weekends to visit his girlfriend in San Francisco. He would return to the prison after spending a few nights there. Through its highly personalized sources of information (informants are often excellent sources of intelligence), the San Francisco Police Department was tipped off to this caper and arrested Sampsell in the apartment of his girlfriend.

Justice Spence's commentary continues:

> ". . .Sampsell, contrary to my recommendation, and despite the terrible record he had, was paroled finally. He got down to San Diego, and he killed somebody in a bank robbery down there. He was charged with murder and convicted of murder. I was on the Supreme Court at the time. I got a letter from him while he was at San Quentin saying that he thought because I had tried the original cases in Alameda County, I was probably disqualified on his appeal. Of course I was not technically disqualified but I never wanted any man whose life was at stake to feel any doubt about the qualification of the men judging him. I just suggested to the Chief Justice that he put somebody in my place on the day that the Sampsell case was to be heard. Justice Maurice T. Dooling went in my place."

ALAMEDA GRAFT

One afternoon an intense crowd of men and women came roaring up the long steps of the old courthouse at Fifth and Broadway in

Oakland. I was standing at the head of the top flight of steps and saw in the crowd some prominent citizens whom I knew from the city of Alameda. In the front rank was a doctor I had known for many years as a most stable, calm and restrained personality. On this occasion, as he rushed up the steps two at a time waving his arms, he was obviously quite excited. I learned from my friend that the crowd had just come from a meeting in Alameda at which it was decided to call on Earl Warren immediately to take action with respect to conditions in the government of that city.

I went back to Warren's office and reported the situation. He instructed me to return to the lobby, which was jammed to overflowing, and tell the crowd to select three leaders whom he would talk to in his private office. This was a wise move because the group was a greatly agitated mob. I took the three representatives to Warren's office where he listened patiently to them at length. Their agitation gradually subsided. Their complaints involved a series of management episodes by city officials and the political clique which was running the city government.

Seeing this group—of which I knew many to be normally stable, sober, respectable citizens—charging up the courthouse steps in wild–eyed excitement demanding action by the district attorney, was a lesson in mob psychology. The frenzy of a motivated crowd can result quickly in a riot and mob violence.

In spite of this incident, the highhanded activities of the political clique under the leadership of the city manager continued until, suddenly, an attorney employed part–time as a consultant to the city attorney resigned. This increased Warren's suspicions, which up to this point had been based largely on rumor and hearsay, about the situation in Alameda, so he called the grand jury to investigate the operation of the city government. The part–time consultant claimed the attorney–client privilege with respect to much of his relations with the city attorney and city officials. However, we continued to subpoena city employees and officials of the city before the grand jury. Frankly, we were digging without sufficient evidence to support indictments.

Finally, an appointed official cracked while testifying before the grand jury, and we hit paydirt in certain other discussions, which came together to supply a framework of charges upon which, by further investigation, we were able to build cases against the city manager, the mayor, the city attorney and two city councilmen. They were charged with conspiracy to violate certain statutes having to do with unlawful use of the services of city employees, theft of building materials belonging to the city, unlawful solicitation and receipt of salary kickback payments from city employees for a political campaign fund, and solicitation and acceptance of bribes from persons doing business with the city. In the case of the city manager, a charge of perjury was also made, predicated upon the testimony of certain city employees who were unhappy about having to contribute parts of their wages or salaries to the political machine which controlled the city government.

The city manager, who was head of the machine, was tried first upon the perjury charge, convicted and sentenced to San Quentin. This helped to loosen up some of the employees who, perhaps through fear of reprisal, had been reluctant to cooperate in the investigation.

The trial of the mayor, the city attorney and two councilmen proceeded to the conclusion of arguments and submission of the case to the jury. After a period of deliberation, the jury informed the bailiff that they had a verdict. When the jury was brought into court and announced that its verdict was guilty on each defendant and on each count, I asked the court to postpone having the clerk record the verdicts.

Under the law of California, when a verdict of guilty on a charge against a public official involving moral turpitude is recorded, the official is automatically disqualified and his tenure is terminated. Had the verdicts been recorded, the city of Alameda would have been without a mayor, who was also a member of the City Council, and two councilmen. In other words, with only two councilmen out of the five member Council left, the Council could not function officially and city government, if any, would become de facto.

At a meeting of the Council, called that evening, one of the convicted councilmen resigned, whereupon the remaining four councilmen appointed a man to fill the vacancy. Then another convicted councilman resigned and was replaced with a new Council member. Then the mayor resigned and a new mayor was selected by the newly constituted Council. The next day the verdicts were recorded, and in due course sentence was imposed.

Since that day there has been no official misconduct or trouble in the government of the city of Alameda. The use of the grand jury to probe the situation and question city officials under oath made it possible to develop proof to support the indictments and convictions.

LIQUOR LAW GRAFT

After the constitutional amendment repealing Prohibition, the California state Legislature put control and administration of laws concerning alcoholic beverages in the hands of the California Board of Equalization. This Board consisted of four elected officials, each representing a geographic district of the state. Another state official, the controller, was ex–officio a member of the Board.

This was at a time when the Board of Equalization was used to doing little to disturb the status quo and when the quality of the Board's membership was at a low ebb. Public administration of laws affecting the fast–growing liquor business presented many problems. Each member had practically absolute and exclusive power of administration in his own district. This meant approval of licenses, regulations and cancellation for violations of law. Board membership was elective and political considerations prevailed.

The chief enforcement officer of the Board of Equalization in the Alameda—Contra Costa County district shook down a licensee for $500 to square a citation for a minor infraction of regulations. Rumors of lax administration had been spreading, and a newspaper chain had been gathering information prior to initiating a crusade for legislative action establishing a separate agency for liquor control.

Warren called the grand jury on the matter involving the enforcement officer and the media exploded. A committee of the Legislature had been prying into Board operations in the liquor business and the Hearst newspapers were itching for something about which to crusade. The liquor business and the Board of Equalization were ready targets.

When the furor subsided, the chief enforcement officer in Alameda County, his assistant, and an attorney who was a close friend of a Board member were indicted and convicted. The Legislature subsequently enacted legislation taking administration of liquor laws away from the Board of Equalization and creating a whole new government colossus (Alcoholic Beverage Control Board) with complete authority over the business of intoxicating liquor.

Our investigation, having started with a $500 payoff for fixing a minor infraction of a liquor business regulation in Niles, progressed to an extensive and thorough investigation of enforcement and administration of the liquor laws. Eventually the whole business of liquor came in for a thorough overhaul. This was another impact case resulting in better enforcement and administration of liquor control laws. It was also a case in which Warren's timing was right and where he hit a jackpot of favorable state–wide publicity.

WARREN'S SHIP MURDER CASE

The so–called "ship murder case" was probably the most highly publicized of the many important cases during Warren's regime as district attorney. This was a period of intense activity among radical elements in labor unions and competition for members between the conservative Seamen's Union of the Pacific and the Firemen, Oilers, Wipers and Water Tenders Union, the latter controlled by radical leadership whose head was Earl King. This was the decade of the Depression when one–third of eligible workers were unemployed and conditions were ripe for subversive propaganda and activism. Radical leadership had gained control of the International Longshoremen's and Warehousemen's Union (ILWU). Maritime workers who incurred the wrath of radical union leaders were brutally worked over by "goon" squads to the extent, on occasion, of murder.

Warren described conditions as follows:

"Some of the Maritime Unions were dominated by extremists,

> and 'goon squads' operated along the waterfronts of both San Francisco and Oakland to physically intimidate any opposition. Occasionally, the trussed up body of a waterfront personality would be found floating in San Francisco Bay."[15]

An officer of a ship approaching San Francisco disappeared mysteriously at sea and was never found. The chained body of a crewman of another ship was found floating in shallow water on the edge of the Bay in Alameda County.

On March 22, 1936, the mutilated body of George Alberts was found lying in his stateroom on the *S.S. Point Lobos,* a cargo ship lying at anchor alongside a dock at the Encinal Terminal in Alameda, at a quiet time when there was no activity on the ship. Alberts had been beaten, stabbed and slashed with a sharp knife and had bled to death. Alberts, who was the chief engineer on the ship, had been involved in a dispute over payment of overtime wages to a member of his crew. Alberts was described by Warren as being "known for his resistance on his ship to Communist influences which were so prevalent in Maritime circles at that time."

For sometime after Alberts' death, the identity of the killer or killers was unknown. There was much talk on the waterfront about Alberts' murder, and, in due course, scuttlebutt surfaced to the effect that King had directed the goon squad to the ship to teach Alberts a lesson, and that Alberts, a strong man, had put up a fight and was killed. In due course also, the scuttlebutt identified others involved as: E. G. Ramsay, a grievance adjuster for the union; Frank J. Conner, a member of the ship's crew, who directed the goon squad how to find Alberts; and George Wallace, a member of the union, who boarded the ship with a nondescript radical fireman named Ben Sakowitz, who dropped completely out of circulation after the killing.

Wallace was arrested in Brownsville, Texas, apparently enroute to Mexico, and was returned, in custody, to Oakland, where he confessed that he had boarded the *S.S. Point Lobos* with Sakowitz, but

[15]Earl Warren, *Memoirs of Earl Warren*, 1st ed. (Garden City, NY, Doubleday, 1977), p. 113.

had not entered Alberts' room. Conner admitted telling Wallace and Sakowitz where to find Alberts and later recanted this statement.

King, Conner, Wallace, Ramsay and Sakowitz were indicted and, with the exception of Sakowitz, went to trial. Selection of the jury lasted a month. The trial lasted three months. During the trial, harassing phone calls threatening harm to Warren's children were received at his home. Pickets paraded around the courthouse during the trial, especially while the jurors were entering and leaving.

Wallace was represented by Willard Shea, the public defender, and testified in his own defense. The other defendants did not take the stand. During the trial, the new courthouse at 1225 Fallon Street was completed, and the case was moved there for closing arguments. The jury deliberated less than four hours before delivering a verdict. All the defendants were found guilty of murder second–degree and sentenced to San Quentin.

During World War II, about five years after the trial, Sakowitz was located in the French Foreign Legion and turned over to U.S. Army headquarters in Europe. He was returned to the United States in the custody of a provost marshal, and, upon arrival in New York Harbor, he escaped. He has not been heard from since. According to rumor, he fled to Russia and was killed later in the war, fighting for the Soviets.

About three years after the trial, while Warren was attorney general, Governor Olson caused the state Parole Board to release on parole King, Conner and Ramsay. He did nothing for Wallace. Warren criticized Governor Olson vigorously because of the parole and made it one of the issues of his campaign for governor against him.

Warren considered the "ship murder case" the most important case of his regime as district attorney. Unquestionably, it contributed in no small measure to his election as attorney general and governor. It was another impact case which, Warren said, slowed down goonism and reduced the number of its victims found floating in the Bay.

A CASE OF MISTAKEN IDENTITY

In 1931 there had been a series of aggravated rape cases in Oakland in which young white girls had been forcibly raped by a black. Among these cases were two in which the victim of the rape had been sitting in an automobile with her boyfriend. In each case a black approached the automobile on the driver's side with a knife in his hand, threatened to stab the boy, and ordered him to get out of the automobile. The black then got into the car and drove it, with the girl, to an isolated park where, at the point of the knife, he took the girl from the automobile into some bushes and raped her, holding a knife in his hand and threatening to kill her if she made an outcry. The rapes occurred under similar circumstances at different times in west Oakland.

A young black named Waller* was arrested by the Oakland Police Department and placed in a lineup in which he was positively identified by the two girls and their boyfriends. At the preliminary hearing, the two girls and the two boys again identified Waller as the perpetrator of the crime.

Waller was held to answer to the Superior Court and while the case was awaiting trial, Raymond Ferrario, assistant public defender, talked to me and said that his client, Waller, vigorously protested his innocence. Ferrario asked me to have the case reinvestigated. I did so and found that Waller and a friend of his named Turner,* who was also a black and about the same size as Waller, had been living together in west Oakland about the time that the rapes were committed. It also developed that Waller had a checkered overcoat which he sometimes loaned to Turner and that a similar overcoat was worn by the person who committed the rapes of the two girls.

I traced Turner to Seattle, Washington, where he was in custody for a felony offense in that jurisdiction. I communicated with the Seattle authorities, explained the circumstances, and asked them to interrogate Turner about the Oakland rapes. He admitted he was the one who had committed the rapes in Oakland. I questioned the four witnesses, showing them pictures of Turner and Waller and explaining the circumstances, including Turner's confession and Waller's persistent denials. At the time, the maximum penalty in California for forcible rape was fifty years in state prison.

I explained to the witnesses that, under the circumstances, there was at least a reasonable doubt as to Waller's guilt and that the case should be dismissed. The witnesses, upon being presented with all the facts, expressed a doubt as to the identification of Waller. I reported this to Warren, and recommended dismissal of the case against Waller. District Attorney Warren instructed me to present the facts to the grand jury and obtain from the grand jury a recommendation that the case be dismissed. This was done and the case was dismissed.

Many years later, while Warren was governor of California, he received a letter from Waller, who was in the Army in the South Pacific during World War II. In this letter he stated that he had made good and thanked Warren for saving him from serving a long term in state prison.

AN UNUSUAL DRUNK DRIVING CASE

During early morning hours, a large Packard automobile, traveling at a high rate of speed on 8th Street, struck the side of a Chevrolet as it was crossing 8th Street at Fallon Street. The owner of the Packard was a San Francisco contractor named Thomas Sharman, Jr. The driver of the Chevrolet was Frank Dutra, and the passenger was his 14 year old son, Frank, Jr.

The Chevrolet was knocked a considerable distance and almost broken in half as it hit a tree. The force of the collision was such that Dutra and his son were both killed instantly. The Packard turned on its right side and skidded about half a block along 8th Street. When it came to a stop, a man was seen to crawl out of the driver's side, which was facing upward, and disappeared. This man was later identified as Borelli, an employee of Sharman's. In the automobile, draped over the back of the front seat with his head hanging down in the rear compartment, was Sharman who at the time was badly injured and unconscious.

Borelli told the police that Sharman was the driver of the Packard and that he, Borelli, had been riding with him. Investigation developed that Sharman was a very heavy drinker and, prior to the accident, had been drinking for a number of hours.

Sharman, after being unconscious at the county hospital for several days, was questioned by the police and said that he had no recollection of what had happened and that he did not know whether or not he had been driving the automobile at the time of the accident.

The witness who had seen a man climbing out of the driver's side of the Packard had not been interrogated by the police nor had witnesses who had seen Sharman's Packard pass them on 8th Street before the accident.

Sharman was charged with two counts of manslaughter, and, at the preliminary hearing, Borelli testified as a witness for the prosecution that Sharman was the driver of the Packard at the time of the accident. He again so testified at the trial of Sharman in the Superior Court.

After the prosecution rested, defense counsel put witnesses on who testified that, as they were driving westerly on 8th Street, a Packard automobile passed, and that the driver had on a coat of a different color than that which Sharman was found to be wearing after the accident. I cross–examined the defense witnesses thoroughly and was unable to shake them.

At the noon recess, I reported this to Earl Warren and said that in my opinion there was a reasonable doubt as to Sharman's guilt. Warren authorized me to dismiss the case. I returned to court, and when the defense rested I made a motion for dismissal in which I criticized the police for incompetence in not having interrogated all witnesses at the scene of the crime. I also said that if I had had an opportunity to interrogate the defense witnesses prior to the trial, there would not have been a trial. The judge granted my motion whereupon I instructed the bailiff to arrest Borelli, who was sitting in the courtroom. The jury was discharged and Borelli was taken to the county jail, where he was interrogated by an inspector from the Oakland Police Department. Borelli confessed to the inspector that Sharman was so drunk that he couldn't drive the car, and that he, Borelli, sat on Sharman's lap and was steering the car at the time of the collision. Borelli was later charged with perjury and convicted.

Warren criticized the police for careless work and the trial judge, Fred V. Wood, declared the case was the most unusual he had experienced in his many years as a judge.

AN EXCEPTIONAL MANSLAUGHTER

Charles Maxim, age 53, a quarrelsome cantankerous person when drinking, picked a fight with Healey* in a tavern in Berkeley. Maxim was very insulting in his language toward Healey, and, without provocation, knocked him off of a stool and hit him in the face, causing bruises around his eye and a bloody nose. The proprietor evicted Maxim, after which Maxim stood outside taunting Healey and inviting him to come out and fight. Healey went out and they exchanged blows. Healey, a young man, struck Maxim in the back of the head with his fist. Maxim fell or slipped on the wet street, striking his head violently on the pavement.

The autopsy showed abrasions of the right ear, left eyebrow and left temple region. He died as a result of a brain hemorrhage which the autopsy surgeon testified was caused apparently by a heavy blow to the head. Healey was charged with manslaughter, held to answer, and came to trial before a jury in the Superior Court.

The testimony of persons who witnessed the fight on the street, together with the testimony of the autopsy surgeon, left a reasonable doubt in my mind as to whether the defendant's blows caused the brain hemorrhage or whether it was caused when Maxim's head struck the street.

Under the circumstances, this was a case which should not have been charged or, at least, should have been dismissed on motion of the prosecutor at the end of the preliminary examination. However, this was during a period when Warren had a policy that when a person died as a result of a violent attack, a homicide should be charged.

I assigned the case to a young deputy, William Quinn, son of a veteran Superior Court judge. It was my practice when not engaged in trying a case myself to go into court with a young deputy to give him what help might be necessary. Quinn rested the prosecution's case just before the noon recess.

While walking uptown with Warren for lunch, as we often did, I told him about the case and said "I have a reasonable doubt, and I don't think Quinn should be in the position of asking the jury to convict."

Warren said "If that is how you feel about it, you make the closing argument and tell the jury how you feel."

So before court convened for the afternoon session, I told Quinn about my conversation with Warren and said, "I will make the closing argument."

The witnesses for the defense did not change the picture. In my closing argument I told the jury that it was their function under the law, as to which they would be instructed by the Court, and by the evidence which they had heard, to decide whether the defendant was guilty, but that if I were on the jury I would vote "not guilty."

Counsel for the defendant, a young lawyer recently admitted to practice, read a lengthy argument, after the fashion of some defense lawyers, attacking the District Attorney's Office.

In my rebuttal I repeated that if I were on the jury I would not convict, and closed by saying that I hoped the jury would not hold the ineptitude of defense counsel against the defendant.

The jury was out about two hours and returned a verdict of not guilty. It was learned later that they had considerable discussion during their deliberation as to whether they should censor the defense counsel for his unwarranted attack on the District Attorney's Office. Defense counsel continued to try cases and became a successful practitioner.

A CASE OF ARMED WITHDRAWAL

Minnis,* a resident of a small ranch in Castro Valley, walked into the Hayward branch bank of one of the large state–wide chains and presented a $44,300 check for cashing to the manager. The manager said there was not that much cash in the bank. Minnis asked him if the main office of the bank could cash the check. The manager said "yes." Minnis pulled a gun and ordered the manager to drive with him to Oakland, some fourteen miles distant, to get the check cashed at the bank's main office.

Upon arrival at the main office, the manager walked with Minnis to a teller's window where he was known, and told the teller that Minnis was a customer of his Hayward branch. The teller cashed the check and handed the money to Minnis.

Upon receiving the $44,300, Minnis directed the Hayward branch manager to ride with him back to the Hayward branch bank, where he left him and drove away. The manager reported the whole episode to the police, whereupon Minnis was arrested. Before being arrested, Minnis had buried the cash on his property in Castro Valley.

The District Attorney's Office got into the case and found the buried cash. The whole matter was presented to the grand jury. The branch manager testified. Incredible as his testimony might appear, I believed him, as did Earl Warren. The manager had never been in any trouble and apparently he was the kind of timorous person who could be so scared that such a thing could happen to him. Warren and I informed the grand jury of the manager's clear record and our thinking as to his innocence. We recommended no indictment of the manager and the grand jury agreed.

Minnis was indicted for robbery and pleaded "present insanity"—inability to cooperate with defense counsel. He was found "presently insane" as distinguished from "insane at the time of the offense." After a short confinement in one of the state mental institutions, he was returned to court for trial on the indictment. It was found at the state hospital that he had been malingering during his trial on "present insanity" or that he had recovered his ability to cooperate with his counsel.

Prisoners awaiting trial while incarcerated in jail occasionally develop what is known as "prison psychosis" in which state they can become unable to appreciate their current predicament or to cooperate with counsel. When the anxiety and uncertainty of the trial and trial conditions are eliminated, they can recover completely as far as their mental stability is concerned; in which event, if not already tried, they are subject to prosecution on the charge. Sometimes a person like Minnis is just eccentric enough to concoct a bold and incredible crime such as happened in this case, and sometimes they get away with it.

WARREN AS ADMINISTRATOR AND POLITICIAN

Warren was always strong politically and an excellent mixer, with a great deal of geniality, friendliness and personal charm. While in high school in Bakersfield, he played in a local band and became a member of the musician's union. Through the years, when in labor circles he would flash his union card and challenge anyone to top his tenure in union membership.

While in college at the University of California at Berkeley, he was a member of a fraternity and of the ROTC university band. After finishing college and law school at Berkeley, he joined a local law firm in the Bay Area, served in the United States Army during World War I, returned to California, worked as a clerk of a committee for one session in the state Legislature, then entered the Oakland City Attorney's Office and later the District Attorney's Office. His avowed ambition was to become a prominent trial lawyer.

Although he prosecuted criminal cases while in the District Attorney's Office, his work there, especially after he became district attorney, was largely administrative. As a trial prosecutor he was resourceful, vigorous and successful. As district attorney he was always on top of things, in close touch with the work of the office and the staff members. He demanded and received a high quality of performance, personal integrity and behavior.

He was a joiner, belonging to organizations such as the Elks, Moose, Eagles, Exchange Club, Athens Club and Bohemian Club. He also belonged to Sequoia Country Club for a few years but dropped out because he had no time for golf. Jokingly, he once said to me, "I would rather have a drunkard on my staff than a golfer." I was also a member of Sequoia and played golf there regularly.

He became a very active 33rd Degree Mason, Master of his Lodge, Potentate of the Ashmes Temple of the Shrine and Grand Master of Masons of California and Hawaii. He was always quite visible politically and obviously enjoyed his association with friends. He attended funerals regularly and visited friends who were ill.

He was a strong family man. He had an artist friend who each year would design a Christmas card showing Warren, his wife Nina and his six children, and occasionally the dogs and the pony. The list of the recipients of his Christmas cards was long and widespread geographically. Political acquaintances would say "how in hell can you beat a family like that?"

Although not a teetotaler while district attorney, Warren refrained from alcoholic beverages during the Prohibition era. He was circumspect about his associations and public appearances. Without sermonizing, he simply set an example which was generally followed. Staff members did not visit speakeasies or associate with persons of questionable repute. They simply sensed the boss' preference and quickly absorbed his policies. As a result of the high standards of competence and personal behavior of Warren and the staff, the good reputation of the office was strengthened professionally and politically.

There was no danger of defeat at the polls—a happy thing because there was no civil service in the office and all members served at the pleasure of the district attorney. This condition has continued to date. Over a long period of years there had been, and still is, a tradition of continuity in the District Attorney's Office of Alameda County, by virtue of which an experienced member of the office succeeded the incumbent. When Warren took office as attorney general of California on January 2, 1939, he left the District Attorney's Office in good hands in the person of Ralph Hoyt, who had entered the office in 1919 under Ezra Decoto and served with distinction during his entire incumbency.

WARREN RUNS FOR HIGHER OFFICE

When Attorney General Ulysses S. Webb in 1938 announced that he would retire at the end of his term, Warren announced his candidacy for the office. In California, the method of nominating candidates was by the direct primary system, which enabled any candidate to run simply by filing a petition with a certain number of signatures of his party and paying the filing fee. The candidate, if he wished, could also file for nomination as a candidate of another party by filing a petition with a like number of signatures from that party and paying an additional filing fee. This was known as "cross–filing" and was on the statute books well into the 1950's. If a candidate cross–filed and received the most votes of the party in which he was not registered, he would also have to receive the most votes of his own party in order to go on the ballot as the nominee of both parties. Candidates could cross–file only in elections for state office.

In his campaigns for attorney general and governor, Warren always cross–filed. In his campaign for attorney general, he filed on the Republican, Democratic and Progressive party tickets and received the nominations of all three parties. Later, in one of his three primary elections for governor he received the nominations of both the Republican and Democratic parties. In his other two campaigns for governor (one against James Roosevelt) he was overwhelmingly elected at the general election in November.

The Progressive party, with only about 4,000 members, was a creature of Hiram Johnson's. Practically all of the members of that party were Johnson's friends. Although he was a Republican, he had nurtured the little Progressive party as an ace–in–the–hole in case the Republican "Old Guard" should turn against him, in which event he could shift his party registration to the Progressives and run with cross–filing from that base.

During the Depression era of the 1930's, California had been deeply scarred economically, as had the rest of the nation. The Townsend Pension Plan of "Thirty Dollars every Thursday" had taken hold and received heavy support. Bread lines had been many and long. Unemployment was up around 25 percent. Farmers and urban homeowners, unable to make loan payments, defaulted and lost their properties.

In 1934, the Socialist reformer Upton Sinclair had run well as a Democrat against the Republican Frank F. Merriam in what for many years had been an overwhelmingly Republican state. Warren, as chairman of the Republican State Central Committee, campaigned vigorously for Merriam and the Republican slate. Carrying the torch as a staunch conservative leader of the party in 1936, Warren headed a favorite son ticket for President in the primary against Alf Landon and won. After the primary he withdrew as a presidential candidate.

During the 1930's, hundred of thousands had migrated from Midwestern states in dilapidated jalopies, looking in vain for work. State welfare, unemployment insurance and social security did not start until the mid–1930's. With the Roosevelt Democratic deluge of 1932 and 1936, the great swing of voter registration to the Democratic party had occurred.

4

Ralph E. Hoyt 1939—1947

While Warren was running for attorney general, Ralph Hoyt was running for district attorney from his position as chief assistant district attorney. Hoyt won at the primary election over four opponents and was later reelected in 1942 and 1946.

Hoyt had been a member of the District Attorney's Office since before Warren, and was thoroughly familiar with all phases of the work. During Warren's regime as district attorney, Hoyt handled primarily the Board of Supervisors and other civil work. He also prosecuted important criminal cases. A most able and dedicated public law officer, he refrained from private practice—as did Warren and myself. We were probably among the first full–time, career prosecutors in the nation.

Hoyt's first campaign for district attorney in 1938 did not appear the certainty that it finally proved to be. It was a long and hard campaign. Warren had announced his candidacy for attorney general in February 1938, and the primary at that time was in August. Some years later it was changed to June. Of course, Hoyt had to announce his candidacy for district attorney immediately following Warren's declaration and start working on his campaign. I managed the campaign.

Hoyt was not running—and would not be on the ballot—as the incumbent district attorney, but as chief assistant district attorney. From February through August, six to seven months, is a long time to campaign for public office, especially a county office. In those days the candidate had to cover the county, attending town hall political meetings in the evenings and fraternal organization picnics on Saturdays and Sundays, where the candidate shared food and drink with ethnic groups—who were well organized in the county.

With the exception of a few members of the office who could afford it, no contributions were accepted from anyone in any of Hoyt's three campaigns for District Attorney. This was true with respect to Warren's three campaigns for District Attorney and five of my campaigns. In my sixth campaign in 1966, because of the obviously lavish amount of campaign spending of my opponent and his effort to jell a coalition of racial, radical and other factions, I was advised to accept some financial help. I consented to do so provided there would be no contributions from any questionable source or from persons as to whom there could be a conflict of interest or obligation related to the duties of the District Attorney's Office. The political climate had changed by the mid–1960's, and the county's population had increased to over one million. A candidate for a county office could no longer conduct a successful campaign without some outside financial help.

CORRUPTION ON THE BENCH

Hoyt's chair in the corner office, which Warren had vacated the day before, was barely warm when a case broke involving Hamilton,* a secretary of the defeated governor. He had been appointed a judge of the Alameda County Superior Court by the governor during the waning hours of his term. A high–rolling, uninhibited type, Hamilton had traveled around the state borrowing money from and cashing worthless checks with persons who sought favors from the governor's office or other departments of state government.

While secretary to the governor, Hamilton had received some $2,000 from Nichols* as a consideration for using his influence to obtain a pardon for a prisoner named Lewis* in San Quentin, who was serving time for murder. The money was paid by Nichols at a tavern in San Francisco. Pursuant to Hamilton's direction, an attorney associate of his in Oakland prepared a pardon application for Lewis. Somehow, word of Hamilton's deal with Nichols concerning a pardon for Lewis got around, as did word of some of his other activities and peccadilloes, especially as the governor's term drew to a close with no results from Hamilton's promises. After he was appointed Superior Court judge, the roof caved in on him.

Warren, as the new attorney general, was notified and questioned Hamilton. Warren referred the case to Alameda County where T. W. Harris, the presiding judge, refused to assign any cases to Hamilton. A grand jury investigation on the pardon deal and other activities was begun, and Hamilton resigned as judge. Indictments were returned charging him with receiving a bribe from Nichols and with passing a number of bad checks under circumstances which smacked of bribery.

On the basis of the preparation of the pardon application having been done in Alameda County, Warren and Hoyt theorized that this was an overt part of the action of a conspiracy to accept a bribe, and that it gave Alameda County concurrent jurisdiction with San Francisco to prosecute in the Superior Court of Alameda County. Warren had no confidence in the competence of the San Francisco District Attorney's Office.

He was tried on the Nichols–Lewis bribery charge before Judge Warren Tryon of Del Norte County, sitting *pro tempore* in Alameda County, and convicted. Judge Tryon granted him a new trial on the ground that San Francisco County had exclusive jurisdiction, solely because the money had changed hands in that county, although some overt action had occurred in Alameda County.

The decision of Judge Tryon was appealed and the Appellate and Supreme Courts of California held that Alameda County had jurisdiction under the law, part of the action having occurred in the county, but upheld Judge Tryon's order granting a new trial on the grounds that a trial judge is like a thirteenth juror and, right or wrong, his discretion in granting a new trial must stand.

Hamilton was tried on bad check charges, convicted and sentenced to the county jail. He was defended by Leo Friedman of San Francisco, one–time prosecutor of movie actor Fatty Arbuckle, leading defense trial lawyer and later a judge of the Municipal Court. His appeal from Hamilton's convictions in the check cases failed.

POLICE BRUTALITY

Fred Fernelius, husband of Mabel Fernelius and father of four children, alcoholic, emaciated, height 5'6", weight 135 pounds, at midnight staggered into a building of the Pacific Gas and Electric Company, very much under the influence of liquor. People at PG&E called the Oakland police. He was put in a patrol wagon and delivered to the Oakland city jail where he was confined. Pursuant to custom, he was herded, with other drunks arrested during the night, into a lineup to await being taken to court.

Suddenly, he broke out of line and started running. He ran into a part of the jail where felony prisoners were confined in locked cells—an area from which he could not possibly escape. Two officers on duty in the jail chased Fernelius and caught him. One officer started beating on his head with a police billy club loaded with lead, while the other officer held him. The other officer hit him a couple of times with his handcuffs which he finally fastened on his wrists.

Fernelius, extremely weak, in a state of *delirium tremens*, and unable to put up any kind of resistance, was quickly subdued and knocked unconscious, blood streaming out of his ears. He was taken to Highland Emergency Hospital where he died the next day from the injuries inflicted by the police officers in the jail.

An investigation disclosed that one of the officers was notorious for brutality. The two officers were indicted, tried and convicted. At issue in the trial was whether they had used more than reasonable force in subduing Fernelius. The autopsy showed that his skull had been fractured and his brain was macerated, apparently from being knocked around inside his skull. Legally, a peace officer could use reasonable and necessary force to subdue a prisoner resisting arrest or trying to escape.

A prominent Oakland brain surgeon testified for the defense that Fernelius had in his brain a chronic cerebral hemorrhage which had been there for about eighteen months and that even a slight tap on the head could reactivate the hemorrhage and cause death, thus negating the prosecution's theory that more force had been used than was necessary and reasonable.

I collaborated with Dr. Howard Naffziger, dean of the University of California Medical School, San Francisco, who was one of the world's leading brain surgeons. He advised me, as did Dr. Gertrude Moore, Alameda County autopsy pathologist, that the testimony of the defense expert concerning a standing chronic cerebral hemorrhage in Fernelius' brain was sheer nonsense and medically untenable. Dr. Naffziger advised that he no longer testified in court but recommended a former student, Dr. Lester Lawrence, whom he had trained in medical college and who practiced in Oakland. I used Dr. Lawrence and Dr. Moore as expert witnesses.

They completely repudiated the defense expert, their conclusion being that a hemorrhage in the brain does not remain static or chronic, that the blood is absorbed into the brain tissue and in a short while leaves only a fine microscopic line. In other words, there was no such thing as a chronic standing hemorrhage in the brain as round as a walnut, which the defense expert had testified would have resulted from a head injury which Fernelius had suffered a year or two before.

The defendants were represented by Charles Brennan, a prominent trial lawyer from San Francisco, and Leo Sullivan, leading trial counsel of Alameda County. They were convicted of manslaughter and sentenced to San Quentin by Judge Lincoln Sheridan Church, himself a former trial lawyer of great ability. The convictions were affirmed on appeal.

In a civil action against the city of Oakland, a jury rendered a verdict of $45,000 for the surviving widow of Fernelius. The case became somewhat of a legal landmark creating great interest among liberals and liberal organizations throughout the West. The Supreme Court of California held that the chief of police and the city manager of Oakland and their official performance bondsman, Fidelity and Deposit Company of Maryland, were liable. The case was decided on the pleadings in an appeal from a demurrer which had been sustained by the lower Superior Court. The California Supreme Court held as follows:

> "While superior public officers generally are not liable for the torts of their subordinates where such subordinates are likewise public employees, a superior officer is liable if, having the power and duty of removal, he negligently fails to discharge a known unfit subordinate.
>
> "A city manager and chief of police may be held liable in damages for unlawful acts of incompetent and brutal police officers on the theory of negligent retention of such subordinates, although such officers, on suspension or removal, would have a right of appeal to a civil service board, where the power and duty to initiate any action leading to such removal are vested exclusively in these superior officers. There is no more reason for excusing negligent failure to perform a restricted duty, which if faithfully performed would, in the ordinary course of events, be adequate to prevent the damage, than there is for excusing such failure to perform an unrestricted duty.
>
> "No presumption can be indulged that a city manager or the civil service board will act improperly with regard to the suspension of unfit police officers after previous proper action by the party primarily charged with the duty of removing such officers.
>
> "An individual aggrieved by breaches committed by a police officer may sue on the bonds of a city manager and chief of police, where such bonds are not among those which the city charter specifically requires to be executed 'to the city,' and where the charter provisions are consistent with the right of individual persons, aggrieved by an officer's neglect or wrongful acts, to sue on such bonds under Pol. Code, section 961."

A FRUIT SHAKE CASE

This was a case in which the facts challenge credulity and yet which were unquestionably true, as so found by the trial jury and sustained by both the trial judge and the state Court of Appeal. The facts were as follows:

George Acheson, age 53, a meek and frail man, height about 5'–6", weight about 140 lbs., slender and lame, was a salesman for an oil company in San Francisco which specialized in the manufacture of materials for surfacing roads and highways. Acheson left his home in Berkeley on December 25, 1939, and took a train to Seattle for the purpose of closing a contract with the city of Seattle. He arrived in Seattle on the evening of December 26, 1939, and registered at the Olympic Hotel.

Leaving his room, he intended to go to the coffee shop in the hotel basement, but, after arriving on the first floor, he decided to go out for a short walk. Leaving the hotel, he walked several blocks down Fourth Avenue, and, as he was returning to the hotel, he stopped at a lavatory in the public library. The entrance to this lavatory was on Fourth Avenue and could be entered without going into the library itself.

As he was walking out the doorway to the sidewalk, he encountered a man later identified as Frank L. Sigel, who remarked that the lavatory was untidy. Acheson made some reply in answer thereto and continued on to the Olympic Hotel, which was about a block away.

Sigel walked beside him to the hotel, and, as Acheson approached the entrance, Sigel asked if he lived there. Acheson replied that he was staying there. Whereupon, Sigel asked him if he was in the lumber business, remarked that the wood paneling on the mezzanine floor was of unusual quality and design, and suggested that Acheson see it.

Sigel then turned and walked up a short stairway, followed by Acheson. When Sigel reached the top, he turned around quickly, and Acheson noticed that Sigel's pants were unbuttoned and part of his underclothing was visible. Acheson turned to descend, and, as he did so, a second man appeared and told Acheson that he was under arrest, at the same time holding his hand in his pocket in such a manner as to lead Acheson to believe that he had a gun.

The #2 man exhibited a badge, as did Sigel, who buttoned his clothing and said to the #2 man, "This is the fellow. We caught him." These men then carried on a rapid conversation between themselves, stating that the churches and newspapers of Seattle had been after the police department for a series of sex crimes; that

Acheson was a degenerate; that he was under arrest; and that the chief would be happy in cleaning up the matter.

Acheson was then taken out of the hotel to a car which was parked nearby, where they said to him, "You don't look like a degenerate. My God, you ought to be dead." They told him that they ought to get rid of him and suggested taking him to the hospital to see his victims.

They then got into the car and drove for several blocks to near the police department, where the #2 man got out and informed Acheson he was going in to book him. In a few minutes the #2 man returned and said that they had to go back to the hotel and search Acheson's room at the request of the chief.

After getting to the room, Sigel began going through all of Acheson's luggage and personal effects, while the #2 man itemized the various articles that were found. Among the articles examined was a savings account book from the American Trust Company in Berkeley, California showing a balance in Acheson's name of approximately $20,000.

Acheson was questioned regarding his business, his purpose for being in Seattle at that time, his appointment with the purchasing agent the following day, and also his destination after leaving Seattle and his expected time of departure on the following day for Salem, Oregon.

The following day, Acheson completed his business with the purchasing agent in Seattle, and, in the afternoon, went to the railroad station to board a train for Salem, Oregon, where he planned to transact some further business. While Acheson was waiting in the depot for the train, the #2 man and a man later identified as Elkins appeared.

Elkins flashed a badge and accused Acheson of trying to run away. Elkins told him that the detectives of the night before had not done their work; that they had no business to let him go; and that he would have to return to the police station. During this conversation, Elkins seized Acheson by the arm and shoved him around. He was lame and off balance and he stumbled.

They then left the station, Acheson between Elkins and the #2 man—both holding onto Acheson's arms. They took him two or three blocks away to the doorway of a vacant building and went through his pockets and wallet, where they found certain credentials indicating Acheson was a member of a Masonic Lodge. Upon seeing these credentials, Elkins then said to him it was too bad, he would have to do something for him.

The #2 man then left, saying that he was going across the street to see the judge. The conversation then turned to the matter of a bail bond. Elkins suggested Acheson write a check for $800, and that, plus the $200 which Acheson had in his wallet, would be sufficient bail. Elkins then gave Acheson a fountain pen and the latter wrote out a check[21] for $800 and handed it over, together with the $200 cash. Elkins then took him back to the railroad station, where Acheson boarded the train to Salem.

On February 2, 1940, thirty–eight days later, at about eleven o'clock in the morning, Acheson received a phone call at his office in the Monadnock Building in San Francisco, purporting to come from a man named Davis, relating to life insurance. A few minutes later Elkins appeared and told Acheson to come out in the hallway of the building.

When Acheson got into the hallway he saw a man who was later identified as Walter Simpson. He put something hard against Acheson's back and commanded him to keep walking to the end of the hallway. At that point, Simpson exhibited a badge and stated he was an inspector from the Seattle Police Department; that the other officers in Seattle were on the spot and were going to lose their jobs; and that he would have to return Acheson to Seattle to stand trial for the sex crimes which he had committed. They told Acheson they were going to take him to the San Francisco Police Department.

They took him to Kearney Street, and, on the way, threatened to shoot him. According to Acheson's later statement testifying in this respect: "They referred to these crimes again, as they had in the past,

[21] Endorsement on the cashed check was not in the handwriting of either Sigel or Elkins.

referred to the dirty mess, it would be better to shoot me, to get rid of me, throw me in a slough."

At the end of the first block off Market Street, they pushed him into a doorway, went through his pockets and found his Masonic credentials. Whereupon, the attitude of Simpson changed, professing that he too was a Mason, that he was going to help him; that they could go to the chief of police in San Francisco because he was a Catholic; and that he would call the chief of police in Seattle who was a Mason.

They then took him to the lobby of the Palace Hotel. Elkins stayed with him while Simpson left to telephone. Elkins told him that Simpson could take care of him. Simpson then returned saying he had talked to the chief in Seattle who had told him it would take $2,500 to clear the thing; that Acheson would have to produce $2,500. Acheson told him he did not have the $2,500. They replied, "You've got money in a bank in Berkeley. We will go over to Berkeley and get it."

They then took Acheson and boarded a train to Berkeley. While on the train to Berkeley there was some conversation about Acheson being a degenerate, of taking him back to Seattle to stand trial, which they said would ruin him and his family. Simpson said to Acheson, "If you think we are fooling, feel this." He put Acheson's hand on an object, which Acheson testified felt hard and like a gun of some kind.

Upon arriving at the bank in Berkeley, Acheson withdrew $2,500 from his savings account. The money was handed to Simpson on the train while returning to San Francisco, near Ashby Station in Berkeley. Upon arrival at the Terminal Station in San Francisco, they took him back to the lobby of the Palace Hotel where they told Acheson they were quite sure everything would be all right; that he should go back to his office and go to work; that everything would be taken care of. Simpson told him he would phone him the next morning after talking with the chief in Seattle.

Immediately upon returning to his office, Acheson telephoned Ralph Hoyt, the District Attorney of Alameda County, and reported what had happened. Simpson phoned Acheson later and told him he had been in touch with Seattle; that everything was all right; that the matter had been taken care of.

Acheson told the Berkeley police that he believed Sigel, Elkins and Simpson were corrupt police officers of the Seattle Police Department; that they told him the money was going to the chief of police of Seattle; that Simpson showed him a badge and said he was an inspector of the Seattle Police Department. Acheson said he had paid the money because he feared for his life and that he would be taken back and charged with these sex crimes.

Elkins, when arrested, confessed his participation in the crime and implicated Sigel. The Berkeley police recognized the case for what was known in police jargon as a "fruit shake" bunco. Whether Acheson was a homosexual or just a very timid person and a very gullible victim of a clever team of bunco men was undetermined. He had no criminal record of any kind. Up to the point of his encounters with Sigel, Elkins and Simpson, he had been a successful salesman and continued to be thereafter. Bunco "artists" are shrewd operators and consummate actors who can convincingly maneuver a victim and a situation with great skill.

It was the first bunco case in many years to have occurred under circumstances giving Alameda County jurisdiction. Through photographs of known bunco men, Acheson identified Sigel as the first contact or #1 man of the bunco team; Elkins as the third member of the team who, with #2, contacted him in the Seattle railroad depot and extorted the $200 and the check for $800; and Simpson as the #4 man who, with Elkins, had kidnaped him and robbed him of $2,500 in Berkeley.

An indictment was obtained charging Sigel, Elkins, Simpson and Richard Roe (as the #2 member of the team) with grand theft, robbery, extortion and kidnaping. As anticipated, Elkins and Simpson had left California immediately after obtaining the $2,500, and Sigel, in this case, had never come any closer to California than Seattle, Washington. Sigel's role as the original contact man of the bunco team operation in Seattle qualified him as a principal and co–conspirator in the action and a co–defendant although he had never entered the state.

After a lapse of over a year, Sigel was arrested in Detroit while working in a gambling casino operated by a notorious mob. Extradition papers were issued, and C. H. Ipsen, an inspector of the Berkeley Police Department who wanted to buy a new automobile at a Detroit factory, was assigned to execute the rendition warrant and return Sigel to California, which he did with Mrs. Sigel, an attractive and expensively attired woman, following close behind in a Cadillac El Dorado.

The "rap sheets"—criminal records—of Sigel, Elkins and Simpson were long and varied. They had been arrested numerous times around the nation for bunco crimes, often getting the cases reduced to misdemeanors or dismissed by threatening or buying off victims, or by conning lazy, inept police or prosecutors—a common ploy among seasoned confidence game and bunco artists.

I had warned Acheson that he would be approached by a defendant or their representatives and either threatened with physical harm or exposure to a slanderous attack, and if these threats did not work, they would resort to an attempt to buy him off by returning the money they had stolen from him.

Acheson was contacted through an emissary so as not to incriminate the defendants, but they were unsuccessful. An offer of a plea to a misdemeanor with reimbursement was made to the Berkeley police and to the District Attorney's Office, likewise without success. So the case went to trial against Sigel and Elkins.

Simpson was never found nor was the #2 member of the team. Sigel was represented by Leo Sullivan. Elkins' attorney was the public defender. The only evidence the prosecution had was the testimony of Acheson and the record of withdrawal of the $2,500 in cash by Acheson from his savings account in the Berkeley bank. It appeared that the only identification of Sigel as a participant in the shakedown would be Acheson's testimony unless Elkins testified and implicated Sigel, which would be doubtful. Elkins did not testify. If Sigel took the stand and denied the whole thing, it would be his word against that of Acheson.

A jury was selected the first day of the trial and the next morning Acheson testified. His direct examination concluded and the cross–

examination was almost finished by noon. All that remained of the prosecution case was for me to put on the bank testimony concerning the savings account withdrawal. I anticipated that Sigel might take the stand in his own defense because, up to that point, although arrested many times, he had not actually served time as a convicted felon in a state prison. Consequently, I could not ask him on cross–examination if he had been convicted of a felony.

As was my practice, I had contacted every police department where Sigel had been arrested and obtained what evidence they had, which, however, was hearsay and inadmissible. The victims in those cases proved to be unavailable or unwilling to testify.

At the noon recess, I had lunch uptown and dropped in at the Inspector's Bureau of the Oakland Police Department to talk with an inspector about another case which was pending. While there, I was introduced to John Rauch, Captain of Detectives from the New Orleans Police Department, who happened to be passing through on some business for his department. Having seen on Sigel's rap sheet an arrest in New Orleans, I questioned Rauch about it.

Rauch was a smart policeman known throughout the country for his success in solving crimes. During the founding meeting of the United Nations in San Francisco in 1945, Rauch was one of a select corps of officers chosen to provide protection and security for officials from around the world who were in attendance. Rauch remembered Sigel and all the details involved in his arrest in New Orleans. Sigel's arrest there was an attempt to victimize a clergyman in a typical "fruit shake" scam.

Rauch came back to the courthouse with me, and, before court convened, I had him walk into the courtroom and talk to Sigel to make sure he was the same Sigel listed in the rap sheet. Sigel, of course, pulled away and would not talk with Rauch, but as soon as Sullivan arrived, Sigel was seen in animated conversation with him.

The trial resumed, and, when I finished putting on the bank testimony, I said, "The people rest."

Whereupon Sullivan said, "The defense rests," thus putting on no defense testimony.

Elkins' counsel also rested. Elkins had prior felony convictions about which he could be questioned if he testified. Sullivan was quite aware of the fact that, where possible in any case which I prosecuted, I developed and used similar offense and conspiracy evidence. Apparently, when Sigel told Sullivan that Rauch was present and that he, Sigel, had been arrested in New Orleans on a "fruit shake" case, Sullivan assumed that I was loaded with similar offense evidence and was saving it for rebuttal. By not putting on Sigel or any other testimony, he could shut off all rebuttal.

Under the law in California at that time, the prosecution could comment on the failure of a defendant to testify. The United States Supreme Court later held this law unconstitutional. I disagree with this decision. In my argument to the jury I put particular emphasis on the failure of Sigel to testify, saying that Acheson's testimony stood in the record uncontradicted, and, if it were not true, Sigel could and should have testified.

Sigel and Elkins were convicted and sentenced to San Quentin. Their convictions were affirmed on appeal even though Sigel had not been in California during any part of the action.[22] My theory was that the whole thing was part of a bunco "fruit shake" conspiracy, and that his participation in the conspiracy in Seattle made him guilty as a co–conspirator for what occurred in Alameda County.

One may wonder how things such as happened in the Acheson case could happen in broad daylight in a busy hotel like the Olympic in Seattle or the Palace in San Francisco, in Acheson's building, on the streets of San Francisco, or in a busy bank in Berkeley, with other people present who might be alerted. But again, bunco artists are excellent actors—very bold and resourceful. If their attempt fails, they go on to try again. If they are caught, they try to maneuver their way out of serious trouble by reimbursing the victim or by pleading guilty to a lesser offense. Countless rap sheets of bunco artists around the country bear this out. But these tactics were not permitted in Alameda County, which is why there have been so few bunco cases here. The professional crook, like a pickpocket or a bunco man,

[22] *People v. Sigel, et al,* (1942) 55 Cal.App.2d 279

stays out of a jurisdiction where the odds are against him. Warren, Hoyt and I despised professional crooks and threw the book at them whenever possible.

WHITE HIBISCUS CLAIRE DE LUNE

An unusual case during Ralph Hoyt's administration involved a torrid love affair between Gireth, a prominent Southern California jeweler, and an airline stewardess. The girl's fully clothed body was found on a bed in a motel in Oakland, her crossed hands on her chest holding a white hibiscus. On a phonograph player was a record titled "Claire de Lune."

Gireth had fled, but was found and confessed that he had killed the girl and intended to kill himself but lost his nerve. He said he would plead guilty to murder first degree and wanted to be executed. He refused to cooperate with assigned counsel, was convicted and sentenced to receive the death penalty, which was in due course imposed. He never disclosed his motive and took the secret with him to his death.

When the police arrived at the motel, a few steps ahead of reporters from the police beat pressroom, a vase containing white hibiscus flowers was on a table in the room, as was the phonograph and the record. The newspaper headlines referred to this case as the "White Hibiscus Claire de Lune" murder.

OFFICER JOHNSTON

In 1946, there had been a pattern of home burglaries in the Lake Merritt area of Oakland. Starting at the north end of the lake, the burglaries had moved easterly until one night an Oakland policeman, John Johnston, sitting alone in his patrol car, saw a young man walking along the sidewalk. Apparently, as this person was about to pass his car, Johnston ordered him to stop and submit to interrogation. Later that night, Johnston was found sitting in his car with his open notebook on his lap. He had been shot six times and was dead. There was no living witness to the shooting. Burglaries in the area ceased.

Months later, at a very low tide, a person walking along the bank of a salt water tidal canal between Lake Merritt and the Oakland Estuary saw a pistol lying in the mud of the canal. He took it to the Oakland police, who cleaned it up and examined it carefully. It was a very old gun and badly corroded after lying for months in the mud and salt water.

A ballistic expert from Pasadena, after a most thorough examination of the gun and ballistic testing of bullets fired from the gun and bullets taken from Johnston's body, was able to establish that the gun found in the canal was the same gun used to murder Officer Johnston. The expert spent a long time washing and cleaning the gun to make possible his ballistic comparisons.

A trace put on the gun developed that it had been stolen from the home of a well–known Oakland doctor, who was the son–in–law of Oliver Hamlin, a prominent Oakland lawyer and judge. The doctor had received the gun from Hamlin who, many years before while he was a deputy district attorney of Alameda County, had prosecuted a case in which the gun had been used. The real owner of the gun was not known, so when the loot was being disposed of, Hamlin had received the gun as a souvenir of his effort.

A small impression of part of a fingerprint from the door of Officer Johnston's car was matched up by the FBI with a fingerprint from the doctor's home and with fingerprints from other homes in the pattern of burglaries in the area north of Lake Merritt, contemporaneous with the burglary of the doctor's home and shortly before Johnston's murder. In due course these fingerprints were matched up with fingerprints on record at the FBI and the California Bureau of Criminal Identification. They belonged to one Joe Blaich, an ex–convict who had been released sometime before the Johnston murder.

Blaich was charged with the Johnston murder, convicted and sentenced for life to San Quentin. Folger Emerson, who prosecuted him, was later elected a Superior Court judge of Alameda County, and served with distinction on the California Court of Appeal.

The finding of the gun in the tidal canal was, of course, sheer luck, without which the Johnston killing would have been an unsolved case. But luck does happen sometimes and law enforcement officers need it. Thorough, competent investigation before and after the lucky break also helps, as it did in the Blaich case. A less competent and industrious criminalist might have concluded that the corroded condition of the gun would preclude any effective expert ballistic work on the gun.

TUNNEL ROAD RAPISTS

Another example of such thorough investigative work and examination of possible relevant evidence occurred in the case of Rodgers* and Jackson,* which was prosecuted by Arthur Sherry.

Rodgers, age 24, and Jackson, age 22, came together in Los Angeles, and, after wandering around the country, landed in San Francisco on January 14, 1939. Three nights later, Anderson* and Boyington* were seated in Anderson's car under some trees on Tunnel Road not far from the Claremont Hotel enjoying the view of San Francisco Bay. Suddenly Rodgers and Jackson surged from the darkness against Anderson's car. Rodgers held a pistol. Obviously it was a holdup.

Anderson snapped the lock on his window and tried to start his car. Rodgers smashed the locked window, stuck the pistol against Anderson's head and ordered him to move over. Jackson jumped into the rear seat. Rodgers took the wheel and drove the car up into an isolated area of the Berkeley hills where, at gun point, he and Jackson robbed Anderson and raped Boyington. Both Rodgers and Jackson were wearing leather gloves, and when they had finished their business with Anderson and Boyington, they drove off in Anderson's car. About forty minutes later, Rodgers and Jackson robbed a U.S. Post Office substation in a drug store in Oakland, where they stole $130 cash and a number of blank postal money orders.

The defendants then went to Los Angeles, forged some of the stolen money orders, and boarded a train for Detroit. They were arrested on the train as it pulled into Kansas City, Missouri. A .38 caliber automatic was found in their possession. Returned to San Francisco, they pleaded guilty in Federal Court to robbery of the postal substation in Oakland. After sentencing in the Federal Court, they were remanded to Alameda County for trial on the state charges.

At their trial in Alameda County, Rodgers and Jackson denied committing the offenses against Anderson and Boyington. They used the postal substation robbery as an alibi, claiming that they could not have traveled from where the robbery–rape occurred in the Berkeley hills to the drug store at Park View Terrace and Grand Avenue in Oakland in forty minutes. At the trial, the prosecutor, Arthur Sherry, showed that it could be done.

Dr. Paul Kirk, noted biochemist and criminalist at the University of California, Berkeley, called as an expert by the prosecution, testified that microscopic examination of clothing found in the defendants' luggage when they were arrested and worn by them on January 17, the night of the kidnaping, connected them with the robbery–rape. A glass refraction test disclosed minute particles of glass from the broken window of Anderson's car embedded in Rodgers's clothes, although the clothes had been cleaned.

Other tests disclosed a number of fibers from Boyington's clothing on Jackson's clothing, hair from Jackson's head on Boyington's clothes and spots of blood on gloves and clothes of Rodgers and Jackson, which blood was the same type as Boyington's and not the same as that of either of the defendants or of Anderson. In resisting the defendants' advances, Boyington had sustained a deep cut on her forehead when she was struck by a flashlight in the hand of one of the defendants. Apparently blood from the cut rubbed off on the clothes and gloves of Rodgers and Jackson. The defendants were identified by Anderson and Boyington.

Rodgers was charged with and admitted two prior felony convictions: the first in 1931 in Nebraska for burglary and the second in 1934 in Colorado for robbery with a weapon. He had served time on each conviction in those states' penal institutions. The Alameda County charges included two counts of kidnaping to rob, robbery and two counts of rape.

Both defendants were convicted in Superior Court on all counts. On these convictions they were sentenced to California State Prison for life without parole, under the Little Lindberg Law of the California Penal Code (Section 209). The defendants served time in a federal prison for the postal substation robbery, after which they were released to California prison authorities.

As of this writing, Rodgers and Jackson are on lifetime parole from the California Department of Corrections on the Alameda County convictions. Rodgers was released on lifetime parole in 1961. Jackson was released on lifetime parole in 1963. Forty years ago when Rodgers and Jackson committed the crimes of which they were convicted, they were alert, articulate, well–groomed young men who might have gone far had they pursued an honest living.

A significant thing about this case was the criminalistic testimony of Dr. Paul Kirk, which dispelled any question as to identification and which demonstrated the growing importance of thorough and competent forensic expertise in the prosecution of criminal cases. In a case like this, careful handling of the physical evidence found at the scene of a crime or in possession of a defendant is most important in laying a foundation for expert testimony of a criminalist.

Competent presentation of such evidence and expert testimony is likewise important. This was done by officers of the Berkeley Police Department who had been well trained by August Volmeer, faculty member of the University of California at Berkeley who pioneered continuing education of police, and by the prosecutor, Arthur Sherry, who succeeded Warren Olney III as professor of criminal law at the School of Jurisprudence (Boalt Hall) of the University of California at Berkeley, when Olney became an assistant attorney general of the United States.

PROVEN OIL LAND FOR SALE

For several years, Samuel Hoyt, alias Chait, and his salesmen sold land which they represented as "proven oil land." Their area of operation was mainly in Los Angeles County where their take amounted to several millions of dollars. They had a place of business in downtown Los Angeles, out of which they worked and where they kept their files and records. They advertised regularly in the local newspapers and appeared to be a legitimate organization dealing in oil properties. For years the oil business in California had been a bonanza in which fortunes had been made. This was particularly true in Southern California.

Hoyt had a license to sell real estate and this is what he was doing at amounts ranging from $100 to $500 an acre. Typically, the acreage was in areas which had been explored by oil companies and found to be unproductive. Much of it was in areas where "dry holes" bore witness to the failure to produce. Hoyt and his salesmen, however, represented in glowing terms the wealth in oil beneath the land he was selling and constantly assured people that it was truly "proven oil land." In fact, it was land Hoyt had purchased for $5 to $10 an acre, or less.

The word of his operation spread and other fast–talking hustlers copied Hoyt's method of operation. It was easier than selling stock because the corporation commissioner, up to that time, had paid no attention, and the real estate commissioner did likewise as long as the salesmen had licenses to sell real estate. Hoyt continued to be the leader of the pack, and, when pickings began to grow thin, he strayed into other cities and counties which had not yet been tapped.

One such county was Alameda, where a search of probate records showed an ample supply of well–healed elderly widows. One such prospect was Mrs. Joseph S. Koford of Berkeley, widow of a one–time deputy district attorney who had also been a partner in a very successful law firm. Hoyt, himself, contacted Mrs. Koford and sold her acreage in the eastern hills of Kern County in a badly faulted area which, years before, had been drilled by an oil company and found to be worthless. Hoyt also found ten other prospects and sold them land for $300 an acre for which he had paid $5.

When his promises and representations about large oil companies negotiating to buy the land and preparing to drill for oil failed to materialize, his purchasers began to get impatient. Mrs. Koford came to the District Attorney's Office only after being persuaded by her late husband's law partner that she was probably the victim of a fraudulent operation.

With the help of experts from Standard Oil of California, the California Oil and Gas Division, and others familiar with the areas being peddled by Hoyt, we were able to put together a case for presentation to the Alameda County grand jury. Hoyt and two of his aides were indicted on ten counts of grand theft and one count of violation of the Corporate Securities Act. They were convicted and sentenced to state prison on all counts. The convictions were all affirmed on appeal.

A Corporate Securities Act count was included in the indictment to establish a precedent that, under the circumstances of this case, fraudulent sales of numerous parcels of land for investment purposes was a violation of the Corporate Securities Act. This also was affirmed on appeal, thus giving the corporate commissioner concurrent power to regulate and control such operations.

Governor Warren appointed a new real estate commissioner who, with the incumbent corporate commissioner, proceeded to eliminate the fraudulent sale of $5 an acre pasture land as "proven oil" property for $300 to $500 an acre.

An interesting phase of this case occurred when a portable drilling rig hit a small oil pocket in a spot where two geologic faults intersected. This was on property not far from one of the parcels which had been sold to Mrs. Koford.

Although they should have known better, the lease agents of several large oil companies went berserk trying to outbid each other in signing up land owners on leases for as much as $300 an acre bonus. I told the land owners that the area where the portable drill rig hit oil was badly faulted and that, most likely, there would be no oil any place else for miles around. This proved to be true. But the oil company land agents are an unusual breed who would rather gamble on signing up land owners with generous bonuses in the very keen competition with land agents of other companies, just in case the first oil strike might be the beginning of a new oil field.

There was one such agent, a brilliant and successful performer, who used to start working before dawn. By 10 a.m. he would have completed his work for the day. By 11 a.m. he would be at the Jonathan Club in Los Angeles drinking copious drafts of his favorite liquor (gin) straight. By noon, he was well on his way to being intoxicated. This was a daily routine, which did not seem to impair his performance.

LEONA VLUGHT

Rodney Greig, age 21, member of a well–known and reputable Berkeley family, became interested in Leona Vlught, a tall beautiful cosmetologist and graduate of the University of California. Greig was a competent and respected employee in the office of the Western Pacific Railroad Company in Oakland. He had seen Miss Vlught at an Oakland nightclub but had never dated her.

On the afternoon of December 6, 1938, he bought a six–inch hunting knife enclosed in a leather scabbard. That night he visited the nightclub where he had seen Miss Vlught on previous occasions. They talked, danced and left the club. Greig drove up into the east Oakland hills to a place commonly used by couples for parking.

They sat and talked for a while, and, suddenly, without provocation according to his subsequent confession, he plunged the knife into her chest. She died within a few minutes from the wound. He stood alongside of his car watching her die and smoking cigarettes. When she was lifeless, he dragged her from the car and dropped her body on the ground. He drove home and went to work the next day.

On the corner of 13th and Broadway Streets, adjacent to the building where he worked, he saw a large headline in the newspaper announcing the still unsolved death of Miss Vlught. Greig engaged in conversation with a policeman at the intersection and said, "whoever killed her should be hung," or words to that effect.

Investigation disclosed that Greig and Vlught had been together at the nightclub and had departed together the night of the killing. Police found the knife with blood on it in a leather scabbard under the back seat of his auto. They also found a necklace which was later identified as belonging to Miss Vlught. Greig admitted killing her and said he had taken her hat and purse. A search disclosed the hat and purse in the place indicated by Greig.

Greig later made a full confession, saying that Miss Vlught expressed a state of depression and a thought of suicide; that he tipped her chin with the knife; and that, on a sudden impulse, he plunged it into her chest. His counsel waived jury trial and he pleaded not guilty by reason of insanity. A psychiatrist for the defense testified that he was in a state of an "epileptic equivalent" at the time of the killing. This was denied by psychiatric testimony of the prosecution. He was found sane by the trial judge who imposed the death penalty.

INSIDE JOB

An executive of Owl Drug Company, who was a friend of Ralph Hoyt's, one day said to him, "Someone is stealing us blind . . . cases of barbiturates and Carter's liver pills, which are like money in the bank, are disappearing from our warehouse in San Francisco. Other companies have been hit also. It's got to be an inside job but we have been unable to nail the thief although we have spent a lot of money with a well–known detective agency without results. Recently we employed a small investigative agency, Joseph Kane and his wife, on the case. They seem to be making some progress. I wish you would take a look at it and tell me what you think."

Hoyt agreed and asked me to look into it. I talked with Kane, whom I knew, and was told that he had an informant, who operated a drugstore in San Francisco, working on the matter. The informant had made contact with a man whom he had reason to believe belonged to a ring of thieves in San Francisco which dealt in stolen merchandise. In due course, he started buying from his contact cases of Carter's liver pills and barbiturates at prices well under prevailing wholesale prices. I contacted the San Francisco Police Department and, together with the help of Kane and his informant, we stepped up the investigation.

Shortly, the San Francisco police discovered that the informant's contact man was picking up stolen merchandise around midnight at the warehouse of Coffin Redington, a wholesale drug company in San Francisco. From there he was taking it to the informant's drugstore. The investigation led to a drugstore in Oakland where the proprietor was receiving extra cases of stolen merchandise along with legitimate delivery of merchandise he had ordered, and to others involved in the traffic of stolen property. In the course of the investigation, others were identified as being involved in stealing, selling and buying stolen drugs from the Coffin Redington wholesale warehouse in San Francisco and expensive soaps and toiletries from Colgate Palmolive Company in Berkeley.

At Coffin Redington, a night watchman would come out of a certain exit, look up and down the street and wave his hand. An auto would pull up to the exit, and the watchman would load cartons of barbiturates and Carter's liver pills into the car. The car was followed to the informant's drugstore, where the police arrested the driver as he was delivering the stolen merchandise.

At Colgate Palmolive Company, an inside worker in the warehouse would load extra cases of soap onto a truck which, in making delivery of an order to a drugstore, would be unloaded at a substantial profit to the trucker and the drugstore proprietor. When the Colgate warehouseman confessed, the Colgate management was shocked because this man had been one of their most trusted and reliable employees—a good churchman, family man and avid horticulturist.

The respected proprietor of a prosperous drugstore in Oakland, who was buying the stolen merchandise from the trucker, also confessed. Eventually some ten persons were indicted, eight of whom pleaded guilty.

A significant thing about this case was that inventory checks at Colgate had not disclosed shortages of the stolen merchandise. Needless to say, as a result of this case considerable improvement was made in stock inventory procedures in the warehouses, and traffic in "hot" merchandise in the Bay Area sharply declined.

5

Civil Defense 1940—1961

In 1940, with World War II going poorly for England and the possibility of full–fledged participation by the United States looming, state and local governments were advised by the federal government to prepare civil defense programs. Paperback guidelines issued by the United States Army were based largely upon the experience of London and other cities in England which had taken a pounding from the air. Stress was laid upon protection from air raids, fire damage, and rescue operations to care for persons injured in demolished buildings. Based on the experience of World War I, stress was also laid upon protection from possible poison gas and other chemical warfare attack.

An ordinance initiating a civil defense program for Alameda County was drafted by the District Attorney's Office and enacted by the Board of Supervisors in June 1940. At this time the Board had no staff. There was no county administrator. A deputy county clerk acted as secretary of the Board, kept the minutes and handled Board correspondence. County government was relatively simple. It was on a pay–as–you–go basis with no bonded indebtedness. Although welfare assistance had begun in the mid–1930's, the load was small as compared with postwar years. Budgets, salaries, social services and taxes were minimal. People were not complaining about county government and the press paid little attention to it. For county officialdom it was a benign existence, a calm before the storm. In matters of administration, the Board leaned heavily on the District Attorney's Office, so the Board appointed District Attorney Ralph Hoyt as the new director of civil defense.

With such meager guidelines as were available, Ralph Hoyt started planning for a county civil defense program which, of necessity, would involve cooperation by the cities, special districts, state and federal governments and various other agencies of the public and private sectors. Federal, state and municipal governments would have to use such facilities and personnel as were available, integrating plans so as to coordinate with each other and with county government.

Before Pearl Harbor, some responsible city agencies and officials were slow to respond. Apparently, they did not anticipate war. Consequently, the task of planning and leading an integrated county–wide civil defense program gravitated to the District Attorney's Office. Even after Pearl Harbor, much friction and many conflicts ensued, and city–county coordination was spotty.

In conjunction with Alameda County, the cities would have to work out plans for emergency reciprocal assistance in public and private sectors. This would involve police and fire protection, public utilities, rescue services, doctors, nurses, hospitals, ambulances, air raid shelters, block wardens, blackouts, and logistics which included, among other things, gas masks.

RED ALERT!—ENEMY PLANES APPROACHING

Shortly before the attack on Pearl Harbor, our office was designated by the United States Army as an information and aircraft warning alert center, with the responsibility of communicating warning alert messages received from the Army Filter Center to local governments and other agencies within the county. This would involve a communication operation around the clock.

On Friday afternoon, December 5, 1941, four telephone instruments connecting, by direct wire, our office with the Army Filter Center in San Francisco were installed by direction of the Army. These instruments were placed on a table alongside of our telephone switchboard. It was explained that the phones were to be marked later "yellow," "blue," "red," and "white," respectively, to indicate probable proximity of enemy attack—yellow to mean the attack was some distance away, blue to mean the distance was closing, red meaning great urgency and an attack was imminent. White was to mean all clear, the danger had passed.

Transmission of the messages to cities and other local agencies was up to the District Attorney's Office. At that point, the only quick means was by regular telephone. On this date, Hazel Yoder, veteran operator of our main office telephone switchboard, came out of retirement to operate the board on the night shift—this meant 6:00 p.m. to 6:00 a.m.

The day after the attack on Pearl Harbor, at about 6:30 p.m., Hazel was at the switchboard of the District Attorney's Office on the 9th floor of the courthouse. I was at my desk. Ralph Hoyt and other members of the staff had gone across the street for dinner. Suddenly, an emergency bell, electrically activated by the switchboard operator, began to ring continuously and very loud. Whoever was pushing the bell button on the other end meant business.

I ran from my room to the switchboard to find Hazel, usually a very calm person, in a state of excitement, lifting Filter Center telephone receivers trying to determine which one carried a message and what it was. Finally she heard a voice which said it was a red alert—that enemy planes were approaching San Francisco.

At that time, Army and Navy protection for California was practically nihil. There were just no aircraft interceptor squadrons or planes available or anti–aircraft ordinance operable. If the approaching planes were enemy planes, no one—including the military—was really prepared for such an attack.

The only thing to be done from our office was to get the message by phone to cities and tell them to get the lights out on the streets and in public buildings. Many lights were on. It was December and already dark at 6:30 p.m. in California. I told Hazel I would get on a telephone in an adjoining room to call Oakland, Berkeley, Albany, Emeryville and Alameda, and suggested that she phone the other cities in the county. This was more easily said than done. It was dinner time. Except for police and fire department personnel, jailers, prisoners and janitors, city buildings were empty. To reach police and fire chiefs, even if they were home, through unlisted residential telephones was no simple task. The best thing to do was to get duty officers at the city halls and give them the message.

From a room in the District Attorney's Office, I could look out on Lake Merritt in the heart of Oakland. The usual ring of Christmas lighting, some three miles in length around the Lake, was on full blast—a perfect target for enemy attack. The switch which turned these lights on and off was under lock in a box in Lakeside Park. A gardener employee of the Oakland Park Department had the only key to the box and nobody could find him. Eventually, the box was opened and the lights were doused for the duration of the war.

The lights along Franklin Street in downtown Oakland were something special—new, extra large, and high intensity. These lights were controlled by a different automatic circuit of the Pacific Gas and Electric Company. It took about two hours to get those lights turned off.

From our office on the 9th floor, we could view the results of our efforts to achieve a blackout in the East Bay cities. It took a while and was spotty, but not too bad. From the window behind Hazel, lights at the United States Naval Air Station, across the Estuary in Alameda, could be seen. They were on full power. At least until I was called to active duty, lights at the Naval Air Station continued on every night, as they did at the shipyards which operated around the clock.

At 9:30 that same night, another alert message came from the Army Filter Center. This message was transmitted by telephone from the District Attorney's Office, and the resulting blackouts were roughly complete except for lights on private property. Block wardens and residential zone blackouts came later.

While the warnings from the Filter Center on the night of December 8th were handled with much difficulty by Alameda County, San Francisco was caught totally unprepared. There was no civil defense director or civil defense program. Street lights were not turned off, so people began shooting them out and destroying anything which appeared to be a source of lighting. Electric wires were ripped out and store windows smashed. Conditions became chaotic and riotous. By the next morning, some areas were a shambles of wanton mob violence and destruction.

Sometime later, a retired Navy admiral was appointed civil defense director in San Francisco and a species of a civil defense program was initiated, feebly manned by political appointees. Regular city employees in police, fire and other agencies carried on their usual duties, and there were no more Filter Center alerts to activate San Francisco's so–called civil defense program and procedures. The final surrender of Japan and termination of the war on August 14, 1945, likewise caught San Francisco unprepared for the mob violence, chaos, rioting and destruction which went on for three days and nights.

DOING OUR PART FOR THE DURATION

After December 7, 1941, under most difficult conditions, within what might be classed as a reasonable period, implementation of a rudementary civil defense program was achieved by trial and error. The federal government furnished limited logistic support in the form of information, educational pamphlets and gas masks.

Oakland policemen patrolled downtown beats with gas masks hanging from their shoulders. Policemen patrolling crowded streets festooned with gas masks looked foolish and no doubt felt so. If there ever were a gas attack, the civilians among whom they walked were not so equipped. The gas mask aspect of civil defense was soon discarded.

Finally, under the direction of World War I veteran Frank Atwill of the Oakland City Engineer's Office, an outstanding civil defense program was put together for that city and coordinated with the county and other cities. Thereupon, Atwill returned to active duty as an officer in the U.S. Army and saw service in Europe, as he had during World War I.

Cities in Alameda County turned to and set up a civil defense headquarters and excellent programs which were organized to operate efficiently throughout the war. Civil defense in Alameda County was highly commended by the United States Army as being one of the best in the nation. A system of instant simultaneous transmittal of warning alert messages from the District Attorney's Office to municipal and other agencies in the county was installed and manned by personnel of the District Attorney's Office around the clock every day and night for the duration of the war.

Civil defense activities, particularly the operation of the warning alert communication system, were performed by office personnel as extra collateral duty without any extra compensation. It was the staff's contribution to the war effort. Court calendars and other office work, both criminal and civil, were carried on as usual, however there was a decline in crime and in the civil law work.

Special civil defense training programs for key personnel were initiated, including, as at Stanford University, identification of various kinds of gases and other chemical warfare agents. Recruitment of citizen volunteers and organization of civil defense services went on apace. It should be said that the response of volunteers was remarkable. The collective composite thinking of disparate persons when aroused is an interesting study in group psychology.

Part of the civil defense program recommended by the Army was an aircraft observation system in which citizen volunteers traveled to and from observation posts on high buildings and hilltops to watch for and report possible enemy aircraft movements. Recruitment, organization and management of this operation was conducted by the District Attorney's Office. It operated only during daylight hours. The service of the volunteers in this operation was a most worthy contribution in the civil defense program, as was the service of personnel of the District Attorney's Office who worked on it under the direction of Inspectors Edwin Schnarr and Louis Nieland.

Another aspect of civil defense involving the District Attorney's Office was education of the public and the media. Naturally, public interest accelerated after Pearl Harbor. There was a demand for speakers at countless forums of churches, schools, and fraternal, civic and business organizations. Much of this kind of education was conducted by members of the District Attorney's Office.

The work of the District Attorney's Office in civil defense was an important contribution to the war effort and a civic community service which benefited a broad spectrum of people, both private citizens and other public servants, at very little extra cost to government.

In the post–war period, with the advance of Communism in Mainland China and the abortive attempt of Communists to take over Greece in 1947, followed by the Berlin Blockade in 1948, and the invasion of South Korea in 1950, the possibility of another world war began to surface. State and local governments were again importuned by the federal government to organize civil defense. Again, the District Attorney's Office was confronted with the task of directing and coordinating a county–wide civil defense program.

At a meeting of the Board of Supervisors, mayors and city administrators in 1950, I was asked to act as chairman of the Joint Cities and County Civil Defense Committee. With the capable assistance of Richard H. Chamberlain, chief assistant district attorney, and others on the staff, reactivation of a Joint Cities and County Civil Defense program was established in conjunction with state and national programs.

Because of our World War II experience, the task of planning and organizing civil defense in 1950 was easier, although here again there was significant foot–dragging by some city officials. However, because of mutual aid legislation and state assistance, a state–wide program integrated with programs of the cities and counties was established, complete with organization of law enforcement, fire and medical services along with air raid shelters, evacuation plans and other essentials of civil defense.

Again, as in World War II, civil defense work was carried on collaterally with the customary duties of the District Attorney's Office and at no additional expense to county government, and again Frank Atwill put together an excellent civil defense program for Oakland.

The performance of the District Attorney's Office in civil defense during World War II and the Korean War was an outstanding achievement in dedicated public service.

6

J. Frank Coakley 1947—1969

In 1947, Ralph Hoyt was offered an appointment to the Superior Court bench by Governor Earl Warren and he decided to leave the District Attorney's Office. At the time, I had been in private practice with my brother Thomas a little over a year, following my own relief from active duty in the U.S. Navy. The Board of Supervisors approached me to ask if I would consider coming back to the District Attorney's Office to replace Hoyt. I agreed.

THE ATTORNEY GENERAL'S GANG

One of the most disgusting cases in memory began shortly after I took over as District Attorney. Zola B. Heller, a large friendly man commonly called "Tiny," was the owner of two buildings, one of which contained a bar and restaurant and the other a business office and hotel at 12th and Franklin Streets in Oakland. In his office he had been brokering bets on elections, boxing, baseball and football games for years. He charged a fee of ten percent on the amount bet. He had never made book on horse racing. He was quite well known by prominent men about town who bet with him, including newspaper reporters. He was conducting the same kind of betting operation as well–known betting commissioners had been conducting for a long time in San Francisco without any protest by law enforcement authorities or the press. Likewise, in Oakland the police paid no attention to Heller.

On November 17, 1947, Charles Hoy, an inspector in the Office of the Attorney General under Frederick Napoleon Howser, identified himself to Thomas Alfred, an Oakland policeman, and asked Alfred to go with him to Heller's hotel.

Hoy, with Alfred in tow, walked into Heller's office and seized his books and records, including some betting markers on a football game. There was no search warrant. No one had complained to law enforcement authorities about Heller or presented any evidence that he was violating the law. Hoy arrested Heller and took him to the central station of the Oakland Police Department where he was booked for bookmaking, a violation of Penal Code Section 337a.

When this happened, I was attending a statewide conference of peace officers in Sacramento, which had been called by Governor Warren in connection with his proposed legislation establishing a commission to study organized crime. I was scheduled to talk as chairman of the Law and Legislative Committees of the California Peace Officers Association. When I received information concerning the Attorney General's arrest of Heller, I returned that night to Oakland and questioned him in the presence of his attorney and Sheriff Gleason.

"It was a shakedown and a double–cross by the attorney general," Heller complained. He said that about a month previous, he had received a telephone call from a bookmaker friend in Los Angeles, who informed him that he should expect to hear later that same day from Walter Lentz, Charles Hoy or Wiley "Buck" Cadell, investigators of the Attorney General's Office, who would see him either at his place of business or at the Mark Hopkins Hotel in San Francisco on a certain date. This friend told Heller that he could continue his betting commission business if he arranged for payoffs to these men.

Heller also said that nobody called on him that day, but that the following day he received a personal visit from a friend who was in the gambling business in Contra Costa County. This person told him that he and his partner were members of a group who were going to control all gambling in Northern California through the Attorney

General's Office, that no gambling would be permitted except on the payment of protection, and that Heller's betting commission business could not be operated unless he paid. Heller also said that this friend claimed he had seen the "boys" and Heller would be allowed to operate his business if he paid them fifty percent of his net profit. The fifty percent would have to be paid under the counter to Heller's gambler friend from Contra Costa County, who would take care of the "boys." In addition, a bookkeeper would be sent up from Los Angeles to keep track of Heller's income so that the proper amount was paid, and the bookkeeper's salary would have to be paid by Heller.

Heller said he told his friend that he was not interested—he had never paid a cent of graft to anyone in his whole lifetime and he was not going to start then. Heller's friend then told him he could finish out the football season, but that he would have to make arrangements for the payment of protection before the beginning of the basketball and baseball seasons.

Apparently, the attempt by self–avowed emissaries of the Attorney General's Office to set up Heller in a bookmaking graft arrangement was typical of what was happening in other parts of the state. According to a Report of the Organized Crime Commission of California, E. L. Price, operator of a big gambling operation in Contra Costa County, told Assistant District Attorney Thomas C. Lynch of San Francisco on March 4, 1947, that "Bones" Remmer, a professional gambler and operator of Cal–Neva Casino at Lake Tahoe, had told him (Price) that he (Remmer) was contributing a lot of money to elect Fred N. Howser Attorney General; that when this was accomplished he (Remmer) was going to take over and be in charge of all gambling in certain counties; and that he was going to cut himself in on the profits of the establishments permitted to operate.

Heller would not name or otherwise identify his Los Angeles gambler friend who had phoned him. Our investigation in preparation for Heller's trial disclosed that Lentz had made a reservation at the Mark Hopkins Hotel for the date the Los Angeles gambler had mentioned.

Heller retained Joseph Deasey, prominent Oakland criminal defense lawyer, to represent him. Shortly before trial, Murray Chotiner, a Los Angeles lawyer, took over the defense of Heller and Deasey was eliminated. When Arthur Sherry, assistant district attorney who prosecuted Heller, rested, Chotiner promptly rested his case without putting on any defense. Heller was an impulsive, loquacious extrovert. In retrospect, I believe that Chotiner came up from Los Angeles to manage the Heller defense and to keep him from testifying, lest he explode on the witness stand and open up a line of cross–examination or an investigation which might involve illegal activities in the Attorney General's Office.

Although there was illegal gambling, including illegal bookmaking, in other counties, the Attorney General's Office made no arrests in such other counties and no effort to suppress such activities. At the time, in the context of gambling conditions which prevailed in Los Angeles County while Howser was district attorney of that county and of his failure as attorney general to take any legitimate action with respect thereto in any county other than in the Heller case in Alameda County—one of the cleanest counties in the nation—it appeared that the unprecedented action of the attorney general's agent in arresting Heller was to pressure him into joining with the attorney general's men in a statewide illegal conspiracy to book horseracing with protection from the Attorney General's Office.

There had been no evidence of a breakdown in law enforcement in Oakland or Alameda County to indicate a necessity for the Attorney General's Office coming into the county to make an arrest. Under the circumstances, Heller's arrest was without precedent and strictly unorthodox. Furthermore, the Attorney General's Office had no complaining witness who had made a bet of any kind with Heller. All Hoy had obtained were some pieces of paper which appeared to be betting markers on football games. When Heller was booked, Hoy departed immediately, without appearing in the District Attorney's Office to sign a complaint. Under orders from Sherry, he was picked up and brought to the District Attorney's Office to sign the complaint.

It was a sloppy piece of work by the Attorney General's Office. Alfred, the Oakland policeman, had never in his life made an arrest for bookmaking on a football game and probably not for any other kind of bookmaking. He was simply a patrolman. Arrests for gambling were the function of the vice squad. Our office had to bolster the case by developing other proof. We received no help in preparation for trial from the Attorney General's Office.

Before the preliminary examination in the Heller case, an associate of Murray Chotiner, in talking with Sherry, inquired whether the case could be summarily disposed of for a consideration. A similar suggestion by Chotiner had been made to Joseph Deasey, original counsel for Heller. Deasey's advise to Chotiner was: "If you are going to make a pitch like that to Coakley, you'd better get behind the bars first, because after you make it, that's where you'll be."

After the preliminary hearing, in which Heller was bound over to the Superior Court for trial, Howser, for some strange reason, wrote a letter to me criticizing the District Attorney's Office for its presentation of the case at the preliminary hearing, although the function of the preliminary examination had been achieved. Howser publicized the letter some days before I received it. When interviewed by the press I said that, "to say the least, Howser is incompetent and doesn't know his business."

The Heller case was an impact case because it demonstrated to anyone who might be interested, or who may have been propositioned by the attorney general's men, that no illegal gambling would be tolerated—and, incidentally, it was not tolerated. Heller was convicted, placed on probation and fined $1,500 by Judge Tyrrell.

There had been enough reports of illegal protection of gambling by the Attorney General's agents in other counties sufficient to alarm Governor Warren and cause him to complain about it to Howser. I did not have sufficient proof to support a prosecution of the attorney general or his agents.

I had clashed with Howser when he, as district attorney of Los Angeles County, had worked to defeat in the state Legislature Senate Bill 33—a potential weapon against organized crime which would strengthen the conspiracy law of California. This bill was the number one priority bill on the Peace Officers and District Attorneys Associations' legislative program. As legal advocate for the Peace

Officers and District Attorneys of the state, I had lobbied for the passage of this bill over Howser's vigorous opposition.

When Ralph Hoyt was district attorney of Alameda County, he had also clashed with Howser in ordering one of his inspectors, Wiley "Buck" Cadell, out of the county. Warren, as governor, had clashed with Howser when, as district attorney of Los Angeles County, Howser had failed to do anything about the gambling ship *Lux*, which was operating off the coast of Los Angeles County. In his 1946 campaign for Governor, Warren had refused to support Howser, the then–nominee of the Republican Party, for attorney general. Warren had told Howser that he did not approve of his conduct as district attorney of Los Angeles County. In his memoirs Warren wrote:

> "Immediately thereafter (Howser's election as Attorney General) the word was out throughout the underworld that the state was to be opened up to gambling and other illegal activities. Enough evidence to assure us that this rumor was not unfounded came to our attention. Howser had brought with him two police officers from the Long Beach Police Department, one called Wiley (Buck) Cadell and the other Walter Lentz. They were to be his principal investigators, and it was not long until their intentions became apparent. I told Howser several times that I understood what was going on. He protested that he knew nothing about it, and would take whatever action was called for. But he never did. I then went to the Legislature and asked it to amend the Board of Corrections Act by authorizing the governor to appoint special crime study commissions to assist the Board of Corrections. The Legislature passed the necessary amendment and I appointed five commissions. Their domains were:
>
> Organized Crime
> Juvenile Justice
> Adult Corrections and Release Procedures
> Social and Economic Causes of Crime and Delinquency
> Criminal Law and Procedure
>
> "They were all important and made valuable contributions, but the most critical commission at the time was the one on organized

> crime. It was composed of particularly distinguished public servants, including five–star Admiral William H. Standley, onetime Chief of Naval Operations and Ambassador to the U.S.S.R."[23]

When the bill to create and fund the Commission on Organized Crime was being heard in the Assembly Judiciary Committee of the Legislature, Howser exercised his influence as a former member of the Legislature and as attorney general by appearing personally before the Committee to argue against the bill. I argued in favor of the bill as the representative of the Peace Officers and District Attorneys Associations of California. The bill was approved by the Committee and enacted by the Legislature.

Warren Olney III, a former deputy district attorney of Alameda County, became executive officer of the Commission and performed outstanding service, in cooperation with the Peace Officers and District Attorneys Associations of California, in combating the efforts of the underworld to reap a harvest in the bonanza that was California after World War II. Olney got no help from the Attorney General's Office. In fact, throughout his term in office as attorney general, Howser attacked the Commission as his agents pursued their nefarious efforts to open up the state to gambling and other unlawful activities.

The concerted performance of the Peace Officers and District Attorneys Associations of California (under the leadership of the Alameda County District Attorney's Office), the Commission on Organized Crime (under Warren Olney III), and federal agencies with the support of Governor Warren did much to prevent big–time organized crime from succeeding in its effort to take over. This performance was a high mark for law enforcement in the history of California and an excellent example of what can be done when law enforcement agencies cooperate and work together. If the attempt of big–time illegal gambling interests, in collusion with the Attorney General's Office, to open up the state had not been stopped, a take-

[23]Warren, pp. 198—199

over by the powerful Midwest Capone Syndicate and the East Coast Costello—Lansky—Siegal combination would not have been far behind. They were already looking at the lush profits to be made by organized crime in California, and by murder they had gained control of a wire service so essential to bookmaking.

In an attempt to flood the many popular resorts in the redwood area of Northern California with slot machines (which were illegal in the state), Wiley "Buck" Cadell called at the home of Sheriff Broaddus of Mendocino County. Cadell told Sheriff Broaddus he wanted to install slot machines in certain resorts, dropped an envelope on the sofa, said there would be more of the same every month and left. After Cadell had gone, Broaddus opened the envelope. It contained six one–hundred dollar bills. Broaddus told the district attorney of his county about it and came to talk to me and Sheriff Gleason. Gleason was president of the California Sheriffs Association and I was still chairman of the Law and Legislative Committees of the Peace Officers and District Attorneys Associations.

By this time Governor Warren's Organized Crime Commission had been established. Rather than risk the possibility that the attorney general's man might do a turn–around and try to prosecute Broaddus, the Commission's chairman, Warren Olney III, decided that Cadell should be charged forthwith.

James Bush, the district attorney of Mendocino County, came to my office and collaborated with me in drafting an indictment charging Cadell with offering a bribe to the sheriff. Bush, in a one–man office, needed help, so arrangements were made whereby I would give Arthur Sherry a leave of absence to be appointed deputy district attorney of Mendocino County to assist Bush in the prosecution. Governor Warren, out of a contingency fund, paid Sherry's salary while he worked in Mendocino County.

Cadell was convicted and sentenced to San Quentin. Before, during and after the trial, the Attorney General's Office did many things to obstruct the prosecution of Cadell. It was obvious the attorney general was endeavoring to achieve Cadell's acquittal. Under the circumstances, District Attorney Bush could expect no help from the Attorney General's Office on the appeal, so I assigned Cecil Mosbacher, who was an assistant district attorney in our office at the time, to write the brief for the respondent State and Mendocino County on the appeal. Mosbacher, a brilliant lawyer, filed the brief and handled the appeal throughout. Cadell's conviction was affirmed.

Incidentally, Mosbacher was very helpful to law enforcement statewide in other respects. As a member of the California Commission on Criminal Law and Procedure, she carried the load in research and draftsmanship. Serving without pay as legal advisor to the Commission, Mosbacher—with the help of Judge Ralph Hoyt, Public Defender Willard Shea and members of the District Attorney's Office—made a complete overhaul of the Penal Code of California. This involved deleting obsolete provisions and rewriting sections of the Code. In effect, a complete new Penal Code was drafted, approved by the Commission and enacted by the Legislature. With various amendments added in subsequent years, it is still in effect, and constitutes one of the most advanced codes of criminal law and procedure in the nation. It had the full support and approval of the Peace Officers and District Attorneys Associations of California.

While an assistant district attorney, Cecil Mosbacher also acted as resident legal advocate at the state Capitol for the District Attorney's Office of Alameda County and for the Law and Legislative Committees of the Peace Officers and District Attorneys Associations of California.

Investigations by the California Commission on Organized Crime disclosed that Cadell and others had been attempting to open up the state to illegal operations of slot machines and branded punch boards approved by the Attorney General's Office.

The assistance given to Mendocino County by the District Attorney's Office of Alameda County was typical of the help given to other jurisdictions. A request for assistance from a district attorney, sheriff or police chief of another county or city was given priority. Such help was often requested by district attorneys and peace officers of other jurisdictions. To help achieve more cooperation and coordination among law enforcement agencies was one reason for my founding of the National Association of County and Prosecuting Attorneys (now the National District Attorneys Association).

In his memoirs, Warren had this to say about Cadell and Howser:

> "Warren Olney III (executive officer of the Commission on Organized Crime) . . . eventually caught up with Buck Cadell, who was tried in Mendocino County, convicted, and sentenced to San Quentin for attempting to set up a statewide system of protection for gambling rackets. Walter Lentz later was charged with tampering with a witness in a libel suit brought by Howser. He was acquitted, but Howser lost his suit. This eclipsed the public career of Attorney General Howser, and in his bid for re–election he lost the nomination of his own party."[24]

DRUG BUST

A case which developed into what Harry J. Anslinger, director of the United States Bureau of Narcotics and Chairman of the Narcotics Commission of the United Nations, said was the biggest case in the history of the Bureau up to that time began in quite an innocuous way in Oakland.

Mrs. Kramer* had been a waitress at a restaurant in Oakland for several years. Mary O'Hearn* came to work at this restaurant, also as a waitress. She was young, immature, inexperienced and seemed decent. Mrs. Kramer tried to help Mary, and she responded by cooperating and helping Mrs. Kramer in any way she could. Mary told Mrs. Kramer that she was a member of a large Irish Catholic family in Chicago. She said she had been working a short while as a waitress back in Chicago when she met her husband Harry O'Hearn. Shortly after their marriage, O'Hearn told Mary he had business on the West Coast and that they would have to go to Oakland, where they would rent an apartment temporarily.

One day Mary told Mrs. Kramer that her husband wanted to take her away for a while on a delayed honeymoon, and they would be

[24]Warren, p. 199

giving up their apartment. While they were away, they might be receiving some mail or packages, possibly some wedding presents, and Mary asked if she would mind if the mail or packages could be sent to Mrs. Kramer's address in San Leandro. Mrs. Kramer agreed and, while Mary was away, a package arrived from Chicago by air freight. A few days later, Mary and her husband came to Mrs. Kramer's house and picked up the package. A week later, another package in the name of O'Hearn arrived, also by air freight, carefully wrapped and weighing over two pounds. Mrs. Kramer became suspicious and called the San Leandro police. The police examined the contents and concluded that they were narcotics. A test of the contents by the state Bureau of Narcotics Enforcement showed them to be a high grade of pure heroin and cocaine—by retail standards, after cutting, worth on the street a large amount of money.

Mrs. Kramer was instructed to tell Mary that another package had arrived. Mrs. Kramer did so. Mary telephoned her husband from the restaurant and was told to tell Mrs. Kramer that they would call for the package the following afternoon, Friday, at a time when she would be home. At the appointed time, a San Leandro policeman was waiting inside a house across the street from Mrs. Kramer's home. A Buick automobile with an Arizona plate stopped at Mrs. Kramer's home. Mary and her husband entered the house, and, in a short while, came out with a package, got in the Buick and drove off. A state narcotics agent followed the Buick, stopped it and arrested O'Hearn and his wife. The package was on the front seat between them. State Narcotics Bureau and San Leandro Police Department automobiles were all around the neighborhood. It was a wonder that O'Hearn did not get wise and keep on driving without stopping at Mrs. Kramer's house.

A search of O'Hearn disclosed an address on the Peninsula across the Bay from San Leandro. The state narcotics agents took O'Hearn and Mary to this address, a second–floor apartment in the city of San Mateo, and directed the manager to open the apartment. They neglected to close the door to the apartment. The apartment was empty. The narcotics agents searched the apartment thoroughly and found milk–sugar and other ingredients and implements for cutting heroin and cocaine.

While they were searching the apartment, a man walked along the hall, gazed through the open apartment door and kept on walking. He drove away. It turned out this man was the notorious "Trigger Abe" Chapman, a mobster with a long criminal record. Documents in the apartment indicated that Chapman resided there. After searching the apartment, the state narcotics agent returned with O'Hearn and Mary to the Alameda County Jail and booked them for possession of narcotics.

The next morning, Saturday, the *San Francisco Chronicle* carried on its front page a big story of the San Leandro bust, of how much the heroin and cocaine were worth cut for retail sale, and with embellishments of the capture of O'Hearn and his wife, automobiles surrounding Mrs. Kramer's house, etc. When I read the paper, I phoned Walter Creighton, director of the California Bureau of Narcotics Enforcement.

"That was a pretty big bust your men made yesterday, but I see no mention of federal narcotics being involved," I said.

"No," Creighton replied, "we didn't contact them and they are mad as hell. They say they had been working on the case for a long time and had a big investment in it—many thousands of dollars in buys, informants, etc."

I phoned the agent in charge of federal narcotics in San Francisco and talked with him about the case. He was thoroughly disgusted with state narcotics for messing up their investigation. The word was already out in underworld circles and among informants that it was a "Trigger Abe" Chapman and Waxey Gordon caper, and that Chapman was the one who had walked past the open apartment door in San Mateo.

I told the agent I would go right down to my office to talk to O'Hearn and his wife, and I asked him to meet me there. He arrived shortly after I did and briefed me on their investigation. I called our special cases team of investigators and stenographers and went to work. Saturdays, Sundays or holidays made no difference to us if there was a job to do.

I started talking with O'Hearn. He was relatively young, good looking and personable. The first thing he talked about was his wife.

"She's good kid," he said. "We've been married for only a short while." Then, with some prompting, he proceeded to tell me the whole story.

He was a two–time loser with a federal felony narcotics record. He had served time in Leavenworth and other federal prisons. When he was released from prison the last time, he intended to go straight, met Mary in a restaurant, fell for her and they were married. They came to Oakland, and, while he was looking for a job, he was contacted by one of the mob, who said it was a chance to make some big money easily—just on the fringe—just to receive a few shipments and deliver the packages—no selling or other involvement. I questioned him at length. He gave me a lot of useful information: names, places, *modus operandi,* etc. Then I talked with his wife, Mary.

She was sitting at a desk in another room in custody of a matron deputy sheriff. She was sobbing and had been for some time. I noticed that she was holding rosary beads in one hand. What she said confirmed what O'Hearn had told me. I felt if the case turned out to be part of a big mob operation, as indicated by the Federal Narcotics Bureau, she and O'Hearn would both need protection, and O'Hearn would be needed as a witness. So I phoned judges in San Leandro and San Mateo, indicated the possible magnitude of the case, and asked them to put $100,000 bail on O'Hearn and his wife in each county. They did so.

I filled in the federal narcotics agent as to my conversation with O'Hearn. I said they would be charged in Alameda County and probably in San Mateo County. He said he would put holds on them for the United States Government and go from there. O'Hearn pleaded guilty in Alameda County Superior Court and was sentenced to San Quentin. Mary was put in custodial care for her own protection. With our help and that of O'Hearn, investigation by the federal government developed a case against twenty–eight defendants, all big operators in narcotics, including "Trigger Abe" and Waxey Gordon, international mobsters in narcotics and other rackets. Arrangements were made with the California Adult Authority and prison officials at San Quentin so that O'Hearn could be taken out occasionally to see his wife, and so that he had adequate protection in prison.

He testified in federal court against the twenty–eight defendants, who were all convicted and sentenced to federal prison. It was the cooperation and testimony of O'Hearn which made the investigation and prosecution by the federal government successful. In so doing, O'Hearn was risking his life from retaliation by the mob. I believe he did so because of his affection for his wife and his desire to save her from prosecution. Although he had been a two–time loser and an associate of dangerous criminals, his sense of decency and fairness prevailed over fear of vengeance by the mob.

With the exception of the ineptitude of the California Bureau of Narcotics Enforcement agents, this case was an example of how cooperation and coordination between law enforcement agencies—in this case the District Attorney's Office of Alameda County and the federal government—can get appropriate results. When the prosecution of the case was finished, Anslinger expressed publicly his appreciation for our help in a statement in which he said it was the biggest and most successful prosecution his department had ever had.

AUTOMOTIVE SALVAGE FRAUD

The West Coast head of the National Auto Theft Bureau and a special service officer of the California Highway Patrol asked me to help them in the investigation and possible prosecution of what they said was a large–scale interstate auto theft ring that was running a "Salvage Switch" operation. They said they had been working on the case for quite some time; that their investigation up to that point indicated that the ring's physical headquarters were in Chico in Northern California; that expensive automobiles were being stolen to order throughout California and Nevada to duplicate, in model, color and year, recently totaled cars—cars which had been written off and sold by insurance companies as totally wrecked non–salvageable automobiles.

As a result of the extensive investigation by the National Auto

Theft Bureau and the California Highway Patrol and Motor Vehicle Department, the persons involved in the mechanical work of the "switch" were identifiable and, among others, an Oakland car dealer named Brockman* was suspected as a purchaser of stolen cars at prices substantially below "blue book." Supplemental work by inspectors of the District Attorney's Office of Alameda County developed what appeared to be at least "probable cause" to support a prosecution of Minaldi,* one of the mechanics, who had eliminated the identification numbers on the engines and bodies of the stolen cars and replaced them with the identifications from the wrecked cars.

James Cox, one of the deputies in the District Attorney's Office, was assigned to prepare the case for presentation to the grand jury, Minaldi, Brockman, Mrs. Brockman, and others were indicted and Minaldi was persuaded by his wife to plead guilty. Minaldi had a criminal record and had served time in Folsom, the top maximum security prison of the California system of penal institutions. He was a tough, hardened criminal. While in prison, he engaged in muscle building and had become quite a sports fan.

In working on the case, Cox spent a great deal of time talking with Minaldi, who was confined in maximum security in the county jail at Santa Rita, some thirty miles distant from Cox's office at the courthouse. In fact, Cox spent so much time at Santa Rita that some of his colleagues needled him, saying he spent more time there than the inmates. Cox was a prodigious worker on any case, and, because of the importance and challenge of this particular case, he pulled out all the stops and put in countless overtime hours. This was Cox's way, and it paid off.

Before entering the District Attorney's Office, Jim Cox had been an outstanding athlete—captain of the football teams at both Stanford University and the University of California at Berkeley. During World War II, while a Marine Corps officer, Cox had some duty with the United States Navy at the University of California. For exercise, he went out for football and was selected captain of the team. He had service with the Marines in the Pacific Theater, and after World War II had returned to Stanford to graduate and study law. While in

Stanford Law School, he was assistant coach to Marchmont Schwartz of the varsity football team and head coach of the junior varsity team. After finishing law school, he did a hitch in professional football with the San Francisco 49'ers before entering the District Attorney's Office. Buck Shaw, the 49'er coach, once said to me, "Jim was on the light side (he weighed 200 pounds) for the line, but what he lacked in weight he made up in fight and hustle."

So when Cox set out to communicate and identify himself with witnesses, as he was in the habit of doing, he and Minaldi made a formidable pair. Minaldi, the sports fan, became a fan of Cox, the pro, and he made an extraordinary effort to assist in the prosecution. During his extensive criminal activities, Minaldi had been honed by the bruising competition of some tough big–time mobster, and he had no fear of any of them. At the trial, Minaldi was the chief prosecution witness, and he made a very good one. Under Cox's skillful guidance, he strengthened the links between the members of the complicated conspiracy and helped to tie the whole case together.

After the trial, in which all of the defendants were convicted, Cox said to me, "Chief, Minaldi has been a big help in the case. Although I did not make any promises, I think he is entitled to some break. His wife is a good woman and she has been helpful. I don't think Minaldi will get into any more trouble. He is a damn good mechanic. He won't have any difficulty finding work. I would like to help him. I made no promise, but I would like to recommend to the judge that his sentence be mitigated and that he not be sent back to Folsom."

Cox made the recommendation and Minaldi was given probation, with credit for the time he had served in the county jail. Cox tells me that Minaldi has made good and that he hears from him regularly. At that time, under the law in California (Penal Code Section 1203), a person convicted of a felony who had a prior conviction of a felony (Minaldi had pleaded guilty and had a prior felony conviction) was not eligible for probation. However, there are times in the administration of justice when a prosecutor and judge should, and do, bend the law in the interest of justice.

Incidentally, Cox went on to a very successful and distinguished private practice. Had Jim stayed in the District Attorney's Office he would have been a natural to become district attorney, or, if he so desired, he could have been appointed United States Attorney or a federal judge. At a relatively young age he was elected to fellowship in the American College of Trial Lawyers. In trying to recall facts to prepare this book, I phoned Jim. He remembered the case and sent a letter in which, in addition to the story of the case, he had some other things to say, generally, with respect to the District Attorney's Office, which are pertinent to the importance of thorough preparation for trial:

> "This case is typical of what I observed once I became a member of your Superior Court trial staff, which I believe occurred in late 1951. Namely, responsible law enforcement agencies with wide jurisdiction would request your office to undertake major prosecutions when an overt act or two, or a particular criminal event out of a number of same, had occurred in Alameda County giving you legal jurisdiction. This case was brought to us by the National Auto Theft Bureau (NATB). Mr. Gene Halm was the West Coast head of the same. Working with Mr. Halm at the time I was first introduced to the case was Murray Wemple, a very professional, experienced, special–services California Highway Patrol officer, working out of Sacramento. As I recall, NATB and CHP were interested in a thorough prosecution of this conspiracy, and were particularly desirous of *discouraging the practice* by, hopefully, charging and convicting a used car dealer of receiving if it were at all possible to do so.
>
> "(Minaldi) was one of the principals in the conspiracy. (Minaldi) had done a good deal of time in prisons such as Folsom, was a weight–lifter, quite a health nut, and despite his sorry criminal history, a pretty responsible, staid individual. As I recall, his wife, whom he met and married after his most recent release from Folsom, very much wanted (Minaldi) to turn state's evidence and cooperate with us after he was arrested. As you know, (Minaldi) saw fit to do this and was a material aid in the conviction of all of the persons charged. The ring's physical headquarters were in Chico and in Orland, California. New cars were stolen to meet the model, color and year of recently totaled cars, and they were stolen in various jurisdictions in California, and I believe, several came from Nevada. (Minaldi) and Co. had a particularly effective operation

in that they took great pains to make the stolen vehicles conform *completely* to the identity of the totaled vehicle, and went further than most, according to my then information, in that they were very careful to dispose of the salvage totally, melting down and burning identifying parts of the totaled vehicle or otherwise hiding same.

"You asked me the names of the people who were charged in addition to (Minaldi) and unfortunately none come to mind. However, I can establish them by role or function in the conspiracy.

"1. (Minaldi) and several others as actual thieves, and mechanics who made the changes of identity.

"2. At least two individuals in the junk business who procured merchantable identities and disposed of the identifying parts of the salvaged vehicles once the switch had been made. For example, I remember "Moose" Nelson, inspector in Oakland P.D. actually taking photographs of scratches on a bridge across the Sacramento River near Redding, where various heavy items had been pushed off the bridge into the river. The individual who was convicted as a co–conspirator confessed after we had taken voluminous statements from him and confronted him with other evidence. He was a young man working in a lumber plant in Corning, California. As I recall, we started at least two trials, selected a jury etc. and the defendants then pleaded guilty, which was a tribute to the thoroughness of the preparation involved by Messrs. Halm, Wemple, Russ Ryan and Moose Nelson and your other inspectors and deputy district attorneys.

"(Brockman), a veteran car dealer on Broadway in Oakland, had purchased at least four or five of (Minaldi)'s vehicles, believing he had a complete defense in that clear title was shown, the title matched the automobile delivered and the like. After several weeks of trial, the jury convicted (Brockman) and his wife of receiving stolen property. NATB and the CHP felt that these convictions would have substantial effect in California used car circles and would tend to minimize the prevalence of this lucrative criminal practice in the future.

"I remember spending so much time at the maximum security facility in Santa Rita interviewing (Minaldi) and preparing him for his appearance on the witness stand, that some people said I spent more time there than a lot of the inmates. The point is, pursuant to the training I received from you and other veterans in your office, I spent *real time* with a key witness, got to know him and vice versa, and established a relationship of trust and confidence.

I still hear from (Minaldi) occasionally, perhaps every three or four years. Further, as you know, hours meant nothing to me or to the fine people working with me. We went out into the country and took in–depth statements of all of the people involved early in the going. These statements helped to make the case for the grand jury and at the trial. In my mind, it was a good example of what thoroughness, hard work and determined professionalism can accomplish. Whatever part I played in it, I think it was largely due to the guidance and direction I received in Coakley College. Frankly, aside from trying a lawsuit with C. Ray Robinson in 1966, I never had any training to begin to equal the training I was afforded in the Alameda County District Attorney's Office."

THE BOXING AND WRESTLING INVESTIGATION

After Jim Cox went into private practice, Governor Goodwin J. Knight asked me for help in directing an investigation of prize fighting and wrestling, which had been receiving unfavorable publicity for several years. Because of the amount of work in my office, I could not take on the investigation personally, so I recommended Jim Cox for the job and agreed to help. I gave Clarence Severin, chief of inspectors in my office, a leave of absence to work on the case with Joel Taylor of the Oakland Police Department, and Elton Billings, an ex–FBI agent.

The investigation was interspersed with hearings conducted by Cox in Southern and Northern California. The hearings, freely publicized locally as well as nationally, were well attended by former 49'er teammates of Jim's, who were pulling for his success as a lawyer. In his letter to me enclosing the Committee Report of the investigation, Jim says:

"Gov. Goodwin J. Knight asked you, as the most outstanding law enforcement figure in California, with a reputation for toughness and independence, to handle a no–holds–barred boxing investigation in this state. . . . You recommended me to the governor, and that's how I got the employment. I think the enclosure sets it forth pretty completely and, as far as I'm personally concerned, it was simply another Alameda County prosecutorial assignment which came about because of the standing of the office. . . . I think most

> professional law enforcement people felt a high–caliber job had been done. I've been told that Crackers Columbo* and Freddy Ponzi* who were convicted of extortion in the Federal Courts in connection with boxing matters, wound up in the dock largely because of our efforts. As you know, the work received favorable comment in national magazines such as *Sports Illustrated* etc."

As a member of the Committee under whose auspices the investigation was conducted, I should say that Jim Cox and his staff not only dug deep into an ugly mess of corruption among fight promoters, managers and underworld characters involving fixed fights, mismatches, tank jobs, short changing of fighters and other abuses, but he courageously challenged some of the toughest hoodlums in the nation, fought them to a standstill and got them expelled from the prizefight business. His work contributed in no small measure to cleaning up a bad situation and improving boxing and wrestling in California.

FISH & GAME BRIBERY

After leaving our office to enter private practice, Jim successfully handled a case as defense counsel against Thomas Buckley of the District Attorney's Office. The case involved violations of the Fish and Game Code in another county by commercial fishermen and conspiracy to bribe Fish and Game Department agents. Jim described his work in this case as follows:

> "Again, it was a wide–spread criminal effort which was brought to Alameda County by the state Dept. of Fish and Game and certain federal wardens. The case had been so thoroughly documented and prepared that our only defense avenue was to admit all the incriminatory facts and contend entrapment. [Alameda County had a small piece of the case because of a telephone conversation in which a bribe offer was made by one of the fishermen to a state agent living in Oakland. The conversation had been tape–recorded by the Fish and Game Department and the recording was garbled and indistinct, as often happens.] In addition to the good training I received from you, we had a lot of luck and got [our clients acquitted]. The result doesn't matter, Chief, what counts is again

the law enforcement authorities, without question, came to the Fallon Street headquarters [Alameda County District Attorney's Office] when they wanted a real prosecution."

In closing, Jim wrote:

> "As you may recall, I feel that the Marine Corps had a great deal to do with whatever commendable qualities of character I have been able to develop. The best training I ever got, aside from the U.S.M.C. was at Coakley College. Like all your alumni, I feel a real debt of gratitude to Alameda County and the fine men I worked with and for there."

MORE BANK ROBBERS

Thompson* and Bowman* had major crime records dating back to their teens. At age eighteen, both started their long history of confinement in state and federal penitentiaries. They were described by parole officers as "professional and sophisticated criminals." They were white, clean–cut and of above average intelligence. Born in Florida of a middle–class family, Thompson had completed the seventh grade when his father died, at which time he was thirteen years old. Bowman was born in San Francisco, where he completed high school. Bowman's father died when he was seven years old. Both Thompson and Bowman had two brothers and one sister. There was nothing in the family histories of either Thompson or Bowman to indicate any anti–social tendencies of parents or siblings.

Thompson and Bowman completed academic courses while serving time in prison. Bowman completed several college extension courses (Sacramento City College and the University of California) while in prison with above–average grades. Tests administered to Thompson and Bowman put them in a superior range intellectually.

Thompson and Bowman were in Louisiana State Penitentiary at Angola, Louisiana, at the same time—Thompson for burglary and Bowman for armed robbery. They were released from this prison in 1950. Bowman was returned to the California State Prison for parole violation and paroled in December, 1951.

In 1952, Thompson and Bowman were identified as the armed robbers of several banks and a savings and loan company in Alameda County and Los Angeles. At the time of the robberies, each defendant was living with a woman on the Peninsula in San Mateo County, south of San Francisco, under a fictitious name. Both Thompson and Bowman represented to their women that they were engaged in writing lyrics and music for musical productions in Los Angeles. The women believed them. From time to time, when they would be away for varying short periods, they would tell their women that they were going to Los Angeles on business. In fact, during these periods they would be planning and executing bank or savings and loan company robberies.

Bowman's girlfriend saw a mugshot photograph of him in a newspaper and remarked to a woman acquaintance that it looked like her boyfriend. The remark traveled and eventually reached the police who arrested Bowman in his girlfriend's apartment. This led to Thompson's arrest, although Bowman or his girlfriend did not inform police of his whereabouts.

Thompson and Bowman were prosecuted and convicted in federal and state courts on the series of bank robberies in Alameda County and Los Angeles for which they would ultimately serve about nineteen years in federal and state prisons.

They were tried first in the Federal District Court in San Francisco, where they received 15-year sentences. They were then turned over to Alameda County for prosecution on the four 1952 Alameda County bank robberies, receiving sentences of five years to life, to run consecutively. They were then returned to federal marshals to serve time on the federal court sentence.

Thompson escaped from custody of federal officers in 1956, was captured in Bakersfield and returned to prison at McNeil Island. Bowman spent time first in Alcatraz before being transferred to Leavenworth Federal Penitentiary and later to McNeil Island.

When Bowman was released from McNeil Island federal prison in 1962 he had served about nine years in federal prisons on the fifteen–year sentence. The sheriff of Alameda County had placed a hold on Bowman with the federal prison authorities so that, when he had served his federal time, he would be returned to county custody to serve time on the 1952 Alameda County bank robberies. Somehow, when Bowman was released from McNeil Island, a local justice of the peace in Washington released him from the Alameda County hold.

A week later he walked into the District Attorney's Office of Alameda County, identified himself and said he wanted to surrender to the district attorney on the holds from Alameda County. The captain of inspectors in the District Attorney's Office asked me if I wanted Bowman searched before I talked with him.

"No. He has been free for a week," I replied. "If he wanted to polish me off he could have done so after he was released. My car is parked across from the courthouse and I have always been visible. Besides, I don't think he would walk into the District Attorney's Office armed. He's too smart for that."

The captain brought him into my office. He was very sunburned. He had been visiting with his son who had been born while he was in prison. As I recall, he said they had been skiing. While waiting trial in 1953, Bowman had married the woman with whom he had been living when arrested. We talked for a while about his confinement and conditions in federal prisons. When we finished our conversation he surrendered to deputy sheriffs who had been notified and were waiting to take him to state prison.

In the meantime, Thompson had been busy challenging in state courts, Federal District Courts and the Federal Court of Appeals the legality of his 1953 convictions in Alameda County. On the basis of his prior convictions in Florida and Louisiana, he had been made an habitual criminal under California law and sentenced to California State Prison for enhanced terms. He claimed that he had not been properly represented or advised by counsel in Florida and Louisiana and that the use of these convictions to enhance punishment on the California and federal court convictions of 1953 was in error. He also made a point in another appeal to the federal courts that the use of these prior convictions to impeach him in these trials was error. The Federal District Court ruled against him but the Federal Court of

Appeals reversed the district court and ruled in his favor. The Federal Court of Appeals also ordered a new trial in one of the Alameda County cases and remanded the federal case to the District Court for resentencing. He had been tried and convicted in two separate trials in Alameda County—one singly and one jointly with Bowman.

In the Alameda County case, the attorney general of California filed for *certiorari* in the United States Supreme Court. This petition was denied. Thompson then filed a writ of *habeas corpus* in the Superior Court of Alameda County to set aside his 1953 convictions. After protracted hearings and arguments, this Court granted the writ. As a result he was released from custody.

Bowman also filed a writ of *habeas corpus* in the Superior Court of Alameda County. On the basis of decisions in Thompson's cases, Bowman's writ was granted. In each case, the prosecution could have appealed and, if prevailing on appeal, could have tried Thompson and Bowman again on the 1953 robberies without charging the prior convictions of Florida and Louisiana or using them for impeachment. However, by 1972 they had already served nineteen years. So, no appeal was taken, and Thompson and Bowman were released from custody.

About four months after their release they were seen at 11 p.m. in an apartment house parking lot in Fremont, changing license plates on a Dodge auto. The woman who saw them phoned the Fremont police. Officer Lawrence, responding in his patrol car, drove into the parking lot and encountered two automobiles—a Dodge and a Chrysler. Thompson jumped into the Dodge and drove toward the only exit of the lot. Lawrence blocked this exit with his car.

Thompson got out of the Dodge, and, as Lawrence approached, Thompson pulled a gun on him and ordered him to stand with his hands up against a wall. While against the wall, Lawrence swung around suddenly and grabbed the gun. Thompson would not release it. They wrestled and fell to the ground. Lawrence was a powerful man, having been a Police Olympics weight lifter. He was unable to wrest the gun from Thompson. A boy watching the episode ran to Lawrence's police car and used the radio to call for emergency assistance, which arrived and assisted Lawrence in taking the gun from Thompson.

Bowman, upon the arrival of Lawrence, tried to drive his Chrysler automobile out of the parking lot but, being blocked, threw an object over a fence, jumped over the fence and escaped. He was later arrested in an apartment in San Jose occupied by some other ex–convicts. In Bowman's car, police found a guitar case containing a fully–loaded carbine rifle, a wig and other paraphernalia generally used in bank robberies. The object thrown over the fence by Bowman proved to be a loaded derringer handgun. The gun taken from Thompson's hand was a loaded .38 caliber revolver.

The circumstances connected with Thompson's arrest in the parking lot, Bowman's escape, and other evidence indicated that they were getting ready to commit another bank robbery. A bank was located a short distance from the parking lot. If they had not been seen changing the license plate, they might have pulled it off the following day. The skill with which they planned and executed their bank robberies was far above average—they were never caught in a robbery or in a flight from one.

During a period of three months after his release from prison in early 1972, while living at the Community Treatment Center in Oakland, Thompson reported that he was employed as a salesman for a vacuum cleaner firm and that he averaged between $1,500 and $2,000 a month in salary and commissions. Whether this was an exaggeration is not known. The total amount of money obtained in the 1952 Alameda County robberies of which they were convicted was around $100,000. Had they put their talents to legitimate pursuits early in life, and with their well–groomed appearance, gregarious personalities and superior intelligence, Thompson and Bowman could have earned many times $100,000. Instead, between 1946 and 1972, with the exception of two interludes of a few months, Thompson and Bowman were confined continuously in federal and state prisons.

Thompson and Bowman were found guilty by a jury on their 1972 Alameda County offenses and sentenced to state prison.

THE MCCLURE CASE

William McClure, lived alone in the rear of his successful hardware store on Foothill Boulevard in the Fairfax business district of Oakland. At around midnight on November 16, 1954, McClure was returning in his automobile from his favorite bar where he had been drinking. In turning left to park in a parking lot across from his store he scraped the fender of a passing car. The driver of this car insisted that the police be called. It was in the jurisdiction of what was known as the Eastern Station in east Oakland. Police arrived and McClure was given a citation for an illegal turn with a notation "H.B.D." meaning "had been drinking."

A mutual friend of McClure and the policemen came into the store and asked McClure for money to take care of the policemen. McClure gave him a fifty dollar bill. Five policemen then entered the store. Police Sergeant Gannon,* although he did nothing with respect to the citation, also came into the store, and, upon leaving, took two boxes of shotgun shells, as did two other officers, without paying for them.

A little while after all had left the store, the sergeant returned alone. He told McClure he could be charged with drunk driving, lose his license, and go to jail for a year, and that it could cost him $1,000. He said McClure could make it easy on himself if he wanted to. Sergeant Gannon also said, "That night I found you asleep in your car I could have rolled you." When McClure asked him what the deal was, the sergeant asked him if it wasn't worth a thousand. McClure took $1,000 from his safe and gave it to him.

The next night, according to McClure, one of the traffic officers who had handled the accident and citation came to his store and demanded money. McClure replied that he had already given the sergeant $1,000 and refused to give the officer any money. This officer, in leaving the store, took a skillet without paying for it and had McClure put it in a box for him.

Shortly thereafter, Sergeant Gannon accosted McClure in a bar in the neighborhood and berated him for telling the traffic officer about the thousand dollars. The sergeant threatened McClure if he talked further he would find himself in the Estuary.

About two weeks later, as McClure came out of a bar late at night, a police patrol car with two policemen in it hailed McClure and offered him a ride home. McClure got into the car. Instead of driving him to his store, the police drove up into the Oakland hills, where they robbed him of over $100 and left him.

McClure finally told his insurance agent the whole story—the accident, the police pilferage, the $1,000 shakedown, the kidnaping and the robbery. The insurance agent knew the chief of police, Lester Divine, an honest and competent policeman who had risen through the ranks from the traffic division. He had moved up over many older officers and, possibly because his experience had been primarily in traffic, some older heads were not too cooperative. They thought they knew more than he about police work. Divine referred the McClure matter to the Internal Security Unit of the Department for investigation. The investigation bogged down. The officers involved denied receiving any money. The officers who took the merchandise likewise denied having done so. McClure was unable to identify them or the two officers who had kidnaped and robbed him. The officers on the beat where he had been kidnaped also denied everything.

Lieutenant Miller,* in charge of the precinct station on the midnight to 8 a.m. watch, after learning of the Department investigation of the McClure shakedown, instructed an officer to pick up McClure and bring him to the station. The lieutenant was present and ordered that McClure be booked. The booking charged "drunk and exposed to public view," which required a $10 bail. McClure was called a "fink" and a "ringer" by other officers and taken to Central Station in a patrol wagon where the words "creating a public disturbance" were added to the original booking. The bail on this charge was $25.

McClure was not drunk and he had created no disturbance. In other words, he was being framed. The inference was clear that he was being intimidated, with the lieutenant's knowledge and approval, because of the investigation of the shakedown. The officer who had picked up McClure was simply following orders of the lieutenant, and was not a party to the booking or the events which followed.

An internal police department investigation like this is not easy to contain indefinitely. Rumors began to leak and newspaper reporters on the police beat began to probe. I heard about it and instructed Laurence Dayton, assistant in charge of the Oakland branch office, to look into it. For many years before being appointed to the District Attorney's Office, Dayton had been a newspaper reporter with the *San Francisco Call*, the *San Francisco Bulletin*, the *San Francisco Examiner* and the *San Francisco Chronicle*. He talked with Chief Divine who told him what he knew. Dayton pursued an independent investigation and got no further than the police investigation. He felt, as I did, that the policemen involved were giving him and Chief Divine a runaround.

Journalism thrives on controversy and scandal. This is especially so when it involves a local police department and competing newspapers with substantial local circulation. A man at the city desk, risen from the ranks of the police beat, with the backing of a publisher with great political power and awareness, can generate and exploit a lot of controversy, especially if it involves alleged police misconduct. To be scooped or beaten to the story is a cardinal sin not to be tolerated by a city editor with the clout of a powerful local daily.

The course of a police chief or a district attorney who tries to be his own man and do a fair and competent job without being bludgeoned into premature disclosures or half–baked conclusions in pending investigations can be, and often is, a bruising one, and such a situation is not in the best interest of sound law enforcement and justice over the long pull.

A police chief once told me that the city editor of a prominent local daily used to try to generate a feud between him and me by telling him that I made disparaging remarks about him which reflected on his honesty and competence. In fact I had never made such remarks.

We had on duty at the time of McClure's arrest a seasoned grand jury which was about to be discharged. The McClure case was so sensitive, I had taken over the investigation personally and would present it to the grand jury. Herbert Shuey, a man of great integrity and high repute in the community, was foreman of the grand jury. During the investigation, I talked with Shuey about the case and its seriousness in the context of the police department and law enforcement in Oakland if allowed to go unnoticed or without appropriate penal or disciplinary action. There was obvious concerted defiance on the part of a few officers to cover up criminal conduct by members of the police department. Shuey and I talked with the judge who had impaneled the grand jury and it was decided to hold the grand jury over until after the McClure case was presented.

McClure testified before the grand jury, as did Sergeant Gannon, the officers who were suspected of stealing the merchandise, the lieutenant, the wagon officers and others involved in the booking procedures.

The police witnesses stonewalled any incriminating participation and disclaimed any knowledge of how McClure's booking report had been changed. When asked about McClure's arrest and the booking, the lieutenant's answer before the grand jury, over and over to every question, was, "I have no recollection whatsoever."

The sergeant was indicted for extortion and taking a bribe of $1,000, and the lieutenant was indicted for perjury on the theory that his repeated testimony disclaiming any knowledge of events which occurred in his presence at the precinct station was false. He was also charged with conspiracy to cause a false arrest and imprisonment. They were prosecuted and convicted. On appeal their convictions were affirmed.

The conviction of a witness for perjury in disclaiming recollection of events he was in a position to observe and should have known established somewhat of a legal landmark. With respect to the perjury charge, if the lieutenant had simply testified that during McClure's booking he was in and out of the room and otherwise occupied and not paying attention, he may not have been indicted for perjury although he would have had difficulty explaining why he ordered McClure's arrest. He was probably advised by some lawyer that if he said he had no recollection he would not be charged as a party to the intimidation of McClure. But he laid it on too thick in his repeated "no recollection whatsoever" testimony.

The impact of the McClure case was a shakeup in the police department and the passage of Charter provisions relating to the basic structure of the department. Chief Divine, who had been contemplating retirement because of a cardiac condition, retired. In his place Wyman Vernon, chief of police of the city of Richmond, was appointed chief of the Oakland Police Department by City Manager Wayne Thompson, an able young executive who had come to Oakland from Richmond where he had also been city manager. Thompson knew Vernon and was aware of the excellent job he had been doing since leaving the Oakland Police Department to become chief in Richmond. Vernon, having served in the Oakland Police Department, where he had a fine record, knew what to do to improve the department. He and I collaborated, and out of it came a greatly improved police department.

GRAND JURIES

So far as I knew, there was no organized corruption in the Oakland Police Department, but there had been some individual mooching, petty larceny, drunk rolling and brutality by some officers. According to Earl Warren, some years prior to his regime as district attorney, a police chief had an understanding with bunco men that if they would not operate in Oakland they could reside there.

In the relatively small Chinatown, Chinese lotteries and pai–gow games ran with what amounted to an official tolerance. The police would make regular monthly raids on the lotteries and arrest a Chinese operator and a few players. The next morning, a Police Court judge would impose a fine of $25 on the operator and $5 on each player. The Chinese operator would pay all the fines, return to his operation to continue the play, and wait for the next periodic raid, with the same routine result. This had been the system for years. District attorneys complained in vain. This, in effect, was a type of license from the city and a source of revenue.

A carnival with a merry–go–around, shooting gallery and crooked wheels of fortune and shell games would come to town, rent space from the city in a centrally located public park at a very substantial fee, and start operating—unmolested by the police. The shell games and wheels of fortune were illegal and a criminal fraud on the public. Official tolerance of such conditions are conducive to corruption and reduced morale among police.

Warren and Hoyt had put pressure on the city government to eliminate these conditions with intermittent effect. Before the McClure case, the lotteries, pai–gow and carnivals had been stopped under my threat to call the mayor, city manager and the chief of police before the grand jury to explain why they could not be stopped.

When fairly and competently used, a grand jury is a very useful weapon against official corruption or toleration of illegal business operations. During the regime of District Attorney William Hynes, an Oakland police chief was indicted. Corruption in the department and negligence in city government was aired by a well–publicized grand jury report and corrected, even though the chief was acquitted. Reforms often fade and old tricks and conditions resurface. Warren's use of the grand jury in the Bail Bonds Broker Scam case cleaned up a messy situation in the Oakland Police Department and the bail bond racket, as did his use of the grand jury in the Street Paving Graft case, corruption in certain cities, the sheriff's administration in county government and other situations. To succeed in such investigations, a district attorney must have a staff of competent prosecutors who are above reproach and impervious to criticism, and competent investigators on the payroll of the district attorney's office, who must be willing to put in plenty of hard work and overtime investigating cases. Cases involving official malfeasance or police criminality are difficult and require tough, hard, persistent digging.

Warren, Hoyt and I worked closely with the grand jury, being present when they convened to hear evidence of criminal offenses, or concerning the operation of county government. I always participated in the presentation of matters to the grand jury and went with them to court when True Bills were submitted. A relationship of respect and confidence between a district attorney and a grand jury is conducive to effective action by both. Competence, honesty and fairness on the part of a grand jury, police department, district attorney and courts can go a long way towards maintenance of healthy conditions of law and order in a city or county.

Warren used to say that in a city or county where the police, prosecution and courts are honest and competent, organized crime cannot operate. I would add to that adequate budgeting to employ sufficient well–trained help and necessary equipment. I would add also maintenance and exchange of intelligence among law enforcement agencies on federal, state and local levels, and plenty of well–designed and directed coordination among responsible police and prosecution officials.

Established operating channels of contact and coordination between law enforcement agencies, whereby attorneys general, district attorneys, United States attorneys and top level investigative representatives of federal, state and local enforcement agencies meet regularly for exchange of information and reciprocal assistance, would also improve law enforcement. This is an area where we focused much attention.

To combat juvenile crime in Alameda County, with the help of Laurence Dayton, Albert Hederman, Probation Officer Lorenzo Buckley, Sheriff Gleason and police chiefs of the thirteen cities in the county, we set up a mutual aid unit called the "Juvenile Officers Coordinating Council" which met monthly for lunch to exchange information and discuss problems. The Juvenile Court judges and representatives of the schools often attended these meetings and collaborated. This unit has been operating for many years to the mutual satisfaction of the agencies involved. It has generated better knowledge, understanding, cooperation, and coordination among law enforcement agencies, and especially among officers engaged in the important work of crime prevention and youth welfare.

Another unit, called the "Public Agencies Coordinating Council"—consisting of representatives of the schools, the county Welfare Department, the Sheriff's Office and police departments—was set up under the direction of Edwin Meese III in each of seven districts roughly corresponding area–wise to the township boundaries of the county. The function of this organization was to study crime conditions and law enforcement problems, receive information from citizens and pass it on to public agencies having responsibility to take appropriate action.

A unit of intelligence officers of the law enforcement agencies of the county was also set up to meet regularly and exchange information. However, because of reluctance on the part of intelligence officers of certain departments to disclose information and sources, this operation was not as effective as it might have been. Unless intelligence is carefully circumscribed and the competence and integrity of police assigned to intelligence work are assured, such reluctance to disclose information sources is understandable.

Of course, none of these law enforcement coordinating councils could replace the grand jury as an investigating tool. Over the years, the grand juries of Alameda County have been outstanding groups, chosen by chance from carefully selected names submitted by Superior Court judges. Because they have been fair, they have been highly respected by the citizens of the community and the press.

Pursuant to instructions by the impaneling judge, the grand jury, during its one–year tenure, oversees and reports on the operation of county government, causes an audit of county government to be made by a reputable accounting firm, and hears such cases as the district attorney desires to present. In practice, prior to the *Hawkins v. Superior Court*[25] decision of the California Supreme Court in November 1978, the policy of the District Attorney's Office of Alameda County had been to present selected criminal cases of more than ordinary importance. We would present cases involving corruption in government; police misconduct cases; long complicated conspiracy cases involving numerous suspects and victims which, if presented in a preliminary hearing in a Municipal Court, would further congest an already over–congested calendar; cases involving carnal abuse of victims of tender years; or cases in which it was deemed advisable to afford witnesses protection from injury, harassment or intimidation.

A grand jury can be useful also for investigative purposes in such

[25]*Hawkins v. Superior Court* (1978) 22 Cal.3d 584

cases where no one will sign a complaint; where the then–available evidence is insufficient to support a criminal complaint and a hearing before a magistrate, but which can be developed by subpoena and examination of uncooperative witnesses; or where the suspect is missing and it might be necessary to get an indictment in order to toll the statute of limitations.

However, because of the *Hawkins* case, which holds that, regardless of whether an indictment is returned, the accused is entitled to a preliminary hearing, the use of grand juries in criminal cases will be redundant and rarely used with the possible exception of an investigation, in which event if an indictment is returned a defendant is still entitled to a preliminary hearing. A preliminary hearing must be a public hearing unless the defendant requests a closed hearing.

Although a defendant is entitled to obtain, by discovery procedures, full information of prosecution evidence, there is some advantage to a defendant in the opportunity to cross–examine prosecution witnesses under oath if he is willing to spend the time on a preliminary hearing. But if all that defense counsel wants is knowledge of the prosecutor's or police department's evidence, which is usually the case, such evidence was available under the previously existing law. Like decisions which expostulate the exclusion principle, the *Hawkins* case is another manifestation of distrust of law enforcement officials and of overreaction of courts in favor of the defense.

As herein indicated, the age–old use of grand juries has been effective and salutary in the investigation of cases resulting in indictments and convictions which were affirmed by higher courts. Without the use of the grand juries for the purpose of investigation there would have been many miscarriages of justice or inability to prosecute persons guilty of serious crime.

Apropos of the trend of our courts to increase the difficulties of police and prosecutors, the following words of the great Justice Learned Hand of the United States Court of Appeals in the case of *In re Field* seem relevant:

> "The protection of the individual from oppression and abuse by the police and other enforcing officers is indeed a major interest

> in a free society; but so is the effective prosecution of crime, an interest which at times seems to be forgotten. Perfection is impossible; like other human institutions criminal proceedings must be a compromise. . . . Were it inevitable that all the privileges of an accused should be treated alike, so far as my vote was concerned, I should compel the accused to postpone even a constitutional objection until the trial. I should choose to impose upon him whatever risk that might entail, rather than to hobble the prosecution of crime by mincing the trial into successive separate determinations."[26]

as do his words in the case of *United States v. Garsson*:

> "Under our criminal procedure the accused has every advantage. While the prosecution is held rigidly to the charge, he need not disclose the barest outline of his defense. He is immune from question or comment on his silence; he cannot be convicted when there is the least fair doubt in the minds of any one of the twelve. Why in addition he should in advance have the whole evidence against him to pick over at his leisure, and make his defense, fairly or foully, I have never been able to see. No doubt grand juries err and indictments are calamities to honest men, but we must work with human beings and we can correct such errors only at too large a price. Our dangers do not lie in too little tenderness to the accused. Our procedure has been always haunted by the ghost of the innocent man convicted. It is an unreal dream. What we need to fear is the archaic formalism and the watery sentiment that obstructs, delays, and defeats the prosecution of crime."[27]

PROSTITUTES & REPORTERS

Another impact case involved a young woman, badly bruised and disheveled, who walked into the Oakland Police Department and accused her husband of trying to put her into the prostitution racket and of having beaten her when she protested. He was the proprietor of a posh and well–known tavern in Oakland. In talking with her, I was

[26] *In re Field* 161 Fed.2d 453 at 465
[27] *United States v. Garsson* (1923) 291 Fed 649

informed that her husband was trying to put her into a type of organized crime which involved a circuit of houses of prostitution located in various cities in California and other states. The prostitutes were rotated from city to city. A thorough investigation of the prostitution racket was made with the idea of eliminating it as much as possible in Alameda County. Pimps and panderers were rousted and ordered out of the county. Where there was sufficient evidence to charge, they were prosecuted. The girl's husband was indicted, tried and convicted.

To protect his wife from harassment or harm we put her in the custodial care of Inspector George Irwin and his wife until after the trial. The Irwins owned a ranch near Santa Cruz, an apple growing area. There was an apple orchard on Irwin's ranch in which the girl worked picking apples. During the trial, her cross examination went somewhat as follows:

Q. "Where have you been living since you left the defendant?"
A. "Near Santa Cruz."

Q. "Where in Santa Cruz?"
A. "With Mr. and Mrs. Irwin."

Q. "What have you been doing there?"
A. "Picking apples."

Defense counsel probably thought that she would say she was working in a house of prostitution. A reporter for one of the local newspapers, in his zeal to scoop other papers, apparently did think so, and, without waiting for the answer, rushed out of the courtroom to phone his city desk in time to beat a deadline for the home edition. This edition carried a story to the effect that the witness testified that she had been working as a prostitute, which was untrue, and generated threats of a libel suit.

During World War II, San Francisco was a place of heavy traffic in servicemen moving to or from service overseas in the Pacific Theater. A serious problem for the military was drunk–rolling of servicemen, who were stupefied and robbed as a result of Mickey Finns served by bartenders in collusion with loitering prostitutes and barmaids. After passing out and being robbed, the servicemen would be shoved out onto the sidewalk to be picked up by the police as drunk, oftentimes missing ship or being disciplined for absence without leave.

Instructions were given by the District Attorney's Office to the Oakland police that there was to be none of that in Alameda County. Furthermore, there were to be no shills or B–girls cadging drinks or waitresses drinking with customers. After World War II, the state Legislature belatedly enacted legislation with respect to the problem (California Penal Code Sections 303 and 303a). The police in Alameda County cooperated and the lid got so tight that taxi drivers told patrons they were unable to find a bordello. Those who wanted the service of a house of prostitution would go to San Francisco, where there was plenty of such activity. Because of the tremendous loss of manhours from venereal disease, the policy of the armed forces had been to ask local law enforcement to eliminate houses of prostitution and, as much as possible, prostitution.

In recent years there has been an increase in open solicitation by street prostitutes, who in some cases are teenage girls and boys. Where bordellos, barfly prostitutes and street solicitation are tolerated, it becomes a dirty racket in which young persons are seduced by pimps, panderers and organized criminals who try to corrupt policemen to the detriment of the community and law enforcement. Organized crime and prostitution, where tolerated, are closely allied with the narcotics racket.[28]

SMUT

Sex Life of a Cop or *10:04 Sgt. Thorne*, as it was originally entitled, was a crudely written obscene paperback novel replete with various alleged sex relationships committed by a sergeant in a police

[28] *Final Report of the California Special Crime Study Commission on Organized Crime*, pp. 30, 92.

department, a judge of a local court, their wives and other persons, male and female, in a fictional typical American city. The underlying theme of this book, as of other productions of its publisher, was extreme incompetence and a low ebb of morality of American public officials. The author and publisher had been a policeman.

The mother of a teenage boy in Hayward found a copy of the book in her son's room and took it to the police department for appropriate action. A policeman purchased another copy of the book at a store, and, in due course, a criminal complaint was issued by William Ahern, deputy district attorney in charge of the Hayward branch of the District Attorney's Office, charging Hopper,* owner of Vega Books and other publishing firms in Fresno, California, and Speer,* wholesale distributor of books and magazines in Oakland, with a violation of Penal Code Section 311.2. This statute defines sale, distribution, publication, etc. of any obscene matter as a misdemeanor. Herman Mintz, one of Oakland's leading criminal lawyers, filed on behalf of the defendants a demurrer to the complaint and a voluminous legal brief in support of the demurrer. If the defendants had pleaded guilty in the Hayward Municipal Court, the judge would probably have imposed a fine or a summary probation with a condition to refrain from distribution of the book in Alameda County.

When Ahern called my attention to the fact that a certain Los Angeles law firm, which specialized in defending obscenity cases, had entered the case on behalf of Hopper, we decided to present the case to the grand jury on the theory that it was a felony, a violation of Penal Code Section 182, Subdivision One—viz. conspiracy to commit a violation of Penal Code Section 311.2—in as much as several persons were involved in the production, sale and distribution of this and other obscene books.

Up to this point in time, we had not had any appreciable problem in Alameda County with pornography, although it had burgeoned in other parts of the state, especially Los Angeles. An inquiry had been made of the Oakland Police Department by a woman whose minor child had received in the mail a publication of erotic content. The district attorney of Marin County, California, Roger Garrity, had filed a criminal complaint against a seller of *Tropic of Cancer*. On

Courtesy *Oakland Tribune*

Above: The old courthouse at 5th & Broadway, 1872—1937

Below: District Attorneys of Alameda County
(l to r) Charles E. Snook, 1892, 1894; John J. Allen, 1898, 1902;
Everett J. Brown, 1906; William H. Donahue, 1910;
William H. L. Hynes, 1914; Ezra W. Decoto, 1918, 1922;
Earl Warren, 1925, 1926, 1930, 1934 to 1939

Current Courthouse
1225 Fallon Street in Oakland.

Earl Warren
District Attorney of Alameda County
1925—1938

Ralph E. Hoyt
District Attorney of Alameda County
1939—1947

Above: SS Point Lobos; the scene of Warren's Ship Murder Case.

Below: Induction of Ralph E. Hoyt as Judge and J. Frank Coakley as District Attorney by Judge Edward J. Tyrrell.

J. Francis Coakley
District Attorney of Alameda County
1947—1969

Above: Stephanie Bryan's gravesite in Trinity County

Above: Burton Abbott conferring with counsel during a trial recess.

Left: Prosecutors Folger Emerson (l) and J. Frank Coakley (r).

Courtesy *Oakland Tribu*

News reporters and photographers during a trial recess in *People v. Abbott*.

Front row (l to r): Ken Durham, *Columbia Broadcasting System* (kneeling); Harold V. Streeter, Associated Press; John Campbell, *Oakland Tribune*; Carolyn Anspacher, *San Francisco Chronicle*; Art Johnson, *San Francisco Chronicle*; Jack Ryan, *Oakland Tribune*; Bill Crouch, *Oakland Tribune*; Clarence Hamm, Associated Press; Seymour Snaer, *San Francisco Examiner*.

Second row, seated (l to r): Harriet Martin, Western Union; Lloyd Boles, *Oakland Tribune*; Jane Conant, *San Francisco Call-Bulletin*; Virginia Dennison, *Oakland Tribune*; Jim Edelen, *Oakland Tribune*; Ed Montgomery, *San Francisco Examiner*; Charles Crutenden, *San Jose Mercury-Herald* and *San Jose News*.

Third row, standing (l to r): George Draper, *San Francisco Chronicle*; Dorothy Cuthbertson, *Hayward Review*; Havelock Hunter, *Oakland Tribune*; Bill Fiset, *Oakland Tribune*; John Keyes, *San Francisco Call-Bulletin*; Jim Nichol, *San Francisco Examiner*; Ralph Craib, *Oakland Tribune*; Gale Cook, *San Francisco Examiner*; Sam Blumenfeld, *San Francisco Examiner*; John Hines, *San Francisco Call-Bulletin*; Ken McLaughlin, *San Francisco Chronicle*; Sid Tate, *San Francisco Call-Bulletin*.

Courtesy *Oakland Tribune*

Above: Black Panthers and their supporters demonstrating on the courthouse steps during the first of Huey Newton's murder trials.

Below: Black Panther leader Huey Newton's mugshot taken by the Oakland Police Department.

Above: Bullet–riddled patrol car of Officers Darnell and Jensen.

Right: Mugshot of Bobby James Hutton.

Below: The arsenal recovered from the suspects and their vehicles.

Courtesy Oakland Tribune

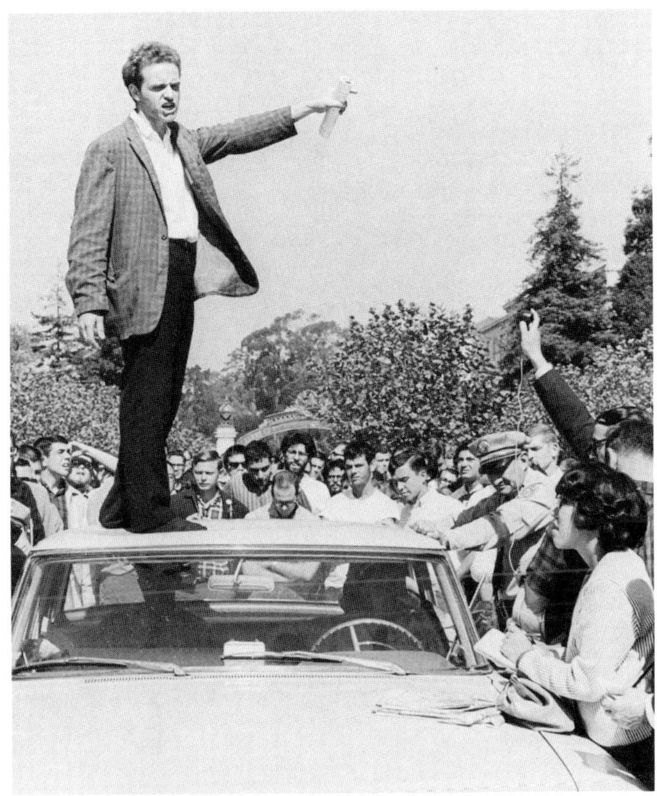

Left: Mario Savio addressing the crowd from atop a campus police car on Upper Sproul Plaza in front of Sproul Hall administration building.

Below: Policemen toppled in surge of Free Speech Movement demonstrators in the entranceway to Sproul Hall.

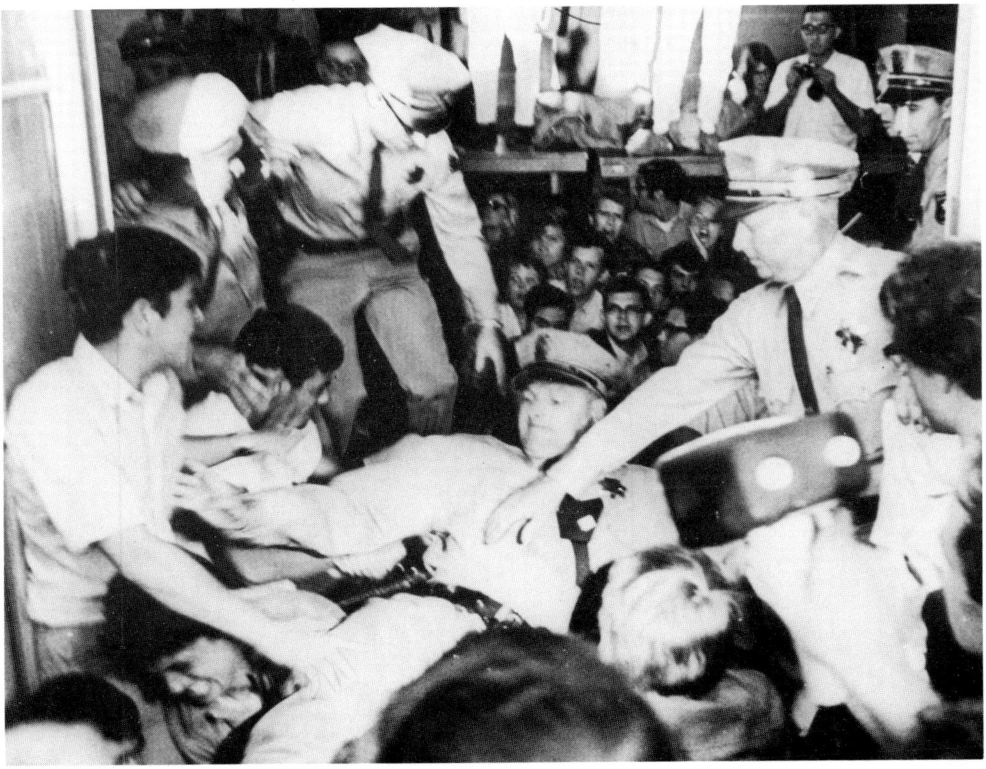

Courtesy Oakland Tribune

Above: Vietnam Day Committee march in Berkeley

Below: Buses with draftees arriving at the Armed Forces Entrance and Examining Station in Oakland during Stop The Draft Week demonstration.

Above: National Guardsmen in riot formation on Upper Sproul Plaza between Sproul Hall and the Student Union building.

Left: National Guardsmen and police confront the mob at the so–called People's Park 2 blocks south of campus in Berkeley.

National Guardsmen and police occupy Sather Gate
at the north end of Upper Sproul Plaza.

D. Lowell Jensen
District Attorney of Alameda County
1969—1981

John J. Meehan
District Attorney of Alameda County
1981—present

the eve of the trial of this case, a member of the California Attorney General's Office made a widely publicized statement to the effect that *Tropic of Cancer* was not obscene. Whether the *Tropic of Cancer* was then or, in the context of current literature and decisions, is now obscene may be a matter of opinion, but the timing of the statement by the deputy attorney general was improper and prejudicial to Garrity's prosecution.

Until the 1960's, books like *Tropic of Cancer* were classified as obscene and barred from the mails and the country by the United States Post Office Department and United States Customs. They were also banned by the United Kingdom. There was reason to believe that obscenity was increasing and on the way to becoming very big business.

Investigation of the case disclosed that the Hopper organization, which operated out of Fresno, specialized in the production and distribution of paperback obscenity and had interstate distribution; that Hopper had on retainer a Los Angeles legal firm; that this firm prepared printed opinions representing that specific Hopper publications were lawful; and that Hopper had these opinions duplicated for distribution to wholesale distributors who might be hesitant about handling books such as *Sex Life of a Cop*. Hopper's headquarters and warehouse were in a large modern building in Fresno where a large staff was employed. It was a big operation devoted exclusively to the production and sale of poorly written sheer smut.

Search warrants were obtained for the Fresno headquarters and warehouse, for Speer's company and for a printing and lithographing company in San Francisco where the manuscripts were printed before being returned to Fresno for binding. The search warrants were general and particular, listing specifically certain named books and generally all records, books, accounts and documents concerning Hopper's operation, the Speer company and the printing and lithographing firm. At the latter place, some fourteen tons of printed and cut galley sheets, ready for shipment to Hopper's Fresno plant for binding, were seized. Hopper's and Speer's company records were also seized on search warrants.

The proceedings against Hopper and execution of the search warrants were matters which a few years before would have received little, if any, mention in the news media. This case was given what I thought was an unusual amount of publicity even to the extent that one of the large dailies in San Francisco quoted editorially one of their trained seals castigating me, the proceedings and—by implication—the courts for the issuance of the search warrants and seizure of the publications.

In retrospect I have wondered whether this was a time when the media may have been waiting for an opportunity to agitate such a case as a challenge to freedom of the press or whether they were genuinely concerned about a growing menace of obscenity. To us in the District Attorney's Office, these were cases in which crimes were committed, and, arrests having been made, it was our job to prosecute. The media generally campaigned against us, as they did later in the University of California "Free Speech Movement" campus unrest cases, the so–called civil disobedience cases, and the Vietnam Day Committee activities.

The United States Supreme Court had recently issued opinions in the *Roth/Alberts* cases stating that:

> "The test (of obscenity) in each case is the effect of the book, picture or publication considered as a whole, not upon any particular class, but upon all those whom it is likely to reach. In other words, you determine its impact upon the average person in the community. . . . Does it offend the common conscience of the community by present day standards? . . ."

and inferentially adopted the definition of the American Law Institute Model Penal Code as follows:

> ". . . a thing is obscene if, considered as a whole, its predominant appeal is to prurient interest, i.e., a shameful or morbid interest in nudity, sex, or excretion, and if it goes substantially beyond customary limits of candor in description or representation of such matters . . ."

The United States Supreme Court stated further that:

> "The impact of the publication, book or picture upon the average person shall be determined by the jury according to present day standards of the community."[23]

After a verdict of acquittal in Garrity's prosecution of the *Tropic of Cancer* case, most of the district attorneys backed off from initiating prosecutions for sale of obscene printed material because of difficulties encountered in the courts. Much time would be consumed counteracting expert testimony introduced by defense counsel at trials and it was a futile and frustrating experience for the police and prosecutors. However, I decided to proceed under the definition of obscenity by the United States Supreme Court.

Thomas Buckley, one of our assistant district attorneys who handled grand jury matters, presented the Hopper case to the grand jury. Because of the United States Supreme Court's definition of obscenity, the book *Sex Life of a Cop* was identified as evidencc and had to be read in its entirety to the grand jury, who returned an indictment charging Hopper and other members of his staff with conspiracy to violate Section 311.2 of the Penal Code, a felony. Hopper's attorneys challenged vigorously every step of the case as to the sufficiency of the grand jury evidence to support the indictment, the search warrants, and the seizures under the warrants.

The case went all the way up to the Supreme Court of California—where they eventually lost, although this Court questioned some of the broad allegations of the search warrant issued by a magistrate in Fresno County and remanded this aspect of the case to this magistrate for further consideration. The magistrate emasculated the case by ordering the books, accounts and records seized on the search warrant returned to Hopper. However, the District Court of Appeal

[23]*Roth v. United States* (1957) 354 U.S. 476 affirming the decision in *People v. Alberts* (1955) 138 Cal.App.2d Supp. 909

of California denied a hearing—in effect holding the search warrant and the grand jury evidence sufficient legally. Defense counsel took the Alameda County case to the United States Supreme Court on a petition for *certiorari.* The Court denied their petition for a review—thus allowing the decision of the California Appellate Court in favor of the prosecution to stand.

The investigation and proceedings in Alameda County caused Hopper to close operations in Fresno. He surfaced later in Burbank, California, where Ahern collaborated with the Burbank Police Department and the Los Angeles District Attorney's Office in the prosecution of Hopper in Los Angeles County. Hopper sued Ahern unsuccessfully for a million dollars for putting him out of business. Ahern followed through completely in the case and collaborated with the FBI in the investigation and prosecution of Hopper and his two aides in the federal courts, where the defendants were eventually convicted and sentenced to long terms in federal prison by a United States District Court judge.

When last heard of, Hopper and his companies were out of business. Thus ended the operations of one of the biggest purveyors of obscene literature in the United States. Its distribution at one point had been intercontinental.

The proceedings in Alameda County and the federal courts took several years, during which period pornography in San Francisco and Los Angeles increased—not only in printed material but in movies, in live–conduct exhibitions, and in recruitment and traffic in juvenile girls, boys and young children for photography of perverse sex acts. However, as a result of the vigorous prosecution of Hopper and those associated with him, the pornography business in Alameda County was eliminated.

Ahern was uniquely qualified for his vigorous and successful pursuit of Hopper and his publications. Educated at St. Joseph's High School in Alameda by the Brothers of Mary, Ahern was a graduate of Santa Clara University where he was an outstanding athlete and member of one of the great Santa Clara basketball teams. He was also a graduate of the Jesuit–operated University of San Francisco

Law School, a fighter pilot in the United States Navy during World War II and a father of teenage children at the time he encountered the Hopper operation. Ahern was not about to pull his punches in the Hopper case.

ACCESSORY TO A PSYCHOPATH

People vs. Janda and Webber was an unusual case in which a person was convicted of manslaughter for criminal negligence in lending or selling another person a loaded pistol under circumstances indicating that he had reason to believe the lethal weapon might be used to kill another person, although he was not present at the killing and said he did not believe the killer would use the pistol to kill.

Reinhart,* son of a retired white Navy officer and a black woman, was raised a Catholic, converted to the Moslem faith and had his name changed legally to Mohammed Janda.* As a boy he was precocious. He started to read and write at age three, started school at the second grade and thereafter skipped three grades, graduated from high school at age fifteen, was awarded several scholarships, attended Long Beach City College and the University of California at Berkeley, at which point he was very large physically and mentally alert. As a child he had been active in the Catholic church and in a Moslem church in San Francisco while at the university, where he gave talks on religious subjects and conducted a Sunday School class for small children.

A psychiatrist testified that Janda had a personality character disorder, a history of psychoneurotic traits, abnormal phobias and superior abstract intelligence. He also had a history of abnormal psychotic behavior. At age sixteen he started a fire in his home because he had promised his mother that he would burn the house and kill her, saying that his mother was "a pig and women are born without souls, so it doesn't matter whether I kill her or not." He claimed that God had given him permission to kill his mother, further professing that a woman's only function was to bear children, and after childbirth they should be exterminated along with older men. He said that he disapproved of our form of government and believed in a modified form of Nazism. On the arson charge, he was committed by a Juvenile Court to a state hospital for observation, and then returned to juvenile authorities and released. Another psychiatrist found that he had a behavior disorder, a schizoid personality and was emotionally immature.

He spent two years at the University of California at Berkeley, where his grades were satisfactory, but he withdrew in his senior year because of trouble he had in harassing and threatening Sonja Huff, a fellow student whom he professed to love. He had asked her to marry him, but there was no evidence of any sexual advances. She rejected his marriage proposals. He saw her frequently at the university, where they both studied Islamic history and philosophy. There were many instances when he threatened to kill her, threatened to commit suicide and threatened to or did injure others whom he thought were unduly attentive to her. Sonja was critical of Janda because he smoked and drank alcoholic beverages, which she contended were contrary to the precepts of his Muslim religion. Although their relationship was far from tranquil and she had appealed to the campus police for help, she was too kind or sympathetic to cut him off abruptly.

Janda had an apartment in Berkeley, and, after his withdrawal from the university, he continued to live there. An avant garde of the non–student Sproul Plaza dissidents, he circulated among this fringe crowd and used the enormous library facilities of the university, as did countless other non–student so–called "beatniks." Among his friends was Webber,* who owned several guns.

Eight days before he killed Sonja, Janda told Webber he wanted to kill her and needed a gun. Webber gave him a gun and Janda returned it saying he did not have the "guts" to use it. Spasmodically, Janda made statements to the effect that he would kill Sonja and himself. Others heard these statements, as did Webber. A week before the murder, Pope,* a student friend of both Janda and Webber who had heard of Janda's threats to kill Sonja, warned Webber of Janda's mental condition and urged him not to give Janda a gun. Webber replied that if any of his friends needed anything he would give it to them.

According to Janda's trial testimony, he told Webber on July 13th he wanted a gun to "protect" himself; that Webber said he might as well sell him a gun; that he paid Webber $20 for a gun and promised to pay $20 more later; that Webber told him it was loaded. Janda also testified that he put the gun in his pocket while Webber was out of the room; that they went to a cafe, had a beer and parted. Later that day, by prearrangement, Janda went to the campus library to meet Sonja. There, while she was seated at a table, they had a short conversation, after which Janda turned away to leave, pulled the gun which he had obtained from Webber, shot Sonja in the back of her head twice and then shot himself in the head.

In various conversations with police and others after the shooting, Webber admitted the gun was his, that he did not think Janda would use it, and that in letting him have the gun on a prior occasion he was giving Janda a psychological test.

Janda withdrew his plea of "not guilty because of insanity" before trial and was tried jointly with Webber on a charge of murder. Janda testified at the trial but Webber did not testify, so that much of Janda's testimony went uncontradicted, but for rambling and inconsistent extra judicial statements made before trial by Webber.

Janda was convicted of murder first–degree with a death penalty and Webber of involuntary manslaughter on the theory of criminal negligence in selling Janda the lethal weapon or making it available to him. The convictions were affirmed on appeal. Later Governor Edmund G. Brown, Sr. commuted Janda's death penalty to life imprisonment.

PREACHERS & CHARLATANS

James Patterson,* a middle–aged hustler with a criminal record and a spurious diploma–mill degree as a theologist, arrived in Oakland in 1944 and opened a series of evangelical revival meetings at an abandoned old church building in a rundown part of town. According to his own statements, he had no money or other assets at this time. For ten years he had been traveling revivalism's "sawdust trail" with negligible monetary results. Outside of a one–year period in Cleveland, his ten–year missionary effort had consisted generally of one, two or three night stands in small towns in the South and Midwest.

While in Oakland, by his aggressive approach combined with an elaborate advertising campaign in newspapers, radio and sound trucks, he garnered about two million dollars from gullible members of his congregation and other activities, among which were speculations in property and gambling in Nevada. When the District Attorney's Office caught up with him, his bank accounts showed deposits of $1,354,706, of which, after all other possible sources had been eliminated, $691,641 must have come from his congregations.

Originally from Tennessee, Patterson was the son of a four–time convicted bootlegger who served three terms in a federal penitentiary in Atlanta. At seventeen years of age, Patterson was expelled from high school for making whiskey in a school basement. When twenty–one, he was arrested in Florida for transporting stolen automobiles across state lines.

Among people who had come to Oakland during World War II from the "Bible Belt" of the deep South to work in the shipyards and other war connected business, Patterson found a receptive audience and soon began to prosper. The west Oakland scene of operations soon became too small to accommodate the congregation, so Patterson rented space in an auditorium of a large building in the heart of downtown Oakland with a seating capacity of 1200 persons. Spending $5,000 a week on advertising, Patterson was soon performing before capacity crowds and engaged the Oakland Civic Auditorium, with a capacity of ten thousand, for highly publicized sessions. This endeavor lasted several weeks and was well attended.

Patterson, who specialized in appealing for money and collections, had a unique talent for soliciting contributions. In a relatively short time, the money that was being collected was such that he was able to purchase the building in which the congregation was meeting—a first–class, fire proof, five–story building—for $265,000. Patterson represented falsely to his congregation that all of their contributions, including this building and other acquisitions, were contained in a trust arrangement in which they all participated. Under appropriate fanfare, this idea was emphasized in a dedication ceremony.

In his exhortations he would single out a certain member of the congregation and say that God had informed him this member had a specific amount of money which God had ordained this member must contribute. Consistently, he represented that he was in direct communication with God, who had informed him that certain members had specific assets which they were obligated to contribute. Information as to assets of members of his flock he acquired through personal conversations between himself and the member, or between one of his shills and the member, or by other devious means.

A fly in the ointment was a bar and dance hall on the second floor which offended the devout puritanical sensibilities of the congregation. Patterson overcame these qualms by saying that the bar and dance hall operations were in the building on long–term leases. These representations were false because they were actually month–to–month tenancies which could have been terminated at any time. From these concessions Patterson, after acquiring the building, collected $1,000 a month in rent, for which he never accounted to anyone.

As his exhortations accelerated and money kept accumulating, his activities proliferated. First, there was a Bible institute—the name of which was used to apply to the whole complex of his enterprises. Included in these, with headquarters in the building, was the Patterson College and Seminary, an Academy of Christian education, and a music school for the training of choir leaders, gospel singers and church accompanists. The students, mainly members of the congregation, were persons of all ages—elderly widows and widowers, adolescents and their parents, and young veterans for whose tuition Patterson had made arrangements with the United States Government under the G.I. Bill of Rights.

When it came to keeping books or accounting for money collected on his complex speculations in real estate, Patterson specialized in confusion. There was no bookkeeping or accounting. Business was conducted haphazardly and apparently on a strictly cash basis in Patterson's own name. In addition to the property already acquired, he bought two ranches with money collected from the congregation and stocked it with cattle in the name, he said, of the church. This likewise was false, as was the representation as to the ownership of the Oakland property, which he sold when it suited his fancy for $450,000—at a profit of about $200,000. He also sold the ranches which he had pledged to be used as an orphanage in the name of the church and the congregation. Meanwhile he was spending money with great abandon—expensive automobiles, expensive tailor–made clothes, hand–tooled cowboy boots, and ties emblazoned with dollar signs. He used to say the initial "C" in his name stood for "Cash."

During one particular phase of his money raising, Patterson spoke of building a ten–story tabernacle on a high hill overlooking "sinful San Francisco." On this theme he continued to solicit and raise large amounts of money. Other than speculating in real estate, nothing was done on this project except to squander the money collected on his own lavish living. Another project for which he solicited money was a radio station. The achievement of this objective never occurred, perchance because of a Federal Communication Commission investigation and refusal to grant a permit. But money solicited and obtained was not returned to those who made contributions for the project. On occasions, his operations became ludicrous. To give his schools an academic atmosphere, he advertised them as accredited by the University of California. This, of course, was blatantly false. His school had no authentic faculty. What teaching took place was done by Patterson and members of the flock—who had no teaching credentials. Enrollees in the Patterson College and Seminary were sold blue sweaters with a large yellow letter "P" sewn on the chest, after the fashion of a varsity athlete's sweater, and stripes around one arm signifying how many years the enrollee had attended the Patterson college. On one occasion, Patterson solicited contributions which he said would be thrown into Lake Merritt and, strangely, many contributed.

One of his outlets for spending was gambling in Reno, Nevada, where, when losing, he cashed large personal checks—among these were two in the amount of $4,200 which bounced. The Palace Club of Reno, through a collection agency, pressed for payment continuously, during which time Patterson covered the bad checks with other bad checks. Eventually, news of his extra–curricular activities surfaced, and complaints were received by the District Attorney's Office of Alameda County.

After a thorough investigation, the matter was presented to the grand jury. Five years had passed since his modest beginning at the old church in west Oakland. During this period he had collected, by incredible flamboyance and fraud, large amounts of money from his congregation of modest means who could ill afford to part with such money. When called before the grand jury and asked if he believed in God, Patterson refused to answer the question on the grounds that his reply might tend to degrade and incriminate him. He responded in the same way to all other questions. He was indicted on several counts of grand theft, obtaining money by trick and device, and embezzlement. Defense counsel raised the constitutional shield of religious freedom and groups of the congregation were conspicuous around the courthouse during the trial, but to no avail. After four and one–half months of trial, he was convicted and sentenced to state prison.

This case was ably handled by Chief Assistant District Attorney Richard Chamberlain and Assistant District Attorney Cecil Mosbacher, both of whom later were appointed Superior Court judges by Governor Warren. It was investigated by inspectors Clifford Wixon, Lester King and Mark McDonough of the District Attorney's Office. It demonstrated how effective and successful thorough, competent preparation and prosecution can be.

For too long charlatans posing as ministers (than whom there are no more despicable crooks) have beguiled and swindled innocent well–meaning persons who, in their declining years and modest means, can ill afford to be victimized. In recent years, a spurious cultism has emerged among growing numbers of converts, especially of the younger generation. In California, the notorious Aimme Semple McPherson, following one of her earlier evangelistic ventures, was persuaded to leave Oakland by a skeptical police chief. She traveled to Los Angeles and reaped a harvest in a more fertile field of avid followers while she glamorized revivalism.

More recently, an eloquent revivalist named Jim Jones, of Guyana mass–suicide fame, migrated to San Francisco where, in a relatively short time, he captivated a large following of ardent contributors and supporters, including some well–known politicians, and amassed a fortune. By and large, these operators are resourceful and not easy to prosecute. Converts, even after being fleeced, hesitate to complain and cling to their elusive hope. For some reason, in California the potential harvest seems more attractive to the cultist entrepreneur. However, when he engages in criminal conduct he can be cornered and convicted, as in the case of Patterson herein discussed. But it takes a lot of patient, painstaking investigation, which many policemen and prosecutors are either disinclined or too busy to pursue.

COLD BLOODED MURDER

One of the most coldblooded double murders in the history of Alameda County occurred on the night of October 22, 1949. Pursuant to a telephone call from Mrs. Robert Savage in which she said her husband, a pharmacist at the Rose Waterman Drug Store on the corner of 7th and Adeline Streets in west Oakland, had not come home at his usual time, Oakland police officers made a routine stop at the store at 12:05 a.m. Closing time at the store was 9:00 p.m. The front door was locked with keys hanging from the lock on the inside of the door. The officers gained entrance by forcing the door.

On one side of the store was a counter, in back of which was a partition separating the counter area from the prescription drugs and safe area. In this partition was an opening about shoulder high through which the pharmacist, while filling prescriptions, could see who was entering or who was in the store. In the prescription area, Robert Savage, the pharmacist, and Marjorie Wilson, the clerk, were on their knees bent forward with their faces on the floor in pools of blood. Marjorie Wilson was a sister–in–law of a prominent Oakland lawyer. Each had been shot in the back of the head while kneeling and had fallen forward. The two bullets which killed them had gone through their heads and were lying on the floor with two expended bullet casings.

The safe, which was open, had been rifled. Two safe drawers had been emptied and were lying on the prescription counter. Records, books and other articles generally kept in the safe were lying on the floor. The cash register tape showed that $601.34 was missing. The light in the prescription area was still on. Obviously Savage and Wilson had been killed just as Savage finished checking receipts and was getting ready to close up. A tin box also generally kept in the safe was found on a work bench in the rear area of the store. It had been forced open. A hasp in which a padlock secured a door from this area to Adeline Street had been ripped loose and the door was unlocked. A hasty exit had been made from this door to the street.

About ten minutes after nine, Barbara Cruikshank, a teenage girl who lived on Adeline Street, was returning from a store on 7th Street. She looked in the front door of the drug store, and in doing so she bumped her head on the glass door, which was locked. As she looked in the direction of the prescription area opening she saw a person behind the opening whom she recognized as Jerry Newcomb*. When she bumped her head on the glass entrance door, he had turned and looked towards the front door. The prescription area was lighted. She had known Newcomb, an 18 year old, for about five years and attended the samc high school with him. She did not see Robert Savage or Marjorie Wilson, whom she knew quite well. Newcomb also knew Savage and Wilson. Both Cruikshank and Newcomb had been in the drug store many times and were friendly with Savage and Wilson. As she walked up Adeline Street to her home, Cruikshank saw Newcomb's automobile standing at the curb adjacent to the door at the rear area of the store, the same door from which the lock was later found by police to have been torn loose on the inside. The car standing at the curb had been purchased recently by Newcomb, who shined shoes at a pool room in Oakland.

At 11:30 a.m. October 13, 1949, nine days earlier, Newcomb had robbed the Harbor Homes Housing Authority office and obtained a bag containing $1,275. On the rolls of pennies and nickels and empty coin wrappers was written the initials of Alice Rodgers who worked in the Housing Authority office. During the robbery Newcomb said to the manager: "Where is the money. I want the big stuff." In demanding that the manager come out of his office and produce the money, Newcomb had threatened to kill one of the two women employees in the Housing Authority headquarters. He pointed the pistol he was holding at Mrs. Rodgers and pulled the trigger. She heard a click of the gun's hammer, but it did not fire. Newcomb then pushed a magazine of bullets up into the gun's chamber and stood over the manager as he assembled the money and rolls of coins from the safe. In leaving the building, a guard, walking in the vicinity, saw Newcomb running and heard a click as the robber pointed a pistol at him. The pistol did not fire. Expert testimony later developed that this pistol was a very old Army issue, the parts and barrel of which were badly worn.

In investigating this robbery, police inspectors, following up on reports in the neighborhood of Newcomb's purchase of an automobile, heavy gambling and other sudden affluence, went to the pool hall where Newcomb worked. When Newcomb went to a closet to get his coat, police saw the bag containing the money from the Housing Authority and the coin wrappers and took it as evidence. While being questioned about the Housing Authority robbery, Newcomb asked the police inspectors what the penalty for robbery was. On being told what the penalty was, he asked what the penalty was if someone was killed in a robbery. He was told it was a possible death penalty. Thereafter Newcomb confessed that he had committed the Housing Authority robbery. This aroused the suspicion of police as to Newcomb's connection with the drug store murders.

Savage and Wilson were well known and liked by people in the vicinity of the store. These murders were widely discussed by people in the area, which was mostly populated by blacks. Cruikshank had talked to several of her friends about having seen Newcomb in the store after closing time and about seeing his car parked alongside the store at the same time with a man sitting in it. Police picked up this information and, working on that aspect, located Cruikshank, who told them about seeing Newcomb in the drug store the night of the murder as she bumped her head on the locked glass door, and about Newcomb looking at her through the opening of the lighted prescription room. She also said that the day after the drug store murders she had seen Newcomb with what appeared to be a pistol protruding from under his coat.

An old Army issue Colt .45 automatic was found wrapped in cloth in the trunk compartment of the automobile of Newcomb's uncle. Newcomb resided with his uncle and was familiar with his uncle's car and its contents. Newcomb pleaded guilty to the Harbor Homes Housing Authority robbery and admitted to having used this pistol in that robbery.

Newcomb was given a lie detector test by Inspector Al Riedel of the Berkeley Police Department (at the time, the Oakland Police Department did not have a polygraph), following which he confessed he had killed two people in the drug store.

While in the Oakland City Jail awaiting the preliminary hearing, Newcomb informed a fellow prisoner that a girlfriend of his knew what had happened in the drug store but she knew how to keep her mouth shut. Also while in the city jail he asked a fellow prisoner, who as a jail trustee had access to a telephone, to get word to Delores Hansen* to visit him in the jail. He told the trustee that he wanted to talk to her about the drug store case in order to transmit a message to Williams* (a suspected accomplice in the case) and to tell Williams to visit him in jail and to "take it easy."

Williams and Hansen were close friends of Newcomb. A substantial amount of the money stolen at the Housing Authority and the drug store was still unaccounted for, except for Newcomb's statement that he had been gambling heavily. The man whom Cruikshank saw sitting in Newcomb's car on Adeline Street alongside of the drug store at the time of the murders could have been an accomplice, or at least a material witness. Early in the investigation, Cruikshank had identified this man as Williams and later recanted.

The trustee had made notes of Newcomb's request and gave the notes to a police inspector on the case. The inspector obtained authority from his superior in the Homicide Division to install a Dictaphone to record any conversation between Newcomb and Williams or Hansen, in the event that either of them visited him in the jail. Under the circumstances, a recording of such a conversation in the jail would be legal. (California Penal Code Section 653h.)[24]

Dictaphone equipment was borrowed from a private agency and installed by the police. The installation was carelessly done. A microphone was placed in an interview room generally used by defense attorneys and visitors, with a wire from the mike leading to a recording machine in an adjoining room. The machine was to be activated to record any conversation which might occur between Newcomb and Hansen or Williams.

Newcomb's request to the trustee was then to be transmitted by the trustee to Hansen, assuming that Hansen would transmit the message to Williams and that Williams would visit Newcomb in the jail. A jailer on duty when the Dictaphone was installed was instructed to allow no one to use the rooms where the mike and the recorder were located. When this jailer went off his shift, he neglected to so instruct the incoming jailer.

A defense attorney in another case was admitted to the interview room and discovered the mike and the wire, which he ripped out. After looking at the recorder in the next room, the attorney rushed downstairs to the press room, where he informed reporters on the police beat of his discovery. He did not inform the press that when he inspected the recorder in the adjoining room it was not plugged in to an electric socket or that the wire from the interview room was not attached to the recorder. The attorney had been tipped off by a prisoner who had seen the recorder being carried through the jail. The reporters questioned Chief Divine, who checked with the Homicide Division and informed the press in confidence as to the reason for the installation.

A San Francisco newspaper ignored Divine's explanation as to the reason for the installation and his request that the matter be unpublicized. The paper also criticized him editorially. There had been some previous friction between Divine and this paper. One of the

[24]*Bell v. Wolfish* (1979) 441 U.S. 520 and
North v. Superior Court (1972) 8 Cal.3d 301.

defense counsels in the case, a radical Left activist, exploited the situation and criticized the Oakland Police Department. He was quoted extensively by the particular paper, by the Communist *People's World*, and by other media as it served their purpose of distorting the facts to whet a controversial racism theme which had been gathering momentum in the media for some time. This was unfair to Divine and I said so. I upbraided the newspaper for the breach of confidence, which impaired the investigation, and said that the police would have been derelict under the circumstances if they had not prepared to record a conversation between Newcomb and Williams, whom the police had reasons to believe had been an accomplice. Because I defended the police, the newspaper turned on me and wrote that I "admitted hiding the mike in jail," which was completely false. I knew nothing about the mike episode until after it had been publicized by the paper. But you cannot win fighting the media. They have the last word.

Divine asked the Alameda County Bar Association to investigate the matter. This was done and the Bar Association committee report found that there was no misconduct on the part of the police. The attorney who had discovered the mike concurred in the finding. Had he discussed the matter in the first instance with the police, the publicity may not have occurred and important evidence might have been developed. Of course, Newcomb, being forewarned by the publicity, had no conversation in the jail with any visitor thereafter.

Testimony was introduced at the trial of Newcomb's admissions to Inspector Riedel that he had killed the two people in the drug store. Newcomb said later that he was kidding when he made these admissions. The testimony of Inspector Riedel, did not indicate there was any kidding about it. Riedel was a polygraph expert and a man of consummate fairness and integrity.

Dr. Paul Kirk, a professor at the University of California and a ballistic expert, testified that the two .45 caliber bullets which killed Savage and Wilson were fired by the Colt .45 found in the car of Newcomb's uncle. A particularly significant fact of the ballistic evidence, in addition to land and groove comparisons, was that the lethal bullets were fired by an old Army issue .45 caliber Colt pistol, the barrel rifling of which was well worn. This was the condition of the Colt pistol which was found by police in the trunk compartment of the automobile of Newcomb's uncle to which Newcomb had access. Breech block markings on cartridge cases of the lethal bullets coincided with such markings on the test bullets. This same weapon was shown to be the weapon which Newcomb had used in the Housing Authority robbery nine days before the murders in the drug store.

Cruikshank, in stenographically transcribed statements, positively identified Newcomb as the person she had seen looking out from the prescription room of the drug store five or ten minutes after nine on the night of the murders. Under oath at the preliminary hearing, she again identified Newcomb as the person she saw in the store looking out from the prescription area opening. Again before trial, in talking with Assistant District Attorney Laurence Dayton, she said that Newcomb, whom she knew, was the one she had seen in the prescription area opening when she bumped her head on the front door. When called to the witness stand at the trial, Cruikshank refused to testify. Trial judge Donald Quayle arranged for a conference with her parents and attorney, out of the presence of the jury, in which he admonished her of the seriousness of her conduct and the possible result of contempt of court.

She finally agreed to testify, and, when Assistant District Attorney Dayton asked who, if anyone, she saw in the drug store when she looked in the front door, she said she had seen no one and proceeded to accuse the police of coercing and threatening her to get her to testify. This was a blatant fabrication. Dayton claimed surprise and laid the foundation for her impeachment. Defense counsel objected and asked the Court to instruct the jury that the impeaching questions and answers did not constitute evidence and could be considered only with respect to the credibility of the witness. The judge said they had correctly stated the law and that he would fully instruct the jury on the subject of impeachment later, which he did.

The jury convicted Newcomb on two counts of murder first–degree with the death penalty. On appeal, a divided California Supreme Court granted a new trial on the grounds that the trial judge failed to instruct the jury on the subject of impeachment at the time the impeachment questions were asked of the witness, Cruikshank, although the judge said at that time that defense counsel had correctly stated the law in their objection and the judge later covered the subject fully in his final instructions before submitting the case to the jury.

The irony of this contretemps is that a few years later the California Legislature enacted a new Evidence Code in which the instruction concerning the limitation of impeachment testimony to witness credibility was eliminated to provide that such testimony became admissible under the same conditions as other evidence, viz. to constitute substantive proof of fact.

Mr. Justice John W. Shenk, Associate Justice of the California Supreme Court, said in his dissenting opinion:

> "There is abundant evidence in the record to establish the defendant's guilt. He had a full and fair trial and judgment of conviction should be affirmed."

The case was tried two more times without the testimony of Cruikshank because the prosecutor could not claim surprise at the change in her testimony. At the second and third trials, the jury disagreed. Newcomb had been sentenced to state prison on the robbery of the Housing Authority for five years to life. After the third trial, the murder case was dismissed. On the recommendation in the Statement of Judge and District Attorney in the Housing Authority robbery case that he be confined for life, he spent twelve years in state prison before being paroled.

Before the first trial, defense counsel had retained a reputable liberal local trial attorney to assist in the trial. After listening to defense counsel outline the tactics to be used in attacking the police and prosecution, this attorney refused to be a party to it and withdrew from the case.

Between trials, I was harassed continuously with anonymous phone calls during late hours of the night, demanding dismissal of the case. The calls in each instance followed the same radical Left pattern. After persistent questioning by me, one of the callers said his name was Beloit.* At the time a man with the same name was on the editorial staff of the *People's World*, the main Communist newspaper in the Bay Area. This paper published a printed pamphlet portraying Newcomb as innocent and accusing the police of a frameup. The pamphlet was widely distributed, and printed leaflets alleging a frameup of Newcomb were strewn around the courthouse during the trials where jurors might pick them up.

After the verdicts and while trial Judge Donald Quayle was considering imposition of sentence, the propaganda attack from the radical Left, which had permeated the case from the beginning, was stepped up. A petition, spearheaded by the Civil Rights Congress and signed by over 2,500 persons, alleging a frameup of Newcomb and demanding that Judge Quayle grant Newcomb a new trial, was filed with the Court. After sentencing Newcomb on the death penalty verdicts, Judge Quayle read the petition, pointed out the impropriety of the attempt to so influence the Court, termed it contempt of court, and instructed his clerk to file the documents in the case so it would be a matter of public record.

Among others, the Civil Rights Congress alleged that Judge Quayle's action in denying a new trial had brought "southern justice" into Alameda County and accused the judge of "legal lynching." The judge, distraught by these tactics, emphatically denounced such conduct and stated that the defendant had received a fair trial and that the verdicts and sentences were fully justified under the law and the evidence. The Bar Association, which should have initiated disciplinary action against those responsible for the contemptuous tactics, did nothing. The Civil Rights Congress at that time was classed by the "Report on Communist Legal Subversion" of the U.S. House of Representatives Committee on Un–American Activities as one of the most virulent of the Communist front organizations.

Following World War I, a concentration of radical activists settled in the Bay Area and particularly in the East Bay around Berkeley. In 1920, several members of the Industrial Workers of the World (IWW) were prosecuted and convicted in Alameda County for violations of the Criminal Syndicalism Law. After World War II, radical agitation and propaganda attacks on government and the administration of justice, nourished by the liberal climate in Berkeley, increased to the detriment of law enforcement and without effective restraint or criticism from the organized Bar or the press.

Although a significant aspect of this case was that it indicated a trend in the Supreme Court of California in which this Court scrutinizes records on appeal in criminal cases in search of error in the conduct of a trial upon which to predicate reversal of a conviction or reversal of a death penalty verdict—a trend which deviates from the long–standing provision of the California Constitution (Article VI, Section 13) that if the record of a criminal trial contains reasonable and substantial proof of guilt, a conviction is to be upheld in absence of error so prejudicial that it could have effected a miscarriage of justice.

The veteran and highly respected Justice Shenk, in his dissenting opinion in this case, comments on this aspect as follows:

> "Having declared that error was committed, the majority opinion then concludes that a miscarriage has resulted if it cannot be shown that a different verdict was improbable. The language of the Constitutional provision itself should govern. It provides that no judgment shall be set aside 'unless, after an examination of the entire cause, including the evidence, the Court shall be of the opinion that the error complained of *had resulted* in a miscarriage of justice.' That provision clearly calls for a realistic appraisal of the entire record on a case–by–case basis to determine whether in the presence of error a miscarriage of justice has occurred. Here there was no error. Even if there were, the record makes it clear that *no* miscarriage of justice has resulted from the judgment of conviction."

This trend of the California Supreme Court in criminal cases was manifested in the struggling of a divided court on the issue of search and seizure and exclusion of evidence until 1955, when finally one of the justices reversed a position he had held previously to concur with three other justices of the court in *People v. Cahan*[25] to embrace the exclusion principle—a principle designed to afford greater

[25]*People v. Cahan,* (1955) 44 Cal.2d 434

protection to the accused from police misconduct or incompetence and to punish law enforcement officers who, in good faith, may have erred in the seizure of evidence, regardless of how relevant and material such evidence might be.

Thus, in California the basic and long–standing law of this state, first set forth in *People v. Mayen*,[26] was changed. The exclusion principle was later imposed upon the legal systems of all the states in the case of *Mapp v. Ohio*.[27] The application of the exclusion principle to the states by the United States Supreme Court was a departure from the decisions of all the courts of the British Commonwealth and contrary to the famous case of *People v. Defore*,[28] in which the great Justice Cardoza rejected the concept in his classic statement: "The criminal should not go free because the constable blunders." Suffice to note here also that the immortal John H. Wigmore, Dean of Northwestern University and considered world–wide an outstanding authority on the law of evidence, denounced the exclusion principle as "misguided sentimentality."

To the credit of peace officers of California it should be said that the reports of the higher courts of the state disclose relatively few reversals before *Miranda*[29] because of involuntary confessions obtained by force, threats, duress, intimidation or promises, or after *Miranda* because of admission of a confession or an extra–judicial statement after failure by an officer to give the *Miranda* admonition. However, the mandates of the higher courts with respect to exclusion and *Miranda* have resulted occasionally in release without charging and often in frivolous pretrial motions and appeals.

There were other lessons to be learned from some of the misadventures of this case, namely: inept police work and criminalistic expertise, mishandling of the Dictaphone episode, premature disclosure by police to the press of information concerning factual details of the pending investigation, poor timing of press releases by police which

[26] *People v. Mayen* (1922) 188 Cal. 237, 24 ALR 1388
[27] *Mapp v. Ohio* (1961) 367 U.S. 643
[28] *People v. Defore* (1926) 242 N.Y. 13, 24
[29] *Miranda v. Arizona* (1966) 384 U.S. 436

coincided with deadlines of certain media and which antagonized other media whose deadlines were missed.

The effort of Dr. Kirk to match up every land and groove in the photography of his comparison ballistic microscope was another mistake. This was not necessary because his testimony as to breech block markings on the cartridge casings found at the scene, and the indisputable fact that the lethal gun was an old U.S. Army .45 caliber Colt automatic pistol and that the markings from the well–worn rifling of the barrel coincided with worn markings on the lethal bullets should have been sufficient with all the other evidence in the case to convince any reasonable juror. Failure of criminalists called by the defense to concur fully with certain refinements of Dr. Kirk's ballistic testimony and microphotography afforded an opportunity for argument concerning differences of the expert witnesses. Sometimes an expert, in his zeal to wrap up all aspects of a case, goes further than necessary. Something should be left for the jurors to figure out for themselves, that they might come to their own conclusions.

Another aspect involved Newcomb's confession to Inspector Riedel. As soon as Newcomb admitted to Riedel that he had killed the two people in the drug store, Riedel left him and informed Oakland police inspectors, who were in another room, that Newcomb had confessed. This information was passed on immediately by Oakland police to newspaper reporters who were waiting with their photographers, and was widely publicized with pictures of police and Newcomb. Newcomb had been sympathetically portrayed by the liberal elements of the media as a poor black eighteen–year–old shoe shine boy.

This was followed by entry into the case of the Civil Rights Congress and various other activists of the radical Left who sought to propagandize and exploit the rapidly growing black community. From then on, racial aspects of the case were exploited interminably, both during the trial and long after. Before so hastily disclosing to the press the fact of Newcomb's confession to Riedel, the Oakland police inspectors should have interrogated Newcomb further with a stenographer as to all of the details.

Another aspect of this case was the failure of law enforcement, including the prosecution, to anticipate and appraise the impact of the tremendous drive at this time of the radical Left, particularly the Communists, to influence by devious means the large population of the black community in Oakland. Inspector Merle Longnecker of the Oakland Police Department, who worked on the case, said, "The Communists took over."

The witness, Cruikshank, who recanted her original positive identification of her schoolmate at the trial, had disappeared before the trial, and only after considerable effort by the police was she located. She should have been given custodial protection instead of being exposed for months to the pressures of an increasing polarization of blacks and whites. Certainly, the case should have been moved along to an earlier trial.

Publicity during an investigation is generally not helpful. Too much publicity can result in a costly change of venue of a trial to another county. Pretrial publicity is not conducive to orderly investigation and preparation for trial by police, prosecutors or defense counsel. In run–of–the–mill cases there is usually little, if any, interference with a lawyer's preparation, but in a case where there is intense competition among the media there can be, and often is, considerable interference.

The British system, where pretrial publicity is minimal, is better. In the United States, in highly publicized cases competing media can be ruthless in pursuit of new leads. In a 1949 case involving police corruption in Oakland, the city editor of the leading daily got very wound up about keeping the story going. He said to me, "If any other paper scoops us I'll cut your ____ off." In another case, a reporter was ordered by that same city editor to sit in the hall inside the District Attorney's Office, outside of my private office, and to follow me wherever I went.

STEPHANIE BRYAN

On April 28, 1955, Stephanie Bryan, a shy, fourteen–year old honor student at Willard Junior High School in Berkeley disappeared on her way home from school. The daughter of Dr. Charles S. Bryan, a noted and highly respected roentologist, Stephanie lived in the vicinity of the Claremont Hotel in Berkeley with her parents and three siblings.

Stephanie and another young girl of about the same age left school at about 3:15 in the afternoon, and walked along Ashby Avenue to the vicinity of the Claremont Hotel where they parted at about 4 o'clock. Stephanie continued on, ostensibly in the direction of her home, which she never reached. Stephanie was carrying several books, including a French textbook, and a purse which contained a wallet, her picture, name and other identification, and a pair of glasses. She was wearing, among other garments, a navy blue cardigan sweater over a white slip–on sweater, a blue cotton skirt, several petticoats, nylon panties and a brassiere. About 4:15 p.m. on the day Stephanie disappeared, several motorists saw a man struggling with a young girl in a car which had stopped suddenly at the side of a road in Contra Costa County, near the Broadway Tunnel, about a mile north of the Claremont Hotel. The girl appeared to be panic stricken. She was in the back seat of the car and the man, who was leaning over the front seat, was striking at her and pulling her down and away from the rear window. She was wearing a navy blue cardigan garment over something white.

A very extensive search was initiated by her parents, the Berkeley Police Department and other agencies, including the FBI. The latter agency got into the case on the theory that she may have been kidnaped, which brought it within their jurisdiction. A substantial reward was offered for information helpful in solving the case. The search continued for three months without any indication as to how, or under what circumstances, she had disappeared, nor was there any indication as to whether she was dead or alive. The investigation was at a dead end.

On the evening of July 15, 1955, three months after Stephanie had disappeared, Burton Abbott, his wife, his mother and a friend, Otto Dezman, a retired Navy veteran, were talking in Abbott's home in Alameda. Abbott's wife was scheduled to take part in a costume show being presented by an organization of which she was a member. She went to the basement of her home, and, while searching through some cartons for costume material, she found a wallet. The wallet contained the name of Stephanie Bryan and a photograph of a young girl, which was later identified as Stephanie Bryan.

Mrs. Abbott came up from the basement and showed the wallet to Abbott, his mother and Dezman saying, “Isn’t Stephanie Bryan the name of the little girl who disappeared in Berkeley?”

Abbott remarked, “Oh, why no, that wasn’t her name,” although the name had been heavily publicized in the media after her disappearance. Abbott also remarked that the wallet probably belonged to some friend of his wife. His wife had no friend with the name of Bryan.

Dezman suggested, “Let’s phone the Berkeley police and find out.”

Whereupon, Mrs. Abbott phoned the Berkeley Police Department and told them about finding the wallet. They instructed her to hold onto it and told her that they would come over in a little while and examine it. They arrived at the Abbott home about an hour later and questioned Abbott, his wife, his mother and Dezman. They all disclaimed any knowledge of how the wallet got into the carton. The police took the wallet with its contents and left.

In questioning Abbott, the police learned that he attended the University of California at Berkeley. He had enlisted in the United States Army on the last day on which enlistees could qualify for GI veteran benefits from the Korean War. Three months after his enlistment, he was hospitalized and later discharged with a diagnosis of tuberculosis. He was again hospitalized in Livermore Veterans Hospital in Alameda County. There he met the girl who became his wife. She was also a patient at the same hospital. She had been a WAC in the Army during the Korean War. After an operation for removal of one lung, Abbott was released from the hospital. For quite a while before Stephanie’s disappearance he had been attending the University of California at Berkeley on GI veterans benefits.

After the finding of the wallet, an investigation of Burton Abbott’s movements disclosed that he was in the habit of having coffee at a doughnut shop on Telegraph Avenue in Berkeley, a half block from the Willard School which Stephanie attended, and that Stephanie and her schoolmates also visited this doughnut shop. Abbott had been in this doughnut shop and had left there at about 3 o'clock the afternoon of Stephanie's disappearance, which occurred shortly after 4 p.m. The University was in a spring recess. He lived in Alameda about eight miles from the University.

Later investigation of Abbott's movements on the day of Stephanie's disappearance disclosed that he had left his home in Alameda at 10 o'clock that morning, bound for Trinity County where the Abbotts had a mountain cabin. He insisted that he had driven from Alameda straight to Sacramento, where he said he called at the State Bureau of Land Management to check on some homestead property, and then drove to the cabin. His brother and sister–in–law had driven to the cabin two days later, on April 30th. On Sunday, May 1st, his brother and his wife in their car and Abbott in his car had returned to Alameda County via Franklin Canyon Road in Contra Costa County.

The day after Burton's wife discovered Stephanie's wallet in their basement, the media had carried stories about the discovery and reviews of facts of Stephanie's disappearance. From this point on, any quiet unhampered police work to develop facts was impossible. Our further investigation was complicated by competing journalistic investigation and conjecture.

A search warrant was obtained for a search of Abbott's automobile and premises in Alameda, and police and FBI agents started searching and digging. In Abbott's backyard some small wooden blocks had been placed in a pattern in the ground in front of a hedge. Al Reck, a veteran police beat reporter and at that time city editor of the *Oakland Tribune*, was in Abbott's yard telling police officers to dig under the blocks and saying, "The body is under the blocks. That's a shrine."

Lights were rigged in the yard to illuminate the diggings, which went on into the night. As it turned out, there was nothing under the blocks but dirt. FBI agents digging in sand in Abbott's basement found school books of Stephanie's and her brassiere and glasses.

Burton Abbott was questioned by FBI agents and me that night.

He denied any knowledge of Stephanie or her disappearance. After we had talked with him for about two hours, Abbott left with his attorney on the understanding that he would be available for further interrogation the next day, at which time I again questioned him and obtained more details of his movements on the day of Stephanie's disappearance.

After the discovery of Stephanie's wallet, the Berkeley Police Department sent two officers to Trinity County to search Abbott's cabin and vicinity. The FBI also sent two men along on the same mission. After four days, the Berkeley police and the FBI agents returned empty handed, without having developed anything of significance.

Ed Montgomery, a Pulitzer prize–winning reporter for the *San Francisco Examiner*, was sent to Trinity County where he employed a man there who owned two dogs which were famous for locating deceased hunters in the mountains. Taken to Abbott's cabin, the dogs ran up the side of a hill, a distance of some 340 feet, and started barking. Montgomery and the owner of the dogs followed them and saw a piece of a shoe sticking out of the ground. It was a low cut brown and white oxford shoe such as Stephanie had been wearing the day she disappeared. Later examination disclosed that in the shoe were the bones of a decomposed foot.

Before notifying police, Montgomery notified his paper, which scooped all the other media. Also before notifying police, representatives of the *Examiner* talked to Abbott and his attorney about the discovery of the shoe sticking out of the ground near his cabin, thus impeding investigation by the police. Word was then relayed to the Berkeley Police Department, which detailed officers to go to Alameda and arrest Abbott.

That night, with Dr. Reginald Hansen, Stephanie's dentist, Dr. George Loquvam, pathologist and medical examiner for Alameda County, and Captain of Inspectors Charles Ryken, I drove to Trinity County, arriving at the cabin at 8 o'clock the next morning. Already, at that early hour, the place was teeming with people. Newsmen, cameramen of *Pathe News* and other media, the sheriff, his men and local citizens were waiting for our arrival. Dr. Loquvam was an able, certified pathologist who had trained in the Western Laboratory of Alameda County under another able pathologist, Dr. Gertrude Moore, who in turn had trained under Dr. O. D. Hamlin, a famous surgeon who for years performed autopsies for Alameda County. Dr. Loquvam had just returned from vacation the night we drove to Trinity County. His availability was fortuitous because he did a very thorough job.

Dr. Loquvam cleared the dirt over, around and under the body. It was badly decomposed. The heat in the Trinity mountains in the summertime is very high—often running over 100 degrees. The skeleton lay on its back in the grave. Except for some skin on the back of a shoulder which had been in contact with the damp bottom of the grave, there was no other skin on the body. The condition of this skin on the back of the shoulder was a factor in determining the time of death. On the day of Stephanie's disappearance and for several days previous it had been raining and snowing in the Trinity mountains and the grave site and hill opposite the cabin had been covered with snow. The grave had been dug and the dead body of Stephanie had been put into the grave and covered over with dirt and snow. Particles of soil had become enmeshed in her cardigan sweater. Her panties which had been cut through the crotch were knotted around her neck and mouth. The rest of the clothing Stephanie was wearing on the day of her disappearance was on the body except for her brassiere which was found in Abbott's basement.

Because of extensive decomposition, it was impossible to determine by a physical examination whether she had been sexually attacked. Stephanie's body had been buried while in a state of *rigor mortis*, and her arms and hands were crossed over her face. There were multiple compound fractures of the skull and two holes about two inches in diameter through the back of her head. Head injuries were the principal cause of her death. From a description of the clothes worn by Stephanie the day of her disappearance it was clear that the clothes on the body were her clothes. Later they were positively identified by her mother.

The body was exhumed and carefully examined by Dr. Loquvam and then taken over by the Trinity County coroner, who took it to Redding for an autopsy. From his office records, Dr. Hansen identified the teeth as Stephanie's. Dr. Loquvam testified that the large hole in the back of her head had been caused by a violent blow from a blunt instrument. Loquvam estimated the time of death as about three months before, which was approximately the time of Stephanie's disappearance.

Under California law the priority of venue or jurisdiction in a murder case is: (1) in the county where the murder was committed, (2) in the county where the victim dies, or (3) in the county where the body is found. A conference with Sterrett Sheppard, district attorney of Trinity County, the sheriff of Trinity County and myself was held, and it was decided that the evidence in the case should be presented to the grand jury in Alameda County. In Trinity County, with its limited budget, where 80% of the land was uninhabited national forest, and where the sparse population was thinly spread over long distances from the county seat, the conditions were such that a case of the obvious dimensions of Stephanie's kidnaping and murder could not be tried conveniently, if at all.

A search of Abbott's car led to the discovery of two hairs which were indistinguishable from Stephanie's and six which were at least very similar to her hair. Eighteen fibers matching those in four of her garments were also found. There was blood deep in the floor mat in the back of the car, and the absence of blood on the surface indicated that the mat had been washed. Abbott's boots were encrusted with red mud which turned out to be the same as a sample of soil taken from Stephanie's grave at a point nine inches below the surface. Several fragments of bloodstained cleansing tissue, which had been carried by a pack rat from the gravesite to a nearby nest, were of the type used by Abbott.

When first questioned by the police, Abbott described in detail the route he said he had taken from his home in Alameda to the cabin in Trinity County. The route which he described would not have taken him through Sacramento. Abbott's brother told the police that Abbott had told him that he had stopped in Sacramento enroute to the cabin. Upon being informed by the police of his brother's statement, Abbott changed his story and said that he had stopped there at the office of the "State Bureau of Land Management" about 4 p.m., gave a description of the office and drew a diagram of it. The next day he said that, although he had gone to Sacramento, he had not been able to find the office.

The case was presented to the grand jury and an indictment was returned charging Abbott with murder and a violation of Section 209 of the Penal Code, viz. kidnaping in which the victim suffers bodily harm. At that time Section 209 of the Penal Code with bodily harm carried a punishment of death or imprisonment in state prison for life without possibility of parole.

At the trial, Burton Abbott testified that he was not in Berkeley on April 28th, that he started for the cabin from his Alameda home about 10:45 a.m., and that, after stopping to say goodbye to his wife at the beauty shop where she was employed, he proceeded to Sacramento, where he made an unsuccessful search for the land office. He said that he then drove north toward Trinity County and stopped at a restaurant about 3 p.m., where he was served by a waitress who had dusty blonde hair and was 25 to 30 years old. He testified that he also stopped at the Wildwood Inn for a drink about 8:30 p.m. and that he then drove 2 miles to the mountain cabin, built a fire and went to bed.

Abbott's account of his activities on April 28th was in conflict not only with the evidence connecting him with Stephanie's disappearance and death but with other testimony as well. He was seen at the state controller's office in Oakland at 1:30 p.m. and at the beauty shop where his wife worked at about 2:30 p.m. There was no waitress on duty between 2 and 10 p.m. in the restaurant north of Sacramento in which he claimed to have stopped at 3 o'clock, and no waitress who looked like the one described by him had been employed there during April of 1955. The manager of the Wildwood Inn and his wife, both of whom knew Mr. Abbott, testified that Abbott was not at the Inn on the night of April 28th. A man who drove past the cabin shortly after 10 o'clock said that he did not smell any smoke and saw no tire tracks, light or other sign of life there. Abbott's account of his activities on April 28th was in conflict with the evidence connecting him with Stephanie's disappearance and death.

A witness identified the auto which Burton Abbott was driving in

Berkeley on the afternoon of Stephanie's disappearance as the car which went through a red light at about 40 miles per hour, cutting across in front of her at the intersection of Ashby and College Avenues. At about this time, Stephanie and her classmate were walking home from school on Ashby Avenue towards the Claremont Hotel. An employee of the Willard School identified Burton Abbott as being in the doughnut shop that afternoon around 3:20 p.m.

A passenger in a passing car identified Burton Abbott as the driver of the car in which Stephanie was seen gazing out of a rear side window in panic on Tunnel Road, not far from Stephanie's home. Five additional persons testified at the trial that they witnessed the struggle between a man and a young girl on Tunnel Road not far from the Claremont Hotel grounds. One of them identified Abbott as the man in the car, another stated that a picture of Abbott published in a newspaper resembled the man, and a third said that the man was about thirty years of age and had a receding hairline like Abbott's. The other two witnesses described the car in which the incident occurred as similar to Abbott's. Tunnel Road leads to Orinda, where an intersecting road leads to Highway 40 (now Interstate 80), which connects with roads which could be used to reach the area in Trinity County in which Abbott's mountain cabin was located.

On May 2nd, at about 7:30 a.m., four days after Stephanie's disappearance and the morning after Abbott's return from his cabin, David Tyree, his wife and their son, Ernest, were driving along Franklin Canyon Road on their way to drop Ernest off at high school. Having taken a certain medicine the night before, David Tyree needed to relieve himself, so he pulled to the side of the road and got out. On returning to the car, he saw a book lying in the weeds alongside the road. He picked up the book and gave it to his son. The book was wrapped with a paper cover, which Ernest removed and threw away. On arriving at school, he placed the book in his locker. Although not noticed immediately, in the book was the name of Stephanie Bryan. It was her French textbook, one of the books she was carrying on her way home when last seen by her schoolmate.

Sometime later, upon reading in the newspaper of Stephanie's disappearance, David Tyree notified the Berkeley police, who secured the book for evidence. During the investigation which followed Abbott's arrest, it was noted that Stephanie's French textbook, which had been discovered early on the morning of May 2nd lying in the weeds beside Franklin Canyon Road, was clean and dry at the time it was found, although it had rained in the area on April 29 and 30, thus indicating that it had been thrown there after April 30th and before May 2nd. On May 1st, while following his brother, Abbott had driven past the spot where it was found.

On May 2nd Abbott returned to the area in Contra Costa County through which he had traveled the day before on his way home from Trinity County. The credit card records of an oil company showed that Burton Abbott had purchased gasoline on May 2nd at a station located near the place where Stephanie's French book had been found earlier that morning. Abbott admitted being in the vicinity between 11 a.m. and 1 p.m., and said he had gone there to purchase used tires. He was unable to name or describe a place where he had stopped to look at tires and he did not purchase any. The area is about twelve miles north of the University where he had classes scheduled at 10, 11 and 1 o'clock. There was a clear implication that Abbott had thrown Stephanie's French book out of his car the evening before while traveling along Franklin Canyon Road, and had returned the next morning to retrieve it.

Details in Abbott's account, before and during his trial, of his movements and activities on April 28th contained many glaringly irreconcilable contradictions. His alibi as to times and places on that date was completely demolished to the extent that, under cross–examination on the witness stand, he finally said he had "compounded the prevarications." By incontrovertible evidence he was identified as Stephanie's kidnaper. After a lengthy trial, Burton Abbott was convicted on both counts and the jury recommended the death penalty.

Superior Court Judge Wade Snook, an able trial judge, denied a motion for a new trial and imposed the death penalty. The automatic appeal, provided for in California law in the event of a death penalty sentence, proceeded. The convictions and sentences were affirmed by the Supreme Court of California. The unanimous decision of this

Court stated, "The evidence is clearly sufficient to support the judgment." A petition for rehearing was denied and petition for *certiorari* was denied by the United States Supreme Court. Burton Abbott was executed in the gas chamber at San Quentin one year after sentence was imposed by the trial Court.

OFFICERS FREY AND HEANES

Another case which was featured in the media involved the shooting of Oakland Police Department officers John Frey and Clifford Heanes by a young black firebrand, Huey Newton, alleged by the media to be a founder and leader of a militant Black Power organization known as the Black Panther Party.

Actually, according to Phillip Luce, ex–Communist consultant to the House Committee on Un–American Activities, this organization had been founded in Alabama by Stokely Carmichael of Student Non–Violent Coordinating Committee (SNCC) fame. When Carmichael's Black Power militancy occupied him in other endeavors and places, Max Stanford, leader of R.A.M. (Revolutionary Action Movement), another Black Power organization advocating violence, became the leader of the Black Panther Party in New York where it rode along more or less on the coattails of R.A.M. under the leadership of Stanford. R.A.M. was described by FBI Director J. Edgar Hoover to a congressional committee as "a highly militant secretive organization following the Chinese–oriented Marxist–Leninist line that believes in replacing capitalism with socialism. It advocates that Negroes arm themselves and fight violence with violence."

Militant Black Power leaders in the West became involved with the Black Panther movement in the East Bay where it established headquarters. The East Bay organization received considerable notoriety when some of the members paraded into the legislative halls of the state Capitol in Sacramento with drawn guns and were arrested by Sacramento police, and when members with guns were arrested for entering the Hall of Justice in Oakland where a case against one of their colleagues was pending. One of the targets of the Black Panther Party in Alameda County was the Oakland Police Department, whose members, according to them, were discriminating against blacks. The west coast Black Panther Party collected considerable money and published an inflammatory paper in which policemen were lampooned as "pigs."

Newton was a native of Oakland, where he received some attention when he was convicted of assault with a deadly weapon for stabbing another black in the head with a knife at a dinner table because his victim disagreed with him in conversation. On another occasion, when a fellow Black Power activist was being arrested by a Berkeley police officer, Newton tried unsuccessfully to snatch the officer's gun from its holster. Although a radical agitator and recipient of much publicity, Newton did not enhance the cause of the civil rights movement. By his wildly inconsistent gibberish and notorious conduct he did damage to the cause, to himself and to his colleagues.

At about 4:50 a.m. on October 28, 1967, Officer John Frey of the Oakland Police Department, patrolling an assigned beat alone in his patrol car deep in a high–crime area in west Oakland, saw a Volkswagen with two men in it moving ahead of him. As was customary under the circumstances, he called the Oakland Police Department on his radio at 4:51 a.m. and requested a routine PIN check on the license number of the Volkswagen. PIN means "Police Information Network"—a computerized system which stores and reports information concerning outstanding warrants associated with identified motor vehicles. (This conversation and those which followed were recorded automatically on tape, and this tape was later identified and entered into evidence at Newton's trial.)

A minute later, Clarence Lord, the Oakland Police Department radio operator, told Frey, "We've got some PIN info coming on that."

Frey: "Check. It's a known Black Panther vehicle . . . I'm going to stop it at 7th and Willow (Streets). You might send a unit by."

Officer Heanes, who was listening to this conversation in his police car on another beat, called in that he was "enroute" to 7th and Willow Streets. This transmission ended at about 4:52 a.m.

Frey asked Lord what he had on the vehicle and the registered owner. Lord gave him the name "Laverne Williams" and asked him if there were a Laverne Williams in the vehicle. Frey replied in the affirmative.

Lord said there were a couple of warrants issued to Laverne Williams. Lord said he would check to see if the warrants were still outstanding, in which event the officer on the street must ascertain if the driver is the person named in the warrants and take appropriate action. Frey then asked Lord for an address and a description of the Laverne Williams and for a birthdate.

Frey: "1 Adam, its the same address he has on his registration, 1114 12th Street."

Lord: "What's his birthdate?"

Fry: "He gave me some phony. I guess he caught on."

Lord: "We're checking him out downstairs. We'll have the info back in a few minutes."

Frey: "Check. Thanks."

The next relevant radio call, received at 5:03 a.m., was a "940 B" (meaning an officer needs help), from Officer Heanes at 7th and Willow Streets.

Officer Heanes testified that he arrived at 7th and Willow in three or four minutes after Frey's "cover call." Frey's police car was parked at the south curb of 7th Street, east of Willow facing east. A Volkswagen was parked directly in front of it, also facing east. Heanes parked his car behind Frey's, alighted and walked to the right rear of the Volkswagen. Two men were seated in the Volkswagen, both in the front seat. Frey was standing near the driver's door writing a citation (Heanes at the trial identified Newton as the driver). Heanes followed Frey to the latter's vehicle where he heard Frey talk to police radio about an address and birthdate. When Frey finished the radio call he told Heanes that the driver, when asked for identification, had produced the Volkswagen registration and had given his name as "LaVerne Williams."

Heanes walked forward to the driver's side of Volkswagen, addressed the driver (Newton) as Mr. Williams and asked if he had any further identification. Newton, still seated in the Volkswagen, said, "I am Huey Newton."

Frey approached the Volkswagen and conversed with Heanes, who asked Newton to get out of the car. Newton asked, "Is there any particular reason why I should."

Heanes asked him "if there was any reason why he didn't want to."

Although neither Frey nor Heanes were aware of it at the time, Newton had a loaded 9mm Luger semi–automatic pistol tucked between his belt and his stomach. For a convicted felon this in itself was a felony. Upon Newton's refusal to get out of the car, Frey informed him that he was under arrest and ordered him out of the car.

Heanes testified that Newton got out and walked "rather briskly in a westerly direction away from the Volkswagen and to the rear of Frey's police car. Frey followed three or four feet behind Newton and slightly to his right. Heanes followed them but stopped at the front end of Frey's police car. Newton walked to the "rear part" of Heanes' car with Frey still behind him. Newton turned around suddenly, assumed a stance with his feet apart, knees flexed, both arms down at hip level in front of his body.

At this point Heanes heard a gunshot and saw Frey fall toward Newton. Heanes then drew his gun in his right hand, and, as he raised his arm, a bullet struck his right forearm. He grabbed his arm (which later medical testimony showed was seriously injured and of no use) momentarily and talked to Newton's passenger, McKinney, who had gotten out of the Volkswagen. This man said he was not armed, that he intended no harm, and raised his hands, which were empty.

Heanes then turned his attention to Frey and Newton, who were "tussling" all over the trunk lid of Heanes' car. At the trial, Heanes testified he next remembered being on his knees at the front door of Frey's car approximately 30—35 feet from Frey and Newton, that Newton was then facing him. Heanes testified that, holding a gun in his left hand, he aimed at Newton's midsection and fired. Newton did not fall. Heanes testified he heard other gunshots from the area where Frey and Newton were tussling. Heanes then called "Emergency . . . 940 B" on Frey's radio, after which he saw two men running westerly toward 7th and Willow.

Henry George,* a black retired Navy Warrant Officer, employed as a bus driver by Alameda County Transit Company, sitting at the wheel of his bus within a few feet of the action, saw Newton walking in front of Frey who was directly behind him. According to George, Newton suddenly pulled a gun from inside his shirt, "spun around" and shot Frey. Heanes, who was two car lengths behind Frey, was also hit and fell. After falling, Heanes drew his gun and fired.

George saw Newton, standing in a crouch, fire several shots into Frey's body as Frey was falling forward onto the street—these shots were fired from within a distance of 4 or 5 feet from the midsection of Frey's body. The last shot was fired by Newton directly into Frey's back while he stood over him as Frey lay face down on the street. After firing this last shot into Frey's back, Newton ran diagonally across 7th Street. At the trial, George positively identified Newton in his account of the shooting.

When Officers Gilbert Dehoyos and Thomas Fitzmaurice arrived at the scene in response to the 940 B call for assistance, they found Frey lying on the street near the rear of Heanes' car. Heanes told them his leg and arm hurt and that Newton had done it. He also said that he fired at Newton and he thought he had hit him.

Frey and Heanes were taken to Merritt Hospital where Frey was dead on arrival. He had been shot five times at approximately the same time but in an unknown order. One bullet entered in the front and exited through the back of his right shoulder (the autopsy surgeon, Dr. Loquvam, testified that this would have immobilized Frey's right arm and hand); another bullet passed through his left thigh; also from front to back; a third (the only one recovered from Frey's body) entered the mid–back and lodged near the left hip; a fourth creased the left elbow; another bullet entered the back, traversed the lungs and exited through the right shoulder in front—this wound caused Frey's death within ten minutes. Heanes had three bullet wounds: one in his right arm, one in the left knee and one in the chest. Heanes almost died and has a permanent disability from the wounds.

Three slugs were recovered—one from Frey's hip, one from Heanes' left knee and a third which had been lodged in the front door of the Volkswagen. In addition, two 9mm Luger shell casings were found at the scene; one was in the street between the two police cars, the other near the left front bumper of Heanes' car and approximately where Frey was lying and where Frey and Newton had been seen tussling. The 9mm bullets had been fired from an automatic. Frey and Heanes carried .38 caliber Smith & Wesson revolvers. A live 9mm Luger cartridge was found on the floor of the Volkswagen. Only Heanes's gun was found; he was holding it when the other officers arrived at the scene. Neither the Luger nor Frey's revolver were ever found.

The location of bullet holes on the clothing and bodies of Frey and Heanes, the testimony of John Davis, criminalist and ballistic expert of the Oakland Police Department, the testimony of Heanes and George, and other testimony, including that of Newton himself, in conjunction with Newton's hair–trigger temper, his violent hatred of police and past history of trying to snatch a gun from a Berkeley police officer, were all consistent. When Newton pulled the gun from his shirt and spun around (George's testimony), he shot Frey in his right arm and shoulder (immobilizing it) and then shot Heanes (immobilizing his right hand and arm). Newton's pistol then jammed. He tussled with Frey while pulling Frey's gun from its holster, then shot Frey and Heanes with Frey's gun. Seeing Frey and Heanes on the ground, Newton ran across the street in possession of his own pistol and Frey's Smith & Wesson, followed by his passenger, McKinney. The two of them then commandeered a car driven by a man named Clinton,* Newton remarking to Clinton that he had just shot a couple of dudes (Clinton's grand jury testimony). He then directed Clinton at gunpoint to drive to a specific street corner in Oakland.

Newton's denial that he shot Frey or Heanes or that he carried a gun was contradicted by George and Clinton (grand jury testimony). Newton's testimony that he was searched by Frey was contradicted by Heanes and George, who both testified that Newton was not searched. Newton's testimony that Frey, while searching him, placed his hands inside Newton's trousers and touched his genitals was utterly absurd and incredible. No police officer, not even a rookie—and Frey was no rookie—would stand behind an arrestee, or in front, and place both his hands inside the arrestee's trousers. Such a procedure would be completely contrary to his training and common sense because the arrestee could spin around and overpower the officer. Furthermore, this testimony was refuted by Heanes and George.

According to Newton's trial testimony, Frey told him that he was under arrest while he was still sitting in the Volkswagen. This was contradicted by Heanes who testified it was he (Heanes) who spoke to Newton, asking him to step out of his car. According to Heanes' testimony, when Newton got out of the Volkswagen he "walked briskly" away from Frey towards the two police cars which were parked to the rear of the Volkswagen, at which time Frey followed him close behind. Frey had no chance to search Newton before he pulled his gun, spun around and shot him. Newton's testimony about Frey placing his hands inside Newton's trousers to touch his genitals was simply ridiculous perjury, concocted to prejudice the jury and was quite in line with usual radical brutality propaganda.

Newton's testimony that Frey, in approaching the Volkswagen, exclaimed "Well, well, well, what do we have here, the great, great Huey Newton," was sheer perjury, contradicted by the dialogue over the police radio between Frey and Lord, and Heanes' testimony.

Heanes testified that after his conversation with Frey upon arrival at the scene, he approached Newton who was sitting in the car, addressed him as "Mr. Williams," and asked if he had any further identification; and that Newton, still seated at the wheel, said, "I am Huey Newton." Newton did not say, "your partner knows who I am," as Newton had testified.

At trial, Newton testified that Frey told him, "You can take that book and stick it up your ass, nigger." According to Newton, Frey then struck him in the face, knocking him to one knee, and shot him—causing a "sensation like . . . boiling hot soup had been spilled on my stomach." Newton further testified that he then heard an "explosion" and a "volley of shots" and crawled and remembered nothing else until he found himself at the entrance of Kaiser Hospital with no knowledge of how he arrived there.

Newton's testimony was completely inconsistent with all the other testimony and evidence in the case. In this day and age, to contend that a police officer would strike a person while interrogating him for a traffic offense and then shoot him is utterly absurd. There was no evidence that Frey or Heanes knew Newton. Further, the fact that Newton, after shooting Frey and Heanes, disarming Frey, then shooting Frey and Heanes with Frey's gun, commandeered Clinton's auto, directed him to a specific location where he got rid of Frey's gun and his own, and then got to Kaiser Hospital where, with characteristic arrogance and vituperative verbal abuse of a nurse, he demanded immediate attention, are wholly at variance with the contention or theory of unconsciousness.

There was no plausible evidence to support an instruction by the trial Court of unconsciousness, and, in fact, defense counsel and Newton stipulated that such instruction not be given by the Court. However, the Appellate Court later held that, regardless of the stipulation, it was the obligation of the trial Court and regardless of how inconsistent with the overall case, it should have given such instruction and it was reversible error not to give it. The unconsciousness and self–defense instructions, first requested by defense counsel and later withdrawn, were likewise inconsistent with Newton's testimony that he had no gun and did no shooting. A defense of unconsciousness implies that the overt act of shooting by the defendant did, in fact, occur. The defense of self–defense likewise implies that the overt act of shooting by the defendant occurred and that the defendant, in shooting, consciously believed that he was in jeopardy of death or bodily harm.

When thc case was presented to the grand jury, Clinton testified that Newton and another man jumped into his car, and, at gunpoint, ordered him to drive to a specific location; and that while in Clinton's car, Newton said he had "just shot a couple of dudes." At the trial, Clinton was called to the witness stand by the prosecution and said he could not remember anything about the case.

Lowell Jensen, the prosecutor, tried to refresh Clinton's recollection by showing him his grand jury testimony and asking him to read it. Clinton said he could not read. Then Jensen read his testimony from the grand jury and asked if his recollection was refreshed after hearing it read. Again he insisted that he could not remember anything about the case. Consequently, the trial Court had to dismiss the count charging Newton with kidnaping Clinton.

Newton was convicted of manslaughter at his first trial and, pending a successful appeal, served two and a half years in state prison. His second and third trials ended in hung juries. At this point the case was dismissed on a motion of District Attorney Lowell Jensen.

In reversing the conviction in the first trial, the District Court of Appeal gave as its reason that the trial Court should have given the unconsciousness instruction, although defense counsel and the defendant had stipulated that it not be given. The District Court of Appeals also held that Jensen's reading of Clinton's testimony should not recur if the defendant was retried, although under the circumstances the reading was approved standard procedure. Later, Clinton informed the District Attorney's Office that the reason for his lapse of memory was that he had been intimidated and threatened with death.

McKinney, Newton's passenger in the Volkswagen, disappeared. He was unknown to the prosecution, and was unavailable to the police or the prosecution before the trial. At the trial, he appeared with counsel as a defense witness, and, after giving his name, refused to testify. He stood on the Fifth Amendment. Granted immunity by the prosecution and the Court, he still refused and was sentenced to jail for contempt. However, he still would not testify. At the next trial, he was again accompanied by counsel and again refused to testify on Fifth Amendment grounds that his testimony would incriminate him.

After the third trial for the murder of Officer Frey, Newton became enraged when Katherine Smith, one of a group of street prostitutes, addressed him as "baby" when he was driving past the group. He jumped out of his car and shot her point blank in the face, inflicting a wound from which she died. He was charged with murder for this shooting.

Ten days later, Newton, while bickering with his tailor over the price of a suit of clothes, claimed he was being ripped off. The tailor, an elderly man named Preston Callins, in a friendly vein said, "Oh, baby, don't feel that way." Whereupon, Newton struck Callins violently about the head and face several times with a pistol, inflicting serious injuries, including multiple fractures of his skull.

For this he was charged with assault with a deadly weapon and a violation of the Penal Code section prohibiting a convicted felon from carrying a gun. Newton then fled to Cuba, where he stayed for two years. His bail on the charges was forfeited. After he returned from Cuba, the charges in the murder of Katherine Smith and the assault on Callins were set for preliminary hearings.

Shortly before the preliminary hearing on the murder of Katherine Smith charge, an attempt by three masked men to kill Crystal Gray, one of the prospective prosecution witnesses occurred, during which attempt, through some mistake, one of the assassins, a Black Panther, was killed by a gun blast apparently fired by one of his comrades. Two weeks later, a Panther named Nelson Malloy was left for dead under a pile of rocks in a Nevada desert near Las Vegas. He had been shot several times. As a result of the wounds, he is paralyzed for life from the neck down.

Newton was tried before a jury and retired Judge Joseph Karesh from San Francisco, who was assigned by the California Judicial Council, on the charges of assaulting his tailor and two counts of possession of guns by a convicted felon.

The tailor, called as a witness by Thomas Orloff, the prosecutor, refused to testify on the grounds his testimony might incriminate him, although he was the victim and not charged with any crime. He persisted in his refusal, and was sent to jail for contempt of court for the duration of the trial. Much later, the police were informed that the tailor (who had since died) had received $6,000 which, along with fear of reprisal, influenced his refusal to testify.

At the trial, Newton was acquitted on the assault charge and convicted on two counts of being a convicted felon in possession of a gun. When Judge Karesh remanded him to the county jail pending sentence, Newton repeatedly insulted the Court by flagrantly contemptuous references to the judge's Jewish faith and integrity. A verbatim transcription from the court record of Newton's vitriolic attack on Judge Karesh reflects his attitude and character better than a summary description of the episode: see Appendix E.

Incredibly, following his release and during an extended period of court delays in his cases in the late 1970's, Newton attended classes at the University of California at Santa Cruz, where he was awarded a Ph.D. in 1980. That a person with such mentality and attitude could attain leadership of the Black Panther Party and the Black Power movement, and receive, without generally prescribed credentials, a degree of Ph.D., even from the liberal Santa Cruz branch of the University of California, is difficult to understand. Really, his only claim to fame was the fact that he had killed a police officer by shooting him in the back and had inflicted permanent disability upon another police officer.[30]

AMBUSH IN WEST OAKLAND

On the evening of April 6, 1968, two nights after the assassination of Martin Luther King, Edson Compton,* another leader in the Black Panther Party, met with a group of blacks in Oakland. According to one of the group, Compton said, "We are going to kill some pigs tonight." They were armed with rifles, shotguns and pistols. They got into four automobiles. In addition to the weapons carried by the members of the group, the trunk compartment of one of the four cars, a Toyota, was loaded with a variety of firearms.

For some time before this date, certain members of the Black Panther Party had been carrying guns—allegedly for defense against policemen. Among more militant Black Panthers were those who advocated killing "pigs" (policemen) and "honkies" (whites). They also advocated burning down buildings owned by whites and they graffitied buildings, fences and telephone poles with the words "Burn, Baby, Burn."

Under the leadership of Compton, they cruised around Oakland to a street in west Oakland where three of the cars parked, bumper to bumper, along the curb. The occupants got out of the cars with weapons in hand, and took up positions on the street, around the cars

[30][Publisher's note: At around dawn on the morning of August 22, 1989, Newton was himself shot to death, ostensibly in a dispute over drugs, on an Oakland street corner not far from the scene of the Frey and Heanes shooting. The shooter was Tyrone Robinson, a young street hoodlum apparently anxious to make a name for himself as the man who shot Huey Newton.]

and on the sidewalk. An Oakland Police Department patrol car containing Officers Nolan Darnell and Richard Jensen hove into sight, at which point one of the Panther group moved furtively out from between two of the three cars and then moved quickly back in. Whether this was a decoy movement designed to ensnare the policemen is not known, but it certainly served the purpose of a decoy and the ambush which followed.

Darnell, suspecting a stolen car might be involved, stopped his police car parallel to the three parked cars and stepped out into the street. As he did so, shots flashed from the direction of the Panther cars, seriously wounding both Darnell and Jensen.

Darnell was able to call for help on the police radio and returned fire. A fusillade of bullets hit the police car from various angles. Forty–nine bullet holes were later found in the police car—the location of the bullet holes clearly indicated an ambush attack from all sides.

As responding patrol cars began to arrive, the Panther group fled in various directions, some barging into nearby homes where they were later found hiding under beds and in basements.

Compton and another young black, Bobby Hutton, were seen to run into the basement of a house around the corner from where the ambush of Darnell and Jensen occurred. Arriving policemen began shooting tear gas into the basement into which Compton and Hutton had fled. Many shots were fired from this basement, and an Oakland policeman's cap was pierced by an emerging bullet. Exploding tear gas canisters ignited a fire in the basement, which filled with smoke.

A pistol and a military rifle sailed out of the basement door, followed by Compton, naked with his hands in the air, and Hutton, who made a dash to escape and was shot by policemen from the Oakland or Emeryville departments who had responded to the emergency calls. Hutton later died.

An AR–15 rifle and bullet casings from the AR–15 and the pistol were found inside the basement. Both of these weapons had been fired. In the trunk of the fourth Panther car, parked two blocks from the ambush, were eight loaded rifles and shotguns.

Compton and seven of his group, including a notorious Black Power militant who had threatened to kill the President of the United States, were arrested and indicted on charges of attempting to murder Darnell and Jensen. Darnell had been shot in the shoulder and Jensen had been hit by bullets in eight places. In addition to the 49 bullet holes in their patrol car, clearly indicating that during the ambush the assailants had surrounded the car while shooting, 64 expended bullet casings were found on the street and sidewalk close to the patrol car. It was clearly a conspiracy to commit murder of police officers. The grand jury also filed with the indictment a document exonerating the policemen of unlawful conduct in the shooting of Hutton.

A radical Left attorney was quoted in the media alleging in broad sweeping terms that Oakland policemen were "murderers." A liberal faction of a black organization denounced the shooting of Hutton and the action of the grand jury exonerating the police.

At the time of the ambush, Compton was on parole from state prison on a charge of assault with intent to commit murder. He also had a prior criminal record for burglary and a narcotics offense. Compton's parole was revoked by the Adult Authority and, while out on bail of $50,000 awaiting trial, he fled to Cuba and Africa and was a fugitive for seven years. His bail was forfeited by the Court.

Eight of the ambushing group, including Compton, were linked by abundant criminalistic evidence to the guns, ammunition and the Panther cars from which they had fired at the scene. Seven of the group were convicted and sentenced to jail. Compton, upon his return to the United States, pleaded guilty, and received probation without jail time.

CORRUPTION IN THE ASSESSOR'S OFFICE

A case involving Truett,* the county assessor of Alameda County, was another important impact case because of the far–reaching effect it had on real and personal property tax law and reform of assessment procedures in California.

Late in the afternoon of July 21, 1965, Michael Harris, a feature writer for the *San Francisco Chronicle*, came to the District Attorney's Office of Alameda County and said that, through the cooperation of Thorpe and Cummings, attorneys in San Leandro, he had seen certain files of a tax consultant named Campbell,* and that what he had seen indicated that people in the assessor's offices of the city and county of San Francisco and the county of Alameda had been receiving bribes from Campbell in connection with assessments of real and personal property. He said that he had reported the substance of his inspection of the records to the district attorney of San Francisco and that he was going to break a story about the case in the *San Francisco Chronicle.*

The San Leandro attorneys said that Norman Phillips, an employee of Campbell, was the source of their information as to alleged bribes and that their examination of Campbell's records supported Phillips' story. Because of a disagreement with Campbell over compensation for his work, Phillips, while Campbell was on vacation, moved all of Campbell's records to Cummings' office. Upon discovery of the theft of his records, Campbell had filed suit in Alameda County Superior Court for recovery of the records. This action had been pending for some time before Judge William McGuiness.

At our request, Judge McGuiness made an order impounding the records and issued a search warrant for seizure of the records, placing them in the custody of inspectors in our office so that we could examine them conveniently. A thorough inspection and audit of the records were made and results of our inspection were made available to district attorneys of other jurisdictions in which Campbell had had questionable relations with county assessors or people in their offices.

Campbell at one time had been employed in the Assessor's Office of Alameda County. He left the office to go into the tax consultant business. His business prospered and he acquired clients throughout California and other states.

Efforts by Campbell's counsel to recover Campbell's records failed. Our examination of the records confirmed the statements of

Phillips, Cummings, Thorpe and Harris. With the records in our hands and Phillips' corroboration of them, Campbell was in a bind. Upon advice of his attorney, he agreed to testify for the prosecution in any county in which his testimony was needed. His agreement to testify was made without any promise of immunity or compromise other than a statement to be made to the Court as to the extent of this cooperation as a prosecution witness.

Campbell's records indicated that he had made payments to Truett and assessors in other counties in connection with reductions of assessments. The records indicated that he had paid Truett $16,000, although Truett later said it was only $10,000. Truett put $10,000 cash in a box in his basement. Grimsby, another one–time employee of the Alameda County Assessor's Office and later a private tax consultant, obtained $5,000 of this $10,000 from Truett.

Truett's case was a sad one. He and his first wife had four children. She had died after a long siege of cancer, which had cost him a lot of money in medical bills. He had worked with Campbell in the Assessor's Office and they were close friends. He may have rationalized his acceptance of Campbell's payments in the vein of campaign contributions or gratuities, although it was clear they were connected with reductions of assessments of properties of Campbell's clients. To his credit, it should be said that he did not perjure himself either at the grand jury or at his trial. He simply did not testify in either proceeding. He was convicted and sentenced to state prison. He did not appeal. Two other members of the Assessor's Office were indicted for aiding and abetting and pleaded guilty. They did not appeal.

Working with Campbell's records in our office, district attorneys in San Francisco and San Diego counties put together cases in which their grand juries returned indictments and which resulted in convictions. Campbell also cooperated and testified as needed in several counties and in Oregon and Washington. He pleaded guilty to charges against him in Alameda County. He was sentenced to county jail and a long period of probation.

Truett testified truthfully before the grand jury in a case against

Grimsby, who pleaded guilty and was sentenced to state prison. A powerful political leader and long–time assessor of the city and county of San Francisco was tried, convicted and sentenced to state prison, as were members of the Assessor's Office of San Diego County. The Assessor of that county committed suicide before trial. A tax consultant in Portland, Oregon, who had practiced in the Northwest, pleaded guilty and cooperated in the prosecution of cases which contributed to improvement of property tax law and assessment procedures throughout the West.

After the trials, *The Saturday Evening Post* carried an article in which it said corruption in property assessments nationwide and payoffs by tax consultants were bigger than the Teapot Dome scandal. At least as to Alameda County, this was an exaggeration, if $10,000 was the extent of the bribery as stated by Truett or $16,000 as indicated by Campbell's records.

During the course of the investigation, I recommended that the books of the Assessor's Office be audited and a complete reassessment made, correlated to the assessment in Campbell's records. This phase of the investigation disclosed that under–assessment of certain properties had resulted in under–payment of taxes on real and personal properties of about two million dollars. Alameda County recovered this amount. The deficiency in San Francisco was a great deal more. Campbell, through his expert knowledge and experience with respect to comparative property values and assessment procedures, was able to effect reductions in assessments in many cases by showing that the properties were over–assessed and that the subsequent reductions were legitimate.

As a result of the publicity generated by this case, legislation was enacted providing that the California state Board of Equalization require each county to assess up to 25% of actual market value of the property. This proved to be a windfall for local governments hungering for more tax money. The cities and counties, in their ever–expanding budgets and unending search for more tax revenues, seized on this, and assessors throughout the state, year after year, increased assessed property values which, with the inflated value of the real estate market, brought on greatly increased taxes on homes and precipitated the Constitutional Amendment known as Proposition 13.

The prosecutions of the County Assessor, his colleagues, and Campbell were most ably handled with characteristic competence by the late Assistant District Attorney Frank Vukota, a prodigious worker and able trial lawyer, who preferred to try cases alone. In the preparation and trial of these Assessor's Office cases, he was assisted by Deputy District Attorney Marie Collins, who is now a Superior Court judge.

7

Riots & Demonstrations

The 1960's were difficult years for peace officers, prosecutors and judges. They were years of mounting discontent, open defiance, disrespect for law, and massive protest against government and business, accompanied by both violence and non–violence. At times, there seemed to be an epidemic of unlawful picketing, trespass, lie–ins, sit–ins, rioting, looting, arson, destruction of property, and felonious assault.

Arrests had to be made, and cases had to be prosecuted and adjudicated. Already congested court calendars became more congested. Excessive numbers of criminal cases went up to higher courts before they could be finalized. Courts on trial and appellate levels were swamped with pretrial and after–trial motions made and appeals taken, frequently without merit, by self–styled public interest lawyers, often paid by government. Policemen, highway patrolmen and deputy sheriffs had to be called away from their beats to work at overtime scales, leaving areas of their regular duty unpatrolled and unprotected, all in the shadow of alleged abuse of civil rights, constitutional law and justice, while concerted violations of the legal rights of the law–abiding by various dissident groups were featured in the media.

Ideas and emotions involved in group criminal activity under the direction of irresponsible leadership is a contagion which can spread fast and erupt in dangerous overt mob action that is very difficult to control. Such contagion can also spawn additional individual criminal conduct in major crime categories, such as burglary, robbery, assault and murder. Some persons and segments of the media labeled crime committed in the course of collective protest "political crime," as if to minimize its impact and excuse its criminality.

In certain portions of societal leadership, as regards their inherent responsibility and obligation to restrain collective criminal protest and the proliferation of individual criminal activity, there was at least an acquiescence if not a condonation. Certainly, the influence of parents, teachers, clergy and government waned, and attitudes of youth toward personal and property rights deteriorated. Juvenile delinquency, long a growing problem of law enforcement, increased as neglected children of absent fathers and working mothers moved into their teens in the 1960's.

The events of the 1960's reflected the impact of the persistent Communist effort since World War I to undermine and destroy the democratic system. Their propaganda influenced many persons on many levels and in many places, high and low, as a younger generation known as the "New Left"—not Communist Party members—tried to assume, and often did assume, leadership of the collective protest movement. They were bolder and more openly defiant than old time Party members whose support and encouragement they received. They wanted change in the existing order of things and they wanted it without delay. Many were Marxists and avowed revolutionaries, professional demonstrators and agitators. Many were new–found amateurs who relished the sounds of their own voices, gloated in media exposure and the acclaim of countless receptive audiences, sometimes of sincere well–meaning persons.

A few years after the Communist Party was organized in the United States, San Francisco became the permanent headquarters of District 13 of the Party, which covered California, Arizona, Nevada and Hawaii. Members of the Party and its affiliates became quite active in the Bay Area. Some joined others from around the United States in attending the Lenin Institute in Moscow where they were taught techniques of subversion and revolution. Upon returning to the United States, they practiced what they had been taught, viz. go for the jugular of class and political differences by exploiting various movements: racial and ethnic, youth, labor, education, and even religion. Although relatively small in numbers, by devious methods—deception, intimidation, blackmail and violence—they succeeded in spreading dissension, distrust and confusion.

Some leaders of the so–called "Black Power" and other racial militancy movements reached extreme positions of advocacy. Bill Epton, who in his role as a revolutionary was a member of the Chinese Communist–oriented Progressive Labor Party, told a rally in Harlem one hour before the Harlem riots started:

> "We will not be fully free until we smash this state completely and destroy it and set up a new state of our own choosing and own liking . . . and in the process of smashing this state we're going to have to kill a lot of these cops, a lot of these judges, and we'll have to go up against their army. We'll organize our own militia and our own army."

For two hundred years a melting pot of many races and cultures, California was ripe for the explosion of collective protest. During the Depression, there had been heavy migration of persons from other states. During World War II this movement increased, especially from the deep South, where substantial numbers of migrants had not enjoyed the amount of freedom and largess which they experienced for the first time in California. After World War II, as work in shipyards, aircraft factories and other war–related industries slackened, large numbers of people from other states who had come to work in California remained and became unemployed. Others flocked in to take advantage of an accelerating welfare program, one of the most generous in the nation. Southern California, particularly, and the area on the east side of San Francisco Bay had long been a mecca for eccentrics, bigots, and dissidents as well as ethnic and racial minorities.

SLATE

During the 1950's, a student organization on the Berkeley campus of the University of California known as "Slate" began to hold daily meetings in front of Sather Gate, the main entrance to the university. Acclaimed repeatedly by the campus newspaper, the *Daily Californian*, and other publications, this was part of the beginning of the so–called New Left. From a voice amplification–equipped platform adjacent to Sather Gate, on university property and in front of which thousands of students passed daily, radical firebrands—non–students as well as students—criticized university officials, university administrative policies and various and sundry political conditions of the community, state and nation.

Slate became a campus political organization that grew into an amalgam of groups espousing various causes, including civil rights and ending discrimination against blacks. At this time there were few blacks enrolled in the university. Eventually, students and non–students were using the university and its facilities as a launching pad from which to harass business and government in off–campus communities. They constituted a small percentage of the student body, but they were well schooled in techniques of agitation and of how to dramatize and publicize their protests. Day after day, month after month, they hammered away at the university, which was portrayed as representing "the evil Establishment of Capitalism."

Slate became a close–knit and well–disciplined organization with a publication and a slate of candidates for office in the official university student body organization. Although the Berkeley campus enrollment exceeded 25,000, the average student was apathetic and did not bother to vote at campus elections—the usual total of votes being between 2,000 and 3,000. The radicals did vote and Slate candidates were often elected. Slate activists joined early on in the "Fair Play for Cuba" movement and conducted a public rally for that movement at the San Francisco Civic Center.

In May 1960, the Un–American Activities Committee of the United States House of Representatives met at the San Francisco City Hall in the meeting room of the Board of Supervisors, which was on the same floor as many of the courts. Slate, which had long been advocating abolition of the House Un–American Activities Committee, recruited students from the university and other schools to appear at the San Francisco City Hall to demonstrate against the Committee. Large numbers of university students responded, and, with hundreds of others, proceeded to interrupt the meeting of the Committee by loud and boisterous conduct. This was obviously a well–planned collective demonstration in protest of the hearing. The noise and activity of the demonstrators disrupted the business of the courts and the Committee hearings.

Police were summoned to restrain the disturbance. The demonstrators refused to disperse and forcefully resisted the police. Many of the demonstrators went limp and had to be carried or dragged bodily out of the building. One policeman was hit on the head with a club and seriously injured. Finally, after prolonged efforts by the police to restrain the demonstrators, they were flushed out of the City Hall with fire hoses and two hundred of them were put into police vehicles and taken to the Hall of Justice, where they were booked on a number of applicable charges. With the exception of the person who struck the policeman with a club, charges against those arrested were dropped.

SAN FRANCISCO'S TURN

On September 27, 1966, a riot occurred in the Hunters Point area of San Francisco. In this area were a U.S. Navy shipyard and large public housing facilities occupied by blacks who had come to San Francisco during World War II and remained. The trouble started one unusually warm autumn afternoon when a policeman shot and killed a young car thief who, with his confederates, was running away from a stolen car after being ordered to halt. Within minutes, word of the incident spread through the black community. Within hours, the area was seething with ominous signs of massive retaliation. A state of emergency was declared and a curfew invoked. Major disaster services were alerted and extraordinary police and fire protective measures were activated.

There was much window smashing, looting, burning, shooting, throwing of rocks, bottles and sundry missiles at police and firemen and at police and fire department vehicles. Many persons were injured. City officials and civic leaders of San Francisco went all out to placate and appease the black communities of the Hunters Point and Fillmore districts. The holocaust of the riot in the Watts district of Los Angeles (August 1965) was still fresh in the minds of everyone, especially the police and fire department personnel.

The rioting lasted from September 27, 1966, when the shooting occurred, through October 2, when the state of emergency was lifted. The California National Guard and the California Highway Patrol were called and responded. These agencies remained on duty until October 2nd. When the rioting subsided and extraordinary emergency operations were reduced, the mayor declared an amnesty as to those arrested and the arrestees were released. There were no prosecutions.

Later, the Park District police station in San Francisco was bombed and a policeman was killed. The criminals who committed this bombing and murder were never apprehended. A policeman sitting at his desk in another San Francisco precinct station was shot and killed. The killer or killers were not apprehended.

A mass demonstration against alleged discrimination in employment of blacks occurred at the Palace Hotel in San Francisco in which demonstrators sat and lay on lobby floors, steps and elevators, obstructing business. The District Attorney's Office of San Francisco first brought a civil action to enjoin the demonstration. Because of legal technicalities encountered, this action was abandoned. Whereupon, arrests were made, followed by criminal charges and prosecutions.

Immediately following the Palace Hotel sit–in/lie–in episode, came sit–in/lie–in demonstrations in automobile show rooms on "automobile row." Simultaneously, sit–in demonstrations protesting alleged employment discrimination against blacks occurred at certain drive–in restaurants. During the sit–in/lie–in cases, hundreds of demonstrators were arrested, charged and prosecuted. They had committed crimes of trespass and public nuisance. Jury trials were requested. Court calendars were jammed. Judges from other counties were assigned to preside over cases in San Francisco. The Municipal Court of San Francisco was bogged down for about a and the additional cost to law enforcement exceeded a million dollars.

THE FREE SPEECH MOVEMENT

For many years, the Communist Party of the United States, through its leader, Gus Hall, and others, had been stressing the necessity for the Party to recruit youths on American campuses. Situated as it was across the Bay from the west coast headquarters of the Party and in a community well peopled with Communists, socialists, radicals and other militant liberals, the University of California at Berkeley, one of the largest educational institutions in the nation, was a natural target for the Communist program of youth regimentation. Under continuous pressure from the Left, the Regents' policy against the use of university facilities and property for off–campus causes had eroded and become almost completely ineffective.

The report of a Special Committee, appointed in December 1964 by the Board of Regents to assess unrest on the Berkeley campus, states:

> ". . . to be sure, the administration's handling of the crisis (on the campus in 1964) was indecisive, vacillant and ineffective."[37]

The report indicated that there was dissatisfaction among the students with the system of instruction at the University, which caused a small group of dissidents to focus on educational reform.

The report concluded that:

> ". . . a variety of individuals and groups of a revolutionary Marxist persuasion participated in the demonstrations and in the Free Speech Movement (FSM) leadership, but that the Marxists

[37]Byrne, Jerome C., *Report on the University of California and recommendations to the Special Committee of the Regents of the University of California* (Berkeley, 1965), p. 60.

did not succeed in gaining any kind of control of events, nor indeed did anyone else."[38]

A study by a major national news magazine, discussing Marxist exploitation of campus discontent, quoted Robert Finch, Secretary of the U. S. Department of Health, Education and Welfare as acknowledging that:

"there are some hard–core militants in the SDS[39] who think they can contest, challenge, overthrow these institutions as we know them. . . . The basic problem goes to the higher educational institution, its rigidity and its unwillingness to respond to the demands of the community around it and the students.

"As students became frustrated with their seeming inability to 'get through' to their elders, their tactics became more extreme. In 1964, students at the University of California at Berkeley protested against a university ban prohibiting on–campus political activity. The protest developed into a massive confrontation between students and the administration. Eventually the university was paralyzed, Berkeley made students aware of their potential power, and the students applied this lesson to campuses across the country, all the way to Columbia, on the East Coast. . . .

"University presidents, while trying to avoid the use of outside force, are nevertheless subject to acute provocation by extremists of all Marxist groups. As student leadership becomes increasingly radical, the thrust of campus activity shifts from satisfaction of student needs to fulfillment of Communist political objectives.

"Thus, Marxist extremists are rioting on campuses not to get more rights for students but to get more students for Communist and Marxist movements.

"They are interested in civil rights not to help the black man but to help the Communists multiply their numbers so they will be able to produce a revolution.

"And they are interested in peace movements not so much to end the war in Vietnam as to strengthen communism in the United States.

"In short, any riot, any protest, and any demonstration—whether

[38]Byrne, p. 57.

[39]Students for a Democratic Society—a national New Left group

> for sex, miniskirts, hot air, or cold air—is worthy of support by the Old Left and the New Left so long as the net result serves the Communist objectives: to alienate students from the 'establishment,' radicalize them with Marxist dogma, and then throw them into the 'war against capitalism.'"

In my view of the situation, old–time Communist party members did not take over control at Berkeley although they were quite active and in the background. This was done by a new breed of young activists who quickly and aggressively exploited a situation which had been simmering for a long time.

The 13th Report of the California Senate Factfinding Subcommittee on Un–American Activities had the following to say concerning the erosion over the years of the administration of President Clark Kerr on the Berkeley campus:

> "The gates have been thrown open to Communists, faculty members, students, and anyone else who cares to utilize the university property as a brawling ground for political controversy. Now that the gates have been swung wider and written propaganda has been accorded free access to the university and students, it takes very little imagination to determine what disciplined, dedicated, organized subversive group will be delighted to take advantage of the opportunity. If this is the only way that absolute freedom of speech and freedom of expression can be assured to the state university and its faculty and its students, we wonder how it is that there have been so many successful, well–oriented, unhampered graduates of this institution during the years of its existence when it functioned as a great educational institution and its facilities were not thrown open to this type of controversial and radical agitation."[40]

By the time the Fall semester arrived in September 1964, university students and hanger–on non–students, who had cut their teeth on civil rights marches, picketing, sit–ins, lie–ins and other varieties of collective protest, were ready for action at the university. All they

[40]*Thirteenth Report of the Senate Factfinding Subcommittee on Un–American Activities* (Sacramento, California Senate, 1965) p. 76.

needed was a cause. This they found in a letter promulgated by Dean of Students Katherine A. Towle, a fine lady and a distinguished educator, which announced a rule against solicitation of money at Sather Gate without any accounting or university approval and a statement by Chancellor Edward M. Strong to the effect that university facilities were not to be used for mounting of social and political actions directed at the surrounding communities.

During the Fall semester in 1964, the first serious demonstration after a number of skirmishes occurred adjacent to Sather Gate on Sproul Plaza in front of Sproul Hall (the Administration Building) on October 1st. This episode was precipitated by the refusal of Jack Weinberg, a non–student New Left activist, to desist from collecting money for the Congress on Racial Equality (CORE) at a card table in an area proscribed by Dean Towle's letter.

After Weinberg was told a number of times to remove the table and stop collecting, a police car pulled up near the table and campus police arrested Weinberg who went limp as he was placed in the car by the police. Immediately, the car was surrounded by demonstrators, some of whom sat or lay on the ground so that the car could not move. More campus police were called and responded, to no avail. They were greatly outnumbered by demonstrators, who kept the police car surrounded throughout the night and into the next day.

Earlier in the day, Mario Savio and other leaders of the demonstration had arrived with loudspeaker equipment, and, using the top of the police car as a platform, they proceeded to regale the constantly increasing crowd of students and non–students—some of whom were actually demonstrators, some of whom were curious, some of whom were amused at the impotence of the police and the university, and some of whom were appalled at the amazing turn of events. Sproul Plaza for some years had been a haven for a motley group of non–students of college, pre–college and post–college ages, who were prone to join any kind of demonstration, regardless of the merits of the issue.

The large amount of exposure given by the media to various mass protests undoubtedly helped to attract and swell the crowds. Police from the city of Oakland, some five miles away, and the sheriff's department of Alameda County were summoned. They appeared and stood ready to assist campus and Berkeley police in dispersing the crowd and, if necessary, in making arrests.

Over a period of a week, demonstrations, many of which exceeded reasonable bounds, had been tolerated by the university, and some concessions had been made by university authorities. However, while the police waited in sweltering heat for word to go into action, University President Clark Kerr vacillated and invited Mario Savio and other leaders of the demonstration to a conference in the Administration Building, where the demonstration leaders agreed to disperse under certain conditions. One of these conditions was that the university would not press criminal charges against non–student Weinberg.

Savio emerged, climbed on top of the police car, and made a rable–rousing speech to the effect that the university had capitulated. The Oakland police and Alameda County sheriff's officers departed, thoroughly disgusted with the situation.

After the demonstration terminated, President Kerr remarked to the press that there were followers of the Castro–Mao Communist line deep in the hardcore of the demonstration, which was labeled the "Free Speech Movement" by its leaders and by the *Daily Californian*, the campus student newspaper. President Kerr later retracted his statement about Communist involvement. The label "Free Speech Movement," or "FSM," was adopted by the off–campus media. It was, in fact, a rebellion and was so–called by the California Senate Factfinding Subcommittee on Un–American Activities. In their 13th Report, the following statement appears:

> "An entire volume could—and should—be written about the effect of Castro Communism on the youth of America. President Kerr recognized the impact, very late, when he declared these highly indoctrinated Castroites to be at the heart of the Berkeley Rebellion."[41]

As so–called "civil disobedience" demonstrations over alleged dis-

[41]California Senate (1965), p. 79.

crimination against blacks increased, student radicals at the University of California continued to use campus facilities as launching pads for off–campus protest activities, which sometimes became illegal and were of considerable trouble and expense to merchants and police.

Although not precisely enunciated by the leaders of the Free Speech Movement, there was at the time some legitimate ground for protest. As the university had grown by leaps and bounds and the faculty had ballooned, the relationship between teacher and pupil had deteriorated. Professors and associate professors, engaged in supplementing their salaries by extra–curricular activities, were seeing less of their classes, which too often were being conducted by youthful teaching assistants who, in many cases, were students doing post–graduate work. Too many professors were absent from too many office hours. But to the hardcore leaders of the Free Speech Movement, the essence of the FSM was a protest against the government generally and what they called the "Establishment," which they wanted to tear down and change without any specifics as to what they would put in its place. This was demonstrated by the fact that after each concession by the university to their demands, they would invent new ones or revise old ones in such a way that the university could not accept them.

Mario Savio, Bettina Aptheker (daughter of Herbert Aptheker, theoretician of the American Communist Party), Arthur Goldberg, Jack Weinberg and other leaders of the Free Speech Movement continued to meet at Sproul Plaza in front of the Administration Building, where they would harangue the thousands of students crossing the Plaza on their way to and from classes. In defiance of university regulations, tables were set up and manned daily in front of the Administration Building on the Plaza. Spurious solicitations continued, ostensibly for a variety of radical causes and organizations, with no accounting.

Governor Edmund G. Brown Sr. meanwhile declared, "This is not a matter of freedom of speech on the campuses," but "purely and simply an attempt on the part of the students to use the campuses of the university unlawfully by soliciting funds and recruiting students for off–campus activities. This will not be tolerated. We must have—and continue to have—law and order on our campuses."

After the October 2nd demonstration and agreement, the FSM leaders began preparations for a future confrontation, which they knew they would provoke. In the meantime, FSM leaders were stationing tables, soliciting funds, programming rallies and beseeching the passing thousands of students and onlookers on Sproul Plaza. After the October 2nd agreement between the leaders of the rebellion and President Kerr, relations between the university and local government—already strained—worsened.

A week later, Ed Meese and I met with Kerr and Thomas Cunningham, legal counsel for the university, to discuss the situation. At this meeting, I said that the trouble had not been settled by the agreement and would continue; that more demands, some of which would be completely unreasonable, would be made; that regardless of concessions and modifications made by the university, an impasse would be reached at which point there would be another eruption; and that the police from Berkeley, Oakland, Alameda County and other departments would again have to be called upon for help.

If arrests were made, the District Attorney's Office would have to prosecute. As counsel to the sheriff, we were already involved. I urged the president to finalize university disciplinary procedures according to legal and constitutional principles of due process and to begin using them. I said that the burden of combating mass turbulence resulting from plans made by students using university facilities should not be imposed upon local and state governments, compelling them to divert their much–needed manpower and resources from normal pursuits in order to maintain peace on the campus and process student on–campus misconduct in the already overburdened courts.

California law enforcement was not about to buy left–wing demands that police be barred from college property or demands that a campus be made a sanctuary where students and faculty could violate the law with impunity. After the meeting, I advised the chiefs of the campus police, the Berkeley police, the Oakland police, the sheriff's department and the California Highway Patrol to prepare for another confrontation, so that, if and when it came and mass arrests were made, there would be no question as to sufficiency of proof and identification. In this regard, provision was to be made to photograph each arrestee at the scene. At the time this was a novel procedure.

Arrests, if made, were to be according to law with no physical abuse and with availability of doctors in the event anyone claimed to be injured. As was well known, it was common practice among radicals when arrested to charge "police brutality."

Preparations were begun, and when the next mass arrests became necessary, law enforcement officers were ready and performed so well that when time came for trial, the proof of guilt was irrefutable and there was no basis for claims of police brutality. In fact, no such claims were made.

On November 4, 5 and 6, 1964, FSM demonstrations occurred in front of Sproul Hall. At the November 6th demonstration, Savio declared that the FSM would no longer be bound by existing university regulations and said, "we'll break the regulations again and again and again." On November 9th, Chancellor Strong warned the students against a planned demonstration on the steps of Sproul Hall and threatened disciplinary action. On November 9th, a rally was held in defiance of the administration and tables were maintained and funds solicited in direct violation of campus directives. On November 16th, students were cited by the Chancellor's office for violations of university regulations.

According to the Un–American Activities Report of the California Senate:

> ". . . the entire movement was slowly but surely being taken over by Communist–oriented leaders. University offices and university typewriters, mimeograph machines, and other equipment, were being used by the FSM for its own purposes, and off the campus they had established offices known as 'centrals,' each one handling a special phase of the FSM strategy.[42]
>
> . . . After all, this was the greatest student rebellion in the history of the United States, and it occurred on the main campus of the

[42]California Senate (1965), p. 97.

> country's largest educational institution. The classic united front organization that we described earlier had now become a tightly–disciplined, thoroughly organized, well–equipped movement. And it was about to stage the greatest demonstration of all, which was scheduled for December 2, 1964, with the invasion of beleaguered Sproul Hall."[43]

On November 19th, State Assemblymen–elect John L. Burton and Willie Brown, Jr. (who later became the long–time Speaker of the California State Assembly) sent messages to the university Regents demanding complete freedom on the campus. On December 1st, the press announced that Chancellor Strong had brought disciplinary action against Mario Savio, Arthur Goldberg, Jacqueline Goldberg, and Brian Turner. Savio issued a statement containing a list of five demands by the FSM as follows:

> "1. The dropping of all charges against Mario Savio, Arthur Goldberg, Jacqueline Goldberg and several student organizations cited for breaking university rules.
>
> 2. An Administration guarantee against further disciplinary action until final settlement is reached with the Free Speech Movement.
>
> 3. A statement that no regulations would be adopted by the university restricting students or organizations from exercising their 'political right on the campus.'
>
> 4. An administration agreement that only the courts should have the authority to regulate political activities on the campus.
>
> 5. The adoption of a policy that all rules governing political expression on the campus should be determined and interpreted and enforced by the faculty—students—administration committees whose judgment would be final."

Savio also issued an ultimatum giving Chancellor Strong 24 hours within which to meet these demands or face a massive demonstration. Savio also threatened that if the demands were not met, the university would face a sit–in demonstration and a strike if any police were called to quell the demonstration.

[43] *Ibid.*, p. 98.

By noon the next day, December 2nd, the ultimatum had not been met. At that time, Savio and others made speeches exhorting the crowd on the Plaza to march into the Administration Building and to bring the operation of the university "to a grinding halt." Led by Joan Baez, singing and strumming on her guitar, Savio, Aptheker, Weinberg, Goldberg and about 1,000 others marched into the building and literally took over.

Baez was not a student at the university. She usually resided at Carmel Valley, over 100 miles away. That she, whose singing generally favored large audiences at very substantial prices, was present to lead the march, was an indication that this event was no haphazard affair thrown together on the spur of the moment. It was obviously a well–organized New Left activity. Apparently, the failure of the university to accede to the ultimatum had been anticipated, and the leaders of FSM were well prepared. Baez did not remain for the confrontation with police, which came later.

This was the beginning of "Campus Unrest," a national phenomenon of mass protest, in which apparently intelligent persons—students and some faculty alike—sharing the privileges of higher education at one of the great multiversities of the world, conspired to confer upon their seat of learning the dubious distinction of being the place where it all started.

Over and over they sang, "We shall overcome." The business of the university came to a stop. As the singing mob marched, they carried mattresses, blankets and cartons of food. They were prepared to stay for some time. Having fought the university for two months, they were ready for more dramatic action, regardless of the issues.

Of course, in the background to guide them were professional provocateurs who had been trained and seasoned in countless episodes of concerted protest and mob action. Outside of the New Left leaders who concocted the ultimatum, it is questionable whether the other marchers knew specifically what the demands were or precisely what the purpose of the demonstration was. Generally, they were mad at the university, as the symbol of the "Establishment," and the government and wanted to take over and run things their own way, however vague that way might be.

After marching into Sproul Hall, the demonstrators broke into the offices of university administrative officials and the office of President Emeritus Sproul who had spent a lifetime of great distinction in service to the university. They rifled desks, threw files and papers over the floors, broke furniture and windows, damaged plumbing and committed other acts of vandalism, while sympathetic FSM teaching assistants reported to hold classes.

At 7 o'clock that evening, the usual closing time of Sproul Hall, announcements were made by the campus police that anyone who did not leave the building would be charged with trespassing and refusing to disperse. Between 700 and 800 of the 1,000 who had entered remained. Preparations were then made to make arrests that night. To wait until the next day, when thousands of students and non–students would be milling around on the Plaza, might make the situation more difficult to handle.

During the night, Governor Brown phoned Inspector O'Connell, who was on duty at the university with a contingent of the California Highway Patrol, to inquire about conditions at the university. He also talked with Ed Meese, who advised him of the conditions and told him that David Dutton, the assistant district attorney in charge of the Berkeley branch of the District Attorney's Office, Alameda County Sheriff Frank Madigan, his staff and deputies, and Oakland, Berkeley and university campus police had already begun making arrests. Governor Brown approved. President Kerr was not consulted.

When he heard that arrests were being made and that Governor Brown had approved, Kerr was displeased, but his displeasure was ignored. Dutton, Chancellor Strong, Sheriff Madigan and the officers worked until 5 o'clock in the morning completing the arrests.

Under the direction of Dutton, Chancellor Strong went to each floor to request, on voice amplification equipment, that the demonstrators leave the building. Lt. Chandler, of the campus police, gave an order to disperse. He announced that arrests were to begin and that anyone who refused to leave would be arrested. Seven hundred seventy–one demonstrators refused to leave and were arrested.

Pursuant to arrest procedures approved by the District Attorney's Office, before a person was arrested an officer with a recording device told the person that he could leave the building and if he did there would be no arrest; that if he refused to leave he would be arrested and charged with trespass and refusal to disperse; and that if he went limp, as many did, he would also be charged with hindering an officer in performance of his duty. To increase the difficulties of the police, the demonstrators were told by their leaders to go to the fourth floor of the building. This they did.

As an arrest was being made, a card with a number was held in front of the arrestee and a photograph was taken of the arrestee and the arresting officer. The arrestees were then transported to the Alameda County Rehabilitation Center, a penal institution operated by the Sheriff's Office at Santa Rita in the Livermore area. This facility had been a Naval Training Center and Naval Hospital during World War II.

Doctors were available to examine anyone who claimed to have been injured. There were no cases of injury and no complaints. As commanding officer in the field to all peace officers of whatever agencies involved, it should be said that Alameda County Sheriff Madigan's performance in this situation, as on other occasions, was always outstanding. The same must be said also of the performance of David Dutton who worked in the field with Madigan and other peace officers.

Within hours after booking procedures were completed, all arrestees were released on bail provided by a bail bonds broker in San Francisco who had in the past provided bail for demonstrators and radicals who were arrested.

On Sunday, December 6th, I received a telephone call from Governor Brown who said he was with Clark Kerr. Brown asked me if I would dismiss the charges against the persons who had been arrested. When I said no, Brown suggested that it might suffice if the *leaders only* were charged with a conspiracy. I replied, "Pat, that would make a felony out of it. Do you want to do that?"

Brown equivocated and suggested that I talk to President Kerr. Kerr came on the phone and greeted me with innocuous amenities and said nothing about the Free Speech Movement prosecution or dismissal of the charges. I felt that to have dismissed the cases would have been followed at a later date with another raid on Sproul Hall and loss of face by campus police and other law enforcement officers.

The following day, at a general assembly of students at the Greek Theater on campus, President Kerr announced a general and complete amnesty for misconduct of all students up to the time of his announcement. This announcement applied only to disciplinary action of the university. It had no effect with respect to the charges filed by the District Attorney against those who had been arrested. These were criminal charges in the Municipal Court of Berkeley. There was no amnesty as to these offenses.

Of the 771 persons arrested, nine minors were referred to the Juvenile Court, where they were found guilty and made wards of the court. At all stages, the juveniles were represented by counsel and, with the exception of trial by jury, the usual adversary procedures of an adult criminal case were followed. Of the remaining arrestees, 101 pleaded guilty. The trials of 159 were consolidated. They waived the right to trial by jury and were tried before Municipal Court Judge Rupert Crittenden, who, after a lengthy trial, took the cases under submission.

A university law school professor took a leading role as a member of a panel of defense attorneys. The cases of the remaining arrestees were submitted by stipulation on the evidence introduced at the trial of the 159. All of the defendants were found guilty by Judge Crittenden. The case against one defendant who died before trial was dismissed. Five cases of defendants who had been arrested outside Sproul Hall were dismissed on technical grounds. The case of a school teacher who claimed to be covering the case for a newspaper was dismissed after trial and a hung jury.

A radical Left activist lawyer had been arrested by a deputy sheriff, under instructions at the scene from Deputy District Attorney Ed Meese, when he refused to leave the building after being ordered to do so. Subsequent investigation disclosed that he had been admitted to the building by a policeman when he claimed that he represented clients in the building. His case was later dismissed and his lawsuit against Meese and me was also dismissed.

The convicted defendants were given probation with fines and, in some cases, county jail sentences. The fines totaled $116,710. Appeals were taken from the convictions to the appellate division of the Superior Court and to the U.S. Supreme Court. All convictions were affirmed. This landmark litigation was important in establishing precedents in substantive and procedural law early in the period of campus unrest, civil disobedience and mass demonstrations.

For many months following the arrests, I received hundreds of letters urging me to dismiss individual cases. All of these letters were addressed to me as "Thomas Coakley," which is the name of one of my brothers. At that time he was a Superior Court judge in a mountain county adjoining Yosemite National Park. He had no connection with the litigation. This was obviously a concerted letter–writing operation directed by someone who mistook my brother for me. Judge Crittenden was later appointed to the Superior Court by Governor Brown, and, shortly after his appointment, he died suddenly of a heart attack. The FSM trials were a heavy strain upon a sick man and no doubt hastened his untimely passing. He was subjected to constant anonymous harassment during the trial.

THE VIETNAM DAY COMMITTEE

The Sproul Hall sit–in prosecution kept the Free Speech Movement relatively quiet during the trial and for some time after sentences were imposed. The Free Speech Movement was losing momentum. A new group called the Free Student Union (FSU) emerged on the campus with many of the same leaders, members, and supporters.

The Free Student Union inherited much of the equipment left over from the Free Speech Movement activities—walkie–talkie sets, public address devices, etc. They continued to plague the university administration with demands, and the administration continued to vacillate and placate dissenters, making concessions and further compounding the confusion. With the absence of overt spectacular action, such as the Sproul Hall sit–in, and being immersed in petty wrangling over rules and regulations, the Free Student Union lost the media's interest and faded.

The 13th report of the California Senate Factfinding Subcommittee on Un–American Activities described this stage of campus unrest as follows:

> "The University's public relations department took advantage of the apparent lull to proclaim that the trouble was over, that rules were now being observed by the students. This was an honest statement, because the FSM had badgered the administration into rescinding all the rules it found distasteful. Those that remained were ignored in most cases."[44]

The Free Student Union (FSU) assumed authority to call campus strikes, to raise objections to university action and to handle civil rights and student affairs. The university provided the facilities on campus for Free Student Union meetings and activities. Having milked the Free Speech Movement dry, the Free Student Union looked for new issues.

The Vietnam War was escalating and opposition to it was warming up. This provided a new technique for college and other radicals in an assembly–type rally called a "teach–in." An anti–Vietnam War group, which became known as the "Vietnam Day Committee," appeared on the horizon, and the Free Student Union made arrangements to lend them electronic and other equipment left over from the Free Speech Movement. Leaders of the Free Student Union became active in the anti–war movement.

Under the heading of "Old Leaders—New Cause," the supplement to the 13th report of the California Senate Factfinding Subcommittee on Un–American Activities, published the following year (1966),[45] described the teach–in as follows:

[44]California Senate (1965), p. 76.

[45][Publisher's note: The Senate subcommittee published a supplement to their 13th report the following year, primarily as a rebuttal to specific criticisms leveled at their 13th report by U.C. President Clark Kerr.]

"The origin of the Vietnam Day Committee is obscure. Some claim that its inception was a 'teach–in' conducted in March 1965 by faculty members at the University of Michigan in Ann Arbor. This affair was reported in the press and described by the U.S. Senate Internal Security Subcommittee. Approximately 2,500 people attended this rally which consisted of a series of lectures, open meetings and seminars punctuated by folksinging and bomb scares. In commenting generally on the teach–ins the [U.S. Senate] Subcommittee said:

"'In reality, the great majority of these teach–ins (there were a few notable exceptions) have had absolutely nothing in common with the procedures of fair debate or the process of education. In practice they were a combination of an indoctrination session, a political protest demonstration, an endurance contest and a variety show. At most of the teach–ins the administration's point of view was given only token representation. The great majority of the speakers, by deliberate design, were critics of the administration. At many of the teach–ins, spokesmen for the administration's policy were subjected to booing and hissing and catcalling, so that it was impossible for them to make a coherent presentation of their case. Communist propaganda films were frequently shown. Communist literature was distributed. People of known Communist backgrounds were frequently involved.'

"The [U.S.] Senate Subcommittee found that a majority of those who were participating in the marches, teach–ins and other demonstrations were sincere and loyal dissenters. But it was also pointed out that the situation presented an admirable opportunity for Communists of all complexions to unite in a common front to further the world Party line—and that line was to give all possible aid to the Viet Cong, and to make all possible trouble in this country which would interfere with the war effort."[46]

As the Vietnam Day Committee gathered momentum, it drew sympathetic anti–war groups and Marxist front organizations into its orbit. On May 21 and 22, 1965, with the express permission of the

[46]*Thirteenth Report Supplement of the Senate Factfinding Subcommittee on Un–American Activities* (Sacramento, California Senate, 1966) p. 76.

university and with the use of university equipment and facilities, the widely heralded Vietnam Day Committee teach–in took place on university property adjacent to Sproul Plaza.

Booths and tables were manned by representatives of the Dubois Club, the Progressive Labor Party, the Trotskyites and other radical groups. Pictures and cartoons portraying alleged American tortures and atrocities against Vietcong as well as pictures of Karl Marx were on display in and around the area of the teach–in. About 10,000 attended over the two days. Saturday, the second day, was simply a mass meeting laced with speeches of increasing intensity by leaders of various radical youth groups.

When someone would try to take issue with the propaganda of the Vietnam Day Committee speakers, he would be interrupted with booing, hissing, cat calling and other voices, human and mechanical. For him there was no free speech. The control of this affair followed the familiar Communist pattern with shills circulating through the crowd leading the applause or derision. During the Free Speech Movement demonstrations in 1964, there had been monitors who fanned out through the crowd, keeping the fervor at high pitch and maintaining vigil over the proceedings. At this teach–in there were the customary monitors with their walkie–talkie equipment and authoritative armbands. It was demonstrated that this affair was part of a coordinated world propaganda operation when telegrams of congratulation were read from Communist elements in various parts of the world.

What up to that time had been a loose ad hoc group, became congealed and formalized, under the name of "Vietnam Day Committee" (VDC), the hardcore of which were about 500 university students and a larger number of non–students led by two university professors and non–student Jerry Rubin.

The Dubois Club ground out Vietnam Day Committee anti–war propaganda to pave the way for the next demonstration scheduled for October 15 and 16, 1965. The president of the university defended distribution of Vietnam Day Committee material on the campus as part of "the American tradition of a great university." Rooms in university buildings were being used freely by pro–Vietcong leaders, many of whom had no connection with the university, for the purpose of formulating plans for blocking the movement of U.S. troop trains and staging demonstrations at the Oakland Army Terminal targeted at troops billeted for Vietnam embarkation.

The forthcoming October protest was advertised by the Vietnam Day Committee as "International Days of Protest." After the October demonstrations, the university alumni magazine stated: "The Vietnam Day Committee office at Berkeley was the international headquarters for the October 15–16 demonstrations that took place throughout the world." As the October 15th date for the all–day rally on the Berkeley campus and the march through Berkeley and Oakland to the Oakland Army Embarkation Terminal approached, applications for parade permits were made by Vietnam Day Committee representatives to the cities of Berkeley and Oakland.

Under ordinances of the cities of Berkeley and Oakland, applications for parade permits were subject to approval of the city managers. The VDC applications specified the route of the parade, the date, time and approximate number of marchers (estimated at between 10,000 and 20,000).

The proposed route was along Telegraph Avenue to Broadway in downtown Oakland and west on 7th Street, which were all heavily traveled main thoroughfares through business districts and densely populated areas. The proposed march on 7th street merged into a narrow lane under a number of railroad tracks. The VDC plan was to march through this underpass to the Oakland Army Base on the other side of the tracks, and to bivouac all night outside the wire fences of the base.

The plans included bonfires, amplified rock music, singing, dancing, speeches and distribution of leaflets condemning the Vietnam War and urging the troops not to board the transports. The proposed route would carry the marchers at night through areas in west Oakland where the incidence of violent crimes was high and racial tensions volatile.

Jerry Rubin, who seemed to be acting as chairman of the VDC, and other leaders were invited to a hearing before the city manager of Oakland, the chief of police of Oakland, and myself. The explosive probabilities of the plan were explained to them and they were told that if they insisted on the march after their all–day teach–in rally on the campus, there was a large park adjoining Bushrod School in north Oakland with ample lighting and sanitary facilities, about a mile and a half from the campus, which could be made available to them. This would afford them a march along Telegraph Avenue through Berkeley and into Oakland. They rejected this offer. Their parade applications were denied by the cities of Berkeley and Oakland.

The VDC filed an action in the U.S. District Court in San Francisco to compel the cities to grant parade permits and to enjoin Oakland and Berkeley police from interfering with the VDC parade. Although Alameda County was not made a party to the litigation by the VDC, Judge George B. Harris, presiding judge of the U.S. District Court, asked me to intervene as a friend of the Court. I did so and took a position with the cities which resulted in denial by the Court of the VDC's demands.

The VDC announced that they would proceed to hold the march through Berkeley and Oakland without parade permits, and went ahead with arrangements for a massive rally on the campus. The university administration granted the VDC permission to hold a rally on the campus in the large open area adjacent to Sproul Plaza. The administration also provided a stage and other facilities for the rally, as it did for the VDC teach–in rally of May 21–22.

On Friday October 15, 1965, the well publicized teach–in took place on campus. The teach–in lasted all day and into the night. This affair was similar to that of May 21–22. Speaker after speaker mounted the stage and addressed the crowd. Monitors with armbands and walkie–talkies circulated through the audience.

At about 9 o'clock, the persons on the field, following their leaders' instructions, marched off campus into the intersection of Telegraph and Bancroft, which was the hub of the campus and a business district. They were directed by monitors to march south on Telegraph Avenue. The number of marchers was estimated at around 10,000.

The Berkeley police had a unit of about 50 uniformed policemen stationed at the intersection. The marchers swarmed past them. No arrests were made by the Berkeley police, although the marchers were violating an ordinance. Well led by numerous monitors with walkie–talkies, the marchers walked along one side of Telegraph Avenue toward Oakland.

At the boundary between Oakland and Berkeley, two wedges of uniformed Oakland police were spread across Telegraph Avenue, backed by members of the California Highway Patrol and the Sheriff's Department. When the marchers reached the Oakland police wedge, they stopped. The police would not move. They were equipped with long riot clubs and plastic face helmets. They were obviously prepared for action. The VDC leaders asked Oakland Police Chief Toothman if they could proceed to march into Oakland. This request was refused. The marchers turned and moved back to a park opposite the Berkeley City Hall, where many of them spent the night.

The next day, they organized and again marched toward Oakland along another arterial, Adeline Street, with the mayor of Berkeley riding ahead of the march. When they reached the Oakland city boundary, they found the street blocked by a wedge of Oakland policemen and Alameda County sheriff's officers under the command of Deputy Chief Preston of the Oakland Police Department. Again they asked if they could parade into Oakland. Again their request was denied. Pursuant to instructions from the monitors, the marchers, about 5,000 in number, sat in the street to listen to speeches from the VDC leaders.

About ten black–jacketed motorcycle riders, known as "Hell's Angels," waded into the marchers and proceeded to break up their rally. It could have easily turned into a riot. Oakland and Berkeley police and the Alameda County sheriff's men moved up and pulled the Hell's Angels away, saving many VDC demonstrators from being worked over. The irony of the situation was that the demonstrators, usually hostile to the police, were very glad to have police protection from the Hell's Angels attack.

Although the marchers of Friday night and Saturday were in violation of the city parade ordinance, the city of Berkeley did nothing to stop the marches. These marches and the obstruction of traffic were without permits and in defiance of the city ordinance. In the confrontation which occurred between the Hell's Angels and the VDC marchers, someone in the melee, hit or pushed by a deputy sheriff, fell against a Berkeley Police Department officer, causing him to fall and sustain a broken leg. The city manager of Berkeley demanded that the Hell's Angles be prosecuted for assault on the injured officer and disturbing the peace of the VDC assembly.

A short while later, the VDC rally dispersed. They had failed to march into Oakland or to the Oakland Army Base. The Oakland police, the sheriff's men and the California Highway Patrol were present in force, determined to prevent a march into Oakland. This was obvious to the demonstrators and they backed off. The events of Friday night and Saturday afternoon were highly publicized by the media.

On November 20th, the VDC decided to try again to parade through Berkeley and Oakland to the Oakland Army Base. They made no secret of the fact that they wanted the march to reach the base, where they could dramatize their opposition to the Vietnam War and possibly precipitate a riot, thus provoking desired publicity. Again, they applied for parade permits. Again, they were told they could march from the campus to Bushrod Park and hold a rally there. Again, they refused this offer. Again, their applications were denied, and, again, they filed an action in the United States District Court in San Francisco to compel the cities of Berkeley and Oakland to permit the march through these cities to the Oakland Army Base.

A number of radical Left lawyers, including one from the Lawyer's Guild of New Orleans, appeared for the VDC. The judge, William T. Sweigert, made an order that the VDC could conduct a march on Saturday, November 20th, from the campus to DeFremery Park in Oakland under certain limitations as to form, route and time. The order provided that the march would start at 10 a.m. and end by 5 p.m.; that the marchers would walk four abreast in units of 100, on one side of the street; that the rally could take place in DeFremery Park; that the park would have to be cleared of debris after the rally; and that there would be no peeling off of marchers to go to the Oakland Army Base, which was about two miles distance from the park. The prescribed route of the march went through the cities of Berkeley, Emeryville and Oakland, a total distance of about five miles.

When it became certain that there would be a march in areas where the incidence of violent crimes had been high, Governor Brown became alarmed, lest the march precipitate a riot. The notorious Los Angeles Watts riot had occurred three months earlier, in which some 35 persons had been killed and an estimated $40 million damage had occurred due to fire and looting. The state government had been criticized for tardiness in activating the National Guard and otherwise assisting the city of Los Angeles in its effort to control the riot.

A report of the United States Department of Commerce (April 1965) of a study made of racial tension in the U.S. had named eleven cities in the U.S. where it found that the potential for race rioting was serious. Nine of these cities were east of the Mississippi River. West of the Mississippi, the cities named were Los Angeles and Oakland, in each of which cities there was a heavy concentration of racial minorities.

After the Watts riot and the criticism ensuing therefrom, and with a campaign for reelection coming up in the following year (1966), Governor Brown did not want another race riot in California. He telephoned me and asked me to take charge of coordinating law enforcement agencies in preparation for handling any emergencies which might arise. I had already done this before he called and so informed him.

Since the 1960 demonstration at the San Francisco City Hall, the District Attorney's Office of Alameda County had been closely watching mass protest activities and exchanging information with local, state and federal law enforcement agencies. Prior to the October 15, 1965, VDC attempt to march through Berkeley and Oakland, meetings had been held in the District Attorney's Office attended by the chiefs of police of East Bay cities, the sheriff, representatives of the FBI, U.S. Army, U.S. Navy, California Highway Patrol, California Major Disaster and Mutual Aid Department and the California National Guard.

At these meetings, information concerning VDC's planning and our preparations to handle the situation were discussed and coordinated. Through David Dutton, assistant district attorney in charge of the Berkeley office and Berkeley and campus police, responsible law enforcement agencies were kept informed.

A similar meeting was held before the November 20th march. I asked the governor to have National Guard units standing by to assist local police if it became necessary. Four hundred members of the California Highway Patrol were also committed. When the 5 mile march from the University of California campus to DeFremery Park took place on November 20th, it was well policed by 2,400 police officers and—to the governor's credit—by 400 California Highway Patrol officers, with 450 National Guardsmen standing by, ready for action.

On the morning of November 20th, while the marchers were assembling in Berkeley at the university campus before the march began, I met with VDC chairman Jerry Rubin to outline the provisions of Judge Sweigert's order.

He said he was familiar with the order.

I told him I would explain the order to his monitors and to the assembling marchers.

He said he would do this himself.

I told him to say that there would be plenty of policemen on duty, and that they were assigned to maintain the peace and to protect the marchers from attack as well as to enforce the provisions of Judge Sweigert's order.

This was done by Rubin before the march began. To his credit, it should be said that he relayed accurately our conversation to the monitors and the assembling crowd, and he urged them to comply with the court order. Throughout the day, they followed his instructions and the directions of his monitors. Although among the estimated 10,000 marchers there were many old–line members of the Communist Party and front organizations, they marched quietly and caused no problems. This was a New Left show under their younger and well disciplined control.

Something should be said also about the efficiency of the communication system of the New Left in assembling about 10,000 people to spend a day marching and listening to interminable, redundant attacks on the "Establishment" and the Vietnam War. Needless to say, they had some help from the media. After these speeches, the park was well cleaned up and the rally ended promptly at 5 o'clock.

For the older people, most of whom appeared to be quite sincere, the hours of marching and listening must have been very uncomfortable. No one tried to reach the Oakland Army Base, and there were no arrests. There were no applications for any more such demonstrations.

From 1965 to 1970 there was continuous friction between leaders of the New Left and the university, repercussions of which spilled over into the communities around San Francisco Bay and cost the cities and the state a great deal of money. Almost daily, student and non–student representatives of various radical organizations and causes sat at tables on Sproul Plaza, soliciting contributions while others, through loudspeakers, harangued the thousands who walked by on their way to and from classes.

Among the protest activities spawned on the campus by faculty, students and non–students using university property and facilities, were: attempts to stop troop trains passing through Berkeley enroute to the Army embarkation base in Oakland, sporadic attempts to climb over fences at this base for the purpose of distributing antiwar pamphlets among the soldiers, attempts to stop armed forces recruitment on the campus, bombing of the Naval Reserve Officers Training Corps headquarters on campus, attempts to stop interviews of students for employment by corporations engaged in production of war materials, and attempts to compel the university to give academic credit for attending unauthorized speeches on campus by notorious militant activists and Communists.

The activities of the dissidents included an attempt to cause a strike of students and faculty and a forceful takeover of Moses Hall, one of the oldest and most revered ivy–covered buildings, where a fire was started. Arrests were made by police in the course of this demonstration and prosecutions followed. The large auditorium in Wheeler Hall was gutted by arson fire, at a cost of $500,000 to the university.

Other protest activities involving police action and prosecution were the "filthy speech" episodes, in which New Left activists, led by Arthur Goldberg, fulminated over loudspeakers and portrayed by placards four letter obscenities to students who had to pass along the plaza to and from classes. Other protest activities hatched on the campus were; the mass picketing of the *Oakland Tribune*, a daily newspaper of wide circulation in Alameda and Contra Costa Counties; and a boycott of the Oakland Public Schools, both of which activities proved to be illegal.

Other activities involving students and non–students occurred in the south–of–campus business district on Telegraph Avenue adjacent to Sproul Plaza. This included shoplifting, damage to property, obnoxious noise making, and obstruction of pedestrian and vehicular traffic having business with the stores in this area. The militants went so far as to demand that the Berkeley City Council rezone the area as a nonvehicular mall for dancing, singing and such other activities as might suit the fancy of the militants.

During the 1960's, a strange hodgepodge of slovenly persons loitered on the campus and Telegraph Avenue for a distance of about four blocks south of Sproul Plaza. Some of them were professional, government–subsidized students who had been attending classes at the university for more than the usual four years. Others were non–students living together, commune fashion, sharing food stamps, clothes and marijuana. They became known as the "street people." They had many encounters with merchants and police, and they quite readily joined any of the various demonstrations which occurred.

STOP THE DRAFT WEEK

In 1967, an anti–draft activity was deliberately planned on campus to disrupt a large area in the heart of the downtown business district of Oakland. The objective was to throw a mob around a federal building at the corner of 15th and Clay Streets in Oakland, one half block from the City Hall and diagonally across the street from the parking building for city vehicles. Among other agencies this federal building housed, was the Armed Forces Entrance and Examining Station which processed all persons inducted into the armed forces from

Nevada and all of California north of the Tehachipi Mountains. Every week, Monday through Friday, buses containing young men to be inducted into the military and then transported to basic training were scheduled to arrive at and depart from this induction center.

The planning for this demonstration was complex and extensive, involving, as it did, the organization and training of leaders and transmission of notices and invitations to thousands of persons to assemble in front of the induction center. So that the Oakland police would have advance knowledge of what was going to happen, two young rookie policemen, garbed in the prevailing mode of students, attended meetings of the anti–draft demonstration committee. Leaders of demonstration planning became aware of the presence of the rookie policemen. This did not deter them in their planning. There was no secret about their planning. Many meetings open to the public were held at which the plans were discussed.

A demonstration in the form of mass picketing was to take place every day for a week starting on Monday, October 16, 1967, in front of the Oakland induction center. Via the hardcore leadership of the New Left and various other radical groups, notice would be passed by word of mouth, by leaflet and the media, both underground and legitimate. This was news, and, of course, the radicals could depend upon the media to give their activities full coverage. The life blood of the media is controversy, and the Vietnam War and the draft had become controversial. This was an opportunity for the radicals to receive a lot of free publicity and, incidentally, more money.

Although this was a conspiracy to commit seditious acts against the federal government in time of war, the federal government at no time took preventive or punitive action. In fact, the commanding officer of the U. S. Army embarkation depot in Oakland had been instructed by the federal civil authorities not to make any arrests of civilians who might try to climb over the fences of the depot or of civilians who might try to persuade soldiers bound for overseas duty to disobey their orders. Apparently, the Federal administration did not want a confrontation in the courtroom over the Vietnam War.

Early Monday morning, October 16, 1967, Joan Baez, with members of her family, her manager and about 200 others, sat and stood in the entrance of the induction center at 15th and Clay Streets in Oakland. This was the beginning of the demonstrations of the so–called "Stop the Draft Week." This Monday demonstration was planned to be passive—no violence, no forceful resistance. Joan Baez and her group were pacifists. Upon being requested to leave and stop blocking the entrance, they simply refused to move and submitted peacefully to arrest. They played the role of martyrdom straight and pleaded *nolo contendere* (no contest) to pertinent charges of violations of the California Penal Code. They quietly accepted and served their sentences in the county jail.

Tuesday, October 17, however, was something else. At 5:30 in the morning, people—male and female, young, middle–aged and old—began to assemble at 15th and Clay Streets in rapidly increasing numbers. By 7 o'clock, there were at least 5,000 persons milling around in the intersection surrounding both sides of the induction center and blocking the entrances to the building. The leaders and their militant cohorts came prepared for action. They wore red helmets, carried shields, clubs, placards and walkie–talkies.

Across the street from the induction center, on the third level of the City Hall parking building, Raymond Brown, deputy chief of the Oakland Police Department, was in command. Sheriff Madigan and I were with him. During anti–war demonstrations and possible riot situations, I was present at the scene with the commanding officer of the law enforcement agency in charge to be available to give legal advice if needed.

On the street, uniformed and ready for action, were some 400 members of the Oakland Police Department, the Alameda County Sheriff's Office and the California Highway Patrol. They carried riot batons and wore helmets with plastic shields to protect their faces.

Chief Brown declared the mob blocking the intersection and the center to be an unlawful assembly and ordered them to disperse, as provided in the California Penal Code. He repeated these orders several times. The demonstrators ignored the order.

Many reporters, photographers, and television cameramen were present on the street, mingling with the demonstrators. The policemen stood at parade rest in a double wedge from curb to curb on Clay Street, waiting for orders. The demonstrators taunted them, yelling a variety of obscenities and insults and throwing missiles into their ranks.

Finally, Chief Brown who had been trained in the Marine Corps during World War II, gave orders to his men to clear the streets. The police wedges, in solid lines, moved forward, holding their riot batons in front and pushing the demonstrators from curb to curb along the street away from the induction center.

Newsmen and photographers among the demonstrators were caught in the action, newspaper and television cameras were upended, and some of the media got pushed along with the mob. This infuriated them and they took it out on the police in their news accounts of what happened. They had no cause for complaint. They had been ordered off the street repeatedly and had ample time to get out of the way. The street and sidewalk in front of the draft center were cleared and the demonstrators and newsmen were left to lick their wounds.

Outside of some bruised feelings and ribs, no one was seriously hurt—except two policemen who received broken legs and an officer whose face was slashed to the bone by a thick piece of broken plate glass hurled by a demonstrator into the ranks of the policemen. The white garbed, bearded pseudo–medic demonstrators present did nothing for the injured policemen.

Wednesday and Thursday were more or less a repetition of Tuesday. Apparently, the leaders of the demonstration accelerated their efforts and, with the help of the media, succeeded in swelling the number of demonstrators on Friday to about 10,000. On Tuesday, Wednesday and Thursday, buses carrying the inductees pulled up to the cleared center and discharged their passengers.

On Friday, mutual aid was invoked, and the Oakland, Alameda County and the California Highway Patrol officers were reinforced to about 1,800 officers. An escort of San Francisco Police Department motorcycle officers, with sirens wide open, sped down San Pablo Avenue, a main thoroughfare through downtown Oakland, ahead of the inductee buses and onto Clay Street to the induction center from which the mob had been cleared. Demonstrators along their route scrambled to safety. No one was foolhardy enough to try to stop the escort or the buses, and quite obviously the motorcycle policemen from San Francisco were in no mood to be stopped or delayed.

This was the end of the Stop the Draft Week demonstrations. Radicals had failed to stop or even delay the draft. They did, however, receive a great deal of free publicity, inflict upon local and state governments a good deal of extra expense, and deprive large areas of the rest of the city of police protection for a week. As far as the objects of the demonstrations were concerned, it should be said that the young inductees ignored the demonstrators and walked scornfully past them as they entered the induction center.

As District Attorney and chief law officer of the county, I presided at coordination and planning meetings. As chief law enforcement officer, the sheriff was present and prepared to command mutual aid agencies in the field. Close liaison with the Federal Bureau of Investigation, the armed forces and police departments enabled us to be informed in advance of any major demonstrations the malcontents were planning.

Our policy was to have reliable advance intelligence and to have plenty of muscle—uniformed, riot–equipped policemen—at the place or places where the demonstration was going to occur. We believed that the best deterrent was conspicuous police patrol vehicles and plenty of policemen, in uniform and obviously ready for action, at the scene before or as soon as trouble would start. This policy of rapid deployment of plenty of well–equipped officers paid off in Oakland on several occasions when provocative events occurred without any advance notice or warning and when not being ready might easily have led to a full blown riot, as happened in Watts.

BURN, BABY, BURN

During the 1960's, various off–campus political social–action organizations, under militant leadership and subsidized by the federal government, the Ford Foundation and other organizations, kept agitating the large black population of Oakland. Among these agitator organizations was the Welfare Rights Organization, which received assistance from the University of California under a U.S. Department of Health, Education and Welfare work study program. Among salaried recipients of substantial amounts of money from a Ford Foundation grant to the University of California were two notorious non–student black agitators with criminal records. They were on the editorial staff of an off–campus inflammatory community newspaper called *Flatlands*. A San Francisco State College student was also on the editorial staff. At this time, he was on the payroll of the San Francisco State College Associated Students in a program called the "Community Involvement Program–Oakland Project." The *Flatlands* became a coordinating communication vehicle between members of political action groups who were leading demonstrations against local government.

In 1966, the "Campus Community for New Politics" used Sproul Plaza to mobilize student support for a boycott against the Oakland Public Schools because of alleged de facto segregation of black students. There never had been de jure segregation in California schools. The boycott conspiracy to cause students to stay away from school was illegal and so declared by me as district attorney. At that time, the district attorney was attorney for all the public schools in Alameda County. Along with the Oakland Public Schools, local government and police were also targets of subsidized campus and off–campus attacks.

An ad hoc committee of black leaders urged students and teachers to stay away from the schools and to attend improvised "free schools" set up in churches. I issued a warning that teachers absenting themselves from regular classes to participate in "free schools" would face disciplinary action and possible criminal prosecution for contributing to the delinquency of minors. The constant agitation so polarized the community that the potential for race rioting was close to the surface. The agitation continued with increasing intensity and with emphasis on the proposed boycott.

In October 1966, a group of about two hundred teenage black students rioted at Castlemont High School in Oakland. Five teachers were assaulted, and one male teacher—a Marine Corps war veteran—was robbed, seriously injured and permanently disabled. Much damage to furniture and property also occurred. A supermarket near the high school was ransacked, with damage to property. Bottles of liquor and other merchandise were stolen. Police were summoned and nineteen arrests were made. Castlemont High School was located in a residential area in east Oakland that became heavily occupied by blacks after World War II. At that time it was definitely not a slum or ghetto area.

Later that same day, an incident occurred at a service station on East 14th Street in Oakland. The station personnel summoned police to arrest a black who had caused the trouble. This man was a troublemaker and verbally abused the police as well as resisted arrest. Word of the incident spread fast, and scores of blacks started to congregate on East 14th Street in the vicinity of the service station, which soon became a target for missiles of various kinds. Before long, store windows were being smashed and looting had begun.

Numerous police patrol cars converged on the area and the looting stopped. Merchants started boarding up their windows and entrances with plywood marked with the word "soul brother." Apparently, they anticipated trouble, not knowing when it would come. They were as prepared as they could be under the circumstances. Young blacks began to congregate and stroll along East 14th Street in groups.

For months, "Burn, Baby, Burn" stickers had been appearing on fences, telephone poles and buildings. There was talk among blacks of ripping the town apart. Emotions were running high. Long dormant grievances and resentments, exploited by leaders whose egos were whetted by the applause and adulation of crowds, were ready to be ignited. The danger of extensive rioting, arson and looting was imminent.

The Oakland Police Department mobilized fast. Days off and vacations were canceled. All members of the department were ordered to duty and concentrated in the seething black areas near East 14th Street. Other law enforcement agencies were alerted, although not activated. The California Highway Patrol was called and responded.

A curfew for youths under 18 years of age was activated by the city. Oakland police patrol cars, paddy wagons and uniformed policemen on foot flooded the volatile section. As groups of black youths clustered, police patrol cars arrived ready for action. Weapons or things which might be used for weapons were confiscated. A youth carrying a sack saw a police car, started to run and threw the sack into a vacant lot. It contained "molotov cocktails"—gasoline bombs. This was no time to quibble about technicalities of the 4th and 14th amendments. Police patrol cars and walking policemen kept moving, figuratively putting out fires before they started.

By 2 a.m., things settled down and the roving groups of blacks disappeared. Few arrests had been made. The action was over for the night. Again the next afternoon, the roving groups of blacks began to appear. Reliable informants advised police that there was talk of rioting, looting and burning that night. Again, all members of the Oakland Police Department went into action as on the preceding night. About 2 a.m., things calmed down and police forces were reduced. Again the following day, there was talk of rioting among certain groups of blacks. Again, the Oakland Police Department went into action as on the preceding nights. Again, their controls succeeded, and about midnight things calmed down and forces were reduced.

That was the end of a dangerous situation which, if not so well handled, might have erupted into a major disaster. As at the Vietnam Day Committee marches, the Stop the Draft Week demonstrations and other episodes, the Oakland Police Department had demonstrated that they were well qualified and prepared to handle such emergencies. It had also been demonstrated that when arrests were made, there was sufficient proof of guilt and successful prosecutions followed. The forecast of the U.S. Department of Commerce report that there would probably be a full blown race riot in Oakland did not come true.

In cases of mass protest picketing, the leaders of those involved were instructed by police not to obstruct pedestrian or vehicular traffic or the operation of business. These instructions were usually followed in Oakland. When demonstrators realized that they were dealing with professional enforcement officers who knew their business, violations of civil rights by demonstrators were reduced to a minimum.

PEOPLE'S PARK

After World War II, growth at the University of California, as at other colleges and universities in California, was rapid. By 1960, undergraduate enrollment at the Berkeley campus exceeded 25,000. In 1967, as part of an expansion program, the university's Board of Regents acquired a half–block of property located one block east of Telegraph Avenue in the south–of–campus area. In 1969, they ordered this property to be cleared for use, first for intramural recreation activities and eventually for student housing.

After the property was cleared and before the university's development program commenced, underground Berkeley publications carried suggestions that the property be taken over, by force if necessary, and developed by revolutionaries. Gradually, it was taken over by a mixture of students and "street people."

Although the takeover was sheer unlawful trespass, University Chancellor Roger Heynes was amenable to discussion and negotiation as to appropriate interim uses of the property, pending ultimate construction by the university. He was unable to reach anyone who purported to lead or represent the dissidents who were moving onto the property.

From April 2 to May 14, 1969, the Berkeley Police Department received 48 complaints from persons living in the vicinity, concerning illegal activities at the so–called "People's Park." Among things about which complaints were made, was noise from late night rallies with mass singing and shouting of obscenities to the accompaniment of bongo drumming. People camped on the property with no sanitary facilities. Food was cooked over fires. As it suited their whims, the trespassers walked around completely naked. Neighboring juveniles were exposed to these conditions and, in some cases, became involved in drunken orgies on the property. Arrests were made for narcotics violations. Trees and shrubs, including marijuana, were planted. Holes for a pond and bonfire pits were dug.

A bulletin board was set up, and, in due course, became covered with notices and political pamphlets. One of the leaflets on the board threatened violence if the university interfered. Another leaflet signed by "madmen" read:

> "We need the park to live and grow and eventually we need all of Berkeley. If the university attempts to reclaim $1.3 million worth of land now claimed by the people, we will destroy $5 million worth of university property."

The utter absurdity of the position of the "People's Park" project was illustrated by the fact that the city of Berkeley was then in the process of acquiring and developing, at a cost of $950,000, property for a 2.8 acre park adjacent to Willard Jr. High School, two blocks from "People's Park." As the city manager of Berkeley said, "control over university property seized unlawfully by the activists represented more than just the use of a piece of land. It raised the basic question of who will control the institutions and property in this country, and for what purpose." In brief, the seizure of the university property was simply another issue for confrontation.

While Chancellor Heynes was considering what measures to take to evict the trespassers, David Dutton, still in charge of the Berkeley branch of the District Attorney's Office, advised the Chancellor that in this particular situation a civil action in Superior Court, restraining unauthorized persons from using the property, would be appropriate. This situation was different from a run–of–the–mill criminal offense involving spontaneous obstruction of traffic and immediate damage to person and property. There was no urgency about eviction and a violation of a restraining order could be processed as contempt of court and heard before a judge without a jury.

Dutton's advice to the Chancellor was not followed—the university had its own legal department. On May 14, 1969, "No Trespassing" signs were placed around the perimeter of the property. Within hours the signs were torn down. On the morning of May 15th, a university construction crew, with police protection, began erecting a wire fence around the property. The police ordered the squatters to leave. Those who refused were arrested.

Word of the action by the university spread fast, so by noon a full–blown rally was beginning at Sproul Plaza. Men dressed in white smocks and wearing Red Cross symbols mingled in the crowd—an indication that trouble involving violence was brewing. It did not take long to organize a rally. A list of speakers at the rally included Paul Jacobs, a non–student leftist who, in 1968, had been the Peace and Freedom Party candidate for U.S. Senator and Michael Lerner, who reserved the Sproul Hall steps for a noon rally on behalf of the "New Left Forum" for a talk on the Middle East. Actually there was no talk about the Middle East. The talk at the rally was exclusively about retaking "People's Park." The final speaker was the student body president–elect who exhorted the crowd to go down and take over the park.

Here was an assembly of supposedly intelligent college students. What followed is an illustration of crowd psychology and of how quickly a group can be incited to commit unlawful, irresponsible, riotous conduct. As a result, the city of Berkeley was in turmoil for over two weeks. The crowd took up a chant, "Let's go, let's take the park," and started a march to the property. Quickly, it became a wild unruly mob—screaming, breaking store and automobile windows, throwing rocks, bottles and other missiles. Berkeley police, California Highway Patrol officers and sheriff's deputies tried to stop the march and the damage. The mob swarmed past and over them. People on rooftops along the line of march began throwing rocks, sticks, bricks, pieces of concrete, lengths of pipe and reinforcing steel bars down on the police officers and police vehicles.

Cherry bombs with BB shot glued on to act as shrapnel began exploding in the streets. Officers were hit by objects thrown by persons on rooftops and by the mob on the street. Obviously, persons connected with the "People's Park" movement had anticipated police action and had stockpiled supplies of steel rods, bottles, rocks and other missiles on the roofs. Groups of officers were surrounded by milling mobs and pummeled with clubs and missiles. Rocks were thrown at a fire engine sent to extinguish fires started in parked automobiles by the mob. A mail truck was stopped and ransacked. The tires were deflated and dirt put into the gas tank. The violence of the mob accelerated.

Inside of two hours, much damage to property and persons other than police officers had been inflicted, and the situation was beyond control. Tear gas ran out and proved ineffective, especially against the missile throwers on the roofs. Finally, sheriff's men were instructed by their commanding officer, a Marine Corps combat veteran, to use shotguns firing bird shot as needed. A man on a roof, in the act of pointing what appeared to be a gun, was hit by buckshot from a shotgun fired by a deputy sheriff, and, after surgery at a hospital, died two days later from hemorrhage and shock—possibly as a result of the surgery.

At noon, 163 officers were on duty in the vicinity of the rally at the "Park" (37 Berkeley policemen, 26 sheriff's deputies and 100 California Highway Patrol officers). As the action of the mob and the violence increased, officers on hand were unable to control the situation. Mutual aid officers from surrounding communities were summoned at 2:15 p.m., and by the end of the day there were 791 officers engaged in trying to quell the riot.

At the request of Berkeley authorities and Sheriff Madigan of Alameda County, Governor Reagan ordered three battalions of the National Guard to Berkeley to assist the local police officers. The soldiers assembled during the night and took up stations in the city. By nightfall, 103 local officers and California Highway Patrol men had been injured and hospitalized.

For several days, there were clandestine hit and run skirmishes in which groups of rioting youths vandalized the community, smashing windows, starting fires, and attacking police officers and National Guardsmen with barrages of missiles, among which were rocks, bricks, Molotov cocktails and balloons filled with paint and excreta. Unlawful assemblies, in the form of itinerant rallies and marches, were held, and a total of 768 persons were arrested.

After these arrests, there was a lull while the People's Park protagonists considered their next move. This was not long in coming in the form of letters of protest, letters to the editors, letters to the grand jury, and letters to several government officials, condemning the action of law enforcement officers and the National Guard. The thrust of one prominent San Francisco daily newspaper was anti–law enforcement.

Throughout the turmoil of the FSM, the anti–Vietnam War marches, VDC activities, Stop the Draft Week, People's Park rioting and other collective protest incidents, the response of Sheriff Madigan's department, the California Highway Patrol, and other departments was exemplary. When two or more agencies were engaged, Sheriff Madigan was the field commander. Considering that before FSM they had no actual experience in large scale mutual aid enforcement, their performance was consistently superior.

"People's Park" was a particularly explosive situation which, if not brought under control, could have become much worse than it was. In response to criticism for use of shotguns to repel attacks on officers from rooftops, Sheriff Madigan said, "The choice was to use shotguns because we did not have adequate manpower—or to retreat and abandon the city of Berkeley to the mob."

Complaints by attorneys for the People's Park arrestees for alleged violation of civil rights were pressed against 12 of the sheriff's deputies, and evidence was presented to a new federal grand jury by a lame duck United States Attorney at the very end of his long overextended tenure. The deputies were not permitted to testify before the federal grand jury. The 12 deputy sheriffs were indicted individually for alleged violation of civil rights. In 5 cases selected for trial by the United States Attorney, there was 1 hung jury and 5 acquittals, after which the cases against the other deputies were dismissed.

During the People's Park turmoil, just the cost of maintaining the National Guard alone at Berkeley for 17 days was $764,258. Additional costs would have to include overtime costs for local law enforcement units, logistic costs for local and mutual aid personnel, prosecution and court costs, damage to property and business, medical costs for personal injuries, and legal costs for defense of the 12 deputy sheriffs. The latter costs, about $80,000, were paid by contributions from private donors.

AFTERMATH OF THE 60'S

In April 1970, the so–called Student Mobilization Committee to End the War in Vietnam announced its intention to hold anti–war, anti–ROTC rallies in Berkeley and on the campus. High school and junior high school students were drawn into this campaign and participated in damage to property and injury to police officers. During this period, 23 officers of the Berkeley Police Department and 22 campus policeman were injured, and damage to property ran into hundreds of thousands of dollars. More active members of the mob were prepared for attacks against police with a variety of missiles, shields against attack by police and rags soaked in vinegar and other fluids to ward off tear gas. Among those who made speeches exhorting demonstrators to violence, were Judy Gumbo, recently returned from Sweden, where she claimed to have met Vietcong and other communist so–called "Liberation Front" representatives. Another speaker was the UC student body president.

Many arrests were made, followed by trials in the Berkeley Municipal Court. A polarization among jurors reflected a difference in attitude among citizens of Berkeley and resulted in many hung juries.

Polarization also occurred in the Superior Court of the county after a judge, for the purpose of increasing representation of minorities on juries, dismissed an entire venire and abolished a simple intelligence test which was legal and had been approved by the Alameda County Bar Association and other judges, including the judge who dismissed the venire.

Another anti–war protester who visited Berkeley during the turmoil was Thomas Hayden. Among others, he addressed rallies of high school students and a gathering of University of California Radiation Laboratory workers at Livermore.[47] He told his audiences that they would have to decide whether to let the university exist; that there were people in Berkeley who had been blowing up utility

[47] [later renamed the Lawrence Livermore National Laboratory.]

company towers since 1967 who had not been caught and would not be caught.

Hayden was a leader of the New Left organization called Students for a Democratic Society (SDS), which dominated the leadership of the protest campaign from 1967 to 1970. The main object of their protests was the war in Vietnam generally, and, later, the Cambodian incursion of 1970. Not surprisingly, during the Soviets' crackdown in Czechoslovakia in 1968, where they brutally suppressed a democratic rebellion representing a set of causes similar to that the American New Left purported to espouse, this American cult of so–called liberals had been signally quiet.

After 1970, mass violence in Berkeley tapered off, although some protest and revolutionary activity continued. Bombings of public buildings, public utilities, local draft boards, and senselessly brutal assaults and individual killings increased with a high percentage of non–clearance by police. FBI national crime statistics continued to disclose that the rate of major violent crimes rose much faster than the rate of population increase. Insubordination and disrespect for authority grew, as the use of narcotics mounted and waves of liberalism and permissiveness swept over the nation.

Prosecutors, defense counsel, judges, and corrections personnel were deluged with serious criminal cases. Plea and sentence bargaining ballooned, and only the more violent convicted criminals reached state prisons. Other felons were sent to county jails or given probation. To hold down overloading of state penal institutions in California, the Legislature enacted a law that subsidized counties in which courts put felony offenders on probation. More judgeships were created, and staffs of district attorneys, public defenders and probation officers increased.

Money poured out of Congress to equip local law enforcement with the latest technology and training aids. Congress enacted a Safe Streets Act and created the Law Enforcement Assistance Administration with hundreds of millions of dollars to improve law enforcement and the administration of justice. Additional hundreds of millions poured into education and welfare to improve the quality of life under the slogan of "The Great Society." Yet, paradoxically, crime continued to increase, both in numbers of cases and in depravity. The average age of criminals crept lower and attitudes of youthful violators became more calloused and defiant.

The most serious of the protest movements in Alameda County of the 1960's was what was labeled "campus unrest." In trying to maintain some semblance of law and order, we were confronted with two types of activists: one, the idealistic students and non–students concerned about national and international conditions and trends; and the other, the militant, destructive, annihilistic–oriented activists—fortunately a very small number—who were interested primarily in overthrowing the "Establishment." The attitude of this latter type of activist was described by the Students for a Democratic Society as follows:

> "We are not sure what the new system should be, but we know that the first thing is to destroy the present system. Then we can start thinking about the new one."

This was anarchy—intellectual nihilism. The hazard of this type of concerted protest is that its protagonists, though relatively small in number, are highly motivated, intensely determined, very active and well organized. They are also usually judgment–proof and practically immune from civil liability for damages. So they can be—and are—more bold and brash in their activism.

This type of faculty activist, and there are some, cannot be impartial and scholarly. He is too much of an advocate. As Learned Hand, in his *Essays on Liberty*, said, "You cannot wear a sword beneath a scholar's gown."[48] If, in the name of academic freedom, the teacher advocates the role of the campus as a launching pad for violent social change and revolution, how can he be objective in his teaching and thinking? If, in the name of academic freedom and of protest over alleged censorship, students are permitted to stage public obscenity and smut in order to challenge administrative authority and to test the

[48]Learned Hand, *Essays on Liberty*, 3rd ed., (New York, Knopf, 1960), p.138

limits of faculty permissiveness, is there not reason to anticipate that the next step will be defiance of university rules and destruction of property—all in the name of "Freedom of Speech"?

During the period of FSM activity before the Sproul Hall takeover, there was much confusion and difference of opinion among faculty members and in the Academic Senate. There were those who were opposed to police action on campus and who concurred in President Kerr's appeasement of FSM. Others urged immediate police intervention and prosecution.

At this stage of the skirmishing, I did not believe that the situation was sufficiently aggravated or the evidence strong enough to warrant prosecution, especially in view of the President's capitulation to Savio and his committee. However, I did believe that there would be more turmoil and that prosecution might become necessary later, at which time, police and prosecutors would have to be prepared to handle the situation.

As a result of the efficient handling of the FSM arrests and prosecutions, things calmed down on the campus, and, with the exception of a few minor episodes, there was no more serious trouble calling for outside police intervention until five years later when the "People's Park" protest exploded. From 1964 through 1967, the Oakland Police Department handled 208 demonstrations which involved 59,984 hours of overtime at a cost to the city of $269,540.72, and with no fatalities or life–threatening injury to police or demonstrators.

The performance of the Berkeley Police Department and of David Dutton and his staff in the Berkeley–Albany branch of the District Attorney's Office, under most difficult conditions, was also a superb example of professionalism in law enforcement.

Although attitudes of disrespect for authority among students in the elementary and secondary public schools of Oakland, and vandalism, arson, theft and destruction of property mounted to the extent that insurance coverage was canceled, no massive Watts–type riot occurred.

By and large, a lesson to be learned as a result of the experience in

Alameda County is that, when efficiently and firmly handled by well–trained officers who know their business and when followed by successful prosecution, violent collective protest can eventually be controlled.

8

D. Lowell Jensen 1969—1981

With the begining of the seventies, there was an increase in the volume and violence of senselessly brutal crime. There was an overall increase also in juvenile delinquency, consumer fraud and failure of fathers to support their families and illegitimate children. Consequently, the staff of the District Attorney's Office had to be substantially increased and made to do with very inadequate space and facilities. New quarters had to be obtained for the Consumer Fraud and Family Support Divisions. The staff of the latter unit alone increased by several hundred percent in size—a sad commentary on the basic mores of American manhood.

Operations were compounded by the Constitutional Amendment known as Proposition 13, which reduced property taxes and circumscribed increases in other forms of taxation, greatly reducing the revenue of local government. The difficulties were further compounded by higher court decisions mandating separate trials and counsel in criminal cases involving more than one defendant, and also requiring removal of trials to counties other than where the crime was committed because of possible prejudicial publicity, thus increasing the cost of law enforcement to state and county government. Even though each succeeding session of the state Legislature created new judgeships, court personnel and calendars were swamped.

Without resort to drafting defense counsel for multi–defendant cases and frequent compromise and reduction of charges by plea bargaining, the criminal justice system could collapse completely. If the changes in the law, which have occurred in recent years as a result of higher courts' decisions concerning due process and fair trial, were necessary, one wonders why it took so long for the courts to discover such necessity. How could defendants have received due process and fair trials during preceding decades and centuries of Anglo–American jurisprudence or in legal systems of other cultures?

Violent criminal injury to citizens, especially the elderly, increased so much that the Legislature enacted a law to provide governmental compensation for such injuries—the legal work to be handled by district attorneys. Witness harassment, intimidation and perversion of justice increased so much that district attorneys in larger jurisdictions had to assign additional help to afford protection to witnesses in criminal cases—a further indication of the depths to which criminality had sunk and the enormous problems encountered by law enforcement.

The increasing numbers of murders, rapes and violent assaults often has led to an awful dilemma: the judge and prosecutor frequently must decide whether a case is heinous enough to go to trial. Even in the case of a murder with special circumstances, where the death penalty could be imposed, a lesser offense might be charged in order to conserve legal resources for prosecuting still more depraved defendants. Nevertheless, there are more and more mind–searing jury trials of murder cases while defense counsel, often at public expense, bend every effort to effect a miscarriage of justice.

Among administrative changes in the District Attorney's Office during the 1970's, was the consolidation of consumer fraud cases into a newly created Consumer Fraud Division, in which both criminal prosecutions and civil actions for recovery were handled by an enlarged staff. Cases would be referred by the Better Business Bureaus, so–called "action lines" operated by the media, police departments, and various other agencies.

Before the establishment of a Consumer Fraud Division, completely devoted to alleged business fraud, cases were handled by deputy district attorneys in the various branch offices, largely by means of citation letters and citation hearings. A high percentage of such cases were disposed of out of court by such citation hearings and subsequent settlements. The average police department is not geared or staffed to handle this type of case, and the average citizen cannot afford to employ private counsel.

The Better Business Bureau, action lines, police departments, and other agencies have been trained to refer such complaints to the Consumer Fraud Division of the District Attorney's Office, and many citizens have learned to appeal to the division directly in the first instance. The aggressive and successful operation of this division and the deterrent effect upon the unscrupulous business operator help to reduce a heavy load which would otherwise have to be handled by the courts.

Deputy District Attorney Charles Herbert, a former Oakland policeman, and Connie Youell, former Berkeley policewoman, in developing and training a staff, have done an outstanding job in a growing and much needed phase of law enforcement.

Other developments included expansion of the in–serivce legal education program, called "The Law in Motion," where decisions of the higher courts in criminal cases were summarized and discussed once a week in the main office by Jack Meehan. During this meeting, pertinent office problems and policies were also discussed and recorded on video tape, which was distributed to each of the seven branch offices.

Because of the heavy increase of cases and lack of sufficient personnel, the training in actual trial work of earlier times, in which a junior deputy participated in Superior Court trials with a senior trial deputy, with few exceptions, was not continued. What experience a young deputy got in actual trials, he or she received by working with older deputies in the Municipal Court.

CHOWCHILLA SCHOOL BUS KIDNAPING

One case of note during the 1970's was the incident in which 26 grammar school children from Chowchilla, a small farming community in Madera County, were kidnaped enroute home from school in a school bus. At approximately 4 p.m. on July 15, 1976, three armed kidnapers waylaid the school bus by blocking the road with a white passenger van. One of the masked kidnapers ran up and, at gun point, ordered the bus driver to open the bus door. Immediately, two of the kidnapers entered the bus and commandeered it to a dry slough about one mile away. At the slough were parked a second green passenger van (a former military police prisoner transport vehicle) and a third van to be used as a spare. The kidnapers forced the bus driver and 15 of the children into the green prisoner transport van and the rest into the white van. The third van was not used to carry any of the victims. The kidnapers then drove their victims 140 miles to a rock quarry in the Livermore Valley in Alameda County, where the kidnapers had previously buried a moving van to be used as a prison for their victims.

In preparing the moving van, the kidnapers had cut a hole in the roof as an access hatch. In the wheel wells they had cut holes to act as makeshift toilets. Two small holes were cut in the sides of the van to which were attached a jury–rigged ventilation system operated by 12 volt batteries. Finally, they had buried the truck, leaving a three foot wide hole over the access hatch.

When the kidnapers arrived at the quarry with their victims, they parked the passenger vans and waited until sometime after 3 a.m. the next morning, when they then removed the children and bus driver from the passenger vans and forced them to climb down a ladder into the buried moving van. In the moving van were mattresses, some food and a small quantity of water. Before being made to climb down into the buried van, an article of clothing or other personal possession was taken from each victim and their names were taken down—written on a bag from a fast–food restaurant.

When all the victims were in the buried van, the kidnapers placed a steel plate over the access hole in the roof of the van. They then intended to place two heavy truck batteries (each weighing well over 100 pounds) on top of the steel plate, but on the spur of the moment, one was thought sufficient. This would prove fortuitous, as the original plan almost certainly would have meant the death of the victims.

The kidnapers then placed a sheet of plywood on top of the single large battery and shoveled two feet of dirt into the hole above the plywood. The kidnapers then departed—leaving their victims entombed, presumedly to die.

Many hours later and with great desperation in the dark, suffocating atmosphere, the bus driver, standing on the piled mattresses and assisted by some of the older children, was able to push up on the steel plate over the access hole and scoop handfuls of dirt down into the moving van. Soon, he was able to shift the steel plate from side to side and dislodge the battery above. After hours of work, he was able to push the huge battery to one side and eventually slide it down into the van. Using his hands, the driver was able to break apart the plywood panel, and by scooping handfuls of dirt down into the van, he could finally open a hole big enough to allow their escape.

By sheer coincidence, Alameda County Sheriff's Lieutenant Edward Volpe and his wife, Kathleen, an inspector in the District Attorney's Office, were driving along a country road in the Livermore Valley that evening when they came upon the 26 bedraggled children and their bus driver walking alongside the road. The children and driver were transported directly to the Sheriff's facility at Santa Rita, where they were medically examined, fed, clothed and interrogated.

The mystery of what had happened to the busload of children who had vanished off the face of the earth had been solved. Our investigation began immediately. District Attorney Lowell Jensen took charge, along with Sheriff Tom Houchins of Alameda County. A command post was set up at the Office of Emergency Services building in San Leandro, where the entire investigation was coordinated.

The local, national, and even international press were camped on the doorstep. District Attorney Jensen and Sheriff Houchins did an outstanding job under the mounting public pressure. The teamwork exhibited by all the law enforcement agencies involved, under the leadership of the Alameda County Sheriff's and District Attorney's Offices, was, likewise, outstanding. The Office of Emergency Services command post became the clearing house for all investigative leads and their follow–up. Through serial numbers, it was learned where much of the equipment used by the kidnapers had been purchased, leading to jurisdictions all over the western United States. Some of the equipment had been purchased as surplus from the U.S. Navy. As a result, the Naval Investigative Service became involved. Of course, the FBI had become involved in the case almost immediately, as was virtually every law enforcement agency in the state.

From these leads, the investigation focused on Fred Woods, the 24 year old son of the owner of the quarry where the victims were found and the grandson of the founder of the Newhall Land and Farming Company. Fred Woods lived in the chauffeur's quarters above the garage at the family estate in San Mateo County. San Mateo County officers staked out the Newhall estate.

Jack Meehan of the District Attorney's Office and Ed Volpe of the Sheriff's Office led the investigation team. Investigative leads were funneled to the command post, where each jurisdiction's involvement was directed and coordinated. Search warrants were carefully drafted by Meehan, who, from his long experience directing the "Law in Motion" in–service education program of the District Attorney's Office, was an expert on the changing rules of procedure. Meehan did an extraordinary job of crossing every "t" and dotting every "i" to make sure the case would be error–proof when it went to trial.

As was the law at the time, a search warrant had to be signed by the magistrate in the community where it was to be served. At times, a local judge would be roused from bed in the middle of the night to sign a warrant. As the investigation proceeded, new information was developed and the original affidavit was amended, becoming, in essence, a "rolling search warrant," which grew in size as one search led to another. Lieutenant Volpe flew by light airplane to many of the jurisdictions where warrants were to be served. This was necessary to maintain the continuity of the affidavit, as Volpe was able to swear to his personal knowledge of the investigation to date.

At one point, a warrant was obtained to search a particular space in a rental storage facility. In that space was found one of the vans in which the victims were transported from Madera County to Alameda County. In the next space, over a divider, the investigators could see the other two vans. Reporting this to Meehan, the investigators on the scene were ordered to hold in place while Meehan amended the warrant's affidavit and a new warrant was issued by the local magistrate for searching the additional spaces. No mistakes were made that could cause problems at trial.

Woods' quarters at the Newhall estate were searched, and, among other incriminating items, a detailed written plan for the crime, a draft ransom note, and the fast–food restaurant bag with the victims' names written on it were found. An army of searchers combed the roadside leading from the quarry in Alameda County to San Mateo County. Several of the personal items and clothing taken from the victims were found.

Woods was captured in Vancouver, British Columbia by the Royal Canadian Mounted Police, working in cooperation with the FBI. The FBI had sent a package—ostensibly from a family member—to Woods by mail, and the RCMP staked out the post office. Woods was arrested when he picked up the package. The investigation also implicated two brothers, friends of Woods who lived nearby. One was picked up by an alert stake–out team of San Mateo officers, and the other surrendered, in the company of his counsel, at the Alameda County District Attorney's Office.

The case first was presented to the Madera County Grand Jury by Chief Assistant Dick Haugner of the Alameda County District Attorney's Office with the assistance of Madera County District Attorney David Minier. An Indictment was returned and the case was transferred to Alameda County for trial.

The trial Court conducted a full hearing on the numerous search warrants used to seize the evidence in the case. Deputy District Attorney Rae Boker represented the prosecution at the hearing. The Court ruled that the warrants which had been drafted by Jack Meehan were valid and the numerous items of evidence seized were admissible. The presentation of evidence at the trial in Alameda County Superior Court was made by Dick Haugner and Joanne Parrilli of the Alameda County District Attorney's Office.

Bodily harm was alleged in the case of three of the victims. One of the children had scraped her knee descending the ladder into the buried van, and the bus driver and another of the children had sustained cuts during their escape efforts. As a result of the close conditions in the passenger vans and forced incontinence of the frightened and confused children, the befouled and humid air had caused some symptoms of heat exhaustion among the victims. Some of the children had fainted while others had exhibited stomach distress. Two children had developed nose bleeds.

Under Penal Code section 209, kidnaping with bodily harm was, at that time, an offense punishable by life imprisonment without possibility of parole. As a result of the extremely professional investigation led by the Alameda County District Attorney's Office, the evidence implicating the defendants in the kidnaping was incontrovertible. The defense entered a plea of guilty but reserved the right to contest the bodily harm allegation, and trial proceeded before the Court without a jury. All defendants were convicted of kidnaping with bodily harm and were sentenced to life without possibility of parole. The defendants filed appeals challenging the allegations of bodily harm.

In supporting his finding of bodily harm, the trial judge reasoned that the whole experience had constituted:

> "an ordeal of terror . . . [which] . . . causes suffering. . . . And suffering to me is what this statute is all about."

The trial judge concluded that the nose bleeds, fainting and stomach aches sustained by several of the victims substantiated "the tremendous amount of suffering that was sustained."

On appeal to the California District Court of Appeal, the bodily harm conviction was reversed. The Court ruled that:

> "the *physical* injuries or harm suffered were simply unsubstantial, transitory forms of bodily distress insufficient to rise to the level of bodily harm contemplated by the Legislature in order to automatically trigger the extreme penalty of perpetual imprisonment. While the defendants candidly concede that the record is replete with evidence of *mental* harm in the form of fear and anxiety, it is vigorously contended that the evidence of temporary bodily discomfort sustained by the three youngsters during their confinement does not amount to *substantial bodily injury* within

> the meaning of the enhancement proviso as interpreted by the courts.
>
> ". . . None of the transient physical distresses, consisting of stomach aches, nose bleeds and fainting, amounted to serious or substantial bodily injuries. The minor physical injuries sustained related to the conditions of confinement and were not the result of the application of physical force by the defendants beyond that involved in effecting the instant kidnaping."

In a dissenting opinion, Judge Elkington remarked:

> "I think all would agree that, had defendants punched or kicked their young victims in their faces or abdomens, thus causing bloody noses and abdominal pains or other such trauma, they would have suffered bodily harm as intended by Penal Code section 209.
>
> "My mind rejects the argument that by inflicting such reasonably foreseeable injuries *indirectly* and by threat of death or bodily injury, under circumstances as here shown by the evidence, defendants' crimes were somehow mitigated. Nor am I able to find legal or other authority supportive of such an argument."[49]

CYANIDE BULLETS

Another spectacular case which received international press coverage was the case of Jose Ricardo* and John Roberts,* of the self–styled Symbionese Liberation Army, in which Oakland Public Schools Superintendent Marcus Foster was shot and killed with cyanide–encrusted bullets as he was leaving a meeting of the School Board. The case took a further twist when the Symbionese Liberation Army kidnaped Patricia Hearst, daughter of newspaper owner William Randolph Hearst, who was attending the University of California at Berkeley.

The case of Marcus Foster's killers was transferred from Alameda County to Sacramento County where it was prosecuted by District Attorney Lowell Jensen of Alameda County. In this trial, which

[49]People v. Schoenfeld, et. al., (1980) 111 Cal. 3rd 671

lasted eleven weeks, the jury convicted both defendants. However, the District Court of Appeals was forced to reverse Roberts' conviction because of a ruling of the California Supreme Court. The District Court of Appeals reversed based on the fact that the trial judge, after the jury was out for 11 days, had given a special instruction to the jury urging them to try to reach a verdict one way or another. A verdict convicting Ricardo had been voted but not returned to court before the special instruction was given.

In an opinion in another case, which was decided after the Roberts trial but before Roberts' appeal was heard by the District Court of Appeal, the California Supreme Court held for the first time that giving the jury such an instruction was error, although at the time it was given in the Roberts trial, it was a standard instruction which had been approved in California, in most other states, and in the federal courts. Moreover, the Supreme Court directed that this new rule would be applied retroactively to cases already tried according to the previously–prevailing law. This was a completely unjustified ruling and resulted in a number of important cases, besides Marcus Foster, being reversed.

This was another example of the extent to which the higher courts of California have moved with the stream of liberalism in their effort to achieve an illusory and impractical perfection in defense of the criminal. The number of cases in which appeals to federal courts from proceedings in the state courts are made and granted raises questions as to the quality of work in either the state courts or the federal courts, or both.

The retrial of Roberts was transferred to Monterey County where, seven and a half years after he was arrested and after a second lengthy trial, he was acquitted. During this period, he was confined in state prison after conviction on another charge.

In his criticism of the eagerness of higher courts to change law by judicial decree, the Honorable Macklin Fleming, Justice of a District Court of Appeal of California, in the preface to his book, *The Price of Perfect Justice*, writes as follows:

> "This book argues that, in our perpetual adjustment and tinker-

ing with the Goddess' scales in order to strike a perfect balance, we have allowed her sword to rust and her right arm to atrophy; that, as a consequence of this neglect of the compulsive element, the legal system as a whole has been thrown out of kilter and into disarray."[50]

Concerning retroactivity, Justice Fleming writes as follows:

"Driven by this logic courts have overturned existing judgments in wholesale fashion. Yet practical necessity eventually brings to a halt the process of perpetual change that is the consequence of an unlimited retroactivity. The resulting compromises have led to a crazy quilt of rules of retroactivity in specific situations under which logical distinctions have all but disappeared. Some new rules are fully retroactive; some are not retroactive at all; some are retroactive in all cases whose judgments are not final; and some are retroactive to specific dates, selected almost at random. The bewildering complexity of the current rules of retroactivity provides criminal lawyers and judges with much of their current business.[51]

". . . In picking and choosing among the bewildering variety of possible rules for retroactivity the courts have entered foursquare into the field of legislation. Justice Harlan of the United States Supreme Court, referring to what he called the Court's ambulatory retroactivity doctrine, said in 1971:

"'What emerges from today's decisions is that in the realm of constitutional adjudication in the criminal field the court is free to act, in effect, like a legislature, making its new constitutional rules wholly or partially retroactive or only prospective as it deems wise. I completely disagree with this point of view. . . . (T)he court in deciding these cases seems largely to have forgotten the limitations that accompany its functions as a court of law.'"[52]

[50]Macklin Fleming, *The Price of Perfect Justice; The Adverse Consequences of Current Legal Doctrine on the American Courtroom,* (New York, Basic Books, 1974) p. vii.

[51]Ibid., p. 14

[52]Ibid., p. 19.

THE ULTIMATE MIRANDA CASE

In an extraordinary perversion of the Miranda rule, a son murdered his father, mother and grandfather to obtain their life insurance, and confessed the murders to a deputy sheriff and later to a deputy district attorney. In this case, the District Court of Appeals and the California Supreme Court reversed his convictions because, after being fully advised of his rights under *Miranda*,[53] he made his first confession—at his own request—"off the record." He later made a full confession during a 60 Minutes CBS Television show witnessed by millions. On appeal by the state to the United States Supreme Court, the petition for review was denied. He was later retried and convicted.

OTHER MISCELLANEOUS CASES

Other important cases which passed through the Alameda County District Attorney's Office during the 1970's included: the second and third trials of the Black Panther who shot Oakland Police Officers Darnell and Jensen in an ambush attack; the case of Hell's Angels leader Sonny Barger for murder and narcotics; the triple murders of the drug–dealing Ragusa family, a case with international ramifications; the case of the son of the mayor of Albany who pleaded guilty to the killing of teenage University of California coed Judy Williamson; and the case of the Japanese artist and militant radical for possession of explosives involved in terrorist activities.

[53]*Miranda v. Arizona* (1966) 384 U.S. 436

9

Civil Public Law

Until May 1, 1967, in addition to the prosecution of criminal cases, the District Attorney's Office handled all civil public law work—in and out of court—for all departments of county government, all public school districts and a variety of special districts such as fire districts, police districts, flood control districts, park districts, agricultural districts, hospital districts and mosquito abatement districts. Included was the work of initial formation of new community college districts and a number of agencies, commissions, committees and other public entities. The office also handled bond issues for schools and other public works, eminent domain actions for acquisition of land for public purposes, construction contracts and leases. The office represented the county in matters pertaining to joint highway districts, county fairs and labor contracts. When faced with reluctance on the part of voters to finance construction of certain public buildings and public works by the sale of public bonds, we handled test litigation involving issuance of local government–backed privately–financed bonds.

During the early 1930's, the District Attorney's Office handled legal work involved in formation of the East Bay Regional Park District and continued to do the legal work for this park district—at no expense to the district—until the Board of Supervisors created the County Counsel's Office, at which time the park district employed its own legal counsel. During the time that the District Attorney's Office did the legal work for the park district, it grew to be one of the largest and most beautiful collections of public parks and recreation facilities in the United States.

By 1964, the population of Alameda County had passed the million mark. The county included thirteen cities and a large unincorporated area, and operated with an annual budget of $400 million, exclusive of schools and special districts. The load of civil legal work was heavy. Changing concepts as to the rights and obligations of people and government agencies—federal, state and local—increased the civil legal work of the District Attorney's Office. With the increasing controls and regulations created by the federal government, legal problems and mandated solutions on local levels of government multiplied. The legal ramifications and complexities of a governmental agency far exceed those of an agency in the private sector and are more exposed to pressure and scrutiny by the media and citizenry.

There was no Welfare Department in Alameda County until the mid–1930's. Before that, whatever aid to impoverished or handicapped persons there was came from private institutions, individual philanthropy or minuscule statutory categorical aid doled out sparingly by the Board of Supervisors. Perforce, with the Depression years came various kinds of public assistance for the needy to supplement what the churches and individuals had been doing for centuries.

Slowly but surely, provisions for food, shelter, medical care, employment, education and other things became a legal right of the individual and a legal obligation of government. Concomitantly, the domain of public enterprise expanded, opening a Pandora's box of administrative and legal complications. This took the form of public housing, parks and freeways, public stadia for games to entertain a bored public, and arenas to attract conventioneers and fill business coffers.

Among public projects of major importance involving the District Attorney's Office were: two vehicle tubes under the Estuary between the cities of Oakland and Alameda, highway bridges over the Estuary and San Leandro Bay to Bay Farm Island and the Oakland Airport, and the Oakland—Alameda County Coliseum and Arena. The District Attorney's Office was also involved in acquisition of land and drafting of contracts for construction of public buildings for more courts and jails and more offices for probation, police, health, welfare and other agencies of local government.

In the public sector there are, of course, the day–to–day things that must be done according to law and the occasional event or decision of such magnitude as to affect the lives of millions of individuals for countless years. The challenge of the civil law work to the public law officer and the opportunity, under the lash of necessity, to perform a public service and to be a vital cog in the growth of a community are stimulating and could be, over the long pull, more satisfying than criminal prosecutions.

BRIDGES

Occasionally, the District Attorney's Office became involved in a case which took it into the federal courts. These were cases involving official or public performance bonds where there was a diversity of citizenship, in admiralty against ships for damage to Alameda County bridges over the Estuary, or involving actions with respect to civil rights under federal statutes.

A case by Alameda County against the United States government involved the Fruitvale Avenue drawbridge over the Estuary from Oakland to Alameda. This structure, built in the 1880's by agreement with the United States government and Alameda County, was a combination highway and railroad bridge. Over the years it had become inadequate. Located on a bend in the Estuary, it was a hazard to navigation of ships passing through on strong running tides between San Francisco and San Leandro Bays. During the 1930's, the Board of Supervisors decided to build a new bridge, but Earl Warren, as counsel for the Board of Supervisors, raised a question as to the legality of the county using public funds to build a bridge over which trains for a private railroad company would pass.

In litigation which I handled, a test suit was filed by the District Attorney's Office which raised the question of the liability of the county for construction and operation of the bridge under the contract between the United States and the county. That contract provided that the county should operate, maintain and, if necessary, rebuild the bridge. Prepared during the 19th century by the United States government for the United States Army Corps of Engineers, the contract had in it a clause—in general use at the time with respect to bridges over navigable waters—which stated that the contract was voidable at the option of the United States government.

The contract was held binding on the county by United States District Court Judge Harold Louderback, but on appeal the United States Court of Appeals reversed the District Court and held that the contract was void for lack of mutuality, thus relieving Alameda County of any responsibility for operation, maintenance or reconstruction of the bridge. This also relieved the county of the expense of three bridge operators to operate the bridge around the clock. The savings in money to the county over the years ran into the millions of dollars. This decision set a precedent, in effect holding void other similar contracts between federal, state, and local governments throughout the nation.[54]

With overseas shipping and U.S. Navy air and other activities during World War II, the population and commerce increased in the city of Alameda. As pressure mounted for construction of a new bridge at the Fruitvale Avenue crossing, the United States government built a new bridge for the Southern Pacific Railroad Company, but stalled on building a bridge for pedestrian and motor vehicle traffic. U.S. Senator Knowland and Congressman Miller—both Alamedans—took issue with the holding in our test case, *Alameda County v. United States,* referring to it as the "Nuts and Bolts" case. However, as a result of the decision, the United States continued to operate and maintain the bridge for years. In recent years, it was replaced by the United States government, to be operated at the expense of Alameda County.

[54]*Alameda County v. United States* (1941) 124 Fed.2d 611

In the late 1930's, the San Francisco–Oakland Bay Bridge was completed to replace the ferryboats at a cost of $76 million. This structure was one of the great engineering achievements of the time. With its foundations deep in the Bay, it was built with two levels: the upper level for 3 lanes of automobile traffic in each direction; the lower level for buses, trucks, and commuter trains. The Key System and Southern Pacific Railroad Company electric trains ran on a double set of tracks and took commuters from Alameda and Contra Costa Counties to San Francisco.

Later, after the demise of the train systems and as automobile traffic increased, the two sets of tracks on the lower level of the bridge were removed and the roadbed was converted for automobile use. Following the conversion, the upper level was dedicated to all westbound traffic and the lower level to all eastbound.

A proposal to build a "parallel" or "southern" crossing gained momentum and alternative locations for a parallel bridge began to circulate in business circles and in local and state governments. At the same time, conflicting interests of property owners and political entities in the path of proposed locations for the crossing and its approaches also surfaced.

Frederick Howser, attorney general of California at the time, sent a letter to me, as counsel for Alameda County, and to the city attorney of the city and county of San Francisco, requesting our opinions as to the legality of a parallel bridge. In reply, I pointed out the fact that under statute the tolls on the existing bridge would have to be eliminated when the bridge's construction bonds were retired. In fact, as these bonds approached liquidation, the state Legislature engaged in a species of legislative legerdemain providing that receipts from tolls could be applied to bridge approaches, other Bay crossings and constructions—a performance referred to by one member of the Assembly as a case of "fancy highway robbery." At the present time, the original bonds have long since been paid off, and the bridge tolls have not only remained, but increased manyfold.

THE KEY SYSTEM

One of the related problems which received wide public interest involved rate hearings of the California Public Utilities Commission as to fares on the Key System's East Bay electric street cars and trans–bay trains. This was another of many maneuvers by East Bay cities to transfer the cost of municipal functions to the county government.

Following World War II, the state Public Utilities Commission had granted a succession of fare increases to the Key System. In 1950, when the fourth application within a year for fare increases was filed, the Mayor's Conference of the Cities requested the county Board of Supervisors to share the expense of fighting another rate increase. The rationale for this was that one of the street car lines was located on a small stretch of unincorporated land between San Leandro and Hayward.

The Board of Supervisors agreed and the District Attorney's Office was in the case with the city attorneys for the cities of Oakland, Berkeley, Albany, Emeryville, Piedmont, Alameda, San Leandro, and Hayward of Alameda County, and El Cerrito and Richmond of Contra Costa County. I personally took over the legal work involved and retained, at joint county and cities' expense, a battery of expert witnesses to combat the equipment and operational cost estimates of the Key System and the Public Utilities Commission.

In the District Attorney's Office at the time, was an able young lawyer named David Wendel, who had graduated from the University of California in accounting and from Hayward State College in law. With the help of our rate experts and accountants, we probed into the calculations and methodology of the Key System and Public Utilities Commission witnesses and demolished their presentations.

Part of the case of the Key System was the market value of the Key System stock—around $35 to $36 a share at that time. A probe of this figure by the District Attorney's Office before the California Public Utilities Commission disclosed that Alfred Lundberg, a San Francisco stock broker, had come to Oakland before World War II, and, by cultivating certain leaders of community and fraternal affairs, gained the presidency and management of the Key System. Among his civic activities was the promotion and presidency of the Conference of Christians and Jews—an organization designed to stimulate better inter–denominational relations.

At the time Lundberg arrived on the scene, the Key System's financial condition had been shattered by a series of reorganizations. As a result, the depreciating stock, held mainly by loyal Oakland residents and their estates, had little value or movement in the stock market.

Surreptitiously through an agent, Lundberg began buying up Key System stock at around $5 a share. When he had acquired control by ownership of over fifty percent of the stock, he and his colleagues sold out to National City Lines for $35 a share and made a big profit, to the chagrin of the long–time loyal stockholders of the Key System who had held on through the years of the Depression and other hard times.

At roughly the same time Lundberg was acquiring control of the Key System, the Fitzgerald brothers had parlayed a single dilapidated bus in Minnesota into a vast national chain of municipal bus lines. They had done this by acquiring electric street car transportation systems all over the nation and then phasing them out of business, to be replaced by their buses. This was subsidized by Mack Trucks (General Motors), Firestone Tire and Rubber Company, Phillips Oil Company and Standard Oil of California, each of which stood to profit handsomely by the transition from electric trolleys to buses. They were, in effect, able to fix prices and monopolize the sale of buses, tires, batteries and petroleum products to city bus transportation systems.

We proved at the Key System rate hearing that Mack Trucks, Firestone, Phillips and Standard Oil of California had been convicted by *nolo contendere* in a Sherman anti–trust case brought against them by the United States government for conspiracy in restraint of trade. And, just as happened in other cities where National City Lines had acquired and supplanted electric transportation systems with buses, so it happened in the East Bay cities of Alameda County, where conveniently scheduled electric street cars and trains have disappeared, and carbon–monoxide and smog have increased.

From before the turn of the century until after World War II, the East Bay cities and the rolling hills and valleys of Alameda and Contra Costa Counties were crisscrossed by a network of conveniently scheduled electric street cars and trans–bay trains of the Southern Pacific Company and the Key Route Company (nee the Oakland Traction Company). Much of this train network was installed across the years by the celebrated "Borax" Smith of Twenty Mule Teams and Death Valley fame whose beautiful home and gardens were located on a hill overlooking Oakland, San Francisco Bay and the Golden Gate, and where, once a year, he opened his spacious estate to the citizens of Oakland for a community picnic.

Before World War I, a wholly electrified railroad system, the Sacramento Northern, was constructed to run from downtown Oakland, where ferryboat passengers would arrive from San Francisco, through a tunnel in the east Oakland hills to Moraga, Lafayette, Walnut Creek, Concord, Antioch, across the San Joaquin River and north to Sacramento and Marysville. Spur tracks extended from Walnut Creek to Alamo and Danville, and they could easily have been extended further on level terrain to San Ramon, Dublin, Sunol, Pleasanton and Livermore, thus providing direct electric transportation from large areas of Alameda and Contra Costa Counties to Oakland and San Francisco. The Sacramento Northern was closed down, its tracks pulled up, its electric lines eliminated and buses substituted, which of course increased the income of the automotive and related businesses.

All this was occurring at the same time tens of thousands of residents of San Francisco, Oakland and other East Bay cities were moving over the hills to suburban Contra Costa County. The freeways, tunnels and bridges between San Francisco, Alameda County and Contra Costa County would soon become inadequate.

In the late 1950's, after much controversy and delay, construction of a second parallel Bay Bridge was abandoned and a proposal gained momentum to build an electrified rapid transit system around the Bay Area. Planning for a Bay Area Rapid Transit (BART) system, with a tube under the Bay between Oakland and San Francisco and a new tunnel between Oakland and Orinda, began.

In the meantime, a Bay Area Rapid Transit District was created, and a bond issue of $750 million for construction of the BART system was authorized for submission to the voters of San Francisco, Alameda, Contra Costa, San Mateo and Marin counties. The bond issue was contested in a court action unsuccessfully. The entire cost of this project to the taxpayers raised a bitter controversy, and the vote for BART won by a very small margin in San Francisco, Alameda and Contra Costa counties. San Mateo and Marin counties voted not to participate.

With increased costs of construction because of inflation and design changes, further funding to complete and operate BART had to be provided by the state Legislature in the form of taxes on real property in the three counties. This is an ad valorem real property tax collected by each county. In addition, BART receives one–half of one percent of the sales tax in the three counties, collected by the state.

Here again was an example of questionable leadership in the county and state. Had the Sacramento Northern been maintained and a relatively short spur track installed to cover the distance from Moraga to Orinda, the same territory now serviced by BART and a lot more could have been serviced by existing facilities and at far less cost. The Sacramento Northern was a private enterprise and self–sustaining. Reliable experts advise that BART will have to be sustained by deficit budgeting and taxes indefinitely. Construction of BART overran original cost estimates and completion deadlines by more than double, and once running, the modern high–speed computer–controlled trains have frequently broken down. The rapidly growing areas of Moraga, the San Ramon Valley, Dublin, Livermore, and Pleasanton are still an automobile commute from the nearest BART station.

FREEWAYS

Among clients serviced by the Civil Division of the District Attorney's Office were Joint Highway Districts 13 and 26 for acquisition of property and construction of freeways and freeway tunnels in Alameda and Contra Costa counties.

The contractors, some of the biggest in the nation, ran into unanticipated water seepage trouble on work in the Broadway low level (Caldecott) tunnels and refused to finish the job. The District Attorney's Office sued the surety company on the performance bond and won. The job was finished by the bond company. The now heavily traveled tunnels, named in honor of Alameda County Supervisor Caldecott, are part of the state highway system (Highway 24). Highway 13, which connects with the Caldecott tunnels via Highway 24, was named the Warren Freeway by the Legislature in honor of Earl Warren.

PRIVATE SCHOOLS

An important civil case with anti–religious overtones occurred when certain pressures surfaced to compel all California counties to tax non–profit private elementary and secondary schools.

The real target of this movement was the Catholic schools, which, under a long–standing interpretation of a provision of the California Constitution, had been property tax exempt. In a strange contrast with his leadership in the Conference of Christians and Jews, Alfred Lundberg filed in the Superior Court of Alameda County a so–called class action taxpayers' suit to mandate Alameda County to assess and tax private non–profit elementary and secondary schools, which at that time in all states of the Union were exempt by law from property taxes.

As chairman of the Law and Legislative Committee of the District Attorneys and County Counsels Association of California, I spoke at the annual conference of the Association and said that in my opinion the prevailing constitutional interpretation on tax exempt non–profit schools was valid and that I had so advised the county assessor and the Board of Supervisors of Alameda County. With one exception, all the district attorneys and county counsels of the state concurred. The county counsel of the lone county which did not concur issued an ambivalent opinion which his assessor refused to follow.

To adjudicate this legal hot potato, the presiding judge of the Superior Court of Alameda County assigned three judges; two judges ruled that the schools were taxable and the other ruled that they were exempt. On behalf of Alameda County, I appealed the case to the California Supreme Court, which reversed the ruling of the two Alameda County judges and affirmed the ruling of the lone judge and the theretofore prevailing interpretation. Counsel for the plaintiff took the case to the United States Supreme Court by appeal from the California Supreme Court. The United States Supreme Court granted our motion to dismiss. Shortly after this decision, supporters of the litigation to abolish tax exemption of private non–profit schools got enough signatures to put a proposed initiative amendment to the California Constitution on the ballot. It failed passage at the election by a large margin. If successful, this lawsuit or the initiative constitutional amendment could have been the beginning of a concerted nationwide effort to wipe out private non–profit elementary and secondary schools.

LIVERMORE VALLEY WATER

In the late 1940's, a group of ranch owners, mostly cattlemen from around Livermore Valley, called on the Board of Supervisors to report their concern over a water shortage. They said the water levels in their wells had been getting lower in recent years, particularly during a protracted drought. They also said that the city and county of San Francisco was drawing large quantities of water from nineteen wells around Pleasanton. Each well was five hundred feet deep. The farmers claimed that this was lowering the water table in the Livermore Valley, which, at the time, was primarily farming and cattle country where water was of paramount importance. These farmers and cattlemen were important taxpayers of the county. They were very much disturbed and they felt they were entitled to some action by the Board of Supervisors. As usual, the problem was referred to the District Attorney's Office for investigation and solution.

The investigation disclosed that the water problem in the valley had a long history, some of which was contained in the files of an action by the United States government to acquire land and water rights in connection with proposed Naval training and hospital facilities at Camp Shoemaker during World War II. At one time, the area at the western end of the valley, extending from a small community known as Dublin to Pleasanton and Sunol, had been a low swampland that in wet years would be covered with water. Before the turn of the century, the United States Reclamation Service built ditches, drained the water, and made a large rich area of fine land available for farming and vineyards.

The Spring Valley Water Company, supplier of water for San Francisco, acquired large stretches of land in the valley around Pleasanton and Sunol. Mrs. Phoebe Hearst, mother of William Randolph Hearst, and owner of the famous Hacienda (now Castlewood Country Club), received unlimited water rights in perpetuity in exchange for land conveyed to the Spring Valley Water Company. Later, the Spring Valley Water Company became Hetch–Hetchy with its source of water in the High Sierra Mountains, 150 miles to the east at the headwaters of the Tuolumne River in Yosemite National Park. From the High Sierras, the Hetch–Hetchy aqueduct carried water to San Francisco via the Livermore Valley and reservoirs in the hills south of San Francisco. But before the Hetch–Hetchy system was built, the Spring Valley Water Company had tapped other sources of water in and around Pleasanton and Sunol.

We checked the records of the city and county of San Francisco and Hetch–Hetchy. We found that San Francisco was selling water to other cities around the Bay. We advised the farmers to keep logs of the water levels in their wells and let it be known that we were preparing to file suit to enjoin San Francisco from pumping water from the 19 wells.

I was in the habit of attending the annual meeting of the Cattlemen's Association in Livermore, where I kept them informed as to the progress of our investigation and our plans to file suit. Not long thereafter, San Francisco stopped pumping water from the 19 wells, and the dry years were followed by some wet years. Whether the end of the drought or our investigation caused San Francisco to cease pumping, I do not know, but water levels in the wells of the farmers began to rise and the demands of the cattlemen for action by the Board of Supervisors ended.

THE COLISEUM

The Bay Area for a long time had been good sports territory. Competition, especially collegiate sports in football, baseball and basketball among teams from California, Stanford, Santa Clara, San Francisco and Saint Mary's, was keen and of high quality. Before World War I, Saint Mary's College baseball teams were among the best in the nation. Saint Mary's was in college baseball what Notre Dame became in college football. During spring training, Saint Mary's beat Pacific Coast League professional teams consistently and also beat the Chicago White Sox and the Boston Red Sox during their spring training trips to California in years when those teams had won the World Series. Many Saint Mary's alumni played in the major leagues. There was also substantial interest in and support of horse racing and boxing. As early as 1904, long before the National Football League and when the prevailing competition in the area was rugby, Oakland had professional teams playing American–style football. After World War II, with the expansion of professional sports came publicly financed stadia. Previously, teams had played in private facilities owned and operated by private enterprises.

During the 1950's, a movement was started to build a coliseum complex in Oakland. Financing was considered via bond issues of the East Bay Regional Park District or a public recreation district, but after polls were taken, these methods were discarded. The District Attorney's Office handled legal work for the East Bay Regional Park District and other park and recreation districts. There was controversy between southern Alameda County and Oakland concerning location. Finally a site and a method of financing were agreed upon—viz. the present location in east Oakland—and a private sector bond issue of $26 million to be amortized over a period of 35 years with Alameda County and the city of Oakland as guarantors on the bonds in the event of default. As planned, the coliseum was to seat 48,000 with possible expansion to 80,500. For football and baseball it now has a capacity of 54,000.

The acquisition of a site involved, among other things, an exchange of land between the Pacific Gas and Electric Company and the Oakland Port Authority and resolution of many sticky legal problems in financing and in conditions concerning construction, parking and use of the facilities, which had to be approved by the Oakland City Council and the Alameda County Board of Supervisors. This involved drafting of a contract between the city, the county and the financing institution. It also involved approval by the city attorney of Oakland and the district attorney of Alameda County—certainly no simple task if legal hurdles were to be resolved so that the contract and the bond issue would pass muster for sale of the bonds as tax–free obligations. This meant approval by the United States Treasury Department, the State Franchise Tax Board, private legal counsel of Coliseum, Inc. and financial institutions underwriting the bond issue.

Eventually, the bond issue was underwritten, floated, and the whole $26 million project completed. In the meantime, Oakland had a pro–football team, the Oakland Raiders, in the American Football League. The Raiders were playing temporarily in a small stadium at an Oakland community college, and Oakland was negotiating with Charles Finley to have his Kansas City Athletics of the American Baseball League play in the forthcoming Oakland—Alameda County Coliseum.

Although Coliseum, Inc. had its own legal counsel, decisions had to be made by the city and county, which looked to the city attorney and district attorney for legal advice. Alameda County Auditor Eugene Waring, who under California law was liable on county warrants involved in county expenditures, retained private counsel, which he had a legal right to do because of potentially conflicting interests, since the District Attorney's Office represented both the

Board of Supervisors and the county auditor. I concurred with Waring's counsel that a test case in court be held to resolve any questions as to the legality of the contract and the proposed bond issue.

A trial was held before Superior Court Judge Thomas Caldecott on the pleadings and stipulated facts prepared by Assistant District Attorneys Douglas Dunning, Richard Moore and myself, and agreed to by the city attorney of Oakland, by Gerald Hagger counsel for the Coliseum, Inc. and Paul St. Sure, counsel for the county auditor. Judge Caldecott found all the proceedings legal and gave judgment for Coliseum, Inc. and the city and county. St. Sure's office filed an appeal from this judgment which, if carried to final conclusion, could have delayed construction of the Coliseum for years. There was an ambiguity in the law with respect to the maximum term of the lease and amortization of the bonds.

A recommendation by me for clarification of this ambiguity was approved by counsel for all parties and the Court. The litigation was then finalized, at which time work started and the coliseum complex was eventually completed in 1966.

A few days before the opening game in the coliseum between the San Francisco 49'ers and the Oakland Raiders, the Central Labor Council of Oakland gave strike sanction to the unions involved in the operation of the coliseum. Counsel for the Coliseum, Inc. went to court and obtained a temporary restraining order against the action of the Central Labor Council and against picketing. The Labor Council decided to ignore the restraining order, and so advised Coliseum, Inc.'s counsel. This meant picket lines at entrances to the coliseum and possible work refusal by union employees of Coliseum, Inc. and concessionaires, ticket takers, ushers, vendors and even union members of the private police agency employed by Coliseum, Inc.

At 9 o'clock Saturday night (the game was scheduled for the next day at 1 p.m. and was sold out), counsel for Coliseum, Inc. phoned me to say that he had appealed to the Oakland chief of police to enforce the restraining order and that the chief said, "The Oakland police will do nothing unless advised to do so by Coakley." Because Coliseum, Inc. had contracted with a private police agency, Oakland police were excluded from the property except as paying customers.

I could to help and that I would talk to the police chief. I instructed Coliseum, Inc.'s counsel to have the coliseum manager at the coliseum at 5 o'clock the next morning. Without ticket takers, ushers, vendors, concessionaires and private police, and with 48,000 customers clamoring for service, things could be pretty ugly—certainly a bad start for the coliseum and the East Bay. The next morning, Richard Moore and I met with the coliseum management, employees and concessionaires, and persuaded them to honor their contracts. The chief of police agreed to cooperate and sent the genial and tactful Captain James McCarthy with 25 uniformed Oakland police officers to police the streets at entrances to the coliseum. There were no incidents.

The Coliseum, Inc. employees went to work and the coliseum filled up. Union drivers on buses of the San Francisco team refused to pass picket lines, and the team members had to walk with their gear from the adjacent Nimitz Freeway to their dressing quarters in the Coliseum. The game started on time and San Francisco won when, in the final seconds, a Raider halfback, en route to a touchdown, dropped the ball inches from the San Francisco goal line.

THE SCHOOL DEPARTMENT

From the standpoint of quality, the performance of the staff of the District Attorney's Office assigned to school work was outstanding. From the time when she was appointed a deputy district attorney by Ezra Decoto in 1921, Agnes Polsdorfer, a graduate of Boalt Hall Law School of the University of California, worked in what came to be called the "School Department" of the office. In this work she succeeded Frances Wilson, who resigned when she married Alexander ("Captain") Kidd, the colorful professor of criminal law and evidence at Boalt Hall. Frances and Agnes were among the earliest female lawyers in the West—if not in the nation. Certainly they were pioneers in the field of career public legal service by female lawyers. During her entire forty years in the District Attorney's Office, Agnes Polsdorfer handled school law and bond issue work. School law was

During her entire forty years in the District Attorney's Office, Agnes Polsdorfer handled school law and bond issue work. School law was not on the curricula of law schools and most young male lawyers were not interested in the subject.

Until after World War II, school law was a confusing mixture of case and statutory law. The latter spread without rhyme or reason through various codes until finally, with the help of Agnes and her assistants, Frank Parker, Catherine Carson and Thomas Firby, a revised Education Code was drafted and enacted by the Legislature in 1959. Even then, the indexing left much to be desired, so that the "School Department" of the District Attorney's Office of Alameda County continued to be a guide and a sure source of authentic school law in the state. Agnes was a widely recognized authority on school law. When school districts in other counties needed legal help they often called Agnes.

I recall one time the Attorney General's Office issued an opinion concerning a school board member's interest in contracts with school districts other than his own district which threw all school districts throughout the state into an uproar. The effect of the Attorney General's opinion would have been to subject a school trustee to prosecution or dismissal from office for conflict of interest if the trustee owned a single share of stock in an oil company which sold oil to another school district in a different county, even though the trustee had no personal interest in or knowledge of the transaction or regardless of how small the transaction might be. As a speaker at the annual dinner of trustees and officials of Alameda County schools, I assured them that we would challenge the attorney general's opinion in court.

When Agnes read the opinion she blew a fuse and drafted a letter to all the school boards in Alameda County, instructing them to ignore the attorney general's opinion and informing them correctly as to the law of conflict of interest. A month later, the Attorney General's Office issued what was called a "reconsideration" of the question and concurred in Agnes' opinion as stated in her letter.

Until World War II, the increase in enrollment in Alameda County schools had been slow. Agnes trained her secretary, Grace Keil, and together they handled school legal work. This work involved bond issues, land purchases, building contracts, public bidding, eminent domain actions, tenure, personal injury, workmen's compensation and other personnel problems. With the advent of World War II, immigration to California, especially from the deep South, accelerated and school enrollment rapidly increased. During the war, shortages of material and manpower held up school construction and bond issues. When the war ended, the need for more schools and money to build them ballooned, as did the legal work.

Frank Parker and Thomas Firby were transferred from other office work to the School Department and new deputies, generally fresh out of law school, were assigned to school work to be trained by Agnes who, although very jolly and congenial by nature, was a stern and exacting teacher. Among the rookie lawyers were Phyllis McKay, Catherine Carson, Karman Dudliegh, Lillian Wollitz, Marie Bertillion, Elizabeth Haggood, Alan Lindsay and others, who learned fast and performed yeoman service in a most important and urgently needed public law work.

In the early 1920's there were 54 school districts in the county, some of the one–room one–teacher variety in thinly populated rural areas. Gradually, this number was reduced by unification, so that by 1982 there were 19 districts maintaining grades kindergarten through 12, and 3 community college districts, to serve a population of 1.2 million. Financing the purchase of sites and building of new schools required many bond issues, which were prepared and processed by Agnes and Grace personally. Their work in this field was so excellent that the Alameda County school districts did not have to pay the customary fee charged by Orrick, Palmer, Dahlquist and Herrington for the supervision of the bond elections, and paid a reduced fee for the approval of George Herrington, the firm's bond expert, a validation function required by bond underwriters.

During the long tenure of Agnes Polsdorfer, every bond issue, apportionment authorization, tax anticipation or other revenue proceeding was processed without an error requiring validation by the state Legislature. Every contract involving construction of a new school or an alteration or addition to a school when the estimated cost exceeded $4,000 had to be submitted for approval by the District Attorney's Office, as did bids on public works contracts.

Questions arising in connection with bidding and defaults in performance sometimes had to be litigated in state courts. Where the surety companies on performance bonds were out–of–state corporations, the action was taken to federal courts. Such legal work was highly sophisticated, involving close factual issues, large amounts of money and expert legal skill on the part of counsel for the litigants.

Segregation and integration of school students, which spawned problems and litigation in other parts of the nation, did not seriously aggravate the legal work of the School Department of the District Attorney's Office of Alameda County. Since the 1950's, the Oakland Unified School District, the largest in the county, had open enrollment, whereby any student, regardless of race, could attend a school where there was room for him. In other school districts, any student living in the district could attend any school in a wide attendance area. Soon after World War II, the influx of blacks and other minorities into Alameda County, especially into the cities of Oakland, Berkeley, Alameda and Emeryville, was of such proportions that minorities predominated in most schools. In 1977, sixty–seven percent of the students in Oakland schools were black and 16 percent were white, the balance of 17 percent were of other minority races.

The Berkeley Unified School District, under the direction of a noted superintendent from Prince Edward County, Virginia, and an elective school board, initiated a program of forced busing. Students from schools of predominately white neighborhoods in the hill areas of Berkeley were bused to schools of predominately black neighborhoods in the flatlands in south and west Berkeley. There was considerable dissatisfaction among parents in the white areas, especially with respect to the forced movement of children in lower grades to schools long distances from their homes, but this controversy—though simmering for sometime—cooled as the trend of court decisions favoring busing advanced.

A broad policy of employment of minority teachers and administrative personnel also helped to prevent serious trouble over integration. Income for public schools in Alameda County from local and state taxes plus federal grant subsidies made it possible to provide a good quality of education, not only for regular students but also for special needs—such as handicapped and mentally retarded—students. Because of proximity to educational institutions of great prestige—such as the University of California and Stanford University and other state and private colleges—a high quality of teaching personnel was readily available, so that there was no excuse for complaint about a disparity in competence of teachers.

MILLER'S OPUS AND OTHER INDEXES

Through the years, it was the practice of attorneys working on criminal cases to reduce the results of their legal research to typewritten memoranda. In the office during the 1930's and until his untimely death in the mid–1940's, was a lawyer named Nathan Harry Miller, a Jewish immigrant from Russia, who had worked his way as a street car motorman through college and law school at Boalt Hall. He handled a wide variety of the office work, including probate and criminal cases. The office did the legal work for the public administrator, which was about 10 percent of the probate filings in the county.

Miller was a prodigious worker and a most thorough organizer in classifying, indexing and filing of things he handled. This was especially helpful in complicated multi–defendant business fraud conspiracy cases involving large amounts of documentary evidence and accounts. In some of these cases Miller's indexing was so complete that he had supplemental indexes, facetiously called by less industrious co–workers "the index to the index to the index."

Miller assembled from the criminal files all memoranda on legal questions, classified them, indexed them and had them bound. This project was of great continuing help at a time when there were few such legal publications. These books were filed in our law library and were known as "Miller's Opus." In the continuing education program in the office, which was constantly improved through the years, Miller's work was a real contribution.

He also assembled, indexed and put in loose leaf binders all approved probate forms used in the work for the public administrator, most of which had been drafted and revised by him with the help of Earleen Rutherford, later for many years executive secretary to the district attorney.

Another project of permanent benefit to the office was the classification, indexing and binding of all written civil opinions of the District Attorney's Office. This was a big job conducted by the civil deputies under the direction of Agnes Polsdorfer on Saturdays, holidays, nights and other unpaid overtime. This proved to be a great time–saver as often repeating legal problems arose in the rapidly growing county.

CODE OF COUNTY ORDINANCES

Another interesting and important project was the Alameda County Code of Ordinances. From the beginning of county government in 1853, the Board of Supervisors had been enacting ordinances, first in accordance with state statutes and later under the home–rule county Charter. For many years before the turn of the century, in fact until typewriters came into common use, the ordinances were written by hand. When the California Legislature enacted an enabling statute with respect to the format of comprehensive county ordinance codes, I decided to draft a proposal for a new County Ordinance Code of Alameda County.

Dave Wendel was assigned to this project. Having majored in constitutional law at Hayward, he was uniquely qualified for the task. He collected all the ordinances, researched for constitutionality each one that had not been repealed, and drafted restatements and clarifications of a whole new Code of County Ordinances, which was adopted by the Board of Supervisors.

The Code was arranged into nine titles according to subject matter and the titles were divided into chapters, articles and sections, with blank spacing to allow for subsequent enactments in the same format as current practice for Codes enacted by the state Legislature. It contained a detailed table of contents in which were listed topic headings of the divisions of the Code, as well as a word index. It also contained appendices presenting detailed histories of all ordinances ever enacted by the Board of Supervisors, their final disposition and ordinances not included in the Code because of proposed revision or insufficient general application.

The review of so many county laws, long since obsolete, affecting county government and regulating the lives of people a hundred and more years before, was most interesting and, in many instances, quite humorous.

THE ATHLETIC SAFETY COMMITTEE

On Friday nights in the Fall, my wife and I attended high school football games in which our sons, Tom and John, participated. One such night, Piedmont High was playing Berkeley High in a league game where there was great disparity in the size, ability and experience of the players, heavily weighted in favor of Berkeley. This particular night, Berkeley High—outstanding perennial holder of state and county league titles—averaged 196 pounds from end to end and was almost as heavy in the backfield. It was a mismatch and there were many injuries during the game on the Piedmont team. One Piedmont boy, who played center on offense and linebacker on defense, was knocked unconscious and died a few hours later.

As counsel for the Piedmont School District, I appointed a committee of doctors, coaches and school officials to make a study of high school athletic programs and safety factors in Alameda County. Among the doctors on the committee were: Dr. Harold "Brick" Muller, who was at that time a leading orthopedic surgeon and who had been a member of the famous University of California "Wonder Team," a Rose Bowl star, the first Walter Camp All–American from the West, an Olympic Games medalist, and a professional football player; Dr. Charles "Snook" Mell, also a noted orthopedic surgeon and member of previous great University of California teams; and others who like Muller and Mell had played the game and maintained an active interest through the years following graduation.

Muller, as the regular doctor for the University of California football and track teams, had a vast experience treating injured players.

His expert professional knowledge and advice transcended that of any others in his highly specialized field in the nation. There were other doctors on the committee who had sat on the bench with teams during games, ready to perform any medical service which might be necessary at the time, or who were available on call to handle injuries occurring during practice—as so often happens.

This committee worked hard, spending countless hours without pay at night meetings considering problems and solutions. One very practical and helpful thing they did was to draft a medical questionnaire form for high school athletic coaches to have filled in by parents of players, covering all aspects of physical fitness for sports and designed to ascertain from medical histories any conditions which might constitute a health hazard. This form, with guidelines for its use, was adopted by high schools throughout California and other states.

The medical members and coaches of the committee considered common football injuries, such as knees, legs, ankles, shoulders, necks, vertebrae, head, joints and muscles—also heart, lung and kidney conditions which might be impaired by the bruising action of contact sports.

On the staff of the District Attorney's Office was a lawyer, Dave Luce, who had played varsity basketball at the University of California. He directed the work of the committee and other aspects of the study which looked at such things as field conditions, uniforms, shoes, cleats, helmets (use of plastic was just beginning to replace leather), and face masks. There were no turf playing fields in Oakland. The fields at Oakland's schools and those of many other school districts were of dirt, which in the Fall were baked hard and overrun with rocks. And there were other hazardous conditions.

The report of the committee was widely distributed and was helpful to coaches and school authorities in correcting dangerous conditions and in obtaining funds for better equipment. A project such as the Athletic Safety Committee was, of course, an extra curricular activity for the District Attorney's Office, as it was for the members of the committee, but the generous response of busy professional men who served on the committee without pay and their contribution to better playing conditions in the high schools was an inspiration to anyone who knew about it. For the District Attorney's Office it was another impact situation.

COLLABORATING WITH THE CITY ATTORNEYS

In situations where a city council wanted to enact a city ordinance with penalty provisions, the District Attorney's Office collaborated with the city attorney in draftsmanship, because if such an ordinance were enacted, the District Attorney's Office would be required to prosecute any violations. Generally, the District Attorney's Office had more experience in the criminal field, and prosecution by the District Attorney's Office of all criminal offenses in violation of city or county ordinances as well as state laws, made for a more uniform enforcement policy.

The drafting of a municipal ordinance could be an enormous task, and building, housing or health codes could be quite large, so city attorneys were glad to let the District Attorney's Office do the work,

POLIO VACCINATIONS

Another of many challenging projects was the mass poliomyelitis vaccination (Salk vaccine) of elementary public school pupils of the Hayward School District during a period of experimentation before the Salk vaccine was approved for general public distribution by the United States Food and Drug Administration.

During a nationwide scientific study being made by the medical profession, it was proposed that first, second and third grade children of three representative elementary public schools in the United States be inoculated with the newly developed vaccine for poliomyelitis. The proposed experiment involved use of approved doctors and public health nurses to inject one half of the children with the vaccine and one half with placebos. Among parties interested in the experiment were the National Foundation for Infantile Paralysis, the county medical association, parents and teachers associations, city and county public health officers and many other persons, organizations and groups.

Members of the Board of Trustees of the Hayward School District—the responsible governing body—as well as the doctors and school nurses were concerned as to legal questions and liabilities if any children came down with polio or other illnesses as a result of their participation in the experiment. As counsel for the district, the District Attorney's Office was asked to advise as to the legal procedures and questions involved. Advice was given to the School Board prescribing the conditions under which the experiment could be conducted without liability on the part of the School District or the Board members.

Pursuant to the advice and legal work of the District Attorney's Office, the experiment was conducted without casualty and to the satisfaction of all concerned. In due course, the Salk vaccine was approved by the United States Food and Drug Administration and the medical profession for use by the public.

THE LOSS OF THE WELFARE BURDEN

In the general election of November 2, 1948, a Constitutional Amendment was approved by the people of California to take administration of welfare away from the counties and impose it upon state government under the direction of Myrtle Williams, protege of George McLain, who was a lobbyist for an organization of elder citizens. The result of the vote on this constitutional proposal came as a complete surprise to officials of local and state governments, and the latter were wholly unprepared to make the transition, which would involve the initiation and staffing of a very large department to investigate and disperse welfare to aged, disabled, blind, needy children and persons otherwise unable to support themselves.

At the request of Governor Warren, a committee of county supervisors met in Sacramento to discuss the problem. Douglas Dunning, assistant district attorney of Alameda County, and I met with the committee. The committee decided to propose to state government that it enter into a contract with the 58 counties, whereby the counties would continue to administer welfare as they had been doing but at the expense of the state. Dunning and I were asked to draft a contract for submission to state and county governments.

Being aware of the fact that county Supervisors were generally chary of committing county taxpayers to additional expense, especially when, as in this situation, the Constitutional Amendment had transferred the operation of welfare to the state, we advised the committee that the contract should uniformly apply to each county and so completely relieve the counties of any expense for administration that there would be no opposition to its acceptance by the boards of supervisors of every county.

Time was of the essence; the Constitutional Amendment provided that the transition from county to state operation had to take place on January 1, less than two months away. To make it more acceptable to the county supervisors and reduce delay in approval by local governments throughout the state, we recommended that the contract very clearly transfer to the state all costs of operation and for good measure, that it contain a hold harmless clause to cover any unanticipated expense which might arise, such as suits against a county for injuries to welfare recipients in county buildings, or by misconduct or negligence of county employees. This became known as the "Coakley Clause" and expedited selling the contract to the supervisors.

Dunning traveled throughout the state, explaining the contract to the boards of supervisors and their legal advisors. He succeeded in persuading the supervisors in all 58 counties to approve it. In due course, representatives of state government accepted the proposed contract. The contract became effective on the first business day of January in the new year, with county employees operating as agents of and at the expense of the state.

Needless to say, state officials were not too happy about the comprehensiveness of the contract, but they were in no position to reject its terms. Eventually, the Legislature submitted another Constitutional Amendment to the voters at the next election. This proposal passed, and the administration of welfare at the expense of the counties, state and federal government returned to the status quo of pre–Myrtle Williams.

THE CIVIL—CRIMINAL SPLIT

The split in the District Attorney's Office, separating civil and criminal law work, was a drastic event in the history of the office. Warren, Hoyt and I always believed it was a stronger operation the way it was, with civil and criminal work combined. Young lawyers joining the staff had an opportunity to experience a broader development in the law. They could be, and they were, rotated so that their experience included a variety of courts, from the Justice and Municipal Court up to the Appellate Courts and occasionally even the California Supreme Court and the federal courts, and a variety of legal work—trial as well as office work, the latter with a wide variety of clients and problems.

After experience in both criminal and civil work, a lawyer would adjust to the type he preferred and to which he was more adapted. Lawyers with experience in both, particularly those with proven skill in trial work, could be most useful in handling an important trial in the civil field, as was true in the Fruitvale Bridge case, for example. We thought this broad experience made for better lawyers and a better staff.

There was a strong incentive for young lawyers to participate in such important and far reaching cases as acquisition of land for and construction of the Estuary Tube between the cities of Oakland and Alameda, acquisition of land for and construction of new schools, courts and county buildings after the hiatus in building during the Depression and World War II years.

Doing legal work involving personal contact with a broad range of public officials and private citizens, all departments of county government, schools and various special districts, was mutually beneficial—provided the quality of the work was satisfactory. Public image is important and a successful image means political strength—a desirable factor to a district attorney who must run for election every four years, but also necessary to protect the independence and integrity of his office. A good image is reflected in results obtained in trial courts from judges and jurors as well as the grand jury.

At the time it happened, I did not believe the split was necessary in Alameda County. The civil clients of the District Attorney's Office, county and special district heads, were quite satisfied with the service they were getting. Just two years before the split, the office had handled the disturbing situation in the Assessor's Office successfully, obtaining for the county a windfall settlement of over $2 million in unpaid taxes and cleaning up the situation with dispatch in the criminal case by a conviction of the assessor without appeal and guilty pleas of the accessories.

The quality of legal work of the District Attorney's Office was recognized throughout the state. When Leland Sweeney, a new Supervisor of Alameda County, asked Harold Kennedy, one–time county counsel of Los Angeles County and nationally acclaimed public law officer, whether Alameda County should adopt the county counsel system, Kennedy replied, "As long as Coakley is doing your civil work you don't need a separate County Counsel's Office." William MacDougall, executive director of the County Supervisors Association of California (later director of the United States Commission on Intergovernmental Relations) made the following statement:

> "Frank Coakley's personal efforts in presenting the views of local government to the Legislature have been unselfish, effective, and in the public interest. In the vital field of crime and law enforcement, Coakley has rendered a service matched nowhere else in America."

However, in 1956, Earl Strathman was appointed county administrator. Strathman, trained in county management in Los Angeles County, proved to be a strong and influential administrator, and he gradually assumed all administrative functions, some of which had been performed by members of the Board of Supervisors and the District Attorney's Office in the past. From the time he became administrator, obtaining salary and budget increases for the District Attorney's Office comparable to public law offices in other counties was an annual struggle.

Earl was trained in a county where for years a separate County Counsel's Office had existed. He was familiar with that system and firmly believed a separate office was preferable. He was of the opinion that there would be greater efficiency by greater concentration in particular fields; that a better job could be done by having two departments, one devoted exclusively to criminal and the other to civil matters. In support of his position, he cited the fact that at that time separate offices had been established in 42 of the 58 counties in California.

As previously indicated, I did not agree that it was necessary in Alameda County, nor did Earl Warren or Ralph Hoyt. As a matter of fact, the Chief Justice on one of his last visits to my office, in leaving said, "Don't let them (the Board of Supervisors) split the office."

Nevertheless the Board of Supervisors, despite my objection that, "This could mark the end of one of the great public law offices of the nation," separated the office, an action which I attribute to the recommendations of Strathman.

Frictions between the District Attorney's Office and members of the Board of Supervisors over budgets and salaries were not new. They had occurred in Warren's and Hoyt's time as well as mine, and no doubt before. As mentioned previously, for a long time the Board kept Warren, who started at $150 a month as a deputy district attorney, at a salary of $600 as District Attorney. During his fourteen years as District Attorney his salary never got over $600 a month.

Some of the school districts now retain counsel outside of the County Counsel's Office, as does East Bay Regional Park District and other special districts. Until relatively recent years, no attorney outside the District Attorney's Office or the County Counsel's Office performed legal work for any school district, the Regional Parks or other public clients of the office. Warren used to say, "We are all lawyers. We can do the work as well or better than outside counsel." Hoyt and I felt the same way, as apparently did the clients of our respective administrations. I believe that a public law officer such as a district attorney or county counsel, whose official duty it is to do the legal work for governmental entities and a variety of public clients day in and day out, has more experience in the work and can do a better job, assuming that personal qualifications are on a par.

It should be said that Richard Moore, who became County Counsel when the District Attorney's Office was split, outlived Strathman, and at no time during his regime has he been ordered or asked to change a legal conclusion or decision. He and his staff had been trained in the tradition of the District Attorney's Office. Under Moore's able direction, his office has handled successfully many cases of major importance, and his department is recognized as one of the top public law offices in the state. The quality, efficiency and integrity of his office has continued at a high level.

APPENDIX A

DISTRICT ATTORNEYS OF ALAMEDA COUNTY
1853—1982

The following is a chronological list of District Attorneys of Alameda County, with the year of their election or service:

William H. Combs	1853
John S. Chipman	1854
George M. Blake	1855
William Van Voorheis	1857
William H. Glascock	1859
W. W. Crane	1861
Stephen G. Nye	1863
George M. Blake	1865
O. H. La Grange	1867
S. P. Wright	1869
A. A. Moore	1871–1873
William H. Glascock	1875
Henry Vrooman	1877
E. M. Gibson	1879–1880
S. P. Hall	1882–1886
George W. Reed	1888–1890
Charles E. Snook	1892–1894
John J. Allen	1898–1902
Everett J. Brown	1906
William H. Donahue	1910
William H. L. Hynes	1914
Ezra W. Decoto	1918–1922
Earl Warren	1925, 1926, 1930, 1934–1939
Ralph E. Hoyt	1939, 1942, 1946, 1947
J. Frank Coakley	1947, 1948, 1950, 1954, 1958, 1962, 1966–1969
D. Lowell Jensen	1969–1981
John J. Meehan	1981–Present

CHIEF ASSISTANT DISTRICT ATTORNEYS
1923 — 1982

Earl Warren
Ralph E. Hoyt
J. Frank Coakley
Richard H. Chamberlain
R. Robert Hunter
Albert E. Hederman
Richard A. Haugner
John J. Meehan
Richard B. Iglehart

APPENDIX B

OFFICE EMPLOYEES IN 1982

DISTRICT ATTORNEY

John J. Meehan

ASSISTANTS AND DEPUTIES

John H. Adams, Jr.
Ben Aliza
James H. Anderson
John C. Baldwin
William M. Baldwin
Thomas J. Barni
John A. Bell
William C. Bell
James H. Bellerive
Kathleen E. Bergland
Darryl J. Billups
Linda C. Blackwell
Ronald E. Blair
Lawrence C. Blazer
Gregory S. Boecker
Martin A. Brown
Walter A. Brown, Jr.
Murray P. Brush III
Alfred R. Bucher
John A. Burke
Kenneth M. Burr
Timothy C. Busler
Clifford F. Campbell
Michael E. Cardoza
Colton C. Carmine
Christopher G. Carpenter
Joan S. Cartwright
Robert F. Chambers
Norbert Chu
Carol A. Corrigan
William E. Cosden
Ralph P. Countryman
Jerry Curtis
Clayton W. DaVega
Leopoldo E. Dorado
Paulino G. Duran
Glen E. Duren
Merle R. Eaton
H. James Ellis
Karen D. Campbell
Kathleen C. Famulener
Lisa M. Faria
Charles E. Fraser
Gregory R. Gibeson
Russell J. Giuntini
Jonathan J. Goodfellow
Louis J. Goodman
Shelley A. Gordon
Raymond W. Hamilton
Rockne P. Harmon
Roy Hashimoto
Charles E. Herbert
Jill S. Hiatt
Randall W. Hooper
Jeffrey W. Horner
Joseph R. Hurley
Arthur M. Hutchins
Robert B. Hutchins, Jr.
Richard B. Iglehart
Donald G. Ingraham
Walter J. Jackson
Alan J. Jang
Howard A. Janssen
John W. Jay
Martin J. Jenkins
Gilbert A. Jensen

Marcia L. Jensen
Harry B. Johnson
Christina H. Jones
Ann Kenfield
Joel P. Kew
Kenneth R. Kingsbury
William M. Kleeman
Grover R. Klemmer
Theodore T. Landswick
Jack Leavitt
James M. Lee
Maureen K. Lenahan
Blair W. Lindsay
Sandra L. Margulies
William R. McGuiness
C. Sue McKinney
William A. McKinstry
Dennis J. McLaughlin
Albert W. Meloling
Karen L. Meredith
Charles E. Merrill
Richard S. Michaels
Maryann Migas
James W. Mullally
Henry D. Murphy
Vernon K. Nakahara
Henry E. Needham, Jr.
James M. Nelson
George D. Niespolo
Margaret A. Ong
Thomas J. Orloff
Aaron B. Payne
Karl W. Payne
Anne W. Pearson
Gary M. Picetti
Robert M. Platt
Cheryl M. Poncini
John R. Poppas
Jack R. Quatman
Sandra L. Quist
Jack B. Radisch
Gloria F. Rhynes
Thomas C. Rogers
Thomas A. Ross
Eric P. Schnurmacher
Alexander M. Selvin
Donald B. Squires
Carolyn J. Stein
Diane E. Teilh
Mark N. Thomson
Jon R. Thurston
William E. Tingle
Mary Jane Tocci
Bruce VanVoorhis
Noel T. Walsh
Stacy L. Walthall
David B. Whitman
Donald P. Whyte

INSPECTORS, LIEUTENANTS & INVESTIGATIVE ASSISTANTS

Clifford L. Ojala, Captain of Inspectors

John L. Agler
Manuel L. Avilla, Jr.
Robert A. Ayres
James Robert Barbour
Harold O. Boscovich, Jr.
James E. Carreker
Stanley A. Clifton
James M. Crisolo
Douglas G. Divine
William E. Eller
Robert E. Fernandez
Robert H. Ficken
V. Sue Fivella
John R. Fredriksson
Philip D. Fry
Robert D. Gannon
David W. Gingery
Arthur F. Guzman
Robert J. Hamilton
James O. Hardcastle
Michael P. Harnett
Theodore R. Hill
William P. Holden
Lawrence N. Holman
Bernard P. Hughes
Lee W. Jones
Kevin P. Kennedy
Mark A. Kennison
James E. Kinnison
Kathleen P. Krathwohl
Nicole Lee
Kevin M. Leong
Gerald J. Lindberg
John R. Lovelady
Marvin L. Lyons
Roy H. McCarthy
Clyde M. McCreary
Helen M. McGinnis
Donald R. McWilliams
John I. Mullen
Donald B. L. Neves
Andrew Pringle, Jr.
Richard A. Purdee
Walter C. Rossi
Eugene F. Sabatini
Norman R. Simmons
Alexander W. Smith
James E. Strong
Kathleen V. Volpe
LaValle White
John J. Whitson

SUPPORT STAFF

Ninfa Wood, Executive Secretary

Phyllis A. Arnerich
Yvonne P. Ayres
Mylene P. Baptista
Patricia G. Bentley
Kathryn E. Barnstein
Mary B. Boles
Joy L. Borba
Kimberly A. Boulware
Kathleen M. Branson
Dorothy Bridges
David C. Budde
Draga Canaday
Diana L. Centoni
Janice Cordova
Ingrid B. Cruz
Amelia G. Davis
Edward D. DiGirolamo
Patricia M. Dimond
Rosario D. Dos Santos
Ruth A. Edwards
David Faris
Lynda G. Ferreira
Vicki A. Francisco
Ruby F. Freitas
Arthur L. Garrett
Dorothy L. Garrett
Deborah Gaspari
Joyce E. Glock
Sandra J. Gordon
Carol A. Grant
Karon L. Haga
Sandra M. Hayes
Lenore A. Holle
Lois A. Inferrera
Mary E. Iverson
Bonnie A. Jenezon
Velma E. Johnson
Juanita M. Kindle
Elinor M. King
Barbara I. Klatt
Sharon S. Lane
Jean L. Lima
Vicki L. Long
Elaine J. Lopes
Diane L. Lynn
Ana Liliana F. Maddock
Julie D. Marrow
Barbara J. Marshall
Dolores A. McGrath
Patricia H. McGue
Sue E. Meadows
Hortense A. Meagher
Rose F. Mineo
Ellen J. Muir
Maryann Nicolaus
Michele P. Nolan
Gail C. Oaker
Bettye L. Palmore
Linda J. Paniagua
E. Evelyn Patterson
Anna T. Petersen
Nancy A. Poerink
Rita C. Pollen
Karen P. Pucci
Yvonne J. Rodgers
Angelener V. Sampe
Allison Ann Schantin
Leticia Serna
Sharon K. Serrano
Gregory J. Smith
Shirley M. Smith
Irene Stoucas
Nancy E. Sunday
Marianne A. Spingolo

Jackie J. Thomas
Olivia Tijero
Vangeleen B. Torres
Stacie S. Treposkoufes
Victoria S. Vandergrift
Denise M. Vargas
Barbara E. Westmoreland
Barbara F. White
Rhea Wilbert
Lizabeth L. Young

APPENDIX C

OTHER OFFICIAL POSITIONS HELD BY STAFF PERSONNEL

Carl W. Anderson
- Justice, California Court of Appeals—Chief of Division

Sandra Brown Armstrong
- U.S. Parole Commissioner
- Superior Court of California
- U.S. District Court

St. John Barrett
- Assistant U.S. Attorney General
- Acting General Counsel, Dept. of Health, Education and Welfare

Lloyd Burke
- U.S. Attorney
- U.S. District Court

Ming Chin
- Justice, California Court of Appeals

Frank Coakley
- Senior Judge Advocate, U.S. Navy
- Western Sea Frontier Legal Officer
- Commanding Officer, Legal Component–12th Naval District
- California Commission on Uniform State Laws
- National Commission on Uniform State Laws
- Professor, St. Mary's College Law School
- Lecturer, University of California, Berkeley
- California Commission on Interstate Cooperation

Laurence Dayton
- U.S. Attorney

Ezra Decoto
- California Railroad Commission
- Superior Court

Howard Gilbert
Special Assistant Attorney General
Investigation and Prosecution of Fraud,
Workmen's Compensation Division, Montana
Staff Counsel, U.S. House of Representatives Committee on
Assassinations (President John F. Kennedy's assassination)

Linn Gillard
Referee Bankruptcy

Oliver Hamlin
Superior Court
U.S. District Court
U.S. Court of Appeals

Lois Haight Herrington
Director, U.S. Commission on Victim–Witness Assistance
Assistant U.S. Attorney General–Justice Research

William Hunter
U.S. Attorney

Richard Iglehart
Chief Assistant Attorney General of California–Criminal

Herbert Jackson
District Attorney, Sacramento County

Kennedy Jackson
U.S. Commissioner

Oscar Jahnsen
Assistant Adjutant General, California National Guard
Major General, California National Guard
Chief of Inspectors, California Attorney General's Office

Lowell Jensen
Assistant U.S. Attorney General—Criminal Division
Associate U.S. Attorney General
Deputy U.S. Attorney General
U.S. District Court

Harold Jewett
U.S. Commissioner

Harold Jewett
U.S. Commissioner

Joseph Koford
Superior Court
District Court of Appeals of California

Alan Lindsay
Assistant U.S. Attorney General

David Luce
Assistant U.S. Attorney General
Administrator, Courts of Alaska
Counsel, California Franchise Tax Department
District Attorney, Lake County

Paul McCloskey
U.S. House of Representatives

Edwin Meese III
Counsel to the President of the U.S.
Attorney General of the U.S.

Albert W. Meloling
Special Assistant Attorney General
Investigation and Prosecution of Fraud,
Workmen's Compensation Division, Montana

Harry Melvin
Superior Court
Supreme Court of California

Richard J. Moore
County Counsel–Alameda County

Cecil Mosbacher
California Commission on Criminal Law and Procedure
Superior Court of California

Alan C. Nelson
Assistant Counsel to the President of the U.S.
Commissioner of Immigration and Naturalization Service

James Oakley
Assistant Attorney General, California—Civil

Warren Olney III
Director, California Commission on Organized Crime
Assistant U.S. Attorney General—Criminal Division
Professor, University of California, Berkeley
Administrator, U.S. Courts

Roger Olsen
Assistant U.S. Attorney General–Tax Division

Robert Quall
Chief Deputy District Attorney, Merced County
Municipal Court

Joseph Salgado
Chief, U.S. Border Patrol
Undersecretary, U.S. Department of Energy

John Schauer
Assistant U.S. Attorney General

Stanley Smallwood
Assistant U.S. Attorney General

Eugene Tunney
District Attorney, Sonoma County

Earl Warren
Attorney General
Governor of California
Chief Justice of the U.S. Supreme Court

Theodore Westphal
Chief Assistant Attorney General, California—Civil

Cameron Wolfe
Referee Bankruptcy

JUDGES OF THE SUPERIOR & MUNICIPAL COURTS

Paul Alvarado
Carl West Anderson
Mario H. Barsotti
C. Richard Bartalini
Thomas A. Black
John A. Burke
Joseph J. Carson
Joan Cartwright
Richard H. Chamberlain
William R. Channell
Ming Chin
Marie Collins
John S. Cooper
Carol A. Corrigan
Ezra Decoto
Alfred A. Delucchi
Stephen Dombrink
Leo Dorado
Merle E. Eaton
Folger Emerson
Richard Haugner
Jeffrey W. Horner
Ralph Hoyt
Kiernan R. Hyland
Martin J. Jenkins
Donald R. Kennedy
Kenneth R. Kingsbury
Joseph Koford
John A. Lewis
Bonnie Lewman
Alan A. Lindsay
Myron A. Martin
James F. Mastoris
Donald P. McCullum
William J. McGuiness
William R. McGuiness
William A. McKinstry
Sandra R. Margulies
Edward L. Merrill
Cecil Mosbacher
Vernon Nakahara
George Nicholson
Joanne Parrilli
Gary Picetti
Roy G. Pucci
Robert D. Quall
Ronald Sabraw
Joseph Schenone
Howard L. Schwartz
Alice Duggan Sullivan
John Sutter
C. Zook Sutton
Irene Takahashi
Bruce Van Voorhis
James C. Walsh, Jr.

To make room for increasing volumes of business, earlier records of county government departments were destroyed from time to time by Court Orders. Consequently, records of personnel in the District Attorney's Office over the past sixty years, as contained in Appendices C and D, may be incomplete.

APPENDIX D

FORMER STAFF

FORMER DEPUTY AND ASSISTANT DISTRICT ATTORNEYS

James W. Aaron
Fred E. Abbott III
Frank P. Agnost, Jr.
William H. Ahern
Tony Allard
Paul H. Alvarado
Leroy James Amaral
Carl West Anderson
Ernest L. Anderson
Robert L. Anderson
Saundra Brown Armstrong
St. John Barrett
Mario H. Barsotti
C. Richard Bartalini
Adrionne (Kitty) Beasley
Melville Behrendt
David E. Biasotti
Joseph P. Bingaman
A. Leonard Bjorklund
Thomas A. Black
Thomas A. Blake
Mary E. Bolint
Kym Bollinger
Dan Bowles
Archie A. Briggs
Robert B. Brodie
Eugene E. Brott
Eugene Brown
J. Michael Brown
Terence L. Bruiniers
Brian H. Burke
Lloyd H. Burke
John L. Burris
Lee W. Cake
Joseph J. Carson
Richard H. Chamberlain
Alton M. Chambliss
William R. Channell
Ming W. Chin
William P. Clancy
Edwin A. Clancy
J. Frank Coakley
Michael P. Cole
Marie Collins
Richard D. Comerford
Thomas W. Condit
Richard J. Conti
John S. Cooper
Larry M. Cowan
James E. Cox
James L. Crew
Frank M. Crews
Taylor R. Culver
Gary Cummings
Frederick Paul Dacey, Jr.
Charlotte Danforth
John F. Davis
Laurence E. Dayton
John T. (Tom) Deal
Alfred A. Delucchi
Charles J. Devlin
Stephen Dombrink
Thomas J. Donnelly
Michael I. Dorshkind
David B. Draheim
Fred H. Drucker
William H. DuBois
Douglas R. Dunning
James J. Durney
David C. Dutton
Frederick Ebey
Herbert E. Ellingwood

Folger Emerson
Maury Engel
George K. Faler
Thomas J. Feeney
Thomas J. Fennone
Carol Ann Fickenscher
Thomas E. Firby
Susan Ann Fisher
Thomas A. Flippen II
Glenn A. Forbes
Keith S. Fraser
Keith H. Fudenna
H. Rowan Gaither
G. Patrick Galloway
Michael J. Gannon
Thomas D. Geary
Michael W. Gericke
Francis R. Giambroni
Anthony W. Gibbs
Howard M. Gilbert
Gary P. Glavinovich
Vernon Lee Goodin
Arnold M. Greenberg
Robert J. Greggins
J. Fred Haley
Howard C. Hall
Roy E. Hamrick
Frederick M. Hanelt
Richard D. Hardin
John S. Hartwell
Richard A. Haugner
Albert E. Hederman
Elizabeth Helfrich
Bruce G. Herold
Lois Haight Herrington
Allan D. Heskin
David K. Hicks
William A. Hirst
C.J. Hollander
William G. Holliman, Jr.
James D. Hollister
David Holstrom
Wayne M. Hooper
Laurence P. Horan
Richard E. Hove
Phyllis McKay Howard
Ralph B. Hoyt
Ralph E. Hoyt
Gary J. D. Hubert
William L. Hughes
Richard F. Humphrey
G. William Hunter
R. Robert Hunter
John B. Huntington
Kiernan R. Hyland
William Hynes
H. Herb Jackson
William P. Jaeger, Jr.
D. Lowell Jensen
Cynthia A. Jewett
Harold W. Jewett, Jr.
Gary J. Johnson
Hurl Johnson III
Marion H. Johnson
Richard B. Johnson
William R. Johnston
Richard A. Jones
Donald R. Kennedy
Michael C. Killelea
Robert A. Kincaid
Bernard M. King
Shelby R. King
Richard H. Klippert
Gordon T. Kono
Roger T. Kosel
Peter B. Lauritzen
Dana M. Leahy
Donovan J. Leighton
Richard T. Lemon
George T. Lenahan
Jacob Levitan
John A. Lewis
Bonnie Lewman
Richard Liebman

Howard C. Lincoln
Larry L. Litke
Alan A. Lindsay
Alan Lipton
David A. Long
Bruce P. Loper
David Lowe
David L. Luce
David R. Lucchese
Richard C. Lynch
Clyde L. MacGowan, Jr.
Robert C. MacKichan
James B. Maguire III
John S. Martel
David J. Martin
Gerald P. Martin, Jr.
Jay R. Martin
John F. Martin
Myron A. Martin
Robert A. Martin
James F. Mastoris
Donald P. Mayhew
Robert H. Mazzera
James P. McBride
Michael P. McCabe
John R. McCardle
Paul N. McCloskey, Jr.
Robert D. McCloskey
Samuel B. McCullagh, Jr.
Donald P. McCullum
David McDowell
William J. McGuiness
William H. McInerney
George E. McInnis
William J. McLean
Bruce McLeod
Tim McLeod
Tim McMahon
Daniel Joseph McNamara
Bryand McOmber
Joseph S. Mead
Edwin Meese III
Raymond E. Mellana
Edward L. Merrill
Leon J. Mezzetti
Robert P. Mooney
Harold I. Moore
Richard J. Moore
Charles J. Morehouse
Michael D. Morgan
G. Wright Morton
W. J. Moseley III
Ronald J. Motts
David A. Mulford
Jerry G. Murphy
John J. Murray
Robert W. Musante
Martin M. Nakahara
Doug Nakano
Alan C. Nelson
Michael J. Ney
George W. Nicholson
Wayne Nishioka
Mike A. Nisperos
Herbert W. Nobriga
John W. Noonan III
Marjorie Nowell
George P. Oakes
James M. Oaklund
Garrett Olney
Roger M. Olsen
George E. Ong
George Papagiannis
Frank D. Parker
Joanne Parrilli
Rollie M. Pennington
John A. Pettis
Lawrence Picetti
Thomas N. Prelock
Roy G. Pucci
William A. Pusey
Robert D. Quall
Terry J. Ravazzini
David Reed

John M. Reidenbach
Frederick W. Reyland, Jr.
Jon R. Rolefson
Martin T. Ruane Jr.
Ronald C. Ruiz
Kenneth W. Ruthenberg
Ronald M. Sabraw
Bart J. Schenone
Joseph Schenone
John A. Schneider
Eric P. Schnurmacher
Howard L. Schwartz
Joseph F. Salgado
Manton L. Selby II
Edward J. Semansky
Michael P. Semansky
J. Tony Serra
William F. Sharon
John E. Shelley, Jr.
Gary C. Sheppard
Harry R. Sheppard
Arthur H. Sherry
Lorilyn E. Simkins
Craig A. Sinclair
Adrian Smeltzer
Charles Michael Smith
Ralph Smith
James C. Snell
William S. Snook
Jeffery D. Snow
John P. Sparrow
Justus Spillner
Ernest R. Stent
French Stone
Richard C. Stone
Dale I. Stoops
William A. Struthers, Jr.
Alice Duggan Sullivan
Dennis M. Sullivan
John H. Sutter
C. Zook Sutton
Irene Takahashi
Alfred F. Talley, Jr.
Michael K. Tandy
John L. Taylor
Albert W. Thews, Jr.
Harry J. Traback
James R. Trembath
Charles Jeffrey Trick
William K. Tuck
Stephen T. Tucker
Griffith E. Tully
Gene L. Tunney
Peter M. Turner
Michael H. Valim
Charles T. Van Deusen
Steven R. Van Sicklen
James C. Walsh, Jr.
Michael P. Walsh
David I Wendell
Philip L. Whitehorn
Roberta Willenkin
Dorothy P. Wilson
Elwood J. Wilson
Lionel B. Wilson, Jr.
Dagny K. Winkler
Robert G. Witser
Benjamin H. Zuppan

CAPTAINS OF INSPECTORS 1923—1982

George Helms
Hugo Radbush
Clarence Severin
Howard Tupper
Charles Ryken
Robert Bernard
Cliff Ojala

FORMER INSPECTORS

Jack Abernathy
Earnest Allen
Frederick Anderson
Robert D. Bernard
Ronald Blair
Fred Bormann
Joseph Branden
Larry Cappelli
Boman Coogler
Michael DiMiceli
Chester Flint
George Forth
John Goodman
Gordon Grimes
Robert Hansen
Charles Harrison
George Hard
Albert E. Hederman, Jr.
George Helms
George Henningsen
Charles E. Herbert
Edward "Ted" Hilliard
George Irwin
Oscar Jahnsen
Lloyd Jester
Glen Johnson
Clifford Jones
Donald Jones
Lester King
William Leach
James LeStrange
Donald Lynn
Alvin Mallon
George Mahi
Mark McDonough
Jack McEvers
Donald McNeil
Thomas Monahan
Robert Moore
Robert Neef
John Lewis Neeland
James Noble
Brian Oliver
Robert Parker
Philip Payette
Vernon Peters
Richard Petersen
Hugo Radbruch
Larry Raussa
Jack Richardson
Joseph Rosales
Russell Ryan
Charles Ryken
Edward Schnarr
Clarence Severin
John Shelley
James Silver
Jack Smith

Douglas Stevenson
Robert Swaynie
Kenneth Tiers
Howard Tupper
Michael Valim
Joseph Veretto
William Wagner
Harold Walker
William Walker
Donald P. Whyte
Clifford Wixson
Charles Young

EXECUTIVE SECRETARIES

Olive Bledsoe
Helen MacGregor
Rae Pollard
Dorothy Watson Bate
Earleen Rutherford
Ninfa Wood

SENIOR SECRETARIES

Jill Vukota Ballas
Eleanor Barbagallo
Draga Canaday
Mary Clark
Barbara Klatt
Rita Pollen

SWITCHBOARD OPERATORS

Hazel Yoder
Marcelle "Granny" Cohen
Amelia Davis

APPENDIX E

Proceedings on Sentence in *People v. Huey P. Newton*

Alameda County Superior Court
Judge Joseph Karesh Presiding

"THE DEFENDANT: I hope you have a good Jewish holiday, and I hope you with "Yeswah" (phonetic). He is even Lord of the Sabbath. Therefore he ate upon the Sabbath. He used his discretion to violate Sabbath. So you are a renegade Jew.

"THE COURT: Would you please sit down.

"THE DEFENDANT: No. Send me to jail.

"THE COURT: I don't think the Court has to give a reason because —

"THE DEFENDANT: You don't just say you violate the Jewish law. You are so interested in the biblical law. My father taught me more biblical law than —

"THE COURT: Let me finish.

"THE DEFENDANT: The only way to finish in fairness is violate what is tradition of Yeswah, later called Jesus in Yiddish. In Yiddish he's called Yeswah. And he said —

"THE COURT: Mr Newton —

"THE DEFENDANT: He had court and asked them, he asked: Why do you violate the Sabbath? And he said, don't you know that, Pilate? He is even lower than the Sabbath, and he sends him, Pilate, to jail, the so–called victim. And he says I followed Judaism. He is a violator of the law and of the Ten Commandments, the law of mercy, also the law structurally. But this man will fool those who only are neophytes and students in Judaism, but I am a star and he is a hoop.

. . . .

"THE DEFENDANT: Hang me by the heels.

. . . .

"THE DEFENDANT: I love your faith. I am a Jew and Jews also only make light after they went to Europa.

. . . .

"THE DEFENDANT: I am of your faith. I am a black Jew.

"THE DEFENDANT: His Honor mentioned biblical all through the trial. His Honor mentioned radio/television all through the trial. How can you attack my attorney? Send me to jail, because I will do Mike Kennedy's time. I am my brother's keeper. If I violate you one time, then that requires that I violate you seven times, and seven times seven, and you are to have another Jewish brother to come with you so two of them can bear witness of the violation. So it's our faith, but that's the problem with you light Jews, that you want to be the only Jew.

. . . .

"THE COURT: One thing I want to do, what the Court wants to do, I know Mr. Kennedy has been very anxious to get back to New York, and I don't usually meet on Saturday, but I told you that I wanted this matter considered about —

"THE DEFENDANT: No. Meet on Monday. Then I think you are doing something. That's the Jewish holiday.

"THE COURT: —about this question of whether he should be released.

"THE DEFENDANT: Meet on Monday. As he ate, are you greater than yeswah, later called—who is the Messiah of your people who is trying to save your ass. And then you are also cliquish. You are a racist dog, southern crackers. You violated the law. And I accuse you of being a racist, North American, sir, southern cracker, violating the old law that I follow. Meet on Monday, and then at least you have faith in your faith. Meet on Saturday and you are excaping a violation when I am punished in jail. So I am punished and you have to decide whether guilty or not. Meet on the holiday. Eat upon the Sabbath, because my Lord is Lord of the Sabbath.

"THE COURT: Mr. Newton, it would be inappropriate for me to pass anything—

"THE DEFENDANT: Is that Old Testament or not? Did Yeswah eat upon the Sabbath, and the twelve in Galilee?

"THE COURT: Mr. Orloff, I found that Mr. Kennedy's remark was highly inappropriate, and I am not going to permit that type of remark, and—

"THE DEFENDANT: Didn't Yeswah later, later called Jesus—

"THE COURT: Mr. Kennedy——

"THE DEFENDANT: Is that not true? Do you take the Fifth Ammendment, like you send Callins to jail? Is that a lie, according to the Jewish theologists? Did he not eat upon the Sabbath one time? You cannot answer that, violator. I will drive you from the temple. Let me go to jail."

Index

A

Abbott, Burton
  See Stephanie Bryan Case
Absentia, 49
Accessory to a Psychopath Case, 171
Acheson, George
  See Fruit Shake Case
Acme Builders Swindle Case, 62–65
Africa, 212
Aftermath of the 60's, 260–264
Ahern, William, 166, 170–171
Alabama, state of, 200
Alameda, California, 31, 33, 86, 191, 193, 278–280, 282, 295, 303
  City Attorney, 82–83
  City Council, 83–84
  City Manager, 82–83
  Mayor, 83
  St. Joseph's High School, 170
Alameda County, 285
  Assessor's Office, 212–216, 287, 304
  Auditor, 290–291
  Board of Supervisors, 10, 24, 26, 35, 40–41, 98, 122, 128–129, 277–279, 282, 287–291, 297–298, 304–305
  Budget, 35, 122, 215, 278, 305
  Charter, 26, 35, 40, 297
  Coroner, 41, 72, 102, 194, 204
  County Administrator, 304
  County Clerk's Office, 26, 28, 122
  County Counsel's Office, xiv, 277, 279–281, 303–306
  Courthouse—1225 Fallon St., 124, 143, 151, 177, 186
  Courthouse—5th & Broadway, 7, 18, 28, 81
  Courthouse—San Leandro(1857), 7
  District Attorney's Office, xi–xii, xiv–xv, xix–xxiii, 6, 8, 16, 25–33, 35, 37, 40–41, 43, 48, 50–51, 53–54, 58, 62, 65, 69, 72, 80, 92–95, 109,
  District Attorney's Office (cont'd), 122–129, 132–133, 135, 137, 142–151, 156, 161, 165–166, 168, 174, 177, 190, 208, 213, 229, 233, 235, 240, 244, 251–252, 256, 263, 265–267, 269, 271, 274, 276–280, 282, 286, 288–289, 291–292, 297, 299–306, 346–348
    Civil–Criminal Split, 303–306
    Consumer Fraud Division, 265–267
    Family Support Division, 265
    School Division, 292–296
  Geography, 7
  Grand Jury, xiii, 10, 37, 40–43, 49, 60, 65, 68–69, 74, 82, 84, 89, 93, 143, 147, 156–163, 166, 169–170, 177, 196–197, 205, 207, 212, 214, 304
  Hall of Records—5th & Broadway, 7
  Hospital, 90, 101
  Jail, 5, 14, 19, 53, 90, 100, 140, 143–144, 146, 209, 214, 234, 236, 249, 269
  Jail—5th & Broadway, 7
  Jail—San Leandro (1857), 7
  Oakland—Alameda County Coliseum & Arena, 279, 289–292
  Population, 28, 31, 278
  Probation Department, 13, 160
  Public Administrator, 296
  Public Defender's Office, xix, 26, 35, 87–88, 109
  Sheriff's Office, xxi, 6–7, 19, 33, 37–41, 62, 141, 151, 159–160, 217, 226–229, 233–235, 242–244, 249–251, 257–259, 269, 276
  Squattersville, 8
  Surveyer's Office, 68
  Welfare Department, 122, 160, 219, 278, 302
Alameda County Bar Association, 33, 36, 49, 183, 186, 260
Alameda County Transit Company, 203
Alameda County v. United States, 280

Alameda Graft Case, 81–84
Alamo, California, 284
Alarcon, 1
Alaska, state of, 1, 21
Albany, California, 33, 42, 282
  Police Department, 30
Alberts, George
  See Warren's Ship Murder Case
Alcalde
  See Legal systems—Spanish
Alfred, Thomas, 130–132
Allen, John J., 11, 307
Alvarado, California, 7
  See also Union City, California
Ambush in West Oakland, 210–212
American Bar Association, 49, 75, 346
American College of Trial Lawyers, 145
American Football League, 290
American Law Institute, 75
  Model Penal Code, 168
American League (baseball), 290
American Trust Company, 105
Anderson, ("Bronco Billy"), 16
Anderson, Carl, 65
Anslinger, Harry J., xxii, 138, 142
Anti–Saloon League, 39
Antioch, California, 284
Aptheker, Bettina
  See Free Speech Movement (FSM)
Aptheker, Herbert, 228
Arbuckle, Fatty, 100
Arizona, state of, 2, 218
Armed Forces Entrance and Examining Station (AFEES)
  See Stop the Draft Week
Armed Withdrawal Case, 92–94
Arson, 172, 246
Assault with a deadly weapon, 80, 201, 208
Athens Club, 94
Athletic Safety Committee, 298–300
Attorney General's Gang Case, 129–138
Atwill, Frank, 126, 128
"Automobile Row" Sit–In, San Francisco, 222
Automotive Salvage Fraud Case, 142–147

B

Bacon, Howard, 26
Baez, Joan, 232, 248
Bagshaw, Al, 6
Bail Bonds Broker Scam, 36, 159
Bakersfield, California, 150
Ballistic tests
  See Forensic evidence—ballistic tests
Bancroft, Hubert H., 5
Bank of America, 78
Bank of Italy, 53
Bank Robbery, 77–81, 92–94, 149
Barger, Sonny, 276
Barnett, Frank, 37–39
Barrett, Edward L., xi
Bate, Dorothy Watson, xxiii
Bay Area Rapid Transit (BART)
  See Railroads—Bay Area Rapid Transit (BART)
Bay Bridge
  See Bridges—San Francisco–Oakland Bay Bridge
Bay Farm Island, 279
Bay Meadows Racetrack, 27
Beachey, Lincoln, 38
Becker, Burton F., 37–41
  See also Graft in Emeryville
Beckman, Arnold O., Ph.D., 57–58, 61
Beery, Wallace, 16
Bell v. Wolfish, 182
Belli, Melvin, 73–74
Bennett, Nathaniel, 5
Bergoni
  See Pigeon Drop Case
Berkeley, California, 30, 33, 38, 41–42, 78, 91, 107, 190, 244, 282
  Berkeley High School, 298
  City Council, 247
  City Manager, 240, 243, 256
  Fire Department, 258
  Mayor, 242
  Police Department, xxi, 30, 78, 109, 116, 183, 191–194, 201, 205, 227, 229, 233, 241, 243, 255, 257–258, 260, 263
  Public Schools, 295
  Willard Jr. High School, 190, 193, 198, 256

Bertillion, Marie, 294
Bessie Ferguson Case, 37–38
Better Business Bureau, 266
Bifurcation of capital trials, 74, 80
Billings, Elton, 147
Black Bart, 7
Black Panther Party, 200, 209–212, 276
Black Power
  See specific organization
Blaich, Joe
  See Officer Johnston Case
Blake, George M., 9, 307
Bleuel, Maurice J., 32
Block Wardens
  See Civil Defense
Blue Sky laws, 61
Blum, Edmund, 6
Board of Corrections Act, 134
Bohemian Club, 94
Boker, Rae, 271
Bombing, 45, 222, 246, 260–261
Bonds, performance–liability, 102
Bookmaking, 129–135
  See also Gambling
Boston Red Sox (baseball), 289
Boxing and wrestling investigation, 147–148
Brennan, Charles, 102
Bribery, 41, 83, 99–100, 136, 148, 157
Bridges
  Fruitvale Avenue bridge, 279–281, 303
  "Parallel" or "Southern" crossing, 281
  San Francisco–Oakland Bay Bridge, 281
British Commonwealth Court
  See Courts—British Commonwealth
Broaddus, Sheriff, 136
Broadway Tunnel
  See Caldecott (Broadway) Tunnel
Brooklyn Township, 7
Brothers of Mary, 170
Brown, Edmund G. Sr., 173, 228, 233–234, 236, 244–245
Brown, Everett J., 11, 307
Brown, Raymond, 249–250
Brown, Willie Jr., 231
Brownsville, Texas, 86
Bryan, Dr. Charles S., 191
Bryan, Stephanie
  See Stephanie Bryan Case
Buckley, Lorenzo, 160
Buckley, Thomas, 148, 169
Bunco
  See Fraud
Burbank, California
  Police Department, 170
Burglary, 112, 120–121
Burn, Baby, Burn, 251–255
Burnett, Donald B., xviii
Burton, John L., 231
Bush, James, 136
Bushrod Park, Oakland, 243
Bushrod School, Oakland, 241
Byrne, Jerome C., 223–224
Byrne Report, 223–224

C

Cadell, Wiley ("Buck")
  See Attorney General's Gang Case
Cal–Neva Casino, Lake Tahoe, 131
Caldecott (Broadway) Tunnel, 191
Caldecott, Thomas, 291
Calhoun, 9
California Bar Association, 49, 76
California Chamber of Commerce, 76
California Constitution
  Early history, 4
  Harmless error, 187
  Tax–exempt private schools, 286–287
California Constitutional Amendments
  Justice of the Peace Courts, 20
  Law Enforcement Initiative Package of 1934, 74–77
  Property Tax Limitation (Proposition 13), 216, 265
  Statewide administration of welfare, 301–303
  Tax private schools, 287
California Court of Appeals
  See Courts—California Appellate
California District Attorneys Association, xvi, 74, 76, 130, 133, 135–137, 286, 346–347
California Highway Patrol (CHP)
  See California, state of—Highway Patrol (CHP)

California Institute of Technology, 57, 61
California Peace Officers Association, xvi, 74, 76, 130, 133, 135–137, 346
California Sheriffs Association, 76, 136
California Supreme Court
  See Courts—California Supreme Court
California, state of
  Alcoholic Beverage Control Board (ABC Board), 85
  Attorney General's Office, 30–31, 76, 98, 100, 129–138, 152, 167, 281, 293
  Board of Equalization, 84–85, 215
  Bureau of Criminal Identification, 113
  Bureau of Land Management, 193, 196
  Bureau of Narcotics Enforcement, 139–142
  Commission on Adult Corrections and Release Procedures, 134
  Commission on Criminal Law and Procedure, 134, 137
  Commission on Interstate Cooperation, 347
  Commission on Juvenile Justice, 134
  Commission on Organized Crime, xxi, 30, 130–131, 134–138, 165
  Commission on Social and Economic Causes of Crime and Delinquency, 134
  Controller, 84, 197
  Corporation Department, 57–58, 117–118
  Department of Motor Vehicles, 143
  Fish & Game Department, 148–149
  Folsom State Prison, 81, 143–145
  Franchise Tax Board, 290
  Highway Patrol (CHP), 16, 142–146, 217, 222, 229, 233, 242–244, 249–250, 253, 257–259
  Insurance Department, 70
  Judicial Council, 209
  Legislature, 7, 10, 13, 16, 26, 28, 49, 65, 74, 84–85, 94, 133–135, 137, 165, 185, 200, 231, 261, 265–266, 273, 281, 285–286, 293, 295, 297–298, 303–304
  Major Disaster and Mutual Aid Department, 244
  National Guard, 222, 244, 258–259
California, state of (cont'd),
  Oil and Gas Division, 118
  Parole Board, 79, 81, 87, 116, 149–150, 185, 212
  Public Utilities Commission, 282
  Railroad Commission, 13, 23–24
  Real Estate Commission, 117–118
  San Quentin State Prison, 6–7, 55, 63, 77, 81, 83, 87, 102, 111, 113, 136, 138, 141, 200
  Senate Factfinding Subcommittee on Un-American Activities (CSFSUA), 225, 227, 230–231, 237–238
Camp Shoemaker, 288
Campus Community for New Politics, 252
Canaday, Draga, xxiii
Capital punishment, 8, 74–75, 79–80, 112, 120, 173, 180, 184, 186–187, 197, 199, 266
Capone Syndicate, 136
Cappelli, Lawrence, xxiii
Cardoza, Benjamin N., 188
Carmel Valley, 232
Carmichael, Stokely, 200
Carr, Thomas, 48
Carson, Catherine, 293–294
A Case of Libel, 20–21
Castlewood Country Club, 288
Castro Valley, California, 92
Castro, Fidel, 227
Cattle rustling, 8
Cattlemen's Association, 289
Centerville, California, 15
Cereghinos
  See Poisoner Case
Chamberlain, Richard H., 32, 65, 76, 128, 177, 308
Chandler, Merrill, 233
Change of venue, 265
Chaplin, Charlie, 16
Chapman, "Trigger Abe", xxii, 140–141
Chicago White Sox baseball team, 289
Chicago, Illinois, 45
Chico, California, 142, 145
Chinese Lotteries, 39, 41, 158
  See also Gambling
Chipman, John S., 307
Chotiner, Murray, 132–133

Chowchilla School Bus Kidnaping, 267–273
Chowchilla, California, 267
Christensen, T. L., 35
Christie & McKay Case, 73
Church, Lincoln S., 10, 14, 102
Civil Defense, xv, 122–128
  Education, 127
Civil Rights Congress, 186, 189
  See also Communist influence
Civil Service, xxi, 35
Claremont Hotel, Berkeley, 114, 191, 198
Cleaning & Dyeing Racket, 44–47
Cleveland, Ohio, 174
Clinton, California, 7
"Coakley Clause"
  See Loss of the Welfare Burden
"Coakley College", xiv, 147, 149
Coakley, John M., xviii, 298
Coakley, Kathleen, xviii
Coakley, Thomas, 236
Coakley, Thomas J., xviii, 298, 346
Code of County Ordinances, 297–298
Coffin Redington Company
  See Inside Job Case
Cold Blooded Murder Case, 178–190
Colgate Palmolive Company
  See Inside Job Case
Coliseum, Inc.
  See Alameda County, Oakland—Alameda County Coliseum & Arena
Collaborating with the City Attorneys, 300
Collins, Marie, 216
Colorado, state of, 2
Columbia University, New York, 224
Combs, William H., 307
Comments by trial judges on credibility of witnesses, etc.
  See Testimony—California comment rule
Commonwealth Club of San Francisco, 77
Communist influence, 86, 128, 186, 190, 200, 218–219, 223–225, 227, 230, 238–239, 245–246, 262
Communist Party of the U.S.A. (CPUSA), 183, 186, 218, 223, 225, 228, 238, 245
Community Involvement Program—Oakland Project, 252
Community Treatment Center—halfway house, 153
Concord, California, 284
Concurrent jurisdiction, 42, 100, 141, 145, 147–148, 191, 196, 213
Conference of Christians and Jews, 283
Confidence Game
  See Fraud
Congress on Racial Equality (CORE), 226
Conner, Frank J.
  See Warren's Ship Murder Case
Conspiracy, 41–42, 47, 54, 63, 70, 79, 83, 100, 111, 132–133, 144–148, 157, 161, 166, 169, 212, 234, 248, 252, 283, 296
Constitutional rights, 111, 177, 217, 229, 279, 297
  Fifth Amendment, 60, 75, 111, 208
  Fourteenth Amendment, 75
Contempt of Court, 186, 208–209
Contra Costa County, 7, 37, 84, 130–131, 191, 193, 199, 281–285
Corning, California, 146
Corporate Securities Act, 53, 60, 118
Corruption in the Assessor's Office, 212–216
Corruption on the Bench, 99–101
Costello–Lansky–Siegal Syndicate, 136
Country Judges, 19
County Supervisors Association of California, 304
Courts
  British Commonwealth, 188
  California Appellate, 12, 28–29, 35, 70, 76, 100, 103, 113, 137, 157, 170, 173, 207–208, 236, 272, 274–276, 303
  California Supreme Court, 28, 41, 49, 60, 76, 78, 81, 100, 102–103, 161, 169, 184–185, 187, 199, 274, 287, 303
  Justice Court, 41, 303
  Juvenile Court, 160, 172, 235
  Municipal Court, 31, 33, 41, 101, 161, 166, 222, 235, 260, 267, 303
  Police Court, 25–26, 158

Courts (cont'd),
  Superior Court, 25–26, 28, 31, 33, 76, 78, 88, 90–91, 99–100, 103, 113, 115, 129, 133, 141, 145, 150–152, 161, 170, 177, 186, 199, 207, 213–214, 216, 236, 256, 260, 267, 272, 286–287, 291
  U.S. Court of Appeals, 15, 21, 151–152, 162, 280
  U.S. District Court, 15, 20, 33, 48, 115, 142, 148, 150–152, 170, 241, 243, 280
  U.S. Supreme Court, xiv, xvii, 12, 29, 34, 49, 75, 111, 152, 168–170, 188, 200, 236, 276, 287
Cox Chemical Case, 55–62
Cox, James E., 143–149
Crane, W. W., 9, 307
Creighton, Walter R., 140
Crittenden, Rupert, 235–236
Crosby, Carlisle, 20
Cross–filing for state offices, 96
Cuba, 209, 212
Cummings
  See Thorpe and Cummings, Attorneys
Cunningham, Thomas, 229
Cyanide Bullets Case, 273

D

Danville, California, 284
Darnell, Nolan, 211–212, 276
Davis, John, 205
Davis, William, 20
Dayton, Laurence, 156, 160, 184
Deasey, Joseph, 131, 133
Death penalty
  See Capital punishment
Declaration of Independence, 2
Decoto, Ezra W., xii, 9, 13–24, 28, 35, 95, 292, 307, 346
DeFremery Park, Oakland, 243, 245
Dehoyos, Gilbert, 204
Del Norte County, 100
Democratic Party, 96–97
Detroit, Michigan, 109
Dezman, Otto
  See Stephanie Bryan Case
Dictaphone, 181, 188
Dierke, Anne, xviii, xxiii
Dierke, Dorothy, xviii, xxiii
Dierke, James, xviii, xxiii
Disappearing Wife Case, 43–44
Divine, Lester, 155–156, 158, 182–183
Doheney, E. L., 52
Donahue, Fred, 15
Donahue, William H., 11, 15, 25, 307
Donovan, Augustin ("Mike"), xix, 36
Dooling, Maurice T., 81
Drake Cleaners, 46–47
Dressler, Marie, 16
Driver, Michael, 41
Driving While Under the Influence
  See Drunk Driving
Drucker, Fred, 65
Drug Bust Case, 138–142
Drunk Driving, 15, 89–91
Dublin, California, 17, 284–285, 288
Dubois Club, 239
  See also Communist influence
Dudliegh, Karman, 294
Dunning, Douglas, 291, 302
Dutra, Frank
  See Unusual Drunk Driving Case
Dutton, David, 74, 233–234, 256, 263
Dyer, Glen, 41
Dying statement by a murder victim, 34

E

Eagles, Fraternal Order of, 94, 347
Earthquakes, 7
East Bay Regional Park District, 277, 289, 305
Education Code, 293
Education, continuing, xiv, xxi, 28–30, 62, 73, 116, 267, 297
Eicke, Louie, 18
Eighteenth Amendment
  See Prohibition
Eisenhower, Dwight D., 15
El Cerrito, California, 282
Elkins
  See Fruit Shake Case
Elks, Benevolent and Protective Order of, 94

Ellingwood, Herbert, 65
Embezzlement, 177
Emerson, Folger, 33, 113
Emeryville, California, 13, 38–42, 244, 282, 295
  Police Department, 39, 211
Epton, William, 219
Escape, 79, 81
Essanay (movie studios), 16
Essays on Liberty, by Learned Hand, 262
Exceptional Manslaughter Case, 91–92
Exchange Club, 94
Exclusionary rule, 31, 34, 59–60, 78, 187–188
Extortion, 45, 103–112, 157

F

Fair Play For Cuba, 220
Federal Communications Commission, 176
Federal Housing Administration (FHA), 63
Ferguson, Bessie
  See Bessie Ferguson Case
Fernelius, Fred
  See Police Brutality Case
Ferrario, Raymond, 26, 88
Fidelity and Deposit Company of Maryland, 102
Field, Stephen J., 3
Finch, Robert, 224
Fingerprints
  See Forensic evidence—fingerprints
Finley, Charles, 290
Firby, Thomas, 293–294
Firemen, Oilers, Wipers and Water Tenders Union, 85
Firestone Tire and Rubber Company, 283
Fish & Game Bribery Case, 148–149
Fish & Game Department
  See California, state of—Fish & Game Department
Fitzgerald brothers, 283
Fitzmaurice, Thomas, 204
Fleming, Macklin, 275–276
Fletcher, Lawrence, 32
Florida, state of, 174
Folsom State Prison
  See California, state of—Folsom State Prison
Ford Foundation, 251
Ford Foundation/American Bar Association Study of Prosecutions in the U.S., 30
Ford, Robert M., 32
Forensic evidence
  See also Testimony—Expert witness
  ballistic tests, 113–114, 183, 189, 212
  blood, 43, 115, 196
  bone, 43
  fibers, 115, 196
  fingerprints, 113, 212
  glass refraction tests, 115
  hair, 115, 196
  soil, 196
  teeth, 37
  toxicology, 72, 74
Forsman, Kennett, 26
Foster, Marcus
  See Cyanide Bullets Case
Fox, Christopher, 26
Franciscan Missionaries, 1
Franklin Canyon, 193, 199
Fraud, 21–23, 44, 48, 50–70, 106, 116–119, 177, 296, 348
  Insurance, 70–71
Free Lot Racket Case, 65–69
Free Speech Movement (FSM), 168, 223–239, 259, 263
  "five demands", 231
Free Student Union (FSU), 236–237
Freeman, James H., 32
Freeways, 286
Fremont, California, 31, 152
  Police Department, 152
French Foreign Legion, 87
Fresno, California, 166–167, 170
Frey and Heanes Case, 200–209
Frey, John F.
  See Frey and Heanes Case
Fricke, Charles, 28–29
Friedman, Leo, 100
Fronts
  See Communist influence

Fruit Shake Case, 103–112
Fruitvale Avenue Bridge
See Bridges—Fruitvale Avenue bridge

G

Gadsen Treaty of 1851, 2
Gambling, 39, 41, 46, 129–138, 174, 176
Gannon, William, 19
Garrity, Roger, 166–169
General Motors Corporation, 283
Gibson, E. M., 10, 307
Gilroy, California, 25
Glascock, John R., 9
Glascock, William H., 9, 307
Gleason, Jack H. P., 41, 130, 136, 160
Gold Rush in California, 3
Goldberg, Arthur
See Free Speech Movement (FSM)
Goldberg, Jacqueline
See Free Speech Movement (FSM)
Golden Gate Fields Racetrack, 27
Golet Oil Company Case, 52–53
Golf—Earl Warren on golfers, 94
"Goon Squads"
See Warren's Ship Murder Case
Gordon, Waxey, xxii, 140–141
Gosden, Laura & Louis
See Poisoner Case
Graft, xiii, 36, 40–42, 81–85
Graft in Emeryville, 38–42
Grand jury
See Alameda County—Grand jury
Gray, Crystal, 209
Gray, Leon, 31–32
Greig, Rodney
See Leona Vlught Case
Griffin v. California, 75
Gumbo, Judy, 260

H

Habitual Criminal Law
See Prior convictions
Hagger, Gerald, 291
Haggood, Elizabeth, 294
Hall, Gus, 223
Hall, Samuel P., 10, 307
Halm, Gene, 145–146
Hamilton, William, 24
Hamlin, Dr. O. D., 195
Hamlin, Oliver D. Jr., 15, 113
Hand, Learned, 162, 262
Hansen, Dr. Reginald, 194–195
Harbor Homes Housing Authority
See Cold Blooded Murder Case
Harder, Jacob, 17–19
Harlan, John Marshall, 75, 275
Harlem, New York, 219
Harris, George B., 241
Harris, Michael, 213–214
Harris, T. W., 100
Harris, Walter, 27
Harvard University, 297
Haugner, Richard A., 271, 308
Hawaii, state of, 218
Hawkins v. Superior Court, 162
Hayden, Thomas, 260
Hayward, California, 15, 17, 30, 56, 58, 60, 70, 92, 282
Police Department, 166
Public Schools, 300–301
Hazard, Geoffrey C., xx
Heanes, Clifford
See Frey and Heanes Case
Hearst Newspapers
See Newspapers—Hearst
Hearst, Patricia, 273
Hearst, Phoebe, 288
Hearst, William Randolph, 274, 288
Hederman, Albert E., 160, 308
Hell's Angels, 242–243, 276
Heller, Zola B. "Tiny"
See Attorney General's Gang Case
Helms, George, 26
Hennessey, William, 25–26
Herbert, Charles, 267
Herrington, George, 294
Hetch–Hetchy
See Livermore Valley Water
Heynes, Roger, 255–256
Hidalgo, Father of Mexican Independence
See Treaty of Hidalgo
Higgins, Preston, 15, 35, 38

Highland Hospital
See Alameda County—Hospital
History of the Bench and Bar, by Augustin Donovan, xix
Holohan, James, 6
Hoover, J. Edgar, 200
Horse stealing, 5
Houchins, Tom, 41, 269
Howser, Frederick Napoleon, 130–135, 138, 281
Hoy, Charles
See Attorney General's Gang Case
Hoyt, Ralph E., xi, 15, 25, 28, 95, 107, 112, 123–124, 129, 134, 137, 159, 303, 305, 307–308, 346
Hoyt, Samuel—a/k/a Chait
See Proven Oil Land For Sale Case
Huff, Sonja
See Accessory to a Psychopath Case
Hume, James, 7
Hunter, R. Robert, 308
Hunters Point Riot, 221–223
Hyer, Charles, 24
Hynes, William H. L., 11, 15, 159, 307

I

Iglehart, Richard B., 65, 308
Immunity
See Testimony—immunized
Impeachment of a witness, 184–185
In re Field, 162
Inadmissible Evidence
See Exclusionary rule
Incorporation Doctrine, 75
Induction Center
See Stop the Draft Week
Industrial Workers of the World (IWW), 6, 12, 186
See also Communist influence
Inside Job Case, 120–121
Insurace fraud
See Fraud—insurance
Inter–agency cooperation
See Mutual Aid
International Longshoremen's and Warehousemen's Union (ILWU), 85
Ipsen, C. H., 109
Irwin, George, 164

J

Jacobs, Paul, 257
Jahnsen, Oscar, 41, 59
Jensen, D. Lowell, xi, 29, 74, 207–208, 269, 274, 307, 348
Jensen, Richard, 211–212, 276
Jester, Lloyd, 65
Johnson, Hiram, 26, 96
Johnston, John
See Officer Johnston Case
Joint Cities and County Civil Defense Committee, 128
Jones, Rev. Jim, 178
"judge shopping", 15
See also Speedy trial
Judges' comments in Court opinions
Calif. Supreme Court on liability of public officers for subordinates' actions, 103
Justice Hand on difficulty of prosecutors, 162–163
Justice Harlan on Incorporation Doctrine and California comment rule, 75
Justice Shenk on harmless error, 185–187
Judges' comments—not court opinion
Earl Warren on the attorney general's gang and organized crime, 134–135, 138
Justice Fleming on atrophy of law enforcement, 275
Justice Fleming on retroactivity of new rules, 275–276
Justice Spence on Earl Warren, 80
Justice Spence on the Yacht Bandits, 80–81
Justice Court
See Courts—Justice Court
Justice Without Trial: Law Enforcement in a Democratic Society, by Jerome Skolnick, xix
Juvenile Court
See Courts—Juvenile Court

Juvenile Officers Coordinating Council, 160
See also Mutual Aid

K

Kaiser Hospital, Oakland, 206–207
Kane, Joseph, 120
Kansas City Athletics, 290
Kansas City, Missouri, 114
Karesh, Joseph, 209, 325
Keil, Grace, 294
Kelly, Michael, 24
Kennedy, Harold, 304
Kern County, 117
Kerr, Clark, 225–229, 233–234, 263
Key System Railway
See Railroads—Key System
Keystone comedy, 16
Kickbacks, 83
Kidd, Alexander, M. ("Captain"), 293
Kidnaping, 6, 103–116, 191, 196–197, 267–273
"King of Torts"
See Belli, Melvin
King, Earl
See Warren's Ship Murder Case
King, Lester, 177
King, Martin Luther, 210
Kirk, Dr. Paul Ph.D., 115–116, 183, 189
Klatt, Barbara, xxiii
Klinge, Charles, xviii
Klinge, Clare, xviii
Knight, Goodwin J., 147
Knowland, William, 280
Koford, Mrs. Joseph S., 117–118
Korean War, 192

L

La Grange, O. H., 307
Labor unions
See Specific Union Name
Lafayette, California, 284
Lake Merritt, 112, 125, 176
Lakeside Park, 125
Landon, Alf, 97
Las Vegas, Nevada, 209
Law Enforcement Assistance Administration, 261
Lawrence Livermore National Laboratory, 260
Lawrence, Dr. Lester, 102
Lawyer's Guild of New Orleans, 243
See also Communist influence
Legal Aid, 35
Legal systems
Anglo–Saxon Common Law, 4, 31, 60, 75, 188
Elected Constables, 33
European Continental, 4
Justice of the peace, 5
Justinian, 4
Spanish, 4
Lenin Institute, Moscow, 218
Lentz, Walter
See Attorney General's Gang Case
Leona Vlught Case, 119
Lerner, Michael, 257
Libel, 20
Lindsay, Alan, 65, 294
Liquor Law Graft, 84–85
Little Lindberg Law
See kidnaping
Livermore Valley, 268–269
Livermore Valley Water, 287–289
Livermore Veterans Hospital, 192
Livermore, California, 7, 15, 31, 234, 284–285
London, Jack, 24
Long Beach City College, 171
Long Beach, California, 77
Police Department, 134
Longnecker, Merle, 190
Loquvam, Dr. George, 194, 196, 204
Lord, Clarence T. Jr., 201–202, 206
Los Angeles County
County Counsel's Office, 304–305
District Attorney's Office, 28, 134, 170
Los Angeles, California, 44, 57, 114, 116, 131–132, 150, 167, 178
Police Department, 78
Watts riots, 222, 244, 251
Loss of the Welfare Burden, 301–303

Louderback, Harold, 280
Louisiana, state of
  Angola State Prison, 149
Luce, David, 299
Luce, Phillip, 200
Lundberg, Alfred, 282
Lusitania, Inc. Case, 53–55
S.S. Lux—gambling ship, 134
Lynch, Thomas C., 131
Lynching, 5

M

MacDougall, William, 304
Mack Trucks, 283
Madera County, 268
  District Attorney's Office, 271
Madigan, Frank, 41, 233–234, 249, 258–259
Malloy v. Hogan, 75
Malloy, Nelson, 209
Manslaughter, 89–92, 102
Mapp v. Ohio, 59, 78, 188
Marin County, 6–7, 285
  District Attorney's Office, 166
Mariposa County, 346
Maritime Unions, 85
Mark Hopkins Hotel, San Francisco, 130–131
Market Street Railway Bribe Case, 9
Masons, Fraternal Order of, 55, 94, 106–107
Maxfield, William, 32
Maxim, Charles, 91
McArdle, Phil, xviii
McCarthy, James J., 292
The McClure Case, 154–158
McClure, Donald, 9, 15
McClure, William
  See The McClure Case
McDonough, Mark, 177
McGuiness, William, 213
McKay & Christie Case, 73
McKay, Phyllis, 294
McLain, George, 301
McNabb, Ethan Allen
  See Yacht Bandits Case
McPherson, Aimme Semple, 177
McSorley, Richard, 53
Meehan, John J., xi, xviii, 29, 267, 270–271, 307–308
Meese, Edwin III, 65, 74, 160, 229, 233, 235, 348
Mell, Dr. Charles ("Snook"), 298
Meltzer, Leonard J., 32
Memoirs of Earl Warren, by Earl Warren, 86, 134–135, 138
Mendocino County, 136–138
  District Attorney's Office, 136
Merriam, Frank F., 96
Merritt Hospital, 204
Mexico, 1–3, 86
Mickle, Judge, 19
Miller and Lux, 24
Miller's Opus and Other Indexes, 296–297
Miller, George, 280
Miller, Grant, 41
Miller, Nathan Harry, 32, 296–297
Minier, David, 271
Mintz, Herman, 166
Miranda v. Arizona, 34, 188, 276
    See also Policy—suspect interview
Mission Dolores, 2
Mistaken Identity Case, 88–89
Mitchel, Frank, 15
Moley, Raymond, xix
Monadnock Building, San Francisco, 106
Monterey County, 274
Montgomery, Ed, 194
Moore, A. A., 307
Moore, Dr. Gertrude, 102, 195
Moore, Richard, 291–292, 306
Moose, Loyal Order of, 94
Moraga, California, 284–285
Morehouse, Charles, 74
Morse, Harry, 6
Mosbacher, Cecil, 33, 65, 137, 177
Muller, Dr. Harold ("Brick"), 298
Mullins, John, 24
Municipal Court
  See Courts—Municipal Court
Murder, 5, 43, 70–74, 79, 81, 85–87, 112–114, 119, 173, 180, 184, 196, 208, 212, 222, 276
Murphy, Joseph, 32

Mutual Aid, 123, 128, 136–137, 227, 229, 242, 244, 250–251, 258–259
Mutual assistance, 160
Mutuality principle, 280

N

Naffziger, Dr. Howard, 102
Narcotics, 138–142
National Association of County and Prosecuting Attorneys
See National District Attorneys Association
National City Lines, 283
National College of District Attorneys, 62, 347
National District Attorneys Association, xvi, xxiii, 138, 347
National Foundation for Infantile Paralysis, 301
Native Sons of the Golden West, 8
Nazism, 172
Nelson, "Moose", 146
Nevada, state of, 2, 54, 142, 145, 174, 218, 248
New Haven, California, 7
New Mexico, state of, 2
New Orleans, Louisiana
Police Department, 110
Newhall Land and Farming Company, 270
Newspapers
Daily Californian, 220, 227
Hearst, 38, 84
Oakland Tribune, xxiii, 193, 247, 347
People's World (CPUSA), 183, 186
San Francisco Bulletin, 156
San Francisco Call, 156
San Francisco Chronicle, 140, 156, 213
San Francisco Examiner, 156, 194
Un-named scurrilous or overly aggressive, 20, 38, 156, 164, 182–183, 190, 193, 249–250, 252, 259
Newton, Huey P.
See Frey and Heanes Case and Appendix E
Neyland, John Francis, 38
Nieland, Louis, 127
Niles, California, 15–16, 85
Normand, Mabel, 16
North v. Superior Court, 182
"Nuts and Bolts Case"
See Alameda County v. United States
Nye, Stephen G., 9

O

Oakland Army Base, 240, 243, 246, 248
Oakland Bank of Savings, 10, 77
Oakland, California, xix, 7, 21, 25–29, 33, 38–39, 42–46, 49–50, 52, 54, 66, 70, 77, 81, 86, 88, 93, 102, 125, 138, 143, 148, 174, 244, 303
Castlemont High School, 252
Chief of Police, 102, 159, 178, 182, 240, 242, 292
City Attorney's Office, 9, 94, 282
City Charter, 103, 158
City Council, 290
City Engineer's Office, 126
City Hall, 249
City Jail, 5, 25, 101, 181–182
City Manager, 102, 159, 240
Civic Auditorium, 174
Civil Defense Program, 126, 128
Commissioner of Streets, 42
Hall of Justice, 200
Mayor, 159
Park Department, 125
Police Department, xxi, 23, 25, 47, 53, 62, 88, 90, 101, 110, 126, 130, 146–147, 154–159, 163, 166, 178, 181, 183, 190, 200–201, 205, 211, 226–227, 229, 233, 241–242, 248–250, 253–254, 263, 292
Port Authority, 290
Public Schools, 9, 247, 252, 263, 273, 295, 299
Oakland Estuary, 10, 37, 113, 125, 155, 278–281, 303
Oakland Raiders football team, 290–291
Oakland Street Paving Graft Case, 42–43

Oakland Traction Company
See Railroads—Key System
Oakland Tribune
See Newspapers—*Oakland Tribune*
Oakley, James, 21
Obscenity
See Smut Case
Officer Johnston Case, 112–114
Ogden, Frank M., 74
Olney, Warren III, xxi, 30, 116, 135–136, 138
Olson, Culbert L., 87
Olympic Hotel, Seattle, 104, 111
Organized Crime, xxi–xxii, 44–47, 65–66, 129–147, 160, 164–165, 348
Orinda, California, 198, 285
Orland, California, 145
Orloff, Thomas J., 209
Orrick, Palmer, Dahlquist, and Herrington, 294
Owl Drug Company
See Inside Job Case

P

Pacific Coast League (baseball), 289
Pacific Gas & Electric Company (PG&E), 101, 125, 290
Pai–Gow
See Chinese Lotteries
Palace Club, Reno, 177
Palace Hotel, San Francisco, 77, 107, 111
Sit–In demonstration, 222
Parker, Frank, 293–294
Parole
See California, state of—Parole Board
Parrilli, Joanne, 272
Pasadena, California, 113
Pathe News, 194
Payoffs
See Graft
Peace and Freedom Party, 257
Pearl Harbor, 123–124, 127
People v. Alberts, 168–169
People v. Cahan, 59–60, 78, 187
People v. Defore, 188
People v. Ford, 6
People v. Mayen, 188
People v. Ottey, 76
People v. Phillip Riley
See Case of Libel
People v. Sigel, et al, 111
People's Park, 255–259, 263
People's World
See Newspapers—*People's World*
Perjury, 83, 91, 157
Perkins, George C., 30, 32, 55, 58–59
Phillips Oil Company, 283
Phillips, Norman, 213–214
Phony Baloney Insurance Case, 70
Photographing arrestees, 230, 234
Piedmont, California, 33, 37, 282
Piedmont High School, 298
Public Schools, 298
Pigeon Drop Case, 21–23
Piper, Harry, 43
Pittsburg Building and Loan Company, 54
Plea bargaining
See Policies—plea bargaining
Pleasanton, California, 15, 19, 284–285, 288
Plummer, Charles A., 41
S.S. Point Lobos
See Warren's Ship Murder Case
Point of View, 29
See also Education, continuing
Poisoner Case, 70–74
Police brutality, 101–103, 206, 230, 258–259
Police Brutality Case, 101–103
Police corruption, 36, 40, 129–138, 154–159
See also Graft
Police Court
See Courts—Police Court
Police intelligence gathering, 160–161, 244, 248, 251
See also Mutual Aid
Policies
"No Smoking", 14
plea bargaining, 32, 109, 111, 261, 266
pre–charge review, xxi, 32, 38, 348
suspect interview, 33–34, 90
Polio Vaccinations, 300–301
Political campaigning, 28, 31, 35, 37, 39, 50, 95–99, 134, 244

Polsdorfer, Agnes, 15, 292–294, 297
Pornography
See Smut Case
Portland, Oregon, 58, 215
Portugal, 2
Potel, Vick, 16
Preachers & Charlatans, 173–178
Present insanity, 93
Presidio of San Francisco, 2
Preston, Robert J., 242
Pretrial publicity, 190
Prevost, Marie, 16
Price, E. L., 131
The Price of Perfect Justice, by Fleming, Macklin, 275–276
Princeton University, 61
Pring's Doughnut Shop, 192, 198
Prior convictions, 144, 151
Prison psychosis, 93
Private schools, 286–287
Proctor v. Justice's Court of the City of Berkeley, 42
Progressive Labor Party (PLP), 219, 239
Progressive Party, 96
Prohibition, 13, 39, 48, 84, 95
Prostitution, 13, 25, 40–41, 46, 163–165
Proven Oil Land For Sale Case, 116–119
Public Agencies Coordinating Council, 160
See also Mutual Aid
Public Assistance
See Alameda County—Welfare Department
Public Defender
See Alameda County—Public Defender's Office
Public interest lawyers
See Legal Aid

Q

Quayle, Donald, 184–186
Quinn, Patrick, 19
Quinn, William, 91

R

Rackets
See Organized Crime
Radical Left activists, 6, 183, 186, 189, 212, 220, 223–229, 232–235, 238, 243–248, 251–252, 257, 261–262
Ragusa family murders, 276
Railroad Commission
See California, State of—Railroad Commission
Railroads
Bay Area Rapid Transit (BART), 285
Great Northern, 27
Key System, 281–284
New York Central, 19
Pennsylvania, 19
Sacramento Northern, 284–285
Santa Fe, 27
Southern Pacific, 10, 27, 38, 280–281, 284
Western Pacific & Rio Grande, 27, 119
Ramsay, E. G.
See Warren's Ship Murder Case
Rape, 88–89, 114–116
Rauch, John, 110
Razeto, Emanuel, 347
Reagan, Ronald W., xiv, 74, 258, 347
Reck, Al, 193
Red Light Abatement Act, 13, 39
Redding, California, 146
Reed, George W., 9–10, 307
Reed, Nusbaumer and Bingamin, 10
Referral Deals
See Acme Builders Swindle Case
Remmer, "Bones"
See Attorney General's Gang Case
Reno, Nevada, 176
Republican Party, 96
Reserve Officers Training Corps (ROTC), 94, 246, 260
Revolutionary Action Movement (RAM), 200
Richardson, Friend, 24
Richmond, California, 282
City Manager, 158
Police Department, 158
Richmond, Ralph, 19, 24
Ricksen, Marshall, 32

Riedel, Albert E., 181–183, 189
Riley, Phillip
See Case of Libel
Riots, 6, 82, 126, 219, 221–222, 224, 242–244, 249–254, 257–259
Robbery, 78, 93, 104–110, 112, 114, 116
Robinson, C. Ray, 147
Robinson, Tyrone, 210
Rodgers, Alice
See Cold Blooded Murder Case
Roosevelt, Franklin D., 97
Roosevelt, James, 96
Rose Waterman Drug Store
See Cold Blooded Murder Case
Roth v. United States, 169
Royal Canadian Mounted Police, 271
Royce, Josiah, 5
Rubin, Jerry
See Vietnam Day Committee
Rutherford, Earleen, 297
Ryan, Russ, 146
Ryken, Charles, 194

S

Sacramento City College, 149
Sacramento County, 274
Sacramento River, 146
Sacramento, California, 193, 197
Police Department, 200
St. Francis Hotel, San Francisco, 59
St. Francis Yacht Club, San Francisco, 80
St. Mary's College, xiv, 29, 289, 346–347
St. Sure, Paul, 291
Sakowitz, Ben
See Warren's Ship Murder Case
Salaries, 25–26, 50, 69, 76, 83, 127, 305
Salem, Oregon, 105–106
Sampsell, Lloyd
See Yacht Bandits Case
San Antonio Creek, 9
San Diego County
Assessor's Office, 215
District Attorney's Office, 214
San Diego, California, 1, 79, 81
San Francisco 49'ers football team, 144, 147, 291–292
San Francisco Bay, 37, 86
Ferryboats, 39, 281, 284
San Francisco Chronicle
See Newspapers—*San Francisco Chronicle*
San Francisco State University, 252
San Francisco, California, 1, 7, 21, 36, 39, 46, 59, 66, 69, 77, 81, 178, 218, 281, 285–289
Assessor's Office, 213–215
Board of Supervisors, 220
Chief of Police, 107
City Attorney's Office, 281
City Hall, 220–221, 244
Civic Center, 220
Civil Defense, 125
District Attorney's Office, 100, 131, 213–214, 222
Fire Department, 221
Police Department, 23, 29, 46–47, 78, 81, 106, 120–222, 250
waterfront, 86
San Francisco–Oakland Bay Bridge
See Bridges—San Francisco–Oakland Bay Bridge
San Joaquin County, 7
San Joaquin River, 44, 284
San Jose, California, 6, 16, 153
San Leandro, California, 7, 15, 19, 31, 141, 213, 269, 282
Police Department, 139
San Mateo County, 150, 270–271, 285
San Mateo, California, 139–141
San Quentin State Prison
See California, state of—San Quentin Prison
San Ramon, California, 284–285
Sandborn, Lydia
See Poisoner Case
Santa Anna, General, 2
Santa Clara County, 7, 16
Santa Clara University, 170, 289
Santa Cruz, California, 164
Santa Maria crude oil
See Cox Chemical Case
Santa Monica, California
Police Department, 48

Santa Rita
See Alameda County—Jail
Santa Rosa, California, 5
Sather Gate
See University of California, Berkeley
Saturday Evening Post, 215
Savage, Robert
See Cold Blooded Murder Case
Savio, Mario
See Free Speech Movement (FSM)
Schnarr, Edwin, 127
School busing, 295–296
Schwartz, Marchmont, 144
Seaboard Finance Company, San Diego, 79
Seamens Union of the Pacific, 85
Seattle, Washington, 21–22, 77, 88, 104, 106, 108
Chief of Police, 107
Police Department, 78, 108
Sedition, 248
Separate trials for multiple defendants, 265
Sequoia Country Club, 94
Severin, Clarence, 147
Sevier, Milton, 15, 25
Sex Life of a Cop
See Smut Case
Sharman, Thomas Jr.
See Unusual Drunk Driving Case
Shaw, Buck, 144
Shay, Frank, 15, 24, 35
Shea, Willard, 26, 35, 87, 137
Shellmound Park, 38
Shenk, John W., 185, 187
Shenone, Joseph, 33
Sheppard, Sterrett, 196
Sherman Anti–Trust Law, 283
Sherry, Arthur H., 30, 33, 65, 114–116, 132–133, 136
Shuey, Herbert, 156
Sigel, Frank L.
See Fruit Shake Case
Similar offense evidence, 111
Simpson, Walter
See Fruit Shake Case
Sinclair, Upton, 96
60 Minutes, CBS Television, 276
Skolnick, Jerome, xix
Slate, 219–221
Smallwood, Stanley C., 33, 76
Smith, "Borax", 284
Smith, Fred, 41
Smith, Katherine, 208
Smut Case, 165–171
Snook, Charles E., 10, 307
Snook, Charles Wade, 15, 25, 53, 199
Solon, Leon, 16
Sonoma County, 6, 21
Sonoma, California, 1, 4
Southern Pacific Railway Company
See Railroads—Southern Pacific
Soviet Union, 87
Spain, 1–2
Speakeasies
See Prohibition
Speculating Loan Company Case, 69–70
Speedy trial, 31–32
See also "Judge shopping"
Spence, Homer R., 47, 78, 80
Sports Illustrated, 148
Spring Valley Water Company
See Livermore Valley Water
Sproul Hall and Sproul Plaza
See University of California, Berkeley
Staats, Rudy, 24
Standard Oil of California, 117, 283
Standley, Admiral William H., 135
Stanford University, 127, 289, 296, 346
Law School, 143
Stanford, Max, 200
Stark, Tom, 28
Stenographic Reporting, xxiii, 33–34, 140, 184, 189
Stephanie Bryan Case, xiv, 190–200
Stewart, Potter, 75
Stock market, 69
Stockton, California, 18
Stop the Draft Week, 247–251, 254, 259
Strathman, Earl, 304–306
Street Paving Graft Case, 159
Strong, Edward M., 226, 230–231, 233
Student Mobilization Committee to End the War in Vietnam, 260
Student Non–Violent Coordinating Committee (SNCC), 200

Students for a Democratic Society (SDS), 224, 261–262
See also Communist influence
Styles, Harry, 15
"Suede Shoe" salesmen, 63, 66
Sullivan, Leo, 102, 109–110
Sunol, California, 284, 288
Superior Court
See Courts—Superior Court
Sweeney, Leland, 304
Sweigert, William T., 243, 245
Swindle
See Fraud
Symbionese Liberation Army (SLA)
See Cyanide Bullets Case

T

Tanforan Racetrack, 27
Taylor, Joel, 147
Taylor, Vivian
See Poisoner Case
Teapot Dome Scandal, 215
Tennessee, state of, 174
Testimony
California comment rule, 74–76, 111
Comments by prosecutor on failure of defendant to testify, 163
Expert witness, 51, 61–62, 91, 102, 113, 115–116, 120, 169, 171, 180, 183, 189, 205, 282
See also Forensic evidence
Immunized, 41, 47, 208, 214
Texas, state of, 2
Theft, 83
Thompson, Wayne, 158
Thorpe and Cummings, Attorneys, 213–214
Tiajuana, Mexico, 52
Tilden Park, 277
See also East Bay Regional Park District
Toothman, Edward M., 242
Towle, Katherine A., 226
Townsend Pension Plan, 96
Transamerica, 54
Treatolite
See Cox Chemical Case
Treaty of Hidalgo, 1–3, 8
Trespassing, 222–233
Trinity County, 193–194, 196–197, 199
Coroner, 195
District Attorney's Office, 196
Sheriff's Office, 196
Tryon, Warren, 100
Tunnel Road Rapists Case, 114–116
Turner, Brian
See Free Speech Movement (FSM)
Turpin, Ben, 16
Tyree, David, 198
Tyree, Ernest, 198
Tyrrell, Edward, 25–27, 133

U

Unethical Attorney Case, 47–49
Union City, California, 7
Unions
See Specific Union Name
United Kingdom, 167
United Nations, 110, 138
U.S. Army, 87, 94, 122–124, 127, 192, 244
U.S. Commission on Intergovernmental Relations, 304
U.S. Commission on Uniform State Laws, 347
U.S. Congress
House of Representatives Committee on Un–American Activities (HUAC), 186, 200, 220–221
Safe Streets Act, 261
Senate Internal Security Subcommittee, 238
U.S. Court of Appeals
See Courts—U.S. Court of Appeals
U.S. Customs Service, 167
U.S. Department of Commerce
report on racial tension in the U.S., 244, 254
U.S. Department of Health, Education and Welfare, 224, 252
U.S. Department of Justice
Attorney General's Office, 33, 64, 348
Bureau of Narcotics, xxii, 138
FBI National Academy, Quantico, 62

U.S. Department of Justice (cont'd),
  Federal Bureau of Investigation (FBI), 113, 170, 191, 193, 200, 244, 251, 261, 270–271
  National Auto Theft Bureau, 142–146
  United States Attorney, 259
U.S. Department of the Treasury, 290
U.S. District Court
  See Courts—U.S. District Court
U.S. Federal Prisons
  Alcatraz, 150
  Atlanta, 174
  Leavenworth, 141, 150
  McNeil Island, 150
U.S. Food and Drug Administration, 300
U.S. Marine Corps, 143, 149, 250, 253
U.S. Marshal Service, 150
U.S. Navy, 77, 124, 143, 171, 244, 270, 346
  12th Naval District, 346
  Judge Advocate General Service, 346
  Naval Air Station, Alameda, 125
  Naval Investigative Service, 270
U.S. Post Office, 167, 258
U.S. Reclamation Service, 288
U.S. Supreme Court
  See Courts—U.S. Supreme Court
University of California, Berkeley, 39, 61, 74, 115–116, 143, 149, 168, 171–172, 176, 183, 192, 220, 223–225, 228, 232, 237–241, 245–246, 252, 255, 263, 274, 289, 296, 299
  Bancroft Library, 80
  Boalt Hall School of Law, xiv, 30, 73, 94, 116, 235, 292, 296, 346
  Board of Regents, 223, 231, 255
  Greek Theater, 235
  Moses Hall takeover, 246
  NROTC bombing, 246
  Police Department, 172, 226–229, 233, 235, 257
  Sproul Hall Sit–In, 231–236, 263
  Wheeler Hall arson, 246
University of California, San Francisco, 102
University of California, Santa Cruz, 209
University of Michigan, Ann Arbor, 238
University of San Francisco, 289
  Law School, 171
Unusual Drunk Driving Case, 89–91
Utah, state of, 2

V

Van Voorheis, William, 9, 307
Vancouver, British Columbia, 271
Vega Books
  See Smut Case
Vernon, Wyman, 158
Victory Mutual Life Insurance Company, 54
Vietnam Day Committee (VDC), 168, 236–247, 254, 259
Vietnam War, 224, 243, 261
Vigilante committees, 6
Virginia Hotel, Long Beach, 77
Vladivostok, USSR, 346
Vlught, Leona
  See Leona Vlught Case
Volmeer, August, 116
Volpe, Edward, 269–270
Volpe, Kathleen V., 269
Vrooman, Henry, 9, 307
Vukota, Frank, 216

W

Wade, George "Chick", 26
Wallace, George
  See Warren's Ship Murder Case
Wallman, Bodie A., 53
Walnut Creek, California, 284
Walsh, James C. Sr., 15, 31
Waring, Eugene, 291
Warren as Administrator and Politician, 94–97
Warren's Ship Murder Case, 85–87
Warren, Earl, xii–xviii, xx–xxi, 23–97, 112, 118, 129–130, 133–136, 158–160, 177, 279, 301, 303, 305, 307–308, 346
  Memoirs, 134–135, 138
Warren, Nina, 95

Washington, state of, 214
Webb, Ulysses S., 95
Wehr, Charles D., 32
Weinberg, Jack
See Free Speech Movement (FSM)
Welfare Rights Organization, 252
Wells Fargo Company, 7
Wemple, Murray, 145–146
Wendel, David, 282, 297
Western Laboratory, 43, 195
Westphal, Theodore A., 32
Wexler, Irving—a/k/a Waxey Gordon
See Gordon, Waxey
White Collar Crime
See Fraud
White Hibiscus Claire de Lune Case, 112
White, Byron R., 75
Whitney, Anita, 12
Wigmore, John H., 188
Wildwood Inn, Trinity County, 197
Wilke, Howard, 32
Williams, Myrtle, 301–303
Williamson, Judy, 276
Wilson, Frances, 293
Wilson, Marjorie
See Cold Blooded Murder Case
Witness protection, 190, 266
Witschen, Theodore, 24
Wixon, Clifford, 177
"Wizzard of Warrants"
See Meehan, John J.
Wolfe, Cameron W., 33
Wollitz, Lillian, 294
Woman's Christian Temperance Union, 39
Wood, Fred V., 14, 91
Wood, Ninfa, xviii
Woods, Fred
See Chowchilla School Bus Kidnaping
Woolner, Ben, 27
World War I, xii, 27, 77, 94, 218, 346
World War II, xv, 30, 87, 89, 122, 143, 164, 171, 174, 219, 234, 346
Wrestling
See Boxing and Wrestling Investigation
Wright, S. P., 307
Wyoming, state of, 2

Y

Yacht Bandits Case, 77–81
Yoder, Hazel, 124
Yosemite National Park, 236, 288
Youell, Connie, 267

About The Author

James Francis Coakley was born and raised in Oakland, California and educated at St. Mary's College, Stanford University, and Boalt Hall law school of the University of California at Berkeley. In later years he taught law at both Boalt Hall and St. Mary's.

Frank joined the Alameda County prosecutor's staff on February 21, 1923, as a deputy district attorney, following his graduation from Boalt Hall. He served under three predecessors: Ezra Decoto, Earl Warren and Ralph Hoyt. Under Warren, Frank served as assistant head of the Criminal Division. Later, under Hoyt, he served as chief assistant.

Having served in the U.S. Navy during World War I, participating in the expedition to Vladivostok, Frank was recalled to active duty during World War II as a Commander in the U.S. Navy's Judge Advocate General service, serving as chief prosecutor for court martial cases in the 12th Naval District.

Following the war, Frank briefly entered private practice with his brother, Thomas, who later became a Superior Court judge in Mariposa County. That interlude was short–lived, as Ralph Hoyt soon decided to move on to the bench himself. Frank was called to take over for Hoyt immediately. Although Frank had discovered private practice to be more lucrative, he knew his heart was with the Alameda County District Attorney's Office, and that was where he belonged.

During his tenure as district attorney, he maintained his record as a great trial lawyer, conducted the civil business of the county with efficiency and imagination, contributed significantly to the legal growth of the state of California as chairman of the Law and Legislative Committees of both the District Attorneys Association and the Peace Officers Association, and built his office into one recognized publicly by the American Bar Association as the nation's finest.

Active in civic as well as public life, Frank served as chairman of the St. Mary's College Board of Regents and was an active member of the local council of the Boy Scouts of America. He was awarded the International Civic Award of the Fraternal Order of Eagles in 1958, and in 1965 was honored as "Outstanding Prosecutor in the United States" by the National District Attorneys Association, a group he was instrumental in founding in 1950, and which he served as its first president. Following his retirement, the NDAA presented him with its "Furtherance of Justice Award". In giving him that award, the NDAA said, "To this man the words, 'Furtherance of Justice' became the foundation on which he built his life." In the years that followed, he served as then–Governor Ronald Reagan's appointee to the California Commission on Interstate Cooperation, and the Commission on Uniform State Laws, and as the director of curriculum and president of the Board of Regents of the National College of District Attorneys, which he also helped found.

In 1952, on his way to the Republican National Convention as a candidate for President of the United States, then–Governor Warren detoured to the annual convention of the California District Attorneys Association at Santa Cruz. In addressing this convention, Governor Warren said:

> "Frank (Coakley) came to the District Attorney's Office in Alameda County in 1923. I was a deputy myself at that time in the office and for fifteen years he and I had a deep association that was most pleasant to me throughout. I want to say to you that I believe in the last quarter of a century there is no man in this state who has contributed more to good law enforcement than has Frank Coakley."

Upon his retirement in 1969, the *Oakland Tribune* said, "Coakley, who has served longer in his post than any other man—an unprecedented six terms—is regarded nation–wide as the dean of American district attorneys." Alameda County Supervisor Emanuel Razeto summed up the sentiments of his fellow supervisors: "The highest compliment that can be paid to you, Frank, is that you kept this county clean."

According to Frank Coakley's successor, Lowell Jensen (who later became head of the Criminal Division of the U.S. Attorney General's Office and then Deputy U.S. Attorney General under another Coakley–trained prosecutor, Edwin Meese III):

> "The District Attorney's Office is really the pivotal office in the whole criminal justice process. . . . The district attorney is a discretionary executive officer who makes the decision as to what offenses are prosecuted and how they are disposed of. The standard of law enforcement in the county is to a great extent dependent upon what the district attorney does. Under Frank Coakley . . . there was a standard of law enforcement which was as tough as you could get. As far as Coakley was concerned, you don't have consumer fraud rings, you don't have organized crime and you don't have corruption in governmental functions. He viewed the role of district attorney as one that was absolutely incorruptible and fearless."

Throughout his life, J. Frank Coakley stood as a tough and aggressive advocate . . . *For the People.* He stood before the bar of final judgment on January 16, 1983.

Eratta

The following errors occured in the 1st printing of *For The People; Sixty Years of Fighting for Law & Order*:

In the Table of Contents, on Page X, the first line is repeated from the previous page.

On Page 222, the last line has a word missing. The sentence should read:

> "The Municipal Court of San Francisco was bogged down for about a year and the additional cost to law enforcement exceeded a million dollars."

On Page 293, the first two lines of text are repeated from the previous page.

On Pages 196 and 338, the type was mis–cast, but all information on those pages is correct.

We express our regret if any of these eratta have caused confusion. They will be corrected in the next printing.

THE PUBLISHER